West's Law School
Advisory Board

PRINCIPLES OF INTELLECTUAL PROPERTY LAW

Second Edition

By

Gary Myers

Dean & Earl F. Nelson Professor of Law
University of Missouri School of Law

CONCISE HORNBOOK SERIES®

A Thomson Reuters business

Mat #41186131

Concise Hornbook Series and Westlaw are trademarks registered in the U.S. Patent and Trademark Office.

© West, a Thomson business, 2008
© 2013 Thomson Reuters
    610 Opperman Drive
    St. Paul, MN 55123
    1–800–313–9378
Printed in the United States of America

ISBN: 978–0–314–27779–4

For my students, past and present, who have engaged in the issues presented by Intellectual Property law.—GM

Summary of Contents

v

Table of Contents

Page

CHAPTER 14. PATENT OWNERSHIP

CHAPTER 15. PATENT INFRINGEMENT

CHAPTER 16. PATENT DEFENSES

CHAPTER 17. PATENT REMEDIES

CHAPTER 18. TRADE SECRET LAW

CHAPTER 19. IDEA PROTECTION & MISAPPROPRIATION

CHAPTER 20. SUI GENERIS INTELLECTUAL PROPERTY RIGHTS

PRINCIPLES OF INTELLECTUAL PROPERTY LAW

Second Edition

INTRODUCTION

PRINCIPLES OF INTELLECTUAL PROPERTY

Almost everyone is talking about issues related to Intellectual Property ("IP") law today. Consider this list of topics:

— using images and music in social media,

— the newest iPhone or iPad from Apple

— downloading electronic versions of books on Amazon

— file sharing on the Internet

— the costs and benefits of genetically modified foods

— the latest new medical treatment or drug

— patent disputes among Silicon Valley companies

— the hottest new brand of children's toy.

Fundamental questions related to Intellectual Property are almost always involved in any of these discussions.

Intellectual Property is, in my opinion, the most fascinating, rapidly changing, and analytically complex area of the law that you will encounter today. Intellectual Property protections—which include the law of copyright, patents, and trademarks—come into play in fields as diverse as entertainment, sports, aviation, biotechnology, and retail franchising. Every new movie, song, pharmaceutical product, brand-name product, and video game presents material that is protectable under one or more Intellectual Property paradigms. As this book went to press, for example, Apple won a $1 billion verdict against Samsung for infringement of Apple's patents. In the same month, Apple became the largest public company as measured by market capitalization.

Consider this panel discussion at the 2012 South By Southwest (SXSW) Interactive Festival about IP issues in social media:

> Social media have made sharing information with friends and followers easier and quicker, but federal copyright law is struggling to adapt to the challenges presented by these tools. When hot news breaks, how soon can it be tweeted? If an image is shared via Flickr or Facebook, can it be used for news or marketing purposes? Is it fair use to post portions of song lyrics, news articles, or YouTube videos on your Tumblr? What legal ramifications do mock Twitter accounts face? Will Creative Commons save us all? This panel of attorneys, scholars

and media professionals discuss how courts and the industry have been handling these issues and some possible solutions to resolve them.[1]

Intellectual Property plays an integral role in our culture and in public policy discussions. It is a cutting edge subject, and one that should interest non-lawyers as much as those trained in the law. It is also a bedrock of our information economy. One study showed that about 80 percent of the market capitalization of the companies in the S & P 500 was attributable to intangible value (mainly IP), as compared to ownership of tangible assets.[2] According to some estimates, Intellectual Property plays a role in 45 percent of the United States Gross National Product.[3]

This book is designed to provide an overview of the entire field of Intellectual Property, covering the three main areas of federal Intellectual Property, as well as related state rights. The focus is on United States law, but relevant international treaties and some points of comparative law are also addressed. This is an ambitious task, and some narrow topics will necessarily receive only brief treatment, as each of the major topics in Intellectual Property could fill an entire book of this size.

This book includes changes and developments in the law through August 2012. Intellectual Property is a rapidly changing field. Since the first edition of this book was published in 2008, Congress has made significant amendments to the patent laws, in the 2011 Leahy–Smith America Invents Act (or AIA). The main and most widely publicized change made by the AIA is to move patent law in the United States from a first-to-invent to a first-to-file (or first-to-publish) rule for determining ownership of an invention (taking effect in March 2013). In light of this change, delays in filing patent applications take on much greater significance than under prior law. The Supreme Court has issued important rulings in patent law, such as *Ebay v. MercExchange* (setting the standard for granting injunctions in patent cases), and in copyright law, such as *Golan v. Holder*, which addressed the validity of statutes that restored copyright protection for foreign works that had forfeited

---

1. http://lanyrd.com/2012/sxsw-interactive/spmym/ (last visited June 13, 2012).

2. James E. Malackowski, Keith Cardoza, Cameron Gray, & Rick Conroy, The Intellectual Property Marketplace: Emerging Transaction & Investment Vehicles, The Licensing Journal, February 2007, Volume 27, Number 2, pages 1–11 (discussing upward trend). *See also* http://www.buildingipvalue.com/05 _ TI/ 031 _ 034.htm (reporting similar percentage for Fortune 500 companies); http://www.wipo.int/sme/en/documents/ valuing_patents.htm (45–75 percent, based on a 2002 study).

3. Miranda Jones, Casenote, Permanent Injunction, a Remedy by Any Other Name Is Patently Not the Same: How *Ebay v. MercExchange* Affects the Patent Right of Non–Practicing Entities, 14 GEO. MASON L. REV. 1035, 1035 & n.2 (2007).

their copyright based on technical violations of prior United States law. In both copyright and trademark law, lower courts have handed down groundbreaking new rulings on the scope of IP protection on the Internet.

Organization:

The structure of this book follows a consistent pattern throughout the various areas of Intellectual Property law. With regard to each type of Intellectual Property right, the book addresses issues of validity, ownership, infringement, defenses, and remedies. Validity is concerned with the threshold for establishing a particular type of right; ownership addresses the establishment of priority in those rights, while infringement addresses the proof that must be adduced to show a violation of the right. The discussion of defenses focuses on limitations on Intellectual Property rights and affirmative defenses that can be asserted even if the plaintiff establishes a prima facie case of infringement. Finally, the book briefly surveys remedies available for violation of each Intellectual Property right.

Acknowledgements:

I gratefully acknowledge Bridget Kevin Myers for her comments on book drafts, Lee Ann Lockridge for reviewing several patent sections of this book, and Brittany Bartley for her research assistance. Small portions of this book are drawn from material I have authored, including my casebook on Intellectual Property, the accompanying teacher's manual, and published and unpublished articles. This book is designed to be used with any Intellectual Property casebook, but it includes discussion of many of the cases featured in Lange, LaFrance, Myers & Lockridge, Intellectual Property: Cases & Materials (Fourth Edition 2012 Thomson West), the casebook that I coauthored with David Lange, Mary LaFrance, and Lee Ann Lockridge. This book can also serve as a free-standing introduction to Intellectual Property.

Chapter 1

OVERVIEW

Table of Sections

¶ 1.01 Types of Intellectual Property & Key Terms

It is probably useful to begin by distinguishing the three major areas of federal Intellectual Property. The first is copyright law, which protects creative works and other works of authorship—from a John Grisham novel or movie to computer software or architectural plans—as soon as they are embodied in some tangible form or medium. The second is patent law, which primarily protects useful inventions of various kinds—such as the Wright Brothers' airplane, the Apple iPhone, or the Amazon Kindle Fire e-book reader—as well as providing exclusive rights in ornamental designs and new plant varieties. The third is trademark law, which protects marketing information, such as brand names, logos, slogans, and other indicators of the source of goods or services. Classic examples might include the McDonald's brand and the "golden arches," as well as perhaps the overall appearance of a McDonald's fast food restaurant. In each of these main areas, Intellectual Property plays an increasingly important role in the national and in the world economy. This growth is a result of the expansion in the subject matter, scope of rights, and remedies available.

There are state law counterparts to each of these three federal Intellectual Property schemes. The state laws vary in terms of their modern significance. With regard to copyrights, state copyright law has been largely preempted by the federal Copyright Act of 1976, although there remains some state copyright protection for certain "unfixed" works, such as an unscripted and unrecorded speech or improvised song. Before the 1976 Copyright Act, state law played a more important role in protecting creative works, as will be discussed in Chapter 2, ¶ 2.07.

4

The most important state law claim is most likely to be the law of trade secrets, which protects proprietary innovations and is therefore the state law counterpart to patent protection. As will be seen, trade secret protection plays an important role in protecting various forms of confidential business information, including a variety of subject matter that would not qualify for federal patent protection. Finally, with regard to trademarks, state law provides protection through a variety of state trademark laws, as well as the law of unfair competition. In addition, the state law right of publicity provides an important form of protection, particularly as to product endorsements and other uses of a person's name, image, or other identifying characteristics in the marketing of goods or services.

¶ 1.02   Historical Notes

Trying to provide an overview of a field as all-encompassing and crucial as Intellectual Property is a daunting task. One useful way to begin is to look at how Intellectual Property has been viewed historically, starting with one of the Founding Fathers, Thomas Jefferson. The following quote is frequently cited by commentators in the Intellectual Property field, although they often only include the first four sentences, rather than the five that are quoted here:

> [An idea's] peculiar character, too, is that no one possesses the less, because every other possesses the whole of it. He who receives an idea from me, receives instruction himself without lessening mine; as he who lights his taper at mine, receives light without darkening me. That ideas should freely spread from one to another over the globe, for the moral and mutual instruction of man, and improvement of his condition, seems to have been peculiarly and benevolently designed by nature, when she made them, like fire, expansible over all space, without lessening their density in any point, and like the air in which we breathe, move, and have our physical being, incapable of confinement or exclusive appropriation. Inventions then cannot, in nature, be a subject of property. Society may give an exclusive right to the profits arising from them, as an encouragement to men to pursue ideas which may produce utility, but this may or may not be done, according to the will and convenience of the society, without claim or complaint from any body.[1]

---

1. Thomas Jefferson, Letter from Thomas Jefferson to Isaac McPherson (Aug. 13, 1813), *quoted in* Justin Hughes, Copyright and Incomplete Historiographies: Of Piracy, Propertization, and Thomas Jefferson, 79 S. Cal. L. Rev. 993 (2006).

This letter from Thomas Jefferson to Isaac McPherson, expresses several meaningful thoughts about Intellectual Property.

Jefferson's first insight is that ideas and information are very different from natural resources such as land, oil, or wheat. If someone occupies a field, it prevents others from making use of it. So too when oil is burned or wheat is consumed—there is less available for others to use. The supply of these resources is necessarily limited, and one person's consumption reduces the quantity available for others to use. Information, by contrast, is relatively inexhaustible. If one person reads a William Faulkner novel or a paper by Albert Einstein, it does not preclude others from reading these works or making use of these thoughts. So too when the Wright Brothers invented the airplane, their innovation can be used and built upon by others, who might build better and faster planes.

The second point found in Jefferson's letter is that information is not readily appropriated. This fact is one of the fundamental conundrums of Intellectual Property—once information is created, it is difficult to prevent others from making use of it. Unlike fencing a field, storing oil in a tank, or harvesting grain, there is no readily apparent way to appropriate or take control of Intellectual Property, particularly in a state of nature. Without the legal constraints of Intellectual Property law, information would be free. Unfortunately, however, there would be no financial incentive to create new information or innovations.

The third point is that society might choose to provide Intellectual Property rights in order to stimulate and reward the creation of Intellectual Property. Without this incentive, there would be little or no financial reward for the creation of Intellectual Property, because it would be quickly used by others without any payment or permission. Jefferson made a philosophical observation here as well—suggesting that there is no "natural right" to Intellectual Property, and that instead the basis of Intellectual Property protection is the overall benefit that inures to society from the creation of Intellectual Property. This viewpoint differs substantially from the natural rights theory, which is much more influential in Continental Europe and elsewhere in the world, and which suggests the rights to creative works inherently belong to their creators by virtue of their labor and efforts. Interestingly, Jefferson (in his capacity as Secretary of State) was previously responsible for the operations of the patent office

Consider this quotation from Abraham Lincoln's Second Lecture on Discoveries and Inventions, which was delivered to the Phi Alpha Society of Illinois College in 1859: "Next came the Patent laws. These began in England in 1624; and, in this country, with the adoption of our constitution. Before then, any man might instantly use what another had invented; so that the inventor had no special advantage from his own invention. The patent system changed this; secured to the inventor, for a limited time, the exclusive use of his invention; and thereby added the fuel of *interest* to the *fire* of genius, in the discovery and production of new and useful things."[2] Lincoln is expressing the same concept as Jefferson—society can and should reward innovation by providing Intellectual Property rights to those who create and innovate.

¶ 1.03 Economic & Natural Rights Perspectives

"Like many businessmen of genius he learned that free competition was wasteful, monopoly efficient. And so he simply set about achieving that efficient monopoly."

—Mario Puzo, The Godfather, Book 3, ch. 14 (1969) (describing Don Vito Corleone).

The jurisprudential basis for Intellectual Property has both theoretical and practical significance. On a theoretical level, it is important to understand why IP rights are granted, for example, to the maker of a hit movie or a blockbuster pharmaceutical product. On a practical level, courts often look to the underlying purposes of patent, copyright, and trademark law in order to decide close cases. Unlike some areas of the law, IP issues are often not clear-cut, and the policy rationales for IP protection can help guide courts in drawing the lines between permissible and unlawful uses of IP-protected materials. For instance, whether a particular use of a copyrighted work using modern technology infringes on a copyright may well hinge upon the extent to which that use would frustrate the incentives that authors have to create the work in the first place. Thus, compare the analysis of copying a thumbnail version of a photograph onto Google's search engine with wholesale copying of musical works using file-sharing technologies.

As mentioned earlier, there are two competing theories for why Intellectual Property protection might be granted. The first, which is predominant in the United States, focuses on the overall benefit that inures to society from the creation of Intellectual Property. This approach is commonly known as the economic or the incentive theory for IP protection. In short, IP protection is a necessary evil that provides a financial reward for creative and inventive effort. IP rights are granted to serve the greater public good. This utilitarian philosophy is reflected even in the text of the IP Clause of the

---

2. Abraham Lincoln, Second Lecture on Discoveries and Inventions, Delivered to the Phi Alpha Society of Illinois College at Jacksonville, Illinois (February 11, 1859), *quoted in* 3 Collected Works of Abraham Lincoln 357 (Roy P. Basler, Ed., 1953).

Constitution, which grants Congress the power: *"to Promote the Progress of Science and useful Arts*, by securing for limited Times to Authors and Inventors the exclusive Right to their respective Writings and Discoveries."* This language, found in Article I, Section 8, Clause 8 of the Constitution, clearly sets forth a general public purpose for IP protection, rather than an emphasis securing the inherent rights of authors and inventors.

The economic approach differs substantially from the natural rights theory, which is influential in Continental Europe and elsewhere in the world. Under this view, the rights to creative works inherently belong to their creators by virtue of their labor and efforts, or by virtue of being an extension of their personhood. The first of these philosophical justifications, most closely associated with John Locke, emphasizes that creative works are the product of the labor and efforts of those who created them, which entitles them to property rights as a matter of natural right. The second view, associated with George Wilhelm Friedrich Hegel, focuses on how creative works are an extension of their creators' personhood, which justifies their ownership of these works. Both of these natural rights justifications have their proponents, as well those who claim the theories in fact do not justify IP rights. The natural rights view generally is seen has supporting stronger IP protections, including moral rights, which are discussed in discussed in Chapter 4, ¶ 4.03.

Viewed from an economic or incentive theory, Intellectual Property is an example of a public good. A public good is a product or service that has two basic characteristics. First, it is not appropriable—the producer of the public good cannot prevent it from being used or consumed by others. Second, it is inexhaustible. The use of the service by some does not diminish the ability of others to use the service. Because of the inability to appropriate the service, thus allowing only those who paid for it to receive its benefits, public goods are underproduced in the absence of government or other intervention. National defense provides an example of a public good. Establishing a nuclear arsenal to protect a country would present appropriability problems, as it would be practically impossible to provide the protections of a nuclear umbrella only to those who pay for the national defense. Moreover, once national defense is provided, an increase in the number of people protected by the arsenal would not impose additional costs, as long as the same geographic area is involved. Hence, tax money is used to provide national defense because it would not be adequately produced in a free market.

Similarly, an invention or book has the characteristics of a public good. Once it is produced, others can imitate or copy the innovation or creative effort. These imitators or copiers are known as free riders. To solve this free rider problem, Intellectual Property law provides property rights in the invention or creative work. Absent these protections, there would not be sufficient incentives for investment in research and development or creative endeavor. Yet the fundamental irony of Intellectual Property is that once the invention or creative work has been made, the use of that Intellectual Property by others does not diminish it. This is Thomas Jefferson's point in the quotation above.

Intellectual Property law is designed to accommodate these conflicting aspects of the public good problem. On the one hand, Intellectual Property law provides property rights to encourage invention and creativity. On the other hand, the Intellectual Property Clause, which is found in Article I, Section 8, Clause 8 of the Constitution, mandates that copyright and patent rights cannot be perpetual, so that upon expiration the Intellectual Property can be freely used at no cost: "to Promote the Progress of Science and useful Arts, by securing for limited Times to Authors and Inventors the exclusive Right to their respective Writings and Discoveries." Thus once a copyright or patent has expired, the information protected by these IP rights will fall into the public domain, as discussed below.

Intellectual property is one of the most heavily debated areas of the law, particularly as to the scope of rights that inhere to owners of patents and copyrights. Intellectual property has grown in importance, particularly as the economy has grown to be more service- and information-based. Music file-sharing, biotechnology, prescription drugs, and software are leading topics of the day. The growing importance of these rights has only heightened the importance of Intellectual Property policy. Fundamentally, Intellectual Property rights offer exclusivity—a kind of monopoly in some instances (though the patent or copyright does not necessarily confer market power in an economic sense, because there may be substitute products available to give consumers an alternative to the patented or copyrighted item).

These exclusive rights are nominally antithetical to the fundamental economic policy goal of having competitive markets in order to promote efficiency and consumer welfare. Hence, some commentators focus on the inherent conflict between Intellectual Property rights and competition. On the other hand, patents and copyrights offer incentives for research and development and artistic creativity, helping to address the public good problem. Under this view, Intellectual Property is not problematic from an economic efficiency standpoint, but rather is necessary to promote innovation and creativity.

It is appropriate to focus not only upon the rights of authors and inventors, but also upon the interest of society in promoting competition, expanding its base of knowledge, improving technology, and protecting consumers. Intellectual Property law should maintain a focus on its constitutional roots and fundamental purpose—"To promote the Progress of Science and useful Arts."[3] This approach suggests a basis for stronger Intellectual Property protection in some circumstances—such as when piracy or counterfeiting has become so rampant that the incentive to create may be destroyed. At the same time, courts and legislatures should resist the impulse to offer overly broad Intellectual Property rights that are inconsistent with the fundamental statement of purpose set forth in the Intellectual Property Clause: "to Promote the Progress of Science and useful Arts, by securing for limited Times to Authors and Inventors the exclusive Right to their respective Writings and Discoveries."[4] There is much debate among commentators, practicing lawyers, and judges regarding the proper balance to be struck in such areas as the duration of copyrights, the scope of copyright, patent, and trademark protection, and the proper balance between IP and the First Amendment.

¶ 1.04   The Public Domain

The public domain is a commonly used term in IP, referring to material that is unprotected by IP rights, either because the rights have expired, been forfeited, or abandoned/waived. On the importance of the public domain, consider David Lange's comments in his seminal work on this topic: "The problems [of expanding Intellectual Property claims] will not be resolved until courts have come to see the public domain not merely as an unexplored abstraction but as a field of individual rights fully as important as any of the new property rights. The field of Intellectual Property law at large sometimes seems to be beyond the possibility of exhaustion. But then, that was the view taken by the public toward the buffalo as they were being hunted one hundred years ago. And where are the buffalo now?"[5]

Professor Lange's suggestion to address this concern merits quotation as well:

> What I would suppose, then, is not that Intellectual Property is undeserving of protection, but rather that such protection as it gets ought to reflect its unique susceptibility to conceptual imprecision and to infinite replication. These attributes seem

---

3. U.S. Const., Art. I, § 8, cl. 8.

4. U.S. Const., Art. I, § 8, cl. 8.

5. David L. Lange, Recognizing the Public Domain, 44 L. & Contemp. Probs.

147, 168 (1981). *See also* David Lange, Reimagining the Public Domain, 66 Law & Contemp. Probs. 463 (2003).

to me to require the recognition of two fundamental principles. One is that Intellectual Property theory must always accept something akin to a "no-man's land" at the boundaries; doubtful cases of infringement ought always to be resolved in favor of the defendant. The other is that no exclusive interest should ever have affirmative recognition unless its conceptual opposite is also recognized. Each right ought to be marked off clearly against the public domain.[6]

Many other scholars also have focused their attention on the importance of the public domain.[7] A key tenet of Intellectual Property is the idea that information should fall into the public domain upon expiration of the patent or copyright. This concept is consistent with the constitutional dictate that copyrights and patents can exist for "limited times." The policy remains ingrained in both copyright and patent law, even though copyright and patent terms have been the subject of rather recent extensions. In *Brulotte v. Thys*,[8] the Supreme Court held that a patent owner could not enforce a contractual provision requiring payment of patent royalties after expiration of the patent. The Court did not have the same concern in *Aronson v. Quick Point Pencil*,[9] where it upheld a license for an invention that was the subject of a pending patent application. Both *Brulotte* and *Aronson* are discussed in *Baladevon, Inc. v. Abbott Laboratories, Inc.*[10]

In *Lear, Inc. v. Adkins*,[11] the Court "held that a person licensed to use a patent may challenge the validity of the patent, and that a licensee who establishes that the patent is invalid need not pay the royalties accrued under the licensing agreement subsequent to the issuance of the patent. Both holdings relied on the desirability of encouraging licensees to challenge the validity of patents, to further the strong federal policy that only inventions that meet the rigorous requirements of patentability shall be withdrawn from the public domain."[12] Allowing licensees to challenge the validity of patents furthers Intellectual Property policy by allowing knowledgeable market participants (including those who obtained licens-

---

6. David L. Lange, Recognizing the Public Domain, 44 L. & CONTEMP. PROBS. 147, 148–50 (1981).

7. Yochai Benkler, Free as the Air to Common Use: First Amendment Constraints on Enclosure of the Public Domain, 74 N.Y.U. L. REV. 354 (1999); Diane Leenheer Zimmerman, Is There a Right to Have Something to Say? One View of the Public Domain, 73 FORDHAM L. REV. 297 (2004); Jessica Litman, The Public Domain, 39 EMORY L.J. 965 (1990); Robert P. Merges, A New Dynamism in the Public Domain, 71 U.

CHI. L. REV. 183 (2004); Pamela Samuelson, Enriching Discourse on Public Domains, 55 DUKE L.J. 783, 786–813 (2006); Symposium, The Public Domain, LAW & CONTEMP. PROBS., Winter/Spring 2003, 1.

8. 379 U.S. 29 (1964).

9. 440 U.S. 257 (1979).

10. 871 F.Supp. 89 (D. Mass. 1994).

11. 395 U.S. 653 (1969).

12. *Id.*

es) to bring forward information relevant to the validity of the Intellectual Property right.

Although it might generally be thought that Intellectual Property protection is always an impediment to a free and open public domain, the protections of copyright law (for example) can actually further some goals of those who favor a robust public domain. For example, the Creative Commons (CC) allows authors to license their works to the public so long as they comply with obligations to make any resulting work available to the public. Similarly, "open source" software, such as Linux, can be made available for public use, again with some restrictions as to how resulting innovations must be treated. Another example is the GNU General Public License, which again requires that those who adapt open source software must make their innovations available to the public.

¶ 1.05   Intellectual Property & The First Amendment

In addition to considering the importance of the public domain, a recurring issue involves the interaction of IP law and the First Amendment. This intersection is most prominent in the copyright field, as that is the area of law that protects expressive works and thereby might also impinge upon the ability of others to use creative expression that is protected by someone else's copyright. The issue arises too in the use of trademarks for expressive purposes.

"Few topics in the study of intellectual property are as important, or as aggressively disputed, as the relationship between the conventional IP doctrines and the First Amendment."[13] The First Amendment familiarly states that "Congress shall make no law abridging freedom of speech or of the press...." The following abstract explains some of the issues that can arise. The Supreme Court's 2012 ruling, alluded to in the excerpt, is discussed later in this book, in Chapter 3, ¶ 3.03.

> *Does copyright violate the first amendment? Professor Melville Nimmer asked this question forty years ago, and then answered it by concluding that copyright itself is affirmatively speech protective. Despite ample reason to doubt Nimmer's response, the Supreme Court has avoided an independent, thoughtful, plenary review of the question. Copyright has come to enjoy an all-but-categorical immunity to first amendment constraints. Now, however, the Court faces a new challenge to its back-of-the-hand treatment of this vital conflict. In Golan v. Holder [609 F.3d 1076 (10th Cir.2010), cert. granted, 131 S.Ct.*

13. LANGE, LaFRANCE, MYERS & LOCKRIDGE, INTELLECTUAL PROPERTY: CASES & MATERIALS (Fourth Edition 2012), at 27.

1600 (2011)] the Tenth Circuit considered legislation (enacted pursuant to the Berne Convention and TRIPS) "restoring" copyright protection to millions of foreign works previously thought to belong to the public domain. The Tenth Circuit upheld the legislation, but not without noting that it appeared to raise important first amendment concerns. The Supreme Court granted certiorari. Our essay addresses the issues in this case, literally on the eve of oral argument before the Court. We briefly consider the Copyright and Treaty Clauses, and then turn our attention to the relationship between copyright and the First Amendment. In the course of our discussion we endorse an understanding of that relationship in which the Amendment is newly seen as paramount, and copyright is newly seen in the image of the Amendment.[14]

14. *Abstract*, from Lange, Weaver & Reed, *Golan v. Holder: Copyright in the Image of the First Amendment*, 11 John Marshall Review of Intellectual Property Law 83 (2011). For more information on the interplay between copyright and the First Amendment, see Robert Denicola, *Copyright and Free Speech: Constitutional Limitations on the Protection of Expression*, 67 Calif.L.Rev. 283 (1979); Paul Goldstein, *Copyright and the First Amendment*, 70 Colum.L.Rev. 983 (1970); Melville B. Nimmer, *Does Copyright Abridge the First Amendment Guarantees to Freedom of Speech and Press?*, 12 UCLA L.Rev. 1180 (1970); Jed Rubenfeld, *The Freedom Of Information*, 112 Yale L.J. 1 (2002). See also Yochai Benkler, *Free As The Air To Common Use: First Amendment Constraints On The Enclosure Of The Public Domain*, 74 N.Y.U. L. Rev. 354 (1999); Neil Weinstock Netanel, Copyright's Paradox (Oxford Press 2010).

Chapter 2

COPYRIGHTABLE SUBJECT MATTER

Table of Sections

"Copyright is the Cinderella of the law." Zechariah Chafee, *Reflections on the Law of Copyright*, 45 COLUM. L. REV. 503, 503 (1945).

¶ 2.01 Introduction

Copyright law protects creative works such as music, movies, software, and books. Because of its interesting subject matter, it is indeed the "Cinderella of the law." It is also a field about which many intelligent people have serious misconceptions. In the vein of David Letterman, the following is a "top ten" list of copyright myths:

10. If a work is old, I can always copy it.

9. If a work can be found on the Internet, I can freely copy and use it.

8. If I bought a copy of a work, I can make additional copies of it or use it as I please.

7. Any personal use of copyrighted works is permitted.

6. Copyright owners do not really care if I copy a work, and they will not catch me.

5. If I add my own material to someone else's work, there is no copyright violation.

4. If I do not make a profit on my use of a copyrighted work, there is no copyright violation.

3. If there is no copyright notice on a work, I can copy it.

2.   Educational or news reporting uses are always fair use.

1.   The First Amendment is a complete defense to copyright claims.

The extent to which each of these ten assertions are incorrect (at least in part) will become clear in the next several chapters. Within each major field of Intellectual Property, this book is organized based on the main elements of an Intellectual Property claim. Consider the case of a copyright. Those elements are:

— subject matter and validity issues (whether the copyright at issue is within the subject matter of copyright law and whether it satisfies the requisites for protection);

— ownership and duration issues (who owns and can assert the copyright claim, and how long does the copyright last);

— infringement issues (what showing must be made to establish a violation of a copyright);

— defenses to claims of infringement, such as fair use in copyright law;

— remedies, such as injunctive relief and damages.

¶ 2.02   Types of Copyrightable Subject Matter

Section 102 of the Copyright Act sets forth a general definition of copyright subject matter and then identifies eight illustrative categories of copyrightable subject matter:

Copyright protection subsists, in accordance with this title, in original works of authorship fixed in any tangible medium of expression, now known or later developed, from which they can be perceived, reproduced, or otherwise communicated, either directly or with the aid of a machine or device. Works of authorship include the following categories:

(1) literary works;

(2) musical works, including any accompanying words;

(3) dramatic works, including any accompanying music;

(4) pantomimes and choreographic works;

(5) pictorial, graphic, and sculptural works;

(6) motion pictures and other audiovisual works;

(7) sound recordings; and

(8) architectural works.

As the Copyright Act expressly states, this listing is not an exclusive cataloguing of the types of works protected under copyright law. Instead, it is clear that any original work of authorship is eligible for copyright law's benefits once it is fixed in a tangible medium of expression.

The scope of copyright's subject matter has grown considerably from the first American copyright law, the Copyright Act of 1790, which protected only books, charts, and maps. This first statute provided:

> An Act for the encouragement of learning, by securing the copies of maps, Charts, And books, to the authors and proprietors of such copies, during the times therein mentioned. Section 1. Be it enacted by the Senate and House of Representatives of the United States of America in Congress assembled, That from and after the passing of this act, the author and authors of any map, chart, book or books already printed within these United States, being a citizen or citizens thereof, or resident within the same, his or their executors, administrators or assigns, who halt or have not transferred to any other person the copyright of such map, chart, book or books, share or shares thereof; and any other person or persons, being a citizen or citizens of these United States, or residents therein, his or their executors, administrators or assigns, who halt or have purchased or legally acquired the copyright of any such map, chart, book or books, in order to print, reprint, publish or vend the same, shall have the sole right and liberty of printing, reprinting, publishing and vending such map, chart, book or books, for the term of fourteen years from the recording the title thereof in the clerk's office, as is herein after directed: And that the author and authors of any map, chart, book or books already made and composed, and not printed or published, or that shall hereafter be made and composed, being a citizen or citizens of these United States, or resident therein, and his or their executors, administrators or assigns, shall have the sole right and liberty of printing, reprinting, publishing and vending such map, chart, book or books, for the like term of fourteen years from the time of recording the title thereof in the clerk's office as aforesaid. And if, at the expiration of the said term, the author or authors, or any of them, be living, and a citizen or citizens of these United States, or resident therein, the same exclusive right shall be continued to him or them, his or their executors, administrators or assigns, for the further term of fourteen years; Provided, He or they shall cause the title thereof to be a second time recorded and published in the same manner as is herein after directed, and that within six months before the expiration of the first term of fourteen years aforesaid.[1]

1. Copyright Act of 1790, Section 1, 1 Statutes At Large 124.

Thus, the first copyright law protected only a map, chart, book, or book already printed. A variety of categories of works were added in succeeding years: designs, prints, etchings, and engravings in 1802, musical compositions in 1831, dramatic compositions in 1856, photographs and negatives in 1865, and statuary in 1870. In 1891, Congress finally permitted copyright protection for works of foreign origin. In essence, the United States took a very narrow view of copyright protection for its first century, but then joined the world copyright economy in its second century. In its third century, the United States gains substantial export revenues from foreign sales of software, movies, books, music, and other material protected by copyright law.

In the 1909 Act, Congress provided a general description of copyrightable subject matter: "The works for which copyright may be secured under this title shall include all the writings of an author."[2] Technology continued to advance, and thus in 1912 Congress added "motion pictures" to the illustrative list. Despite its existence for many years before this date, Congress did not add "sound recordings" until 1971, a topic discussed in Chapter 4, ¶ 4.02.

The most recent category of copyrightable works to be added to the list was architectural works, which were not expressly included until 1990. This is a significant category of creative endeavor, and the Architectural Works Protection Copyright Act of 1990 offers important protection for the work product of architects.[3] An "architectural work" is defined as "the design of a building as embodied in any tangible medium of expression, including a building, architectural plans, or drawings. The work includes the overall form as well as the arrangement and composition of spaces and elements in the design, but does not include individual standard features."[4] Accordingly, a set of architectural plans are copyrightable, and can be infringed if the plans are duplicated or reproduced—including by construction of a building or home based on the plans. This right thus vindicates the architect's efforts from imitation by others seeking to simply replicate the original architectural design. These were rights required to be protected under the Berne Convention, an international treaty to which the United States has adhered and which sets forth minimum copyright protections. Congress ratified the Berne Convention in 1988.

Copyright protection for architectural works presents some challenges—some unique and some frequently encountered in copy-

2. Act of Mar. 4, 1909, ch. 320, § 4, 35 Stat. 1075, 1076.

3. Architectural Works Protection Copyright Act of 1990, Pub. L. No. 101–650, 104 Stat. 5133 (1990).

4. 17 U.S.C. § 101 (2000).

right law. A unique problem is how to deal with photographs of buildings that are designed by an architect—does the photograph infringe the copyright in the work of architecture? Section 120(a) of the Copyright Act expressly prevents assertion of such a claim, providing as follows: "The copyright in an architectural work that has been constructed does not include the right to prevent the making, distributing, or public display of pictures, paintings, photographs, or other pictorial representations of the work, if the building in which the work is embodied is located in or ordinarily visible from a public place." Moreover, section 120(b) permits the alteration or destruction of buildings without the consent of the architect (or other copyright owner): "Notwithstanding the provisions of section 106(2), the owners of a building embodying an architectural work may, without the consent of the author or copyright owner of the architectural work, make or authorize the making of alterations to such building, and destroy or authorize the destruction of such building."

A more typical copyright problem is differentiating between protected expression and unprotectable ideas, *scenes á faire* (stock background material), and the like (these topics are discussed later in this book). This issue is addressed in general terms in the legislative history of the Architectural Works Act. The creative effort in architecture can involve either (1) the selection, coordination, or arrangement of unprotectible elements into an original and protected whole; (2) incorporating new, protectable design features in otherwise standard and unprotected building features; or (3) creative interior architectural elements. Copyright protection does not extend to individual standard features, such as windows, doors, and other standard building components. There is also no copyright protection for design elements that are functionally required.[5]

Current Copyright Law

The general scope of copyright subject matter is set forth in section 102(a): "Copyright protection subsists, in accordance with this title, in original works of authorship fixed in any tangible medium of expression, now known or later developed, from which they can be perceived, reproduced, or otherwise communicated, either directly or with the aid of a machine or device." The statute proceeds to identify eight categories of material that are included within the definition of works of authorship:

(1) literary works;

(2) musical works, including any accompanying words;

(3) dramatic works, including any accompanying music;

(4) pantomimes and choreographic works;

---

5. *See* H.R. Rep. No. 101–735, at 18–21 (1990).

(5) pictorial, graphic, and sculptural works;

(6) motion pictures and other audiovisual works;

(7) sound recordings; and

(8) architectural works.

Most of these terms are seemingly self-explanatory, but several have specific definitions found in section 101 of the Copyright Act and thus are "terms of art." When one is in doubt about the meaning of a term in copyright law, it is important to review the definitions in section 101, which sometimes provide clear and unequivocal answers to the issue.

Literary works are defined as "works, other than audiovisual works, expressed in words, numbers, or other verbal or numerical symbols or indicia, regardless of the nature of the material objects, such as books, periodicals, manuscripts, phonorecords, film, tapes, disks, or cards, in which they are embodied."

Audiovisual works are "works that consist of a series of related images which are intrinsically intended to be shown by the use of machines, or devices such as projectors, viewers, or electronic equipment, together with accompanying sounds, if any, regardless of the nature of the material objects, such as films or tapes, in which the works are embodied."

Motion pictures (movies) "are audiovisual works consisting of a series of related images which, when shown in succession, impart an impression of motion, together with accompanying sounds, if any."

Pictorial, graphic, and sculptural works "include two-dimensional and three-dimensional works of fine, graphic, and applied art, photographs, prints and art reproductions, maps, globes, charts, diagrams, models, and technical drawings, including architectural plans. Such works shall include works of artistic craftsmanship insofar as their form but not their mechanical or utilitarian aspects are concerned; the design of a useful article, as defined in this section, shall be considered a pictorial, graphic, or sculptural work only if, and only to the extent that, such design incorporates pictorial, graphic, or sculptural features that can be identified separately from, and are capable of existing independently of, the utilitarian aspects of the article."

Sound recordings "are works that result from the fixation of a series of musical, spoken, or other sounds, but not including the sounds accompanying a motion picture or other audiovisual work, regardless of the nature of the material objects, such as disks, tapes, or other phonorecords, in which they are embodied."

Utilitarian Objects

What about works that have utilitarian functions? The copyrightability of such works depends on their nature. Consider the classic case of *Mazer v. Stein*. In that case, the creative work was a statuette of a dancing figure, whose copyrightability would not be in doubt but for their mass production for use as lamp bases. The court found that the inclusion of the statuette in the overall final product—the lamp—does not render the work uncopyrightable, given that the statuette could be independently perceived as a creative work. Section 101 of the Copyright Act defines a useful article as "an article having an intrinsic utilitarian function that is not merely to portray the appearance of the article or to convey information." In a somewhat circular note, the statute also provides that "[a]n article that is normally a part of a useful article is considered a 'useful article'."

Certainly mass production does not itself deprive a work of copyright protection, as indeed such mass production is the very purpose of many creative works. Nor does a commercial purpose or use in advertising result in a forfeiture of copyright. Consequently, Justice Holmes writing for the Court in *Bleistein v. Donaldson Lithographing*[6] held that a poster used to advertise a circus was protected by copyright law:

> It would be a dangerous undertaking for persons trained only to the law to constitute themselves final judges of the worth of pictorial illustrations, outside of the narrowest and most obvious limits. At the one extreme, some works of genius would be sure to miss appreciation. Their very novelty would make them repulsive until the public had learned the new language in which their author spoke. It may be more than doubted, for instance, whether the etchings of Goya or the paintings of Manet would have been sure of protection when seen for the first time. At the other end, copyright would be denied to pictures which appealed to a public less educated than the judge. Yet if they command the interest of any public, they have a commercial value,—it would be bold to say that they have not an aesthetic and educational value,—and the taste of any public is not to be treated with contempt. It is an ultimate fact for the moment, whatever may be our hopes for a change. That these pictures had their worth and their success is sufficiently shown by the desire to reproduce them without regard to the plaintiffs' rights.

Justice Holmes' observation regarding the need for courts to avoid aesthetic or stylistic arguments is an important one. Copyright law protects any type of work that fits within the statutory definition,

---

6. 188 U.S. 239, 251–52 (1903).

regardless of its artistic merit or lack thereof. Humble works, such as advertising copy or imagery, or software code to operate garage door openers or computer printers, are within the scope of copyrightable subject matter.

On the other hand, a purely useful object does not qualify for copyright protection, even if it has a pleasing aesthetic appearance. *Brandir International, Inc. v. Cascade Pacific Lumber Co.*[7] is a good example of this type of situation. The plaintiff developed a ribbon-rack style bicycle rack. It was inspired by an abstract sculptural work—a jagged-edged ribbon-like metal piece. Someone suggested that the work could serve as a model for a useful bicycle rack, but of course the final version of the bicycle rack incorporated a number of design changes that made it much more useful as a bike rack. For example, the bicycle rack included smooth round surfaces and symmetrical spacing to enable as many bicycles as possible to be stored and easily removed from the rack. Not surprisingly, the court held that the design of the bicycle rack was driven by its function, and thus it was not copyrightable. (Of course, the functional design could theoretically be protected by a utility patent, but only if the requirements of patent law are satisfied, a subject addressed in Chapter 12.)

¶ 2.03   The Minimum Standard of Creativity

"Individual perception of the beautiful is too varied a power to permit a narrow or rigid concept of art."[8]

The starting point for any analysis of copyrightability is the Supreme Court's landmark decision in *Feist Publications, Inc. v. Rural Telephone Service Co.*,[9] a 1991 Supreme Court decision. An understanding of *Feist* is crucial to analyzing questions of copyrightability. In that case, the Court considered the copyrightability of a typical "white pages" telephone directory (listing names alphabetically, along with addresses and telephone numbers). Substantial portions of the directory were directly copied verbatim by a competitor telephone directory provider. Justice O'Connor's opinion for the Court noted two basic starting points—(1) facts are not copyrightable; and (2) compilations of facts generally are copyrightable. "Each of these propositions possesses an impeccable pedigree. That there can be no valid copyright in facts is universally understood. The most fundamental axiom of copyright law is that '[n]o author may copyright his ideas or the facts he narrates.' "[10] Moreover, as Justice O'Connor noted: "The sine qua non of copyright is original-

---

7. 834 F.2d 1142 (2d Cir. 1987).

8. *Mazer v. Stein*, 347 U.S. 201, 214 (1954).

9. 499 U.S. 340 (1991).

10. *Id.* at 344–45 (quoting *Harper & Row, Publishers, Inc. v. Nation Enterprises*, 471 U.S. 539, 556 (1985)).

ity. To qualify for copyright protection, a work must be original to the author. Original, as the term is used in copyright, means only that the work was independently created by the author (as opposed to copied from other works), and that it possesses at least some minimal degree of creativity."[11]

The Court made it clear that the originality requirement has a constitutional dimension:

> Originality is a constitutional requirement. The source of Congress' power to enact copyright laws is Article I, § 8, cl. 8, of the Constitution, which authorizes Congress to "secur[e] for limited Times to Authors AAA the exclusive Right to their respective Writings." In two decisions from the late 19th century—*The Trade-Mark Cases*, 100 U.S. 82, 25 L.Ed. 550 (1879); and *Burrow–Giles Lithographic Co. v. Sarony*, 111 U.S. 53, 4 S.Ct. 279, 28 L.Ed. 349 (1884)—this Court defined the crucial terms "authors" and "writings." In so doing, the Court made it unmistakably clear that these terms presuppose a degree of originality.[12]

The Court then explained how this principle places powerful limitations on the ability to protect factual material:

> It is this bedrock principle of copyright that mandates the law's seemingly disparate treatment of facts and factual compilations. . . . This is because facts do not owe their origin to an act of authorship. The distinction is one between creation and discovery: The first person to find and report a particular fact has not created the fact; he or she has merely discovered its existence. To borrow from *Burrow–Giles*, one who discovers a fact is not its "maker" or "originator." 111 U.S., at 58, 4 S.Ct., at 281. "The discoverer merely finds and records." Nimmer § 2.03[E]. Census takers, for example, do not "create" the population figures that emerge from their efforts; in a sense, they copy these figures from the world around them.[13]

Justice O'Connor next turned to what is known as the "sweat of the brow" or "industrious collection" theory, in which "the underlying notion was that copyright was a reward for the hard work that went into compiling facts." The Court unequivocally and unanimously rejected this doctrine:

> The "sweat of the brow" doctrine had numerous flaws, the most glaring being that it extended copyright protection in a compilation beyond selection and arrangement—the compiler's original contributions—to the facts themselves. Under the doctrine, the only defense to infringement was independent cre-

11. *Id.* at 345 (citations omitted).   **13.** *Id.*
12. *Id.*

ation. A subsequent compiler was "not entitled to take one word of information previously published," but rather had to "independently wor[k] out the matter for himself, so as to arrive at the same result from the same common sources of information." "Sweat of the brow" courts thereby eschewed the most fundamental axiom of copyright law—that no one may copyright facts or ideas.[14]

As the Court noted, when it enacted the Copyright Act of 1976, Congress removed language referring to "all the writings of an author" and replaced it with the phrase "original works of authorship."[15] The Copyright Act also specifically delineated those elements of a work for which copyright is not available. As 17 U.S.C. § 102(b) states: "In no case does copyright protection for an original work of authorship extend to any idea, procedure, process, system, method of operation, concept, principle, or discovery, regardless of the form in which it is described, explained, illustrated, or embodied in such work." The Court observed that section 102(b) is universally understood to prohibit copyright protection for facts.

For a factual work to qualify as a copyrightable compilation, the Court noted that three elements must be met: "(1) the collection and assembly of pre-existing material, facts, or data; (2) the selection, coordination, or arrangement of those materials; and (3) the creation, by virtue of the particular selection, coordination, or arrangement, of an 'original' work of authorship."[16] The Court went on to note that the crucial statutory requirement is the second one: "It instructs courts that, in determining whether a fact-based work is an original work of authorship, they should focus on the manner in which the collected facts have been selected, coordinated, and arranged. This is a straightforward application of the originality requirement. *Facts are never original, so the compilation author can claim originality, if at all, only in the way the facts are presented. To that end, the statute dictates that the principal focus should be on whether the selection, coordination, and arrangement are sufficiently original to merit protection.*"[17] Finally, the Court noted: "Not every selection, coordination, or arrangement will pass muster. This is plain from the statute. It states that, to merit protection, the facts must be selected, coordinated, or arranged 'in such a way' as to render the work as a whole original. This implies that some 'ways' will trigger copyright, but that others will not."[18]

---

14. *Id.* at 253.

15. *Id.* (citing 17 U.S.C. § 102(a)).

16. *Id.* at 357 (citing 17 U.S.C. § 101).

17. *Id.* at 358 (emphasis added).

18. *Id.* at 359.

Applying these principles to the white-pages telephone directory, the Court found it failed to satisfy the minimum standards required by the Copyright Act and the Constitution:

> The selection, coordination, and arrangement of Rural's white pages do not satisfy the minimum constitutional standards for copyright protection. As mentioned at the outset, Rural's white pages are entirely typical. Persons desiring telephone service in Rural's service area fill out an application and Rural issues them a telephone number. In preparing its white pages, Rural simply takes the data provided by its subscribers and lists it alphabetically by surname. The end product is a garden-variety white pages directory, devoid of even the slightest trace of creativity.
>
> Rural's selection of listings could not be more obvious: It publishes the most basic information-name, town, and telephone number-about each person who applies to it for telephone service. This is "selection" of a sort, but it lacks the modicum of creativity necessary to transform mere selection into copyrightable expression. Rural expended sufficient effort to make the white pages directory useful, but insufficient creativity to make it original.[19]

Further, the Court found that Rural's laborious and thorough coordination and arrangement of facts in alphabetical order is not "remotely creative" and "is an age-old practice, firmly rooted in tradition and so commonplace that it has come to be expected as a matter of course."[20]

Thus, *Feist* indicates that copyrightability entails two elements. The first is originality, which means simply that the work must originate with the plaintiff, as opposed to being simply copied from the work of another. The second element is a minimal showing of creativity. Applying this standard, the Court held that the white pages directory—with its mere alphabetical listing of names, addresses, and phone numbers—did not satisfy the minimum threshold of creativity in light of its entirely mechanical arrangement of uncopyrightable facts.

The Court's holding and reasoning in *Feist* is clear and easily defended, despite its allowing the wholesale copying of the database that Rural Telephone had meticulously gathered and maintained. As the Court noted, most copyrighted works easily make the grade—for example, a work of fiction or an oil painting is obviously creative enough to satisfy the minimum standard set forth in *Feist*. The difficulty is in the application of the *Feist* standard to cases involving factual arrangements that are somewhat more creative or

---

19. *Id.* at 362–63.   **20.** *Id.* at 363.

arbitrary than the phone book's alphabetical list. Several cases provide useful illustrations of this question. Consider first a yellow pages categorization intended to be used by Chinese–American consumers, which was the work at issue in *Key Publications, Inc. v. Chinatown Today Pub. Enterprises, Inc.*[21] The court found that the selection and arrangement was sufficiently creative to make the grade. Next, what about a list of the 100 best lawyers in the United States? This selection would surely involve sufficient judgment to merit copyright protection. These illustrations show that the copyright standard is quite low, and that aside from purely mechanical listings, most works are readily protectable.

Yet the court in *Key Publications* ultimately found that the defendant had not taken any copyrightable expression. The court noted that if the defendant's phone directory had "exactly duplicated a substantial designated portion of the 1989–90 Key Directory—for example, all its listings of professionals such as medical doctors, lawyers, accountants, engineers and architects, an infringement action would succeed. However, there is no claim that such duplication occurred here."[22] Accordingly, the case reaffirms the point that copyright protection in factual compilations is often "thin" or of limited scope. Similarly, anyone can develop their own list of the 100 best lawyers in America, and there may be some overlap between the lists of each author, as long as there was no wholesale copying of the particular selections.

Some have argued that United States law should provide *sui generis* protection for databases of the type not protected under the reasoning of *Feist*. A *sui generis* form of protection is essentially a free-standing or unique form of Intellectual Property. Some examples of *sui generis* laws include the Semiconductor Chip Protection Act of 1984 and The Vessel Hull Design Protection Act of 1998. The Vessel Hull Design Protection Act, Title 17, Chapter 13 of the United States Code, was enacted on October 28, 1998 and provides protection for original designs of boat hulls. The law grants an owner of an original vessel hull design exclusive rights provided that application for registration of the design with the Copyright Office is made within two years of the design being made public. The law protects vessel hull designs embodied in actual vessel hulls that are publicly exhibited, publicly distributed, or offered for sale or sold to the public on or after October 28, 1998. Similarly, the Semiconductor Chip Protection Act of 1984 protects original mask works and related semiconductor products upon proper registration with the Copyright Office. A mask work is a two or three-dimensional layout or topography of an integrated circuit, i.e. the ar-

21. 945 F.2d 509 (2d Cir. 1991).   **22.** *Id.* at 517.

rangement on a chip of various semiconductor devices (e.g., transistors and resistors).

Bills have been regularly proposed in Congress to provide specialized legal protection to the creators of databases, as the European Union has already done.[23] Laboriously gathered databases would be eligible for protection under the EU Database Directive. But to date, Congress has not enacted similar protection under United States law.

Were Congress to enact a database law, a preliminary question that would have to be addressed is the source of its authority to do so. The Court in *Feist* clearly established that the Intellectual Property Clause does not authorize copyright protection for works that do not satisfy a minimum standard of creativity, as well as that the Copyright Act does not cover such works. In that sense, the ruling in *Feist* has a constitutional, as well as statutory, dimension. The Intellectual Property Clause states: "to Promote the Progress of Science and useful Arts, by securing for limited Times to Authors and Inventors the exclusive Right to their respective Writings and Discoveries."[24] By its terms, copyrights can only be granted to those who qualify as authors of a writing.

The constitutional holding of *Feist* implies that the Intellectual Property Clause would not provide Article I authority to Congress for a database law. The alternative, of course, is for Congress to anchor the database law in its Commerce Power. It is clear that the development, marketing, and sale of databases would be activity in interstate and foreign commerce, and thus within Congress' power to regulate. The real issue would be whether using the Commerce Clause as a basis for the database law constitutes an impermissible end-run around the limited authority Congress possesses under the Intellectual Property Clause. This fundamental question is the subject of considerable scholarly comment. For instance, Yochai Benkler contends: "While Congress may regulate information markets under the Commerce Clause, it may not do so by creating exclusive private rights in information in a way that circumvents the substantive limitations placed on its power by the Exclusive Rights Clause [i.e., the Intellectual Property Clause]."[25] Marci A. Hamilton, on the other hand, argues that Congress has the power

---

23. *See* Jonathan Band & Makoto Kono, "The Database Protection Debate in the 106th Congress," 62 Ohio St. L.J. 869 (2001); Jane C. Ginsburg, "Copyright, Common Law, and Sui Generis Protection of Databases in the United States and Abroad," 66 U. Cin. L. Rev. 151 (1997); J.H. Reichman & Pamela Samuelson, "Intellectual Property Rights in Data?" 50 Vand. L.Rev. 51 (1997).

24. U.S. Const., Art. I, § 8, cl. 8.

25. Yochai Benkler, Through the Looking Glass: Alice and the Constitutional Foundations of the Public Domain, 66 Law & Contemp. Probs. 173, 178 (2003).

to enact database legislation under the Commerce Clause as long as the legislation does not "create copyright rights in information."[26]

Absent a database law like those found in Europe, there is an important group of copyright cases involving somewhat arbitrary lists or categories, such as lists of automotive parts. The goal of these lists, like the white pages telephone directory, is to be completely inclusive, so no creative selection is involved. On the other hand, these lists often do involve somewhat arbitrary organization and assignment of numbers or codes to the items in the list. Courts have struggled with whether this type of listing is copyrightable under United States law, and the outcomes have varied.

A number of federal appeals courts have addressed the copyrightability of numbering systems in light of *Feist*. A recent decision is *ATC Distribution Group, Inc. v. Whatever It Takes Transmissions & Parts, Inc.*[27] In that case, ATC claimed that the defendants infringed its copyrights in a transmission parts catalog, the individual part numbers contained in the catalog, and its "Numbering System Manual." The main issue in the case was whether these items were eligible for copyright protection. Both the district court and the unanimous Sixth Circuit panel held that the catalog, part numbers, and manual lacked the originality required for copyright protection, and thus the defendants' admitted copying of these works was not copyright infringement as a matter of law.

The plaintiff asserted two theories for copyrightability of its works. First, it claimed the "catalog is a creative classification scheme, or taxonomy, which sorts parts into categories and subcategories, and allocates numbers to each part. Under this theory, the individual part numbers would be protected as the copyrightable expressions of the overall taxonomy. Second, ATC argues that even if the numbers themselves are not protected by copyright, the catalog as a whole is protected as a creative and original compilation of data." The court rejected both theories.

ATC's part classification scheme divided transmission parts by brand, transmission type, and type of part. An additional field was available for different types of parts. Each specific part

---

26. Marci A. Hamilton, A Response to Professor Benkler, 15 BERKELEY TECH. L.J. 605, 623 (2000). For additional commentary on the database law, see Yochai Benkler, Constitutional Bounds of Database Protection: The Role of Judicial Review in the Creation and Definition of Private Rights in Information, 15 BEREKLEY TECH. L.J. 535, 546–48 (2000); Paul J. Heald & Suzanna Sherry, Implied Limits on the Legislative Power: The Intel-

lectual Property Clause As an Absolute Constraint on Congress, 2000 U. ILL. L. REV. 1119, 1178–79; Malla Pollack, The Right to Know? Delimiting Database Protection at the Juncture of the Commerce Clause, the Intellectual Property Clause, and the First Amendment, 17 CARDOZO ARTS & ENT. L.J. 47 (1999).

27. 402 F.3d 700 (6th Cir. 2005).

could be identified by a specific number, between five and nine digits long. The court noted that some of the classifications were obvious while others were "less obvious, and require[d] decisions such as whether to have a single category of rings, of which some are sealing rings and some are O-rings, or to have two distinct categories, sealing rings and O-rings."[28]

The plaintiff asserted that its numbering scheme involved creativity in deciding what information to convey in part numbers, leaving slots open in a given sub-category to allow for new products, deciding when to add new categories of parts, designing the part numbers, and creating an overall "taxonomy" of part categories. Citing section 102 of the Copyright Act, the court found, however, that "the creative aspects of the ATC classification scheme are just that: ideas. ATC cannot copyright its prediction of how many types of sealing rings will be developed in the future, its judgment that O-rings and sealing rings should form two separate categories of parts, or its judgment that a new part belongs with the retainers as opposed to the pressure plates." By way of analogy, the court noted that "permitting copyright protection for ATC's choice of where in the catalog to locate a new part would be akin to granting copyright protection to a grocer who decides to display a new type of heirloom tomato with the gourmet produce, as opposed to with the other tomatoes or the locally grown produce."[29]

The *ATC Distribution Group* court found that the expression of the plaintiff's ideas, i.e., the classification system, is barred by the merger doctrine—"For almost all of the types of creativity claimed by ATC, there is only one reasonable way to express the underlying idea. For example, the only way to express the prediction that a maximum of four additional types of sealing ring might be developed is to leave four numbers unallocated, and the only way to express the idea that a novel part should be placed with the sealing rings rather than with the gaskets is to place that part with the sealing rings. Under the merger doctrine, 'when there is essentially only one way to express an idea, the idea and its expression are inseparable [i.e., they merge,] and copyright is no bar to copying that expression.' "[30]

---

28. *Id.* at 705–06. Some parts were numbered in order, "with gaps being left in each sub-category to accommodate new parts in the future. Although all parts within a sub-category are numbered sequentially, the ordering of the sub-categories within a field, or the parts within a sub-category appears to be random. As such, the fact that an 'O-ring pump' and an 'O-ring pump bolt' are in the same general range of numbers is no accident. But the fact that O-rings in general are numbered in the 300's, and the fact that these two parts are numbered 311 and 312 rather than 341 and 342, are accidental." *Id.* at 706.

29. *Id.* at 706 n.4.

30. *Id.* at 707–08 (citing *Kohus v. Mariol*, 328 F.3d 848, 856 (6th Cir. 2003)).

Rejecting the plaintiff's claim that the numbering itself constituted copyrightable expression, the court noted:

> Even assuming, arguendo, that some strings of numbers used
> to designate an item or procedure could be sufficiently creative
> to merit copyright protection, the parts numbers at issue in the
> case before us do not evidence any such creativity. ATC's
> allocation of numbers to parts was an essentially random
> process, serving only to provide a useful shorthand way of
> referring to each part. The only reason that a "sealing ring,
> pump slide" is allocated number 176 is the random ordering of
> sub-categories of parts, and the random ordering of parts
> within that sub-category. Were it not for a series of random
> orderings within each category field, a given part could be
> 47165 or 89386. As such, the particular numbers allocated to
> each part do not express any of the creative ideas that went
> into the classification scheme in any way that could be consid-
> ered eligible for copyright protection. These numbers are no
> more copyrightable than would be the fruit of an author's
> labors if she wrote a book and then "translated" it into
> numbers using a random number generator for each letter in
> every word.[31]

Further, the court noted that courts should exercise great
caution in considering the copyrightability of numbers, just as in
the case of short words and phrases. The court cites the Copyright
Office prohibition on registering short names, phrases, or expressions such as the name of a product or service, even if it is novel or
distinctive. 37 C.F.R. § 202.1 indicates that short phrases, names,
and similar material not subject to copyright protection.[32]

The court then highlighted a fundamental policy set forth in
Feist: "While the use without compensation of one's labors may
seem unfair, this is not 'some unforeseen byproduct of a statutory
scheme.' It is, rather, 'the essence of copyright,' and a constitutional requirement. The primary objective of copyright is not to reward
the labor of authors, but 'to promote the Progress of Science and
useful Arts.' Permitting uncopyrightable materials to receive protection simply by virtue of adding a number or label would allow an
end run around that constitutional requirement."[33]

Finally, with regard to the plaintiff's claim that the arrangement of product categories is copyrightable, the court noted that
the creativity bar is low. For example, in *Publications International*

---

31. *Id.* at 709 (citing *Mitel, Inc. v. Iqtel, Inc.*, 124 F.3d 1366, 1374 (10th Cir.1997) ("[T]he random and arbitrary use of numbers in the public domain does not evince enough originality to distinguish authorship.")).

32. *See also* Copyright Office Circular 34 (available at http://www.copyright.gov/circs/circ34.html).

33. *Id.* at 710 (quoting *Feist*, 499 U.S. at 349).

v. Meredith Corp.,[34] the court held that the selection and arrangement of recipes was sufficiently creative to constitute original compilation. Similarly, in *CCC Information Services, Inc. v. Maclean Hunter Market Reports, Inc.*,[35] the court found that a collection of used car values was copyrightable and was infringed. In *ATC Distribution Group*, however, the court ultimately found that the plaintiff's parts catalog did not meet this minimal level of creativity, as the choice of headings and arrangement of the parts into categories was " 'typical, if not inevitable,' and lacking in the 'requisite creativity for copyright protection.' "[36]

Another leading case is the Third Circuit en banc decision in *Southco, Inc. v. Kanebridge Corp.*[37] Written by Judge (now Justice) Alito, this case also concerned a serial numbering system for a variety of products, including rivets, latches, handles, screws, and captive fasteners. "Southco has referred to one of the numbers at issue in this case, part number 47–10–202–10, to show how the system works. The first two digits ('47') show that the part falls within a class of captive screws. Other digits indicate characteristics such as thread size ('632'), composition of the screw (aluminum), and finish of the knob ('knurled')."[38]

Judge Alito found that the plaintiff's product numbers lack originality, because the numbers are rigidly dictated by the rules of its system. The system itself, the court noted, is an uncopyrightable idea, and the numbers themselves lack any creativity. "To be sure, before any Southco product could be numbered, Southco had to create the numbering system applicable to products in that line. It had to identify the relevant characteristics of the products in the class (that is, the characteristics that would interest prospective purchasers); it had to assign one or more digits to express each characteristic; and it had to assign a number or other symbol to represent each of the relevant values of each characteristic. For example, Southco might decide that, for a class of screws, composition was a relevant characteristic; it might assign the eighth digit to indicate composition; and it might use the number 1 to indicate aluminum, 2 to indicate steel, and so on."[39]

Having established this system (an uncopyrightable idea), there was no creativity in assigning numbers to products. "Indeed, if any creativity were allowed to creep into the numbering process, the system would be defeated. Suppose, for example, that the person given the task of actually numbering the products in the class in accordance with the applicable rules of the system decided that it

---

34. 88 F.3d 473, 481 (7th Cir.1996).

35. 44 F.3d 61, 67 (2d Cir.1994).

36. 402 F.3d at 709.

37. 390 F.3d 276 (3d Cir. 2004) (en banc), *cert. denied*, 546 U.S. 813 (2005).

38. *Id.* at 278.

39. *Id.* at 282.

would be more fitting to indicate aluminum composition with the number 13 (its number in the periodic chart) rather than the number 1. Customers who wished to purchase aluminum screws but were unaware of this variation would be befuddled. In short, an essential attribute of the numbering process and the resulting numbers is an utter absence of creativity." The product numbers are the result of "mechanical application of the system, not creative thought."[40] The court also cited a number of treatises that find uncopyrightable product numbers that represent "an inevitable sequence dictated by the logic of the parts system."[41] Consequently, the en banc Sixth Circuit concluded that the plaintiff's product numbers were not protected by copyright law because they were mechanically produced by the inflexible rules of the Southco system.

As the court noted in *Silverstein v. Penguin Putnam, Inc.*,[42] "if the selection process imbues a compilation with the requisite creative spark, the compilation may be protected so long as there are indicia that principles of selection (other than all-inclusiveness) have been employed." Similarly, the court in *Matthew Bender & Co. v. West Publishing Co.*,[43] held that West's decision to include every record of Supreme Court opinions in a database constituted "no 'selection' at all" for copyright purposes. In contrast, the Eighth Circuit's pre-*Feist* decision in *West Publishing Co. v. Mead Data Central, Inc.*[44] held that West's selection and arrangement of cases was protected under copyright law. Whether that decision remains good law after *Feist* is certainly open to question, as the *West Publishing v. Mead Data Central* court arguably appeared to apply the "sweat of the brow" approach that the Court repudiated in *Feist*. On the other hand, Judge Sweet's dissent contended that the West selection and arrangement was sufficiently creative to satisfy the standard established in *Feist*.

Illustration: Copyright Protection for "Taxonomies"

There is some case authority upholding copyright protection for taxonomies in some circumstances. Most prominently, the Seventh Circuit's decision in *American Dental Ass'n v. Delta Dental Plans Ass'n*.[45] should be considered. In that case, the court found

40. *Id.*

41. *Id.* (quoting 1 WILLIAM F. PATRY, COPYRIGHT LAW AND PRACTICE 46 (2d ed.2004)); 1 JOHN W. HAZARD, JR., COPYRIGHT LAW IN BUSINESS AND PRACTICE § 2.58 at 2–79 to 2–80 (2002) (distinguishing between numbers assigned pursuant to process that requires creativity and numbers assigned under system that leaves no room for creativity).

42. 368 F.3d 77, 83 (2d Cir. 2004), *cert. denied*, 543 U.S. 1039 (2004).

43. 158 F.3d 674, 687 (2d Cir. 1998). *See also Matthew Bender & Co. v. West Publ'g Co.*, 158 F.3d 693 (2d Cir. 1998).

44. 799 F.2d 1219 (8th Cir. 1986).

45. 126 F.3d 977 (7th Cir. 1997).

that the American Dental Association's Code on Dental Procedures and Nomenclature is copyrightable subject matter. This volume classifies dental procedures into groups; each procedure is indicated by a number, a short description, and a long description. "For example, number 04267 has been assigned to the short description 'guided tissue regeneration-nonresorbable barrier, per site, per tooth (includes membrane removal),' which is classified with other surgical periodontic services."

Although on the surface, this decision appears to conflict with *Southco* and *ATC Distribution,* Judge (now Justice) Alito addressed this point in *Southco, Inc. v. Kanebridge Corp. (Southco I).*[46] *Southco I* is a prior panel opinion in that litigation, and this opinion was not superceded by the en banc opinion, and indeed was reaffirmed by the en banc panel. In this ruling, Judge Alito noted:

> We believe that there are important distinctions between *American Dental* and the present case. The long and short descriptions of the various dental procedures are obviously very different from the part numbers at issue in the present case, and therefore the Seventh Circuit's decision that these descriptions are copyrightable has no application here. Moreover, even the numbers assigned to the procedures appear to be quite different. These numbers were not chosen randomly, as were the numbers in *Toro* or the computer codes in *Mitel,* and they were not the mechanical results of a numbering system, as are the part numbers in question in this case. Rather, the numbers in *American Dental* reflected creative thought. The entries in the ADA's Code were originally developed by a committee comprised of representatives from interested organizations. When new procedures were developed or other changes to the system became necessary, this committee collected written proposals submitted by state dental societies and national dental organizations. The committee then debated, edited, and voted on the proposals. Although the ADA eventually changed this process, the new process still involved significant debate and editing of proposals by this committee.[47]

Moreover, "[a]ssigning a number to a particular dental procedure reflects a decision about the distinctiveness and prevalence of the procedure and its relationship to the other procedures in the Code."[48] In short, the ADA Code possessed sufficient creative elements in its descriptions, arrangement, and overall expression to warrant copyright protection. In contrast, where the numbering system is simply a random or mechanical system, with rudimentary

---

46. 258 F.3d 148 (3d Cir. 2001).   **48.** *Id.* at 156.

47. *Southco Inc.,* 258 F.3d at 155–56 (citations omitted).

description of the relevant products (e.g., red, blue, green, or 1–inch, 2–inch, 3–inch), the numbering system is not copyrightable. It is useful to compare this distinction with a selection of the 100 best lawyers in the state of Missouri, as compared to an alphabetical directory listing of all 100 lawyers who practice in the city of Columbia, Missouri.

Judge Posner has written a helpful summary of this area of the law—"The obvious orderings, the lexical and the numeric, have long been in the public domain, and what is in the public domain cannot be appropriated by claiming copyright." *Assessment Technologies of Wisconsin, LLC v. WIREdata*, 350 F.3d 640 (7th Cir. 2003).

Illustration: Copyright Protection for Photographs

Photographs somewhat surprisingly present a challenge for copyright law, in spite of the inclusion of photography within the subject matter of copyright since 1865. An early case, *Burrow–Giles v. Sarony*,[49] concerned the copyrightability of famed photographer Napoleon Sarony's image of the author Oscar Wilde. This photograph was apparently so popular that the defendant was about to sell 85,000 lithograph copies of the Sarony image without the photographer's consent. In defending against Sarony's claim of copyright infringement, Burrow–Giles asserted that the image was merely a mechanical reproduction taken from life and thus was not copyrightable. The Court rejected this argument, finding that Sarony's work was in fact a creative work of authorship qualifying for copyright protection. The Court noted:

> *We entertain no doubt that the constitution is broad enough to cover an act authorizing copyright of photographs, so far as they are representatives of original intellectual conceptions of the author.*

> But it is said that an engraving, a painting, a print, does embody the intellectual conception of its author, in which there is novelty, invention, originality, and therefore comes within the purpose of the constitution in securing its exclusive use or sale to its author, while a photograph is the mere mechanical reproduction of the physical features or outlines of some object, animate or inanimate, and involves no originality of thought or any novelty in the intellectual operation connected with its visible reproduction in shape of a picture. That while the effect of light on the prepared plate may have been a discovery in the production of these pictures, and patents could properly be obtained for the combination of the chemicals, for their application to the paper or other surface, for all the machinery by

49. 111 U.S. 53 (1884).

which the light reflected from the object was thrown on the prepared plate, and for all the improvements in this machinery, and in the materials, the remainder of the process is merely mechanical, with no place for novelty, invention, or originality. It is simply the manual operation, by the use of these instruments and preparations, of transferring to the plate the visible representation of some existing object, the accuracy of this representation being its highest merit. *This may be true in regard to the ordinary production of a photograph, and that in such case a copyright is no protection. On the question as thus stated we decide nothing.*[50]

Burrow–Giles v. Sarony thus expressly refused to state that all photographs are copyrightable, and indeed the issue continues to arise. The Sarony photograph appears to be an easy case for copyrightability, as a perusal of the photograph demonstrates its creative rendition and composition (the photograph is easily found on the Internet by searching "Napoleon Sarony Oscar Wilde photograph"). The Court identified a significant number of creative features in the Oscar Wilde photograph:

[I]n regard to the photograph in question, that it is a "useful, new, harmonious, characteristic, and graceful picture, and that plaintiff made the same ... entirely from his own original mental conception, to which he gave visible form by posing the said Oscar Wilde in front of the camera, selecting and arranging the costume, draperies, and other various accessories in said photograph, arranging the subject so as to present graceful outlines, arranging and disposing the light and shade, suggesting and evoking the desired expression, and from such disposition, arrangement, or representation, made entirely by plaintiff, he produced the picture in suit." These findings, we think, show this photograph to be an original work of art, the product of plaintiff's intellectual invention, of which plaintiff is the author, and of a class of inventions for which the constitution intended that congress should secure to him the exclusive right to use, publish, and sell, as it has done by section 4952 of the Revised Statutes.[51]

At the other extreme is *Bridgeman Art Library, Ltd. v. Corel Corp.*,[52] which involved the Bridgeman Art Library's collection of photographic reproductions of major public domain works of art, such as Vincent van Gogh's Sunflowers (oil on canvas, 1888).

The goal of the Bridgeman collection was to have a completely accurate replication of the original work, and hence it is not

---

50. *Id.* at 58–59 (emphasis added).
51. *Id.* at 60.

52. 36 F.Supp.2d 191, 197 (S.D.N.Y. 1999).

surprising that the court found no creative element worthy of copyright protection. The court found: "plaintiff by its own admission has labored to create 'slavish copies' of public domain works of art. While it may be assumed that this required both skill and effort, there was no spark of originality—indeed, the point of the exercise was to reproduce the underlying works with absolute fidelity. Copyright is not available in these circumstances." Accordingly, the very thing that made the Bridgeman collection useful—its verisimilitude with the works of the great masters—is what rendered its final product unworthy of copyright protection.

What of the photograph that is not pure replication like the Bridgeman reproductions, but also not as creative as the works of Napoleon Sarony? That is where the copyright creativity standard becomes unclear. Judge Kaplan's opinion in *Mannion v. Coors Brewing Co.*[53] offers three touchstones for creativity in photographs: rendition, composition, and timing. This framework is useful for analyzing the validity of copyrights in photographs, and of course suggests a broader basis for assessing any other particular creative field. The focus is first on the level of creativity in the photographer's rendition—choices of settings, camera, lighting equipment, lens, development (in the case of film), and perspective. Consider Ansel Adams' skills in taking his famous "Moonrise" photograph, or the "Midnight in the Garden of Good and Evil" photograph at issue in *Leigh v. Warner Brothers, Inc.*[54] Second, there may be creativity in the composition—the manner in which the subject is posed, the creation or selection of background, choices in attire, and lighting. The Sarony photograph is a good illustration of creative composition. Third, the timing of a photograph can involve creative effort, or at least protected serendipity. The Ansel Adams photograph Moonrise involved such good timing, as does the famous Zapruder film of the Kennedy assassination.

¶ 2.04   Uncopyrightable Material—The Idea/Expression Distinction

There are important limits on the subject matter of copyright. The most important can be found in section 102 of the Copyright Act, which precludes protection for ideas and methods: "In no case does copyright protection for an original work of authorship extend to any idea, procedure, process, system, method of operation, concept, principle, or discovery, regardless of the form in which it is described, explained, illustrated, or embodied in such work."[55] Hence, an idea—no matter how original and creative the inspiration might be—is not copyrightable, and may be freely used by

---

53. 377 F. Supp. 2d 444 (S.D.N.Y. 2005).

54. 212 F.3d 1210 (11th Cir. 2000).

55. 17 U.S. C. § 102(b).

others. Thus, Einstein's theory of relativity and his insight that is found in the formula, $E=mc^2$, are not copyrightable, though of course, the extended expression of these ideas in a book or article would be copyrightable. In other words, others can take and use the ideas and theories, but they cannot reproduce a 200–page discourse on the subject.

The distinction between ideas and expression has been the subject of many copyright cases. A good illustration is *Hoehling v. Universal Studios.*[56] Hoeling wrote a book about the Hindenberg disaster in which he posits that the ill-fated German dirigible was deliberately sabotaged by Eric Spehl, who was an employee on board and who sought to impress his anti-Nazi girlfriend. This hypothesis is a good example of an uncopyrightable idea. Universal produced a movie on the Hindenberg disaster, which incorporated the Speil thesis into its plot development. Hoeling's extended discussion of this topic, of course, is entitled to copyright protection, but Universal did not take Hoeling's copyrightable discussion of the thesis. As a result, Universal did not infringe on Hoeling's book despite the overlap in the ideas presented.

Moreoever, Hoeling highlighted a number of other similarities—such as a beer hall scene, and scenes with Nazi uniforms, songs, and greetings. These similarities, the court found, are examples of *scenes á faire*—inevitable background scenes that are common to the particular type of work at issue. In other words, it is inevitable that a movie depicting pre-World War II Germany would include beer hall scenes, Nazi uniforms and greetings, and other stock background items. The *scenes á faire* doctrine has many important applications. A movie about the Revolutionary War, for example, would include rag-tag colonial fighters, spiffy but ill-fated redcoats, raucous colonial taverns, and a magisterial George Washington figure riding tall on his proud horse.

Interestingly, a recent study of the Hindenberg disaster reveals that it may have resulted from a spark causing a flammable coating on the dirigible's surface to ignite. Whatever the actual cause of the disaster, the Spehl hypothesis may well be false. This brings to light an important point about copyright law—the fact that the Spehl hypothesis turned out to be incorrect does not change its status as an uncopyrightable idea or "fact." Indeed, if a particular work is represented by the author to be factual, its actual veracity or accuracy is irrelevant. The author is deemed to have presented facts, which the author is estopped from recapturing as protectable fiction. As the court stated in *Houts v. Universal City Studios, Inc.*:

> The basic tenet of copyright law is that copyright protection is
> predicated upon originality. No one, however, may claim origi-

---

56.   618 F.2d 972 (2d Cir.), *cert. de-*
nied, 449 U.S. 841 (1980).

nality as to facts. Facts may be discovered, but they are not created by an act of authorship. Consequently, the copyright protection afforded to fictional works differs from that afforded to factual works. In the case at bar, plaintiff claims that his book is an amalgam of fact and fiction, and hence it is entitled to full copyright protection. The general rule is that fictional elements, or fictionalized versions of factual elements, of an otherwise factual work are protectable under copyright law. Copyright estoppel is an exception to the general rule. Under the doctrine of copyright estoppel, *once a plaintiff's work has been held out to the public as factual the author-plaintiff cannot then claim that the book is, in actuality, fiction and thus entitled to the higher protection allowed to fictional works.*[57]

On the facts of that case, the author and publishers made numerous representations about the book's factuality, including:

(a) the book jacket of the American hardcover edition extols the books as "real life detective stories";

(b) the spine of the Dell paperback edition has the notation "N–F," expressly informing the public that the book is non-fiction; and

(c) the first page of the paperback edition proclaims that "[h]ere is a book that shows that truth can be more brutal than fiction."[58]

The idea/expression dichotomy reflects an important balance in copyright law, as it provides rewards for creative expression, while at the same time allowing the public to gain access to new ideas, facts, histories, and the like. The line between ideas and expression is not always clear, of course, and some cases present a particular challenge when there is only one way (or perhaps a very small number of ways) to express a specific idea or concept. This might be a concern, for instance, with regard to lines of computer software code that are designed to accomplish a particular result. It may be that there is only one efficient way to set forth this code.

Copyright law prevents the author of the code from usurping this idea or method under a doctrine know as "merger," which allows copying when necessary to obtain the uncopyrightable idea, method, or other public domain information. The merger doctrine is an important delimiting tool in copyright law. Under this doctrine, if there is only one or a very limited number of ways to express a particular idea, then the specific manner in which the idea is expressed is not copyrightable. Judge Hand, in *Nichols v.*

---

57. 603 F.Supp. 26 (C.D. Cal. 1984) (emphasis added). *See also Oliver v. Saint Germain Foundation*, 41 F.Supp. 296, 299 (S.D. Cal.1941).

58. 603 F.Supp. at 28.

Universal Pictures Corp.,[59] noted that ideas are not protected by copyright, and if the idea is so intertwined with the expression that it is impossible to separate them, then the expression is said to have "merged" with the idea. The merger doctrine was recognized in the First Circuit's opinion in *Morrissey v. Procter & Gamble Co.*,[60] which stated that merger takes place when "the topic necessarily requires, if not only one form of expression, at best only a limited number, to permit copyrighting would mean that a party or parties, by copyrighting a mere handful of forms, could exhaust all possibilities of future use of the substance." Morrissey involved a set of contest rules for a promotional sweepstakes, which were found to have merged with the contest idea.

The distinction between unprotected facts/ideas and protected expression is a fundamental one. It is not only a bedrock principle underlying copyright law, but also a crucial way in which copyright law accommodates First Amendment considerations. As the Supreme Court explained in *Eldred v. Ashcroft*:

> In addition to spurring the creation and publication of new expression, copyright law contains built-in First Amendment accommodations. First, it distinguishes between ideas and expression and makes only the latter eligible for copyright protection. Specifically, 17 U.S.C. § 102(b) provides: "In no case does copyright protection for an original work of authorship extend to any idea, procedure, process, system, method of operation, concept, principle, or discovery, regardless of the form in which it is described, explained, illustrated, or embodied in such work." As we said in *Harper & Row*, this "idea/expression dichotomy strike[s] a definitional balance between the First Amendment and the Copyright Act by permitting free communication of facts while still protecting an author's expression." Due to this distinction, every idea, theory, and fact in a copyrighted work becomes instantly available for public exploitation at the moment of publication.[61]

¶ 2.05   Uncopyrightable Material—Useful Articles

Copyright protects creative features but not functional ones. When a creative element is added to a functional object, it can still be copyrighted if it is conceptually separable from the useful features. An influential test for addressing this issue was developed by Professor Robert C. Denicola. The Denicola article notes that "the statutory directive requires a distinction between works of industrial design and works whose origins lie outside the design process, despite the utilitarian environment in which they appear."

---

59.   45 F.2d 119, 121 (2d Cir. 1930) (Hand, J.).

60.   379 F.2d 675, 678 (1st Cir. 1967).

61.   537 U.S. 186, 219 (2003).

He notes that "[c]opyrightability, therefore, should turn on the relationship between the proffered work and the process of industrial design" and suggests that copyrightability "ultimately should depend on the extent to which the work reflects artistic expression uninhibited by functional considerations."[62]

The court in *Brandir Intern., Inc. v. Cascade Pacific Lumber Co.* formulated the Denicola test for conceptual separability as follows: "if design elements reflect a merger of aesthetic and functional considerations, the artistic aspects of a work cannot be said to be conceptually separable from the utilitarian elements. Conversely, where design elements can be identified as reflecting the designer's artistic judgment exercised independently of functional influences, conceptual separability exists."[63]

The conceptual separability test is not always easily applied. Is an ornate design on a belt buckle copyrightable? The court in *Kieselstein–Cord v. Accessories by Pearl, Inc.*[64] held that it is, as the design could appear independently as a copyrightable work (jewelry), somewhat akin to the statuette lamp base in *Mazer v. Stein.*[65] On the other hand, what about a jeweled pin with in the shape of a bee? In *Herbert Rosenthal Jewelry Corp. v. Kalpakian,*[66] the court held that copying of expressive elements of the bee pin was not barred because the idea of a jeweled bee pin and the expression of that idea was inseparable.

Can a fashion design be copyrighted? Traditionally, fashion designs were viewed as mere crafts or useful objects that do not warrant copyright protection. The fashion industry has generally flourished in spite of this general lack of copyright protection, but with increasing levels of style piracy, there have been calls from some in the industry for stronger Intellectual Property protection.[67] Modern technology now makes it possible for fashion designs displayed for the first time at a show in New York or Paris to be very quickly replicated and produced in garment factories worldwide. One proposal would provide copyright-like protection for original clothing designs. If such a scheme were enacted, "[n]o longer would designers have to send models down the runway with their latest creations only to find that, through the wonders of digital cameras, the Internet, and mass-production facilities in faraway lands,

62. *Id.* at 741.

63. 834 F.2d 1142 (2d Cir. 1987).

64. 632 F.2d 989, 993 (2d Cir. 1980).

65. 347 U.S. 201 (1954).

66. 446 F.2d 738 (9th Cir.1971).

67. *See* Kal Raustiala & Christopher Sprigman, The Piracy Paradox: Innovation and Intellectual Property in Fashion Design, 92 Va. L. Rev. 1687 (2006) (questioning the need for copyright protection in fashion design). *See also* Julie P. Tsai, Fashioning Protection: A Note on the Protection of Fashion Designs in the United States, 9 Lewis & Clark L. Rev. 447, 447 (2005).

knockoffs had arrived in discount stores seemingly before the model had finished her last sashay.''[68]

An example of such a proposal is the Design Piracy Prohibition Act, H.R. 2196, 111th Congress, 1st Session. To date, no fashion bill has been enacted. In the past, the fashion industry has attempted to self-police imitators through boycotts of retailers who sold pirated designs, but this led to a well-known antitrust case, *Fashion Originators' Guild of America, Inc. v. FTC,*[69] which held that the group boycott violated section 1 of the Sherman Act. So the fashion industry has no collective recourse against imitators, and as of today must rely on general copyright protection, which is highly unlikely to be successful in most instances.

¶ 2.06   Uncopyrightable Material—Words & Short Phrases, Governmental Works

By regulation, the Copyright Office prohibits the registration of short names, phrases, or expressions such as the name of a product or service, even if it is novel or distinctive. See 37 C.F.R. § 202.1 provides that short phrases, names, and similar material not subject to copyright protection.[70] Judge Alito's Third Circuit opinion in *Southco, Inc. v. Kanebridge Corp.,*[71] suggests an alternate ground for invalidating product numbering systems on the ground that words, short phrases, names, titles and similar items are unregistrable and uncopyrightable.

A category of works specifically excluded from copyright protection are works of the United States Government. Section 101 defines this term as "a work prepared by an officer or employee of the United States Government as part of that person's official duties." Thus, material such as court opinions, congressional documents, and executive branch and agency materials are in the public domain by statute under U.S. law. The content of most law casebooks, for instance, includes a large number of court opinions, which can be used without consent or payment. These casebooks provide a good illustration of whether the selection, arrangement, and editing of the public domain court opinions is sufficiently creative to give copyright protection to casebook authors. As the coauthor of three casebooks, it would be my (not wholly unbiased) view that such efforts are sufficiently creative to make the grade for copyrightability.

68. Henry Lanman, Copycatfight: The Rag Trade's Fashionably Late Arrival to the Copyright Party, Slate, Mar. 13, 2006, http://www.slate.com/id/2137954 (last visited Jan. 31, 2008).

69. 312 U.S. 457 (1941).

70. *See also* Copyright Office Circular 34 (available at http://www.copyright.gov/circs/circ34.html).

71. 390 F.3d 276, 285–87 (3d Cir. 2004) (en banc).

There may be a question as to the copyright status of a work to the extent it has been officially incorporated into the governmental bidding or procurement process. For example, in *Veeck v. Southern Bldg. Code Cong. Int'l, Inc.*,[72] a website operator who posted municipal building codes, developed by a private party, on a website sought a declaratory judgment that he did not violate the Copyright Act. The court held that copyrights were valid until the cities adopted the codes; upon adoption, the codes essentially became facts and thus entered the public domain.

¶ 2.07 Fixation in a Tangible Medium of Expression

Under present United States law, section 102 of the Copyright Act states that copyright protection attaches as soon as the work is "fixed in any tangible medium of expression, now known or later developed, from which they can be perceived, reproduced, or otherwise communicated, either directly or with the aid of a machine or device." Elaborating on this point, section 101 of the Copyright Act provides that a work is fixed in a tangible medium of expression "when its embodiment in a copy or phonorecord, by or under the authority of the author, is sufficiently permanent or stable to permit it to be perceived, reproduced, or otherwise communicated for a period of more than transitory duration. A work consisting of sounds, images, or both, that are being transmitted, is 'fixed' for purposes of this title if a fixation of the work is being made simultaneously with its transmission." In other words, as soon as a creative work is written down or recorded in some tangible form, copyright protection is triggered. Examples of ways in which to fix a work include writing a novel on paper (if anyone still uses paper!) or storing it to a computer hard drive or on an iPad or in the "cloud," recording a baseball game on a camcorder as it is being played, or memorializing a song by writing down its musical notes or recording the song as it is being played by a band. In each of these instances, copyright protection attaches at the very instant that the work is fixed or recorded in tangible form. As section 101 states: "A work is 'created' when it is fixed in a copy or phonorecord for the first time; where a work is prepared over a period of time, the portion of it that has been fixed at any particular time constitutes the work as of that time, and where the work has been prepared in different versions, each version constitutes a separate work."

Whether a fixation is sufficiently permanent to trigger copyright protection is an issue that a number of courts have addressed. In *MAI Systems Corp. v. Peak Computer, Inc.*,[73] the court addressed

---

72. 293 F.3d 791 (5th Cir. 2002).

73. 991 F.2d 511, 518–19 (9th Cir. 1993).

the issue of whether recording a work in a computer's random access memory or RAM is sufficiently permanent given that this particular memory storage ceases to retain the work if the computer's power is turned off or disconnected. The court defined RAM as "a computer component in which data and computer programs can be temporarily recorded."[74] Thus the RAM memory can be contrasted with more plainly permanent methods of fixation, such as storing a work on the computer's hard drive, to a compact disc or memory card/stick, or in the "cloud," each of which undoubtedly would be permanent enough to quality as a fixation. The court held that storing a work in the RAM was indeed sufficiently permanent to establish copyright protection. Accordingly, software copied into RAM was thereby fixed in a tangible medium and was sufficiently permanent or stable to permit it to be perceived, reproduced, or otherwise communicated for a period of more than transitory duration. This conclusion is sensible, as many methods of recording a work are subject to damage or destruction and yet are deemed sufficient. It is possible, for example, to erase or seriously damage many methods of storing information by use of a strong magnet, which can erase certain types of electronic storage devices.

In contrast, the court in *Cartoon Network LP v. CSC Holdings, Inc.*, 536 F.3d 121 (2d Cir. 2008), held that digital video recorder (DVR) systems, such as those used by TiVo, or by cable company video-on-demand services that were at issue in the case, do not result in reproduction of copyrighted movies, because any copies made of the works were so transitory in duration that they are not actionable reproductions of the movies.

A recent case involving Dallas artist Chapman Kelley provides an excellent illustration of a rare case in which fixation was a strongly contested issue. In that case, Kelley designed and installed a living wildflower display, called "Wildflower Works," which consisted of two large elliptical flower beds, each almost as big as a football field, featuring a variety of native wildflowers with borders of gravel and steel. Wildflower Works was planted in a city park in Chicago, where it received critical and popular acclaim as "living art." Kelley and a group of volunteers tended the garden, pruning and replanting as needed, but eventually the garden had deteriorated. The Chicago Park District decided to modify the garden, substantially reducing its size, reconfiguring the oval flower beds into rectangles, and changing some of the planting material.

---

74. *Id.* at 519. *See also Perfect 10, Inc. v. Amazon.com, Inc.,* 487 F.3d 701 (9th Cir. 2007) ("A photographic image is a work that is 'fixed in a tangible medium of expression' for purposes of the Copyright Act, when embodied (i.e., stored) in a computer's server (or hard disk, or other storage device). The image stored in the computer is the 'copy' of the work for purposes of copyright law.").

Kelley brought suit against the Park District for violating his "right of integrity" under the Visual Artists Rights Act of 1990 ("VARA"), 17 U.S.C. § 106A, which protects certain categories of works of fine art from alteration. Before getting to any analysis of whether a VARA violation had taken place, the threshold question was whether "Wildflower Works" was a "fixed work," which is necessary in order to have any federal copyright protection at all:

> Simply put, gardens are planted and cultivated, not authored. A garden's constituent elements are alive and inherently changeable, not fixed. Most of what we see and experience in a garden—the colors, shapes, textures, and scents of the plants—originates in nature, not in the mind of the gardener. At any given moment in time, a garden owes most of its form and appearance to natural forces, though the gardener who plants and tends it obviously assists. All this is true of Wildflower Works, even though it was designed and planted by an artist.

> Of course, a human "author"—whether an artist, a professional landscape designer, or an amateur backyard gardener— determines the initial arrangement of the plants in a garden. This is not the kind of authorship required for copyright. To the extent that seeds or seedlings can be considered a "medium of expression," they originate in nature, and natural forces— not the intellect of the gardener-determine their form, growth, and appearance. Moreover, a garden is simply too changeable to satisfy the primary purpose of fixation; its appearance is too inherently variable to supply a baseline for determining questions of copyright creation and infringement. If a garden can qualify as a "work of authorship" sufficiently "embodied in a copy," at what point has fixation occurred? When the garden is newly planted? When its first blossoms appear? When it is in full bloom? How—and at what point in time—is a court to determine whether infringing copying has occurred?

Kelley v. Chicago Park District, 635 F.3d 290 (7th Cir. 2011).

Does an unfixed work have any Intellectual Property protection? The answer is that it does not under federal copyright law, but state law may offer protection for it. Since the enactment of the 1976 Copyright Act, there has been hardly any reported litigation involving state copyright law. Probably the best known state law copyright case is *Estate of Hemingway v. Random House, Inc.*,[75] which predated the 1976 Act. In that case, Ernest Hemingway's estate sought to assert common law copyright protection for conversations Hemingway had with the author of a subsequent book (who wrote down the dialogue without Hemingway's knowledge or con-

---

75. 23 N.Y.2d 341, 346, 296 N.Y.S.2d 771, 244 N.E.2d 250 (1968).

sent, and then included the quotes in the book). The court recognized that a state law copyright might exist in this situation, but ultimately the claim failed because there was no evidence that Hemingway had sought to assert copyright protection for his statements or otherwise reserve his rights to his conversations. The legislative history of the 1976 Act clearly contemplated a small but continued role for state law copyright in the case of unfixed works:

> "[S]ection 301(b) explicitly preserves common law copyright protection for one important class of works: works that have not been 'fixed in any tangible medium of expression.' ... [Unfixed works] would continue to be subject to protection under State statute or common law until fixed in tangible form."[76]

In the Uruguay Round Agreements Act, Congress enacted two "anti-bootlegging" provisions, creating copyright-like protection against the unauthorized fixation, transmission, or distribution of live musical performances.[77] The constitutionality of the federal anti-bootlegging statute has been the subject of considerable litigation for two reasons. First, the law's protections do not have an apparent time limit or expiration. In *United States v. Martignon*,[78] the court upheld the constitutionality of 18 U.S.C. § 2319A because it does not offer copyright protection, but instead only "copyright-like" relief under the Commerce Clause. Second, the law protects unfixed works, which arguably exceeds Congress' power under the Intellectual Property Clause, which is limited to protection for "Writings." In *United States v. Moghadam*,[79] the court upheld the constitutionality of the law, but declined to address whether fixation is constitutionally required under the Copyright Clause. Instead the court resolved "that the Copyright Clause does not envision that Congress is positively forbidden from extending copyright-like protection under other constitutional clauses, such as the Commerce Clause, to works of authorship that may not meet the fixation requirement inherent in the term 'Writings.' "[80]

76. H.R. Rep. No. 94–1476, at 131 (1976), *reprinted in* 1976 U.S.C.C.A.N. 5659, 5747.

77. Pub. L. No. 103–465, §§ 512–513, 108 Stat. 4809, 4974–76 (1994) (codified as amended at 17 U.S.C. § 1101 and 18 U.S.C. § 2319A (2000)). There are civil remedies under 17 U.S.C. § 1101 and provisions for criminal prosecution under 18 U.S.C. § 2319A.

78. 492 F.3d 140, 149–50 (2d Cir. 2007).

79. 175 F.3d 1269, 1274–80 (11th Cir. 1999).

80. *Id.* at 1280. For commentary on these issues, see Susan M. Deas, Jazzing Up the Copyright Act? Resolving the Uncertainties of the United States Anti–Bootlegging Law, 20 Hastings Comm. & Ent. L.J. 567 (1998); Adam Giuliano, Note, Steal This Concert? The Federal Anti–Bootlegging Statute Gets Struck Down, But Not Out, 7 Vand. J. Ent. L. & Prac. 373 (2005); Joseph P. Merschmann, Note, Anchoring Copyright Laws in the Copyright Clause: Halting the Commerce Clause End Run Around Limits on Congress' Copyright Power, 34 Conn. L. Rev. 661 (2002); Andrew B. Peterson, Note, To Bootleg or Not to

Bootleg? Confusion Surrounding the Constitutionality of the Anti–Bootlegging Act Continues, 58 OKLA. L. REV. 723 (2005).

Chapter 3

COPYRIGHT OWNERSHIP

Table of Sections

¶ 3.01 Copyright Authorship & Ownership

The Intellectual Property Clause of the Constitution states that Congress has the power: "to Promote the Progress of Science and useful Arts, by securing for limited Times to Authors and Inventors the exclusive Right to their respective Writings and Discoveries."[1] Quite naturally then, Congress has the power to grant copyright protection to authors. But who is the author?

In the case of the individual artist or novelist, the identity of the author is quite straightforward. Complications arise when two or more people are involved in the creative process, as the question becomes whether a particular contribution merits coauthorship. Courts have actually developed a rather stringent standard for coauthorship, or "joint works." Section 101 of the Copyright Act defines a joint work as: "a work prepared by two or more authors with the intention that their contributions be merged into inseparable or interdependent parts of a unitary whole."

A representative case on this issue is *Childress v. Taylor*,[2] in which a dramatist prepared a play involving Jackie "Moms" Mably, the famous African–American comedienne. As Alice Childress wrote her play, she received and accepted suggestions from actress Clarice Taylor. Taylor's suggestions are delineated in the court's opinion:

> Taylor identifies the following as her major contributions to the play: (1) she learned through interviews that "Moms"

---

1. U.S. Const., Art. I, § 8, cl. 8.   2. 945 F.2d 500 (2d Cir. 1991).

Mabley called all of her piano players "Luther," so Taylor suggested that the play include such a character; (2) Taylor and Childress together interviewed Carey Jordan, "Moms" Mabley's housekeeper, and upon leaving the interview they came to the conclusion that she would be a good character for the play, but Taylor could not recall whether she or Childress suggested it; (3) Taylor informed Childress that "Moms" Mabley made a weekly trip to Harlem to do ethnic food shopping; (4) Taylor suggested a street scene in Harlem with speakers because she recalled having seen or listened to such a scene many times; (5) the idea of using a minstrel scene came out of Taylor's research; (6) the idea of a card game scene also came out of Taylor's research, although Taylor could not recall who specifically suggested the scene; (7) some of the jokes used in the play came from Taylor's research; and (8) the characteristics of "Moms" Mabley's personality portrayed in the play emerged from Taylor's research. Essentially, Taylor contributed facts and details about "Moms" Mabley's life and discussed some of them with Childress. However, Childress was responsible for the actual structure of the play and the dialogue.

The issue was whether Taylor's contributions and role merited elevating her to the status of a joint author. The court concluded that it does not, and on two separate grounds. First, the court found that Taylor had not made independently copyrightable contributions to the work. This was fatal to the coauthorship claim because the court adopted copyright scholar Paul Goldstein's view that coauthorship requires that each author contribute creative expression substantial enough to be independently copyrightable. This approach theoretically avoids some frivolous claims of coauthorship—particularly those in which the claim is that "he took my idea and wrote a book." (The topic of how ideas can be protected under the law is the subject of Chapter 19 in this book.) It also prevents the sort of contributions frequently made by editors, arrangers, and other ministerial types, who often suggest minor changes or provide ideas. This is not to suggest that a particularly creative musical arrangement might not merit copyright protection, but simply that providing an idea or two regarding a note or tempo or the like would not suffice.

Other courts have adopted a similar view of joint authorship. In *Gaylord v. United States*, 595 F.3d 1364 (Fed. Cir. 2010), the Federal Circuit held that the sculptor of a war memorial was the sole author of a commissioned work. The court concluded that government entities were not joint authors because their contributions consisted of uncopyrightable, general suggestions regarding the appearance and positioning of the soldiers depicted in the memorial.

Despite its logic from a copyright standpoint, the Goldstein view is not the only approach that might be taken. The late Mel Nimmer, arguably the leading commentator in the copyright field, contended that if two authors agreed to joint ownership, it should not matter if one of them only contributes uncopyrightable ideas.[3] Indeed, the idea may the a crucial contribution, as important as carrying out the idea in expressive form. Nonetheless, the Goldstein view has been adopted by most courts.[4] For example, the court in *Erickson v. Trinity Theatre, Inc.*[5] criticized the Nimmer approach because it has the effect of extending copyright protection to ideas and concepts, contributions that can be ambiguous in nature and difficult to assess in practice. Thus, for example, a critic, commentator, or editor might claim coauthor status. The *Erickson* court concluded that the Goldstein approach was more consistent with copyright policy and with clarity in the law.

Moreover, most courts have suggested that in such a situation, the two parties can simply agree to joint ownership by contract. In effect, the courts have adopted a "default rule" providing sole ownership to the person who contributed the copyrightable expression. Such a solution does have its drawbacks—it requires contractual alteration and it does not completely avoid the fact that the "author" for copyright purposes remains the person who contributed the expression, even if the rights are then assigned in part to the "idea man." Consequently, for example, the term of copyright will be governed by the life of the first author only, rather than by the lives of both (i.e., joint works are protected based on whoever passes on last). Nonetheless, parties are free to contract for any allocation of relative rights that they choose to provide.

The second requisite for joint authorship is the intent that the contributions be combined into a unitary whole. In *Thomson v. Larson,*[6] the court rejected a claim of joint authorship in the musical play "Rent" because the playwright did not intend to share authorship with his collaborator. The court noted several pieces of evidence on the intent question, including the fact that the principal playwright retained decision-making authority over the final work, that the playwright was billed as the sole author, and that the playwright entered into written agreements with third parties as sole author.

Similarly, in *Clogston v. American Academy of Orthopaedic*

---

3. Melville Nimmer, Nimmer on Copyright § 6.07.

4. *See, e.g., M.G.B. Homes, Inc. v. Ameron Homes, Inc.*, 903 F.2d 1486 (11th Cir. 1990); *S.O.S., Inc. v. Payday, Inc.*, 886 F.2d 1081 (9th Cir. 1989).

5. 13 F.3d 1061, 1070–71 (7th Cir. 1994).

6. 147 F.3d 195 (2d Cir. 1998).

Surgeons,[7] a photographer was not deemed to be a joint author of a book containing his photos because the publisher did not intend to create a joint work. The Ninth Circuit has focuses primarily on the issue of artistic control. In *Aalmuhammed v. Lee,* 202 F.3d 1227, 1234 (9th Cir. 2000), the court held that joint authorship depends on three factors: (1) who exercised control over the creative effort; (2) whether there were "objective manifestations of a shared intent to be coauthors;" and (3) whether "the audience appeal of the work depends on both contributions and 'the share of each in its success cannot be appraised.' "

For examples of joint works as defined by copyright law, many famous songwriting teams have created songs that can be deemed joint works, such as John Lennon/Paul McCartney, Elton John/Bernie Taupin, Mick Jagger/Keith Richards, Alan Jay Lerner/Frederick Lowe, and George & Ira Gershwin. When these songwriters create their songs, they both contribute copyrightable material (whether one writes music or song lyrics or both) and they both intend to combine their efforts into a single song.

Finally, a fundamental distinction in copyright law is the difference between ownership of the copyright (i.e., the intellectual property rights) as distinct from ownership of material object. Section 202 of the Copyright Act states: "Ownership of a copyright, or of any of the exclusive rights under a copyright, is distinct from ownership of any material object in which the work is embodied. Transfer of ownership of any material object, including the copy or phonorecord in which the work is first fixed, does not of itself convey any rights in the copyrighted work embodied in the object; nor, in the absence of an agreement, does transfer of ownership of a copyright or of any exclusive rights under a copyright convey property rights in any material object." In other words, when an artist paints an old painting, he or she is typically the author of that work and the owner of the copyright. When the artist sells the physical object—the painting itself—to a buyer at an art gallery, the buyer then owns that object (the painting), but does not own the underlying copyright to that work unless those rights are specifically transferred to the buyer in a signed written agreement by the artist. Instead, absent a transfer agreement, the copyright remains vested in the artist, which means the artist can decide whether to create derivative works (such as posters or calendars) or otherwise to exercise other rights of the author. The buyer of the painting has only ownership of the physical object, and is entitled (under section 109 of the Copyright Act) to display the painting publicly or to sell the work itself.

---

7. 930 F.Supp. 1156 (W.D. Tex. 1996). *See also Thomson v. Larson,* 147 F.3d 195 (2d Cir. 1998) (requiring mutual intent); *Clogston v. American Academy of Orthopaedic Surgeons,* 930 F.Supp. 1156 (W.D. Tex. 1996) (same).

¶ 3.02   Works Made for Hire

Often copyrighted works are created by someone who is hired and paid to carry out the creative task. In this situation, there is often a question regarding copyright ownership. The key issue is whether a work qualifies as a "work made for hire," which is defined in section 101 of the Copyright Act:

A "work made for hire" is—

(1) a work prepared by an employee within the scope of his or her employment; or

(2) a work specially ordered or commissioned for use as a contribution to a collective work, as a part of a motion picture or other audiovisual work, as a translation, as a supplementary work, as a compilation, as an instructional text, as a test, as answer material for a test, or as an atlas, if the parties expressly agree in a written instrument signed by them that the work shall be considered a work made for hire. For the purpose of the foregoing sentence, a "supplementary work" is a work prepared for publication as a secondary adjunct to a work by another author for the purpose of introducing, concluding, illustrating, explaining, revising, commenting upon, or assisting in the use of the other work, such as forewords, afterwords, pictorial illustrations, maps, charts, tables, editorial notes, musical arrangements, answer material for tests, bibliographies, appendixes, and indexes, and an "instructional text" is a literary, pictorial, or graphic work prepared for publication and with the purpose of use in systematic instructional activities.

The first category of works made for hire includes the standard situations in which someone is employed to perform creative tasks for his or her employer. Simple examples of works made for hire would include the output of staff writers and photographers who are employed by a newspaper or magazine and who create their works in the scope of their duties with the publication. The author and owner of these articles and photographs, for purposes of copyright law, is deemed to be the newspaper or magazine employing these staffers. In contrast, the work of a freelance writer or photographer is deemed to be authored by the writer or photographer, who can of course assign such rights by contract.

The landmark case differentiating between an agent/employee and an independent contractor is *Community for Creative Non–Violence v. Reid.*[8] In that case, the Community for Creative Non–Violence (CCNV), which is a homeless advocacy group led by Mitch

---

8.   490 U.S. 730 (1989).

Snyder, entered into negotiations with famed sculptor James Earl Reid. The CCNV wished to have a sculpture created that would help depict the plight of the homeless. Reid, who would normally command about $100,000 per work, agreed in this instance to donate his services, but requested $10,000 for materials and related expenses. The parties did not discuss or address copyright ownership. In the process of creating the sculpture, which was known as "Third World America," sculptor Reid received some input from Snyder and CCNV. For example, Snyder suggested that the homeless people should be depicted in a reclining position, and urged the inclusion of a shopping cart in the display. Reid created the sculpture in his studio and delivered it to CCNV.

Undoubtedly, CCNV owned the particular physical rendition of the work—the physical embodiment of the sculpture itself. But who owns the copyright? Who owns the right to reproduce the sculpture, in the form of post cards, mugs, calendars, or miniature replicas? The answer to this question is the author, as that term is defined in copyright law, has these rights. If the sculpture was a work made for hire, then CCNV would own the copyright, but if it was the work of an independent contractor, then it was most likely that Reid retained the copyright. Or perhaps the sculpture was a joint work, but only if CCNV could establish such rights. Given the discussion of joint works above, it is highly unlikely that CCNV's contributions to the work were independently copyrightable or that Reid ever intended a joint authorship arrangement with CCNV. Thus, it is highly unlikely that the sculpture was a joint work.

In order to determine whether "Third World America" was a work made for hire, the Court in *CCNV v. Reid* had to resolve the appropriate test for addressing this issue. The circuit courts had previously applied four different tests—(1) the right to control test, which focuses on the ability of the hiring party, CCNV, to control by virtue of a binding contract; (2) the actual control test, which emphasizes the actual control wielded by the hiring party in the creative process; (3) the common law agency standard, which is drawn from the agency/tort law distinction between agents and independent contractors; and (4) the formal, salaried employee test, which would limit works made for hire to situations involving an employee on staff. The first two tests were the easiest to satisfy, giving CCNV an arguable claim that the sculpture was a work made for hire given that CCNV did have some ability to control the final output and provided some actual instructions to Reid. The third test follows the common law dichotomy between agent/employees and independent contractors, and as will be seen it is likely that no agency relationship could be shown between the CCNV and Reid. Finally, it was clear that Reid was not a salaried employee, and thus CCNV would have no claim to a work for hire relationship under this approach.

The Court adopted the common law agency standard. This is consistent with the general language of the statute, which can be said to incorporate the general understanding of terms not otherwise defined. The Court also suggested that such a standard offered predictability and certainty, though how that is so is difficult to fathom. Consider the amusingly long list of factors the Court identifies as relevant to the test:

> In determining whether a hired party is an employee under the general common law of agency, we consider the hiring party's right to control the manner and means by which the product is accomplished. Among the other factors relevant to this inquiry are the skill required; the source of the instrumentalities and tools; the location of the work; the duration of the relationship between the parties; whether the hiring party has the right to assign additional projects to the hired party; the extent of the hired party's discretion over when and how long to work; the method of payment; the hired party's role in hiring and paying assistants; whether the work is part of the regular business of the hiring party; whether the hiring party is in business; the provision of employee benefits; and the tax treatment of the hired party.

The Court then proceeded to examine the circumstances of this particular case in light of the enumerated factors. It determined that Reid was not an employee of CCNV, but instead was an independent contractor. The Court noted that "CCNV members directed enough of Reid's work to ensure that he produced a sculpture that met their specifications. But the extent of control the hiring party exercises over the details of the product is not dispositive. Indeed, all the other circumstances weigh heavily against finding an employment relationship."

Indeed, as it happens, application of this multi-factor test to the particular case of the sculpture was fairly straightforward. Reid is a skilled sculptor who provided his own materials and tools. He worked from his Baltimore studio, not on CCNV's premises. He was retained for less than two months on a one-time transaction, and CCNV had no right to assign additional projects to him. Reid was free to determine his own hours and was paid for completion of a single job. Finally, CCNV did not pay payroll or social security taxes, provide any employee benefits or insurance contributions. Hence, the sculpture was deemed not a work made for hire. The Court remanded for a determination of whether CCNV's contributions might render them joint authors, but such a conclusion is unlikely, as mentioned previously. It is worth noting that Reid's donation of his services and CCNV's status as a non-profit organization had no bearing on the outcome or analysis of the case.

Despite the clear outcome of the agency test in *CCNV v. Reid*, the sheer number of factors in the test makes it difficult to apply in closer cases. The Second Circuit in *Aymes v. Bonelli*,[9] has highlighted five factors to be given particular weight—"(1) the hiring party's right to control the manner and means of creation; (2) the skill required; (3) the provision of employee benefits; (4) the tax treatment of the hired party; and (5) whether the hiring party has the right to assign additional projects to the hired party." In *Hi–Tech Video Productions, Inc. v. Capital Cities/ABC, Inc.*,[10] the Sixth Circuit applied the *CCNV* factors and held that individuals working for a film production company were independent contractors and not employees. The court found that although the hiring party had the right to control and wielded actual control of the video, these two factors alone do turn an otherwise independent contractor into an employee. Instead, because of the economic treatment of the assistants, the skill required of them, and the hiring party's own perception of the assistants' status, these creative contributors were independent contractors.

CCNV v. Reid is a very important copyright law decision as it affects a myriad of situations in which independent contractors are hired for purposes of creative tasks. Quite often the parties do not address copyright ownership, just as in *CCNV v. Reid*. The expectations of the parties in such an instance are often diametrically opposed—the party who hired and paid for the creative work likely imagined that it owns all relevant rights, while the creative contributor likely believes that he or she retains the copyright, while only conveying the physical object or other manifestation of the work to the customer. In fact, absent an agreement to the contrary, the creative contributor would ordinarily be correct.

Consider two examples—a company hires an independent contractor to design its website, rather than having a staff employee develop the website. The contract, if any, does not address copyright ownership. The company will have very limited rights as the copyright is likely to remain with the web designer. Therefore, the company may be unable to alter its website without the consent of the web designer, who demanded further payment. Or take the case of a wedding photographer who provides the happy couple with a set of prints. If the bride and groom desire additional prints, the copyright is likely to remain in the photographer's hands, and any duplication without the photographer's consent would likely violate

---

9. 980 F.2d 857, 861 (2d Cir. 1992). *See also Carter v. Helmsley–Spear, Inc.*, 71 F.3d 77, 85–87 (2d Cir. 1995).

10. 58 F.3d 1093 (6th Cir. 1995).

copyright law. Yet, they might protest, "we paid the photographer to take pictures at our wedding for our use." But *CCNV v. Reid* informs us that this project is not a work made for hire.

The practical implication of this rule is that anyone who hires talent for purposes of making creative works should insure that the relationship between the parties either qualifies as a "work made for hire" under the Copyright Act (so that the hiring party is the author and owner of the copyright) or at least that the hiring party has obtained as many contractual rights as it needs in order to make use of the work, including such things as the right to make alterations, to place the work in a new medium, to use it anywhere in the world (or the universe, as if often provided in modern contracts), and so forth. Ideally, in the latter situation, the hiring party should consider obtaining a complete assignment of the copyright (although even this assignment would not encompass termination rights discussed in Chapter 3, ¶ 3.08.)

Commissioned Works

Section 101 also includes a second category of works made for hire. These consist of specially ordered or commissioned works for certain specific purposes delineated in the statute. The nine specific uses are:

(1) contributions to a collective work, which is defined as "a work, such as a periodical issue, anthology, or encyclopedia, in which a number of contributions, constituting separate and independent works in themselves, are assembled into a collective whole."

(2) a part of a motion picture or other audiovisual work.

(3) a translation.

(4) a supplementary work, which is defined as "a work prepared for publication as a secondary adjunct to a work by another author for the purpose of introducing, concluding, illustrating, explaining, revising, commenting upon, or assisting in the use of the other work, such as forewords, afterwords, pictorial illustrations, maps, charts, tables, editorial notes, musical arrangements, answer material for tests, bibliographies, appendixes, and indexes."

(5) a compilation, which is defined as "a work formed by the collection and assembling of preexisting materials or of data that are selected, coordinated, or arranged in such a way that the resulting work as a whole constitutes an original work of authorship. The term 'compilation' includes collective works."

(6) an instructional text, which is defined as "a literary, pictorial, or graphic work prepared for publication and with the purpose of use in systematic instructional activities."

(7) a test.

(8) answer material for a test.

or

(9) an atlas.

In order to qualify as a commissioned work, the parties must expressly agree in a written instrument signed by them that the work shall be considered a work made for hire.

The inclusion of these categories of specially commissioned works reflects the industry practice and commercial reality that the nine types of works on the list frequently are the result of the effort of a number of creative contributors. In effect, the list of specially commissioned works allows courts to assume, without further inquiry, that a written work made for hire agreement involving these nine categories of works is in fact a work made for hire with no further inquiry into the realities of the business relationship. In short, it is common practice for works on this list to be the result of collaborative creative effort that will be incorporated into a single unified work, generally with a single corporate author and owner, such as a motion picture.

In sum, in order to be deemed a commissioned work, three key requisites must be met: the work must be "specially ordered or commissioned," the work must fit within one of the nine categories identified in section 101's listing, and the parties must agree in writing that the work is made for hire. If the work does not fit within this list, then the general rules discussed above for ordinary types of works would provide the governing rule. As always, the parties are able to modify their relative rights by contract, as discussed above.

¶ 3.03 Copyright Notice

A copyright notice is an indication by the author or copyright owner of its claim to a particular work. The notice consists of the word "Copyright" (or the © symbol), the date of publication, and the name of the author or copyright owner. The notice is to be placed on an inside front cover or other similar place. Thus, for example, this book contains a copyright notice on the inside cover indicating that it is copyrighted by Thomson West in 2012. The copyright notice should be placed on the work in a manner that gives reasonable notice of the claim of copyright. The notice should be permanently legible to an ordinary user of the work under normal conditions of use and should not be concealed from view.

The Copyright Office has issued regulations regarding ways to affix and position the notice.[11]

The following are illustrative locations and methods of affixing copyright notices:

Works Published in Book Form

Title page

Page immediately following the title page

Either side of the front or back cover

First or last page of the main body of the work

Single-leaf Works

Front or back

Works Published as Periodicals or Other Serials

Any location acceptable for books

As part of, or adjacent to, the masthead or on the page containing the masthead

Adjacent to a prominent heading, appearing at or near the front of the issue, containing the title of the periodical and any combination of the volume and issue number and date of the issue

Works Published as Separate Contributions to Collective Works

For a separate contribution reproduced on only one page:

Under the title or elsewhere on the same page

For a separate contribution reproduced on more than one page:

Under a title appearing at or near the beginning of the contribution

On the first page of the main body of the contribution

Immediately following the end of the contribution

On any of the pages where the contribution appears if the contribution consists of no more than 20 pages, the notice is reproduced prominently, and the application of the notice to the particular contribution is clear

---

11. *See* 37 CFR 201.20; *see also* "Methods of Affixation and Positions of the Copyright Notice on Various Types of Works" at www.copyright.gov/title37.

Works Reproduced in Machine–Readable Copies

With or near the title or at the end of the work, on visually perceptible printouts

At the user's terminal at sign-on

On continuous display on the terminal

Reproduced durably on a gummed or other label securely affixed to the copies or to a container used as a permanent receptacle for the copies

Motion Pictures and Other Audiovisual Works

A notice embodied in the copies by a photomechanical or electronic process so that it ordinarily would appear whenever the work is performed in its entirety may be located:

With or near the title

With the cast, credits, and similar information

At or immediately following the beginning of the work

At or immediately preceding the end of the work

The notice on works lasting 60 seconds or less, such as untitled motion pictures or other audiovisual works, may be located:

In all the locations specified above for longer motion pictures; and

If the notice is embodied electronically or photo-mechanically, on the leader of the film or tape immediately preceding the work

For audiovisual works or motion pictures distributed to the public for private use, the locations include the above, and in addition:

On the permanent housing or container

Pictorial, Graphic, and Sculptural Works

For works embodied in two-dimensional copies, a notice may be affixed directly, durably, and permanently to:

The front or back of the copies

Any backing, mounting, framing, or other material to which the copies are durably attached, so as to withstand normal use

For works reproduced in three-dimensional copies, a notice may be affixed directly, durably, and permanently to:

Any visible portion of the work;

Any base, mounting, or framing or other material on which the copies are durably attached

For works on which it is impractical to affix a notice to the copies directly or by means of a durable label, a notice is acceptable if it appears on a tag or durable label attached to the copy so that it will remain with it as it passes through commerce.

For works reproduced in copies consisting of sheet-like or strip material bearing multiple or continuous reproductions of the work, such as fabrics or wallpaper, the notice may be applied:

To the reproduction itself

To the margin, selvage, or reverse side of the material at frequent and regular intervals

If the material contains neither a selvage nor reverse side, to tags or labels attached to the copies and to any spools, reels, or containers housing them in such a way that the notice is visible in commerce.[12]

The significance of copyright notice under United States law has changed dramatically in the last forty years. Prior to the enactment of the Copyright Act of 1976, a copyright notice was mandatory on all published works, and the failure to include such a notice had the effect of forfeiting the copyright. Consequently, if a work was published without the requisite notice, it fell into the public domain. This draconian rule had a disproportionate impact on unsophisticated authors who were unaware of the law, and on foreign authors and publishers because most foreign countries did not impose such a requirement on published works. As will be seen later in this text, Congress eventually ameliorated some of the harsh effects of this rule, particularly as to foreign authors. Controversially, Congress restored copyright protection in some foreign works that had fallen into the public domain. This action led to constitutional challenges under the Intellectual Property Clause and the First Amendment (discussed later), but was eventually upheld by the Supreme Court in 2012.

The Copyright Act of 1976 ameliorated the harsh effect of the copyright notice requirement. This statute continued the prior requirement of copyright notice, but it contained several provisions allowing for curing or excusing of the omission of the notice. Specifically, it provided for cure of the omission in some cases. The cure provision continues to have relevance and effect for works

12. *See* http://www.copyright.gov/ circs/circ03.pdf (last visited June 6, 2012).

published while this statute is in effect. Section 405(a) of the Copyright Act now states:

(a) Effect of Omission on Copyright.—With respect to copies and phonorecords publicly distributed by authority of the copyright owner before the effective date of the Berne Convention Implementation Act of 1988, the omission of the copyright notice described in sections 401 through 403 from copies or phonorecords publicly distributed by authority of the copyright owner does not invalidate the copyright in a work if—

(1) the notice has been omitted from no more than a relatively small number of copies or phonorecords distributed to the public; or

(2) registration for the work has been made before or is made within five years after the publication without notice, and a reasonable effort is made to add notice to all copies or phonorecords that are distributed to the public in the United States after the omission has been discovered; or

(3) the notice has been omitted in violation of an express requirement in writing that, as a condition of the copyright owner's authorization of the public distribution of copies or phonorecords, they bear the prescribed notice.

The next step in the historical development of a relaxed copyright notice rule is the United States adherence to the Berne Convention in 1988. Article 5(2) of the Berne Convention states: "The enjoyment and the exercise of these rights shall not be subject to any formality; such enjoyment and such exercise shall be independent of the existence of protection in the country of origin of the work. Consequently, apart from the provisions of this Convention, the extent of protection, as well as the means of redress afforded to the author to protect his rights, shall be governed exclusively by the laws of the country where protection is claimed." To bring the United States into compliance with the Berne Convention, the notice requirement was eliminated in the Berne Convention Implementation Act of 1988 (often called the Berne Amendment or the BCIA).[13]

The copyright notice serves at least four beneficial purposes: it places published material in the public domain when the author is not interested in maintaining copyright protection, it serves to inform the public regarding whether a particular work is copyrighted, it identifies the copyright owner, and it indicates the publication date. Even under current law, the notice can serve these informa-

---

13. Pub. L. 100–568 (1988).

tional roles, even though the absence of a copyright notice no longer necessarily indicates that the work is in the public domain.

Even after the Berne Amendments, the old rules governing publication of works without copyright notice continue to have relevance today. The Berne Amendments are not generally retroactive. Thus, works by United States authors published prior to the effective date of the Copyright Act of 1976 (which took effect on January 1, *1978*) are still governed by the mandatory notice requirements of the 1909 Copyright Act. Similarly, works published by United States authors prior to the effective date of the Berne Amendments (which took effect on March 1, 1989), are still governed by the pre-Berne rules of the Copyright Act of 1976. In other words, works by United States authors published prior to January 1, 1978 must contain copyright notice. Works published by United States authors in the time frame of January 1, 1978 but before March 1, 1989 are still governed by the mandatory notice and cure/excuse provisions of the 1976 Act. As to foreign works published before the Berne Amendments took effect, section 104A of the Copyright Act governs the conditions and effect of copyright restoration for certain foreign authors who had failed to comply with formalities under United States Law. Works published by any author since March 1, 1989 are not required to have copyright notice.

In 2012, in *Golan v. Holder*, 132 S.Ct. 873 (2012), the Supreme Court addressed the constitutionality of section 104A, discussed above, which restored the copyright in works of foreign origin that had entered the public domain in the United States because of failures to comply with formalities or for other technical reasons. The Court held that restoration of the copyright in foreign works did not violate the Intellectual Property Clause (specifically, the "limited times" and "progress" clauses) or the First Amendment.

Justice Ginsburg authored the 6–2 majority opinion (Justice Kagan recused herself), upholding the copyright restoration in foreign works. Three categories of foreign works were restored under section 104A: (1) works from countries in which United States law did not offer protection at the time of publication; (2) sound recordings fixed before 1972 (the year U.S. sound recordings were finally given protection); or (3) works for which the author had failed to comply with U. S. statutory formalities applicable at the time. The Court's fundamental holding can be easily summarized: "Neither the Copyright and Patent Clause nor the First Amendment, we hold, makes the public domain, in any and all cases, a territory that works may never exit."

The Court in *Golan* highlighted various measures included in the copyright restoration that were designed to ameliorate its effect on the public domain, including the imposition of no liability for any use of foreign works occurring before restoration, a one-year grace period following the law's enactment before any liability can accrue, and detailed provisions dealing with the potential liability of "reliance parties," i.e., those who had used or acquired rights involving material that had been in the public domain.

Addressing the Copyright Clause challenge, the Court noted that the copyright restoration still maintained a limited time period for copyright protection, thus leaving intact the rule against perpetual copyrights. Second, the Court cited past examples of legislation that effectively placed unprotected works back into the public domain, including the Copyright Act of 1790 (the very first federal copyright statute), which offered federal protection for some works that had been left previously unprotected under prior state copyright law. Justice Ginsburg also noted prior restorations of protection under patent law, suggesting by analogy that the Intellectual Property Clause was not a bar to such actions. Next, the Court noted that *Eldred* had previously put to rest the idea that Congress had limited discretion in offering protection under the progress of knowledge preamble to the Intellectual Property Clause. The Court found that incentives to create new works were not the only basis on which copyright protection could be offered; rather, Congress could rationally determine that dissemination of existing works (presumably in a more efficient manner when under copyright protection) could be the basis for copyright protection.

Justice Ginsburg then addressed the First Amendment challenge. The Court reiterated that the analysis in its prior ruling in *Eldred* had noted that the fair use doctrine and the idea-expression distinction (i.e., only expression and not ideas are protected under copyright law) accommodated the potential general conflict between copyright law and the First Amendment. These limitations on copyright protection were the "traditional contours" to which the Court had alluded in *Eldred*. The challengers in *Golan* contended that the inviolability of the public domain was also one of the traditional contours of copyright protection, a claim the Court essentially rejected.

The Court next disposed of the argument that copyright restoration had destroyed "vested rights" held by those who were making use of public domain works. Justice Ginsburg responded as follows:

> As we have already shown, the text of the Copyright Clause and the historical record scarcely establish that "once a work enters the public domain," Congress cannot permit anyone—

"not even the creator—[to] copyright it." And nothing in the historical record, congressional practice, or our own jurisprudence warrants exceptional First Amendment solicitude for copyrighted works that were once in the public domain. Neither this challenge nor that raised in *Eldred*, we stress, allege Congress transgressed a generally applicable First Amendment prohibition; we are not faced, for example, with copyright protection that hinges on the author's viewpoint.[14]

In concluding, the Court noted that Congress has broad authority to implement copyright laws and to participate in international systems designed to offer reciprocal protection for works worldwide:

> Congress determined that U. S. interests were best served by our full participation in the dominant system of international copyright protection. Those interests include ensuring exemplary compliance with our international obligations, securing greater protection for U. S. authors abroad, and remedying unequal treatment of foreign authors. The judgment [copyright restoration] expresses lies well within the ken of the political branches. It is our obligation, of course, to determine whether the action Congress took, wise or not, encounters any constitutional shoal. For the reasons stated, we are satisfied it does not.[15]

Justice Breyer, joined by Justice Alito, dissented. He focused on the importance of copyright protection as a stimulus for the production of new works, something the copyright restoration clearly did not do. To him, the question posed was thus "does the Clause empower Congress to enact a statute that withdraws works from the public domain, brings about higher prices and costs, and in doing so seriously restricts dissemination, particularly to those who need it for scholarly, educational, or cultural purposes—all *without providing any additional incentive for the production of new material*? That is the question before us. And, as I have said, I believe the answer is no. Congress in this statute has exceeded what are, under any plausible reading of the Copyright Clause, its permissible limits." Justice Breyer concluded as follows:

> The fact that, by withdrawing material from the public domain, the statute inhibits an important preexisting flow of information is sufficient, when combined with the other features of the statute that I have discussed, to convince me that the Copyright Clause, interpreted in the light of the First Amendment, does not authorize Congress to enact this statute.

14. *Id.*   **15.** *Id.*

Returning to the statutory notice provisions, to deal with the possibility that someone might obtain a copy of an older work published without notice and assume that it is not under copyright, section 405(b) provides that a party who is misled by the omission of notice in a public distribution (taking place prior to the Berne Amendment effective date) is not liable for actual or statutory for infringements taking place before the party has actual notice of the copyright claim.

A good example of a case applying the 1976 Act's "cure" provision is *Hasbro Bradley, Inc. v. Sparkle Toys, Inc.*[16] In that case, Hasbro obtained the United States rights in copyrighted toys made by Takara, which had distributed toys without notice in Japan, where copyright notice is not required. The court held that Hasbro cured this omission when it registered the works within five years and made a reasonable effort to place copyright notices on toys distributed in the United States after the omission was discovered. In effect, the court found that when a work is published without notice, the copyright owner has an "incipient copyright" for a five-year period, and if the copyright owner cures the omission during that window "the copyright is perfected and valid retroactively."[17]

The case law under the 1976 Act's cure provisions also addresses what a relatively small number of copies might be, with somewhat unclear results. In *Original Appalachian Artworks, Inc. v. Toy Loft, Inc.*,[18] the court found that omission of the notice from one percent of copies distributed was relatively small. In *Donald Frederick Evans & Associates, Inc. v. Continental Homes, Inc.*,[19] an omission from 2.4% of copies was deemed not relatively small.

In light of the Berne Amendments, copyright notice in works published post-Berne is not an issue that is likely to be litigated aside from situations in which the good faith of an alleged infringer is relevant (for example, with regard to damages determinations). Despite the Berne Amendment's relaxation of the notice requirement, however, it makes practical sense for copyright owners to place a notice on their works—the notice informs readers of the copyright claim and provides contact information for purposes of securing licenses and other requests. In short, from a cost-benefit perspective, the notice is an almost costless way to enhance the ability to enforce and possibly to license the copyright in a work.

¶ 3.04 Copyright Registration & Deposit

As previously discussed, federal copyright protection attaches to a work when it is fixed in a tangible medium of expression.

---

16. 780 F.2d 189 (2d Cir. 1985).

17. *Id.* at 194.

18. 684 F.2d 821, 827 (11th Cir. 1982).

19. 785 F.2d 897, 910 (11th Cir. 1986).

Consequently, a copyright is in force even though the work has not been registered with the Copyright Office. Copyright registration is, however, generally a condition precedent to the filing of a copyright infringement suit in federal court. Hence, before a copyright owner can file a complaint regarding copyright violations, it usually must obtain the certificate of registration from the Copyright Office. Section 411 states:

> Except for an action brought for a violation of the rights of the author under section 106A(a), and subject to the provisions of subsection (b), no action for infringement of the copyright in any United States work shall be instituted until preregistration or registration of the copyright claim has been made in accordance with this title. In any case, however, where the deposit, application, and fee required for registration have been delivered to the Copyright Office in proper form and registration has been refused, the applicant is entitled to institute an action for infringement if notice thereof, with a copy of the complaint, is served on the Register of Copyrights. The Register may, at his or her option, become a party to the action with respect to the issue of registrability of the copyright claim by entering an appearance within sixty days after such service, but the Register's failure to become a party shall not deprive the court of jurisdiction to determine that issue.

It should be highlighted that this statutory requirement, by its express language, only applies to a "United States work." Owners of foreign works are not obligated to register their works prior to filing suit in the United States courts.

In addition to the bar to filing suit prior to registration, the copyright owner cannot recover statutory damages and attorney's fees under section 412 when infringement precedes registration (except when registration takes place within 3 months of publication):

> In any action under this title, other than an action brought for a violation of the rights of the author under section 106A(a), an action for infringement of the copyright of a work that has been preregistered under section 408 (f) before the commencement of the infringement and that has an effective date of registration not later than the earlier of 3 months after the first publication of the work or 1 month after the copyright owner has learned of the infringement, or an action instituted under section 411 (b), no award of statutory damages or of attorney's fees, as provided by sections 504 and 505, shall be made for—

> (1) any infringement of copyright in an unpublished work commenced before the effective date of its registration; or

(2) any infringement of copyright commenced after first publication of the work and before the effective date of its registration, unless such registration is made within three months after the first publication of the work.

If the copyright owner obtains the registration certificate before the infringement takes place, the registration will relate back to the date on which the application was completed, and statutory damages and attorney's fees can be recovered. Section 410(d) states: "The effective date of a copyright registration is the day on which an application, deposit, and fee, which are later determined by the Register of Copyrights or by a court of competent jurisdiction to be acceptable for registration, have all been received in the Copyright Office."

Aside from its legal implications, copyright registration provides a useful repository of information regarding the copyright status of a work, and information about the copyright owner. Thus, for example, if someone wishes to know whether the song "Happy Birthday" is copyrighted, as well as the identity of the owner of the work, it is possible to obtain this information from the Copyright Office website, www.copyright.gov. A search for this song reveals that it is indeed copyrighted, and that (as of June 6, 2012) the owner of record for the work is Birch Tree Group, Ltd.

There are a few exceptions to the requirement of copyright registration. Most importantly, registration is not required prior to filing suit in the case violations of section 106A (moral rights, discussed in Chapter 4, ¶ 4.03.) or in the case of Berne Convention foreign works. Nonetheless, foreign copyright owners cannot recover statutory damages or attorneys fees if they have not complied with the registration requirements as set forth above. The foreign copyright owner still gets the standard remedies, both compensatory damages and injunctive, that are available in all copyright cases.

The Copyright Act also specifies the procedures to be followed in the event the Copyright Office declines to register a particular work. Section 411(a) provides that when registration is refused, the plaintiff may still file suit, but must serve notice on the Register of Copyrights so that agency can determine if it wishes to be involved in the copyright suit.

Live broadcasts involve a complicated notification process. Section 411(b) requires copyright owners to notify possible infringers no less that 48 hours *before* the fixation/transmission that the author intends to secure copyright in the work:

> In the case of a work consisting of sounds, images, or both, the first fixation of which is made simultaneously with its transmission, the copyright owner may, either before or after such fixation takes place, institute an action for infringement under

section 501, fully subject to the remedies provided by sections 502 through 506 and sections 509 and 510, if, in accordance with requirements that the Register of Copyrights shall prescribe by regulation, the copyright owner—

(1) serves notice upon the infringer, not less than 48 hours before such fixation, identifying the work and the specific time and source of its first transmission, and declaring an intention to secure copyright in the work; and

(2) makes registration for the work, if required by subsection (a), within three months after its first transmission.

In practical effect, the copyright owner therefore must know the identity of the infringer and of its plan to copy the work. In most instances, the copyright owner will not have this advance knowledge, and so will be limited to the remedies available after it registers the copyright—that is, actual damages and an injunction against future infringement.

A final point on this topic relates to the "poor man's copyright." This is a layperson's term for an author's practice of taking a copy of a work, sealing it in an envelope, and mailing it to himself or herself. This practice has no direct legal significance in copyright law, but is based on the notion that the mailed copy can serve as a record of the work's authorship or provenance. Indeed, this mailed copy can presumably be introduced into evidence in a dispute over authorship, but the poor man's copyright has no formal recognition in copyright law. It would seem that an author's postage money would be better spent on a proper copyright registration in the Copyright Office. Albeit more costly because of the required payment of a filing fee, the copyright registration is obviously the proper manner in which to record the author's copyright claim.

Section 408 of the Copyright Act specifies the requirement of a deposit of one or more copies of a work which must accompany the copyright registration form and fee (which is $65 for paper filings and $35 for on-line filings as of July 3, 2012):

(a) Registration Permissive.—At any time during the subsistence of the first term of copyright in any published or unpublished work in which the copyright was secured before January 1, 1978, and during the subsistence of any copyright secured on or after that date, the owner of copyright or of any exclusive right in the work may obtain registration of the copyright claim by delivering to the Copyright Office the deposit specified by this section, together with the application and fee specified by sections 409 and 708. Such registration is not a condition of copyright protection.

(b) Deposit for Copyright Registration.—Except as provided by subsection (c), the material deposited for registration shall include—

> (1) in the case of an unpublished work, one complete copy or phonorecord;

> (2) in the case of a published work, two complete copies or phonorecords of the best edition;

> (3) in the case of a work first published outside the United States, one complete copy or phonorecord as so published;

> (4) in the case of a contribution to a collective work, one complete copy or phonorecord of the best edition of the collective work.

Copies or phonorecords deposited for the Library of Congress under section 407 may be used to satisfy the deposit provisions of this section, if they are accompanied by the prescribed application and fee, and by any additional identifying material that the Register may, by regulation, require. The Register shall also prescribe regulations establishing requirements under which copies or phonorecords acquired for the Library of Congress under subsection (e) of section 407, otherwise than by deposit, may be used to satisfy the deposit provisions of this section.

This deposit requirement theoretically serves as a record of the copyright claim, although the Copyright Office does not retain a formal repository for the works. Instead, the works are collected by the Library of Congress. Indeed, the deposit requirement is an important source of acquisitions for the Library of Congress, providing it with free copies of works being registered.

Section 407 contains an additional deposit requirement, applicable only to published works. Again, the purpose of this requirement is to add to the collection of works in the Library of Congress. Section 407 states in part:

> (a) Except as provided by subsection (c), and subject to the provisions of subsection (e), the owner of copyright or of the exclusive right of publication in a work published in the United States shall deposit, within three months after the date of such publication—

> > (1) two complete copies of the best edition; or

> > (2) if the work is a sound recording, two complete phonorecords of the best edition, together with any printed or other visually perceptible material published with such phonorecords.

Neither the deposit requirements of this subsection nor the acquisition provisions of subsection (e) are conditions of copyright protection.

(b) The required copies or phonorecords shall be deposited in the Copyright Office for the use or disposition of the Library of Congress. The Register of Copyrights shall, when requested by the depositor and upon payment of the fee prescribed by section 708, issue a receipt for the deposit.

(c) The Register of Copyrights may by regulation exempt any categories of material from the deposit requirements of this section, or require deposit of only one copy or phonorecord with respect to any categories. Such regulations shall provide either for complete exemption from the deposit requirements of this section, or for alternative forms of deposit aimed at providing a satisfactory archival record of a work without imposing practical or financial hardships on the depositor, where the individual author is the owner of copyright in a pictorial, graphic, or sculptural work and (i) less than five copies of the work have been published, or (ii) the work has been published in a limited edition consisting of numbered copies, the monetary value of which would make the mandatory deposit of two copies of the best edition of the work burdensome, unfair, or unreasonable.

Providing a complete copy of some works to the Copyright Office can be impractical. To address this concern, section 408(c) of the Copyright Act allows the Register of Copyrights to permit registration of some types of works without a deposit of a complete copy:

(c) Administrative Classification and Optional Deposit.—

(1) The Register of Copyrights is authorized to specify by regulation the administrative classes into which works are to be placed for purposes of deposit and registration, and the nature of the copies or phonorecords to be deposited in the various classes specified. The regulations may require or permit, for particular classes, the deposit of identifying material instead of copies or phonorecords, the deposit of only one copy or phonorecord where two would normally be required, or a single registration for a group of related works. This administrative classification of works has no significance with respect to the subject matter of copyright or the exclusive rights provided by this title.

(2) Without prejudice to the general authority provided under clause (1), the Register of Copyrights shall establish regulations specifically permitting a single registration for a group of works by the same individual author, all first published as contributions to periodicals, including news-

papers, within a twelve-month period, on the basis of a single deposit, application, and registration fee, under the following conditions—

(A) if the deposit consists of one copy of the entire issue of the periodical, or of the entire section in the case of a newspaper, in which each contribution was first published; and

(B) if the application identifies each work separately, including the periodical containing it and its date of first publication.

(3) As an alternative to separate renewal registrations under subsection (a) of section 304, a single renewal registration may be made for a group of works by the same individual author, all first published as contributions to periodicals, including newspapers, upon the filing of a single application and fee, under all of the following conditions:

(A) the renewal claimant or claimants, and the basis of claim or claims under section 304(a), is the same for each of the works; and

(B) the works were all copyrighted upon their first publication, either through separate copyright notice and registration or by virtue of a general copyright notice in the periodical issue as a whole; and

(C) the renewal application and fee are received not more than twenty-eight or less than twenty-seven years after the thirty-first day of December of the calendar year in which all of the works were first published; and

(D) the renewal application identifies each work separately, including the periodical containing it and its date of first publication.

In some instances, a description of the work being registered will be deemed sufficient. As an example, the author of secure tests (such as the SAT or LSAT) is not required to include copies of these works as part of its registration, for the obvious reason that the contents of the test would be disclosed.[20] In *National Conference of Bar Examiners v. Multistate Legal Studies, Inc.*,[21] the court rejected a claim that the statute and regulations exempting certain works from deposit requirements violated the Intellectual Property Clause.

---

20. *See* 37 C.F.R.§ 202.20.

21. 692 F.2d 478, 482–87 (7th Cir. 1982), *cert. denied,* 464 U.S. 814 (1983).

The deposit requirement can be traced back at least to the first United States copyright law, the Copyright Act of 1790, which stated:

> And be it further enacted, That no person shall be entitled to the benefit of this act, in cases where any map, chart, book or books, hath or have been already printed and published unless he shall first deposit, and in all other cases, unless he shall before publication deposit a printed copy of the title of such map. chart, book or books, in the clerk's office of the district court where the author or proprietor shall reside: And the clerk of such court is hereby directed and required to record the same forthwith, in a book to be kept by him for that purpose, in the words following, (giving a copy thereof to the said author or proprietor, under the seal of the court, if he shall require the same)."District of to wit: Be it remembered, that on the day of in the year of the independence of the United States of America, A. B. of the said district, hath deposited in this office the title of a map, chart, book or books, (as the case may be) the right whereof he claims as author or proprietor. (as the case may be) in the words following to wit: [here insert the title] in conformity to the act of the Congress of the United States, intituled 'An act for the encouragement of learning, by securing the copies of maps, chart, and book, to the authors and proprietors of such copies, during the time therein mentioned.' C. D. clerk of the district of." For which the said clerk shall be entitled to receive sixty cents from the said author or proprietor, and sixty cents for every copy under seal actually given to such author or proprietor as aforesaid. And such author or proprietor shall, within two months from the date thereof cause a copy of the said record to be published in one or more of the newspapers printed in the United States, for the space of four weeks.
>
> Sec. 4 And be it further enacted, That the author or proprietor of any such map, chart, book or books, shall, within six months after the publishing thereof, deliver, or cause to be delivered to the Secretary of State a copy of the same, to be preserved....[22]

¶ 3.05 Copyright Transfers & Recordation of Transfers

Copyright Transfers

The transfer or assignment of copyrights is a subject of great practical significance, given that most authors are not in a position to develop, market, and distribute their creative works. Musicians and song writers need record companies and music publishing entities to produce, market, and distribute their works, at least

---

22. Copyright Act of 1790, Sections 3 & 4, 1 Statutes At Large 124.

before the days of self-distribution via the Internet, as pioneered by Radiohead in 2007. Authors need publishers, again aside from self-publishing. Consequently, the transfer of copyrights often enables the efficient distribution of creative works to those who can make the best use of them, furthering the interests of authors, publishers, and society.

Intellectual property is thus the "currency" of many entertainment and media industries. Copyright law has a number specific rules that have a major impact on these licenses and assignments of rights. Section 204 requires that transfers of copyright be memorialized in a signed writing—in effect, establishing a federal "statute of frauds" (i.e., a mandatory requirement that agreements be in writing) for copyright transfers. Section 204's mandates applies to all copyright transfers except when the transfer occurs by operation of law. This provision states:

(a) A transfer of copyright ownership, other than by operation of law, is not valid unless an instrument of conveyance, or a note or memorandum of the transfer, is in writing and signed by the owner of the rights conveyed or such owner's duly authorized agent.

(b) A certificate of acknowledgment is not required for the validity of a transfer, but is prima facie evidence of the execution of the transfer if—

(1) in the case of a transfer executed in the United States, the certificate is issued by a person authorized to administer oaths within the United States; or

(2) in the case of a transfer executed in a foreign country, the certificate is issued by a diplomatic or consular officer of the United States, or by a person authorized to administer oaths whose authority is proved by a certificate of such an officer.

Like a statute of frauds in contract law, the purpose of the writing requirement for copyright transfers "is to resolve disputes between copyright owners and transferees and to protect copyright owners from persons claiming oral licenses or copyright ownership."[23] For purposes of section 204, an exclusive license is deemed a transfer, but a nonexclusive license is not (and therefore need not be meet the writing requirement). This point is established in section 101 of the Copyright Act, which states in relevant part that a transfer of copyright ownership "is an assignment, mortgage, *exclusive license*, or any other conveyance, alienation, or hypotheca-

---

23. *Imperial Residential Design, Inc. v. Palms Dev. Group, Inc.*, 70 F.3d 96, 99   (11th Cir. 1995).

tion of a copyright or of any of the exclusive rights comprised in a copyright, whether or not it is limited in time or place of effect, *but not including a nonexclusive license.*"[24] Parties can confirm a copyright transfer after-the-fact, via a later-prepared signed writing.[25] This type of ratification of a prior oral agreement upholds the spirit of the writing requirement, as it serves to confirm the intent of the author or other copyright owner to transfer rights to the work.

Scope of Transfers

One of the fundamental rules of licensing in copyright law is that the licensee only receives from the author or copyright owner as many rights as the license provides, along with rights that might flow by operation of law or through implied licenses. Consequently, the purchase of a book might include the right to resell that work, under the first sale doctrine found in section 109 of the Copyright Act. But it does not include the right to make a movie version of the book. Similarly, a license to use a musical work as background music (a public performance license) does not mean that the work can be incorporated into a film or musical theater production (which involves what are known as synchronization rights). An assignment of rights to a work in the United States does not mean the assignee gets rights in the rest of the world. And a right to use a freelance writer's work in a printed newspaper does not necessarily mean that it can be placed into an on-line database, if the contract between the parties does not so provide.

This last scenario led to the Supreme Court's decision in *New York Times Company v. Tasini.*[26] That case involved the New York Times' attempt to place articles written by freelance journalists onto an on-line and CD–ROM database, which was not a right the newspaper had negotiated in its contracts with freelance writers at that time. (No doubt the newspaper revised its contracts after it became aware of the problem.) The Times argued that it nonetheless was entitled to include the freelance articles in its database on the ground that the database was merely a "revision" of the printed edition. Section 201(c) of the Copyright Act does indeed give some revision rights in the case of collective works:

> Contributions to Collective Works.—Copyright in each separate contribution to a collective work is distinct from copyright in the collective work as a whole, and vests initially in the author of the contribution. In the absence of an express transfer of the copyright or of any rights under it, the owner of copyright in

---

24. 17 U.S.C. § 101.

25. *See Imperial Residential Design, Inc. v. Palms Dev. Group, Inc.,* 70 F.3d 96 (11th Cir. 1995); *Arthur Rutenberg Homes, Inc. v. Drew Homes, Inc.,* 29 F.3d 1529, 1532–33 (11th Cir. 1994); *See*

also Magnuson v. Video Yesteryear, 85 F.3d 1424, 1428–29 (9th Cir. 1996) (transfer of 1909 Act work).

26. 533 U.S. 483 (2001).

the collective work is presumed to have acquired only the privilege of reproducing and distributing the contribution as part of that particular collective work, any revision of that collective work, and any later collective work in the same series.

Unfortunately for the Times, the Court held that the database version of the newspaper articles did not constitute a revision under section 201(c), because the electronic and CD–ROM databases containing individual articles from multiple editions of the newspaper were not reproduced and distributed as part of revisions of the individual periodical issues from which articles were taken. The databases were, instead, new electronic forms of the work disconnected from the original print versions. As a result, the Times did not have the privilege of placing individual articles in its databases, absent a license or transfer of copyright from the authors of the individual articles. The Times contended that this led to unfortunate gaps in its on-line database, because it could not include articles for which it did not have express licenses for on-line uses. This undesirable result illustrates the type of problem that can arise from a failure to obtain necessary rights under copyright law.

Recordation of Transfers

Recording of transfers is not mandatory, but information regarding the transfer, assignment, or licensing of copyrights can be filed with the Copyright Office if the parties so choose, as provided in section 205:

> (a) Conditions for Recordation.—Any transfer of copyright ownership or other document pertaining to a copyright may be recorded in the Copyright Office if the document filed for recordation bears the actual signature of the person who executed it, or if it is accompanied by a sworn or official certification that it is a true copy of the original, signed document.

> (b) Certificate of Recordation.—The Register of Copyrights shall, upon receipt of a document as provided by subsection (a) and of the fee provided by section 708, record the document and return it with a certificate of recordation.

> (c) Recordation as Constructive Notice.—Recordation of a document in the Copyright Office gives all persons constructive notice of the facts stated in the recorded document, but only if—

>> (1) the document, or material attached to it, specifically identifies the work to which it pertains so that, after the document is indexed by the Register of Copyrights, it

would be revealed by a reasonable search under the title or registration number of the work; and

(2) registration has been made for the work.

Because of its value as a searchable public record of transfers, a variety of agreements regarding copyrights will be recorded pursuant to section 205. Transfers (including assignments and exclusive licenses), as well as nonexclusive licenses and other documents related to copyright ownership may be recorded. 37 C.F.R.§ 201.4(a)(2) states: "A document shall be considered to 'pertain to a copyright' if it has a direct or indirect relationship to the existence, scope, duration, or identification of a copyright, or to the ownership, division, allocation, licensing, transfer, or exercise of rights under a copyright. That relationship may be past, present, future, or potential."

It is always advisable to record a transfer to obtain priority over conflicting transfers or licenses. Section 205 specifically addresses priority issues as between conflicting transactions:

(d) Priority between Conflicting Transfers.—As between two conflicting transfers, the one executed first prevails if it is recorded, in the manner required to give constructive notice under subsection (c), within one month after its execution in the United States or within two months after its execution outside the United States, or at any time before recordation in such manner of the later transfer. Otherwise the later transfer prevails if recorded first in such manner, and if taken in good faith, for valuable consideration or on the basis of a binding promise to pay royalties, and without notice of the earlier transfer.

(e) Priority between Conflicting Transfer of Ownership and Nonexclusive License.—A nonexclusive license, whether recorded or not, prevails over a conflicting transfer of copyright ownership if the license is evidenced by a written instrument signed by the owner of the rights licensed or such owner's duly authorized agent, and if

(1) the license was taken before execution of the transfer; or

(2) the license was taken in good faith before recordation of the transfer and without notice of it.

Moreover, a security interest in a copyright is also considered a transfer and should also be recorded in order to perfect security interest in copyright.[27]

---

27. See In re Peregrine Entertainment, Ltd., 116 B.R. 194, 201–02 (C.D. Cal. 1990).

¶ 3.06   Copyright Duration

Copyright protection under current United States law generally lasts for the life of the author plus seventy years. Section 302(a) of the Copyright Act states: "Copyright in a work created on or after January 1, 1978, subsists from its creation and, except as provided by the following subsections, endures for a term consisting of the life of the author and 70 years after the author's death." Thus, the term is determined by reference to the triggering event of the author's death. Joint works, which have two or more authors who created the work, are governed by the rule in section 302(b): "In the case of a joint work prepared by two or more authors who did not work for hire, the copyright endures for a term consisting of the life of the last surviving author and 70 years after such last surviving author's death."

If the copyrighted work is a work made for hire (as defined in Chapter 3, ¶ 3.02), the term is instead a flat term of years–95 years from the date of creation of the work or 120 years from the date of publication, whichever comes first. These set terms of years also apply to works published pseudonymously or anonymously, as there is no identified author in such works. An "anonymous work" is a work on which no natural person is identified as author on copies of the work in question. A "pseudonymous work" is a work on which the author is identified under a fictitious name.[28] Section 302(c) sets forth these rules: "In the case of an anonymous work, a pseudonymous work, or a work made for hire, the copyright endures for a term of 95 years from the year of its first publication, or a term of 120 years from the year of its creation, whichever expires first."

In situations involving anonymous or pseudonymous works, section 302(c) permits the author or other interested party to identify the author and revert to the standard life plus seventy year term applicable to works with identified individual authors:

> If, before the end of such term, the identity of one or more of the authors of an anonymous or pseudonymous work is revealed in the records of a registration made for that work under subsections (a) or (d) of section 408, or in the records provided by this subsection, the copyright in the work endures for the term specified by subsection (a) or (b), based on the life of the author or authors whose identity has been revealed. Any person having an interest in the copyright in an anonymous or pseudonymous work may at any time record, in records to be maintained by the Copyright Office for that purpose, a statement identifying one or more authors of the work; the statement shall also identify the person filing it, the nature of that person's interest, the source of the information recorded, and

---

28.   17 U.S.C. § 101.

the particular work affected, and shall comply in form and content with requirements that the Register of Copyrights shall prescribe by regulation.

The copyright term of life plus seventy years is always based on the original author (or authors) of the work. Consequently, if the copyright in a work is transferred, the term is still determined based on the life of the original author. This is similar to the life estate *pur autre vie* ("for the life of another") in real property, where the term of the life estate is determined by reference to a life other than that of the current owner or occupant. Similarly, with regard to an anonymous work or a pseudonymous work, the duration of the copyright is governed by the set term of years provided in section 302(c), unless the original author is identified, in which case the standard life-plus-seventy term governs, again based upon the life of the original author. If the copyrighted work is a work made for hire, the term is set by statute, regardless of later transfers of ownership.

Although the Copyright Act of 1976 governs current works, works published before January 1, 1978 (the effective date of the Act) are still governed by the rules of the Copyright Act of 1909, as amended. As a result, a very substantial body of copyrighted works—essentially those published between 1923 and December 31, 1977 are governed by the 1909 Act framework. Under this framework, the term of copyright is typically now 95 years. There are a number of exceptions to and variations on this rule, depending on the country of origin of the work, the copyright status of the work when the 1976 Act took effect, and other factors.

For example, in general, if a work was published between 1923 and 1963, the copyright owner was required to have applied for a renewal term with the Copyright Office. If the copyright was not renewed, copyright protection for this work expired and the work entered into the public domain. If the copyright did apply for renewal, then the works will have a 95–year copyright term. Thus, for works published during the 1923–1963 time frame, the work will fall into the public domain no sooner that 2018 (95 years from 1923). With regard to works published between 1964 and 1977, copyright renewal is not required; these works automatically have a 95–year term. Works published after January 1, 1978 are of course governed by the copyright terms set forth above under the 1976 Act.

Section 304 of the Copyright Act sets forth the rather complex and specific rules governing subsisting copyrights (i.e., copyrighted works already published when the 1976 Act took effect on January 1, 1978). Helpful charts illustrating various copyright duration scenarios can be found on the following web pages:

http://www.copyright.cornell.edu/public_domain/

http://www.unc.edu/unclng/public-d.htm

The full text of the pertinent portion of section 304 states:

(a) Copyrights in Their First Term on January 1, 1978.—

(1)(A) Any copyright, in the first term of which is subsisting on January 1, 1978, shall endure for 28 years from the date it was originally secured.

(B) In the case of—

(i) any posthumous work or of any periodical, cyclopedic, or other composite work upon which the copyright was originally secured by the proprietor thereof, or

(ii) any work copyrighted by a corporate body (otherwise than as assignee or licensee of the individual author) or by an employer for whom such work is made for hire, the proprietor of such copyright shall be entitled to a renewal and extension of the copyright in such work for the further term of 67 years.

(C) In the case of any other copyrighted work, including a contribution by an individual author to a periodical or to a cyclopedic or other composite work—

(i) the author of such work, if the author is still living,

(ii) the widow, widower, or children of the author, if the author is not living,

(iii) the author's executors, if such author, widow, widower, or children are not living, or

(iv) the author's next of kin, in the absence of a will of the author, shall be entitled to a renewal and extension of the copyright in such work for a further term of 67 years.

(2)(A) At the expiration of the original term of copyright in a work specified in paragraph (1)(B) of this subsection, the copyright shall endure for a renewed and extended further term of 67 years, which—

(i) if an application to register a claim to such further term has been made to the Copyright Office within 1 year before the expiration of the original term of copyright, and the claim is registered, shall vest, upon the beginning of such further term, in the proprietor of the copyright who is entitled to claim the renewal of copyright at the time the application is made; or

(ii) if no such application is made or the claim pursuant to such application is not registered, shall vest, upon the beginning of such further term, in the person or entity that was the proprietor of the copyright as of the last day of the original term of copyright.

(B) At the expiration of the original term of copyright in a work specified in paragraph (1)(C) of this subsection, the copyright shall endure for a renewed and extended further term of 67 years, which—

(i) if an application to register a claim to such further term has been made to the Copyright Office within 1 year before the expiration of the original term of copyright, and the claim is registered, shall vest, upon the beginning of such further term, in any person who is entitled under paragraph (1)(C) to the renewal and extension of the copyright at the time the application is made; or

(ii) if no such application is made or the claim pursuant to such application is not registered, shall vest, upon the beginning of such further term, in any person entitled under paragraph (1)(C), as of the last day of the original term of copyright, to the renewal and extension of the copyright.

(3)(A) An application to register a claim to the renewed and extended term of copyright in a work may be made to the Copyright Office—

(i) within 1 year before the expiration of the original term of copyright by any person entitled under paragraph (1)(B) or (C) to such further term of 67 years; and

(ii) at any time during the renewed and extended term by any person in whom such further term vested, under paragraph (2)(A) or (B), or by any successor or assign of such person, if the application is made in the name of such person.

(B) Such an application is not a condition of the renewal and extension of the copyright in a work for a further term of 67 years.

(4)(A) If an application to register a claim to the renewed and extended term of copyright in a work is not made within 1 year before the expiration of the original term of copyright in a work, or if the claim pursuant to such application is not registered, then a derivative work prepared under authority of a grant of a transfer or license of the copyright that is made before the expiration of the original term of copyright may continue to be used under the terms of the grant during the renewed and extended term of copyright without infringing the copyright, except that such use does not extend to the preparation during such renewed and extended term of other derivative works based upon the copyrighted work covered by such grant.

(B) If an application to register a claim to the renewed and extended term of copyright in a work is made within 1 year before its expiration, and the claim is registered, the certificate of such registration shall constitute prima facie evidence as to the validity of the copyright during its renewed and extended term and of the facts stated in the certificate. The evidentiary weight to be accorded the certificates of a registration of a renewed and extended term of copyright made after the end of that 1–year period shall be within the discretion of the court.

(b) Copyrights in Their Renewal Term at the Time of the Effective Date of the Sonny Bono Copyright Term Extension Act.7—*Any copyright still in its renewal term at the time that the Sonny Bono Copyright Term Extension Act becomes effective shall have a copyright term of 95 years from the date copyright was originally secured.*

If a work was created before 1978, *but not published before January 1, 1978,* which is the effective date of the Copyright Act of 1976, it is governed for the most part by the rules applicable to current copyrighted works:

(a) Copyright in a work created before January 1, 1978, but not theretofore in the public domain or copyrighted, subsists from January 1, 1978, and endures for the term provided by section 302. In no case, however, shall the term of copyright in such a work expire before December 31, 2002; and, if the work is published on or before December 31, 2002, the term of copyright shall not expire before December 31, 2047.

(b) The distribution before January 1, 1978, of a phonorecord shall not for any purpose constitute a publication of the musical work embodied therein.

Finally, section 305 of the Copyright Act establishes the termination date for the duration of all copyrighted works: "All terms of copyright provided by sections 302 through 304 run to the end of the calendar year in which they would otherwise expire." Consequently, all copyright terms expire on December 31 of the year in which they are scheduled to expire.

Copyright Term Extension

Copyright term extensions have been a subject of considerable debate. In 1998, Congress enacted the Sonny Bono Copyright Term Extension Act, which will be referred to as the Sonny Bono law rather than its more cumbersome formal acronym, the SBCTEA. Named for the former Sonny & Cher member and congressman, the Sonny Bono law added twenty years to nearly all existing copyright terms. Accordingly, prior to the Sonny Bono law the standard copyright term was life plus fifty years; the term for works made for hire was 75 years from the date of creation of the work or 100 years from the date of publication (whichever comes first); the term for most 1909 Act works was 75 years. Now the statutory terms (as noted above) are life plus seventy years; the term for works made for hire is 95 years from the date of creation of the work or 120 years from the date of publication (whichever comes first); the term for most 1909 Act works is 95 years. In the case of joint works governed by the 1976 Act, the copyright term is now 70 years from the death of the last surviving author.

Although the Sonny Bono law extended most copyright terms, Congress did make some provision for libraries and archives with regard to older works. In the last twenty years of a published work's copyright term, if copies of the work are not available at a reasonable price, section 108(h)(1) permits libraries and archives to make, distribute, display, and perform copies of the work for purposes of preservation, scholarship, or research:

> For purposes of this section, during the last 20 years of any term of copyright of a published work, a library or archives, including a nonprofit educational institution that functions as such, may reproduce, distribute, display, or perform in facsimile or digital form a copy or phonorecord of such work, or portions thereof, for purposes of preservation, scholarship, or research, if such library or archives has first determined, on the basis of a reasonable investigation, that none of the conditions set forth in subparagraphs (A), (B), and (C) of paragraph (2) apply.

> (2) No reproduction, distribution, display, or performance is authorized under this subsection if—(A) the work is subject to normal commercial exploitation; (B) a copy or phonorecord of the work can be obtained at a reasonable price; or (C) the copyright owner or its agent provides notice pursuant to regulations promulgated by the Register of Copyrights that either of the conditions set forth in subparagraphs (A) and (B) applies.

(3) The exemption provided in this subsection does not apply to any subsequent uses by users other than such library or archives.

The Sonny Bono law also delays preemption of state copyright laws protecting pre-February 15, 1972 sound recordings for an additional 20 years, until February 15, 2067: "With respect to sound recordings fixed before February 15, 1972, any rights or remedies under the common law or statutes of any State shall not be annulled or limited by this title until February 15, 2067. The preemptive provisions of subsection (a) shall apply to any such rights and remedies pertaining to any cause of action arising from undertakings commenced on and after February 15, 2067. Notwithstanding the provisions of section 303, no sound recording fixed before February 15, 1972, shall be subject to copyright under this title before, on, or after February 15, 2067."[29] In light of this provision, state law continues to provide potential copyright protection for older sound recordings.

Many commentators, particularly in the academic community, objected to the Sonny Bono law.[30] In part, this objection stemmed from a general view that copyright terms were too long, but more specifically that adding twenty years to existing copyrights was a windfall to copyright owners, particularly as to retroactive extensions for preexisting works. Critics of the Sonny Bono law raised a myriad of concerns, the most significant of which was that the retroactive term extension exceeded Congress' power under the Intellectual Property Clause. Recall the language of that Clause: "to Promote the Progress of Science and useful Arts, by securing for limited Times to Authors and Inventors the exclusive Right to their respective Writings and Discoveries."[31] Clearly the Sonny Bono law did not provide for a perpetual copyright term, which would undoubtedly exceed Congress' power under the Clause. But does the retroactive extension of the copyright term also exceed its power?

In *Eldred v. Ashcroft*,[32] the Supreme Court resolved this question and held that Congress did not exceed its constitutional authority. Writing for a 7–2 majority, Justice Ginsburg addressed the issue of whether Congress has the authority under the Intellectual Property Clause to extend the terms of existing copyrights. The Court held that "[t]ext, history, and precedent, confirm that the Copyright Clause empowers Congress to prescribe 'limited Times' for copyright protection and to secure the same level and

---

29. 17 U.S.C.§ 301(c).

30. *See, e.g.,* William Patry, The Failure of the American Copyright System: Protecting the Idle Rich, 72 NOTRE DAME L. REV. 907–933 (1997).

31. U.S. CONST., Art. I, § 8, cl. 8.

32. 537 U.S. 186 (2003).

duration of protection for all copyright holders, present and future."[33]

Probably the most persuasive ground for upholding the Sonny Bono law is the long history of prior term extensions, each of which applied retroactively to copyrights still in force. Although the latest term extension was perhaps not the best policy from the standpoint of United States consumers, it was not wholly unjustified. It allowed United States copyright owners to benefit from the life plus seventy term provided under many foreign laws when reciprocally provided under United States law. As the Court noted in *Eldred*: "a key factor in the CTEA's passage was a 1993 European Union (EU) directive instructing EU members to establish a copyright term of life plus 70 years. Consistent with the Berne Convention, the EU directed its members to deny this longer term to the works of any non-EU country whose laws did not secure the same extended term. By extending the baseline United States copyright term to life plus 70 years, Congress sought to ensure that American authors would receive the same copyright protection in Europe as their European counterparts."[34] The Court suggested that the Sonny Bono law might increase the incentive for American and other authors to create and disseminate their works in the United States. Finally, the *Eldred* Court noted that in addition to international trade considerations, "Congress passed the CTEA in light of demographic, economic, and technological changes, and rationally credited projections that longer terms would encourage copyright holders to invest in the restoration and public distribution of their works."[35]

Upholding the Sonny Bono law's term extension was consistent with prior history, and overturning this extension would seem to call into question prior extensions of the copyright term, some of which are also still in force today. Justice Ginsburg summarized the long history of copyright term extensions in her majority opinion in *Eldred*:

> The Nation's first copyright statute, enacted in 1790, provided a federal copyright term of 14 years from the date of publication, renewable for an additional 14 years if the author survived the first term. The 1790 Act's renewable 14–year term applied to existing works (i.e., works already published and works created but not yet published) and future works alike. Congress expanded the federal copyright term to 42 years in 1831 (28 years from publication, renewable for an additional 14 years), and to 56 years in 1909 (28 years from publication,

33. *Id.* at 199.

34. *Id.* at 205–06 (citing EU Council Directive 93/98, Art. 1(1), p. 11; Berne Convention Art. 7(8); Paul Goldstein,

International Copyright § 5.3, p. 239 (2001)).

35. *Id.* at 206–07.

renewable for an additional 28 years). Both times, Congress applied the new copyright term to existing and future works; to qualify for the 1831 extension, an existing work had to be in its initial copyright term at the time the Act became effective.

In 1976, Congress altered the method for computing federal copyright terms. For works created by identified natural persons, the 1976 Act provided that federal copyright protection would run from the work's creation, not-as in the 1790, 1831, and 1909 Acts-its publication; protection would last until 50 years after the author's death. In these respects, the 1976 Act aligned United States copyright terms with the then-dominant international standard adopted under the Berne Convention for the Protection of Literary and Artistic Works. For anonymous works, pseudonymous works, and works made for hire, the 1976 Act provided a term of 75 years from publication or 100 years from creation, whichever expired first.

These new copyright terms, the 1976 Act instructed, governed all works not published by its effective date of January 1, 1978, regardless of when the works were created. For published works with existing copyrights as of that date, the 1976 Act granted a copyright term of 75 years from the date of publication, a 19–year increase over the 56–year term applicable under the 1909 Act.[36]

More broadly, it is the domain of Congress, rather than the courts, to make this judgment. Many academics seem to desire a robust Intellectual Property Clause, expansive First Amendment, and an assertive Supreme Court to serve as a check on the ability of Congress to expand copyright law generally. The courts have not accepted this invitation, and it does seem that Congress is the appropriate forum for making the types of policy judgments and balancing of interests that many copyright issues present. For the contrary view, consider Justice Stevens' concluding point in his dissenting opinion:

> By failing to protect the public interest in free access to the products of inventive and artistic genius-indeed, by virtually ignoring the central purpose of the Copyright/Patent Clause- the Court has quitclaimed to Congress its principal responsibility in this area of the law. Fairly read, the Court has stated that Congress' actions under the Copyright/Patent Clause are, for all intents and purposes, judicially unreviewable. That result cannot be squared with the basic tenets of our constitutional structure. It is not hyperbole to recall the trenchant words of Chief Justice John Marshall: "It is emphatically the

36. *Id.* at 194–95 (citations omitted).

province and duty of the judicial department to say what the law is."[37]

Consider finally the other dissenting opinion, written by Justice Breyer:

> This statute will cause serious expression-related harm. It will likely restrict traditional dissemination of copyrighted works. It will likely inhibit new forms of dissemination through the use of new technology. It threatens to interfere with efforts to preserve our Nation's historical and cultural heritage and efforts to use that heritage, say, to educate our Nation's children. It is easy to understand how the statute might benefit the private financial interests of corporations or heirs who own existing copyrights. But I cannot find any constitutionally legitimate, copyright-related way in which the statute will benefit the public. Indeed, in respect to existing works, the serious public harm and the virtually nonexistent public benefit could not be more clear.

> I have set forth the analysis upon which I rest these judgments. This analysis leads inexorably to the conclusion that the statute cannot be understood rationally to advance a constitutionally legitimate interest. The statute falls outside the scope of legislative power that the Copyright Clause, read in light of the First Amendment, grants to Congress.[38]

The *Eldred* Court also addressed a constitutional challenge to the term extension. The majority opinion indicated that copyright is not "categorically immune" to First Amendment review, but held that the First Amendment was not violated by the term extension on existing copyrights at issue in the case. The Court found that as long as copyright's "traditional contours" remain in place (including the "idea-expression dichotomy" and the fair use defense), copyright need not be subjected to "heightened scrutiny" under the Amendment.

The language in *Eldred* regarding alteration of copyright's traditional contours left an opening for challenge to another congressional action—a restoration of copyright in foreign works that had lost copyright protection on various grounds, including lack of notice required at the time of publication. In *Golan v. Holder*, decided in 2012, the Supreme Court held that the copyright restoration did not violate the Intellectual Property Clause or the First Amendment. This decision was discussed in Chapter 3, ¶ 3.03.

---

37. *Id.* at 242 (Stevens, J., dissenting) (quoting *Marbury v. Madison*, 1 Cranch 137, 177, 2 L.Ed. 60 (1803)).

38. *Id.* at 242 (Breyer, J., dissenting).

¶ 3.07   Copyright Renewal Terms

Prior to the enactment of the Copyright Act of 1976, copyright owners had an initial set term of protection, following by a renewal term. This had been true since the 1790 Copyright Act, and was also true of most prior state copyright laws and the English law of the time, Thus, the copyright term of ownership was split between an original term and a renewal term. In its early form, the renewal term simply served as an extension of the original term. When the first term expired, the author, if living, or the author's executors, administrators, or assigns could invoke and claim the renewal term.[39]

Congress revised the renewal provision in 1831, providing that the author could assign the contingent interest in the renewal term, but could not divest the rights of his widow or children in the renewal term. The 1831 renewal provisions reflected "an entirely new policy, completely dissevering the title, breaking up the continuance ... and vesting an absolutely new title *eo nomine* in the persons designated."[40] Consequently, Congress gave the authors and heirs a second chance to control and benefit from the work. In *Stewart v. Abend*,[41] the Court explained the legislative purpose behind the continued existence of a renewal term in the 1909 Copyright Act:

> In its debates leading up to the Copyright Act of 1909, Congress elaborated upon the policy underlying a system comprised of an original term and a completely separate renewal term. "It not infrequently happens that the author sells his copyright outright to a publisher for a comparatively small sum." The renewal term permits the author, originally in a poor bargaining position, to renegotiate the terms of the grant once the value of the work has been tested. "[U]nlike real property and other forms of personal property, [a copyright] is by its very nature incapable of accurate monetary evaluation prior to its exploitation." 2 M. Nimmer & D. Nimmer, Nimmer on Copyright § 9.02, p. 9–23 (1989). "If the work proves to be a great success and lives beyond the term of twenty-eight years, ... it should be the exclusive right of the author to take the renewal term, and the law should be framed ... so that [the author] could not be deprived of that right." With these purposes in mind, Congress enacted the renewal provision of the Copyright Act of 1909.[42]

---

39. *See* Copyright Act of May 31, 1790, ch. XV, § 1, 1 Stat. 124.

40. *White–Smith Music Publishing Co. v. Goff*, 187 F. 247, 250 (1st Cir. 1911).

41. 495 U.S. 207 (1990).

42. *Id.* at 218–19 (quoting H.R. Rep. No. 2222, 60th Cong., 2d Sess., 14 (1909)).

At issue in the case was a story written by Cornell Woolrich and entitled, "It Had to Be Murder," which was first published in February 1942 in Dime Detective Magazine. In 1945, Woolrich assigned the rights to make motion picture versions of six of his stories, including "It Had to Be Murder." He also agreed to renew the copyrights in the stories and to assign the same motion picture rights for the 28–year renewal term. In 1953, actor Jimmy Stewart and director Alfred Hitchcock acquired the motion picture rights. Stewart, Hitchcock, and Paramount Pictures then produced the movie "Rear Window," which was a motion picture version of "It Had to Be Murder." The central problem was that Woolrich died in 1968, before he could obtain the rights in the renewal term. Woolrich's estate renewed the copyright as provided under copyright law at the time, and the estate assigned the renewal rights to Abend, who then brought suit alleging that "Rear Window" infringed the renewal term copyright in the story.

The Court addressed the issue of whether the movie, "Rear Window," infringed upon the renewal rights now owned by Abend:

> An author holds a bundle of exclusive rights in the copyrighted work, among them the right to copy and the right to incorporate the work into derivative works. By assigning the renewal copyright in the work without limitation, the author assigns all of these rights. . . . [I]f the author dies before the commencement of the renewal period, the assignee holds nothing. If the assignee of all of the renewal rights holds nothing upon the death of the assignor before arrival of the renewal period, then, a fortiori, the assignee of a portion of the renewal rights, e.g., the right to produce a derivative work, must also hold nothing. Therefore, if the author dies before the renewal period, then the assignee may continue to use the original work only if the author's successor transfers the renewal rights to the assignee. . . . Application of this rule to this case should end the inquiry. Woolrich died before the commencement of the renewal period in the story, and, therefore, petitioners hold only an unfulfilled expectancy. Petitioners have been "deprived of nothing. Like all purchasers of contingent interests, [they took] subject to the possibility that the contingency may not occur."[43]

The Court therefore concluded that "the grant of rights in the pre-existing work lapsed and, therefore, the derivative work owners' rights to use those portions of the pre-existing work incorporated into the derivative work expired. Thus, continued use would be infringing; whether the derivative work may continue to be published is a matter of remedy, an issue which is not before us. . . . Whether or not we believe that this is good policy, this is the

---

43. *Id.* at 220–21 (citations omitted).

system Congress has provided, as evidenced by the language of the 1909 Act and the cases decided under the 1909 Act."[44]

Renewal terms continue to have some significance for works published prior to January 1, 1978, the effective date of the 1976 Copyright Act, particularly with regard to the duration of copyrights, as discussed in Chapter 3, ¶ 3.06. Congress replaced the renewal concept with the termination provisions, which are discussed below in ¶ 3.08 of this book.

¶ 3.08   Termination of Transfers

Traditionally Congress has been concerned with the scenario of the struggling musician, writer, artist, or other impecunious author who assigns his or her copyright in a one-sided, take-it-or-leave-it bargain. Copyright law has mechanisms for protecting authors from the results of their bargains, at least in the long run. Under traditional, pre–1976 Act law, the renewal term for copyright offered something akin to a second chance for authors, or more precisely for their heirs. The purpose and effect of the renewal rights was discussed above in ¶ 3.07 of this book

The Copyright Act of 1976 abolished the renewal term concept, and put into place in its stead a single copyright term. For current works, the copyright term is the life of the author plus fifty years, which eventually was expanded by twenty years (in the Sonny Bono Amendments discussed in ¶ 3.06) to life plus seventy years. Without a renewal term to provide authors or their heirs with a second bite at the apple, Congress set forth a new mechanism for protecting the struggling author. The termination of transfers provision, section 203(a) of the Copyright Act, sets forth the conditions in which terminations can occur:

Conditions for Termination.—In the case of any work other than a work made for hire, the exclusive or nonexclusive grant of a transfer or license of copyright or of any right under a copyright, executed by the author on or after January 1, 1978, otherwise than by will, is subject to termination under the following conditions:

(1) In the case of a grant executed by one author, termination of the grant may be effected by that author or, if the author is dead, by the person or persons who, under clause (2) of this subsection, own and are entitled to exercise a total of more than one-half of that author's termination interest. In the case of a grant executed by two or more authors of a joint work, termination of the grant may be effected by a majority of the authors who executed it; if any of such authors is dead, the termination interest of any such author may be exercised as a

---

44. *Id.* at 235–36.

unit by the person or persons who, under clause (2) of this subsection, own and are entitled to exercise a total of more than one-half of that author's interest.

(2) Where an author is dead, his or her termination interest is owned, and may be exercised, as follows:

(A) The widow or widower owns the author's entire termination interest unless there are any surviving children or grandchildren of the author, in which case the widow or widower owns one-half of the author's interest.

(B) The author's surviving children, and the surviving children of any dead child of the author, own the author's entire termination interest unless there is a widow or widower, in which case the ownership of one-half of the author's interest is divided among them.

(C) The rights of the author's children and grandchildren are in all cases divided among them and exercised on a per stirpes basis according to the number of such author's children represented; the share of the children of a dead child in a termination interest can be exercised only by the action of a majority of them.

(D) In the event that the author's widow or widower, children, and grandchildren are not living, the author's executor, administrator, personal representative, or trustee shall own the author's entire termination interest.

(3) Termination of the grant may be effected at any time during a period of five years beginning at the end of thirty-five years from the date of execution of the grant; or, if the grant covers the right of publication of the work, the period begins at the end of thirty-five years from the date of publication of the work under the grant or at the end of forty years from the date of execution of the grant, whichever term ends earlier.

(4) The termination shall be effected by serving an advance notice in writing, signed by the number and proportion of owners of termination interests required under clauses (1) and (2) of this subsection, or by their duly authorized agents, upon the grantee or the grantee's successor in title.

(A) The notice shall state the effective date of the termination, which shall fall within the five-year period specified by clause (3) of this subsection, and the notice shall be served not less than two or more than ten years before that date. A copy of the notice shall be recorded in the Copyright Office before the effective date of termination, as a condition to its taking effect.

(B) The notice shall comply, in form, content, and manner of service, with requirements that the Register of Copyrights shall prescribe by regulation.

(5) Termination of the grant may be effected notwithstanding any agreement to the contrary, including an agreement to make a will or to make any future grant.

The termination provision basically provides a five-year window beginning thirty-five years from the original transfer during which either the author or the author's heirs or estate can terminate the transfer of copyright. So in essence, this provision allows the author (or heirs or estate) to renegotiate the original deal the author struck 35 years earlier. This result is decreed by section 203(b), which states:

Effect of Termination.—Upon the effective date of termination, all rights under this title that were covered by the terminated grants revert to the author, authors, and other persons owning termination interests under clauses (1) and (2) of subsection (a), including those owners who did not join in signing the notice of termination under clause (4) of subsection (a), but with the following limitations:

(1) A derivative work prepared under authority of the grant before its termination may continue to be utilized under the terms of the grant after its termination, but this privilege does not extend to the preparation after the termination of other derivative works based upon the copyrighted work covered by the terminated grant.

(2) The future rights that will revert upon termination of the grant become vested on the date the notice of termination has been served as provided by clause (4) of subsection (a). The rights vest in the author, authors, and other persons named in, and in the proportionate shares provided by, clauses (1) and (2) of subsection (a).

(3) Subject to the provisions of clause (4) of this subsection, a further grant, or agreement to make a further grant, of any right covered by a terminated grant is valid only if it is signed by the same number and proportion of the owners, in whom the right has vested under clause (2) of this subsection, as are required to terminate the grant under clauses (1) and (2) of subsection (a). Such further grant or agreement is effective with respect to all of the persons in whom the right it covers has vested under clause (2) of this subsection, including those who did not join in signing it. If any person dies after rights under a terminated grant have vested in him or her, that person's legal representatives, legatees, or heirs at law represent him or her for purposes of this clause.

(4) A further grant, or agreement to make a further grant, of any right covered by a terminated grant is valid only if it is made after the effective date of the termination. As an exception, however, an agreement for such a further grant may be made between the persons provided by clause (3) of this subsection and the original grantee or such grantee's successor in title, after the notice of termination has been served as provided by clause (4) of subsection (a).

(5) Termination of a grant under this section affects only those rights covered by the grants that arise under this title, and in no way affects rights arising under any other Federal, State, or foreign laws.

(6) Unless and until termination is effected under this section, the grant, if it does not provide otherwise, continues in effect for the term of copyright provided by this title.

Congress also addressed termination rights with regard to pre–1978 works that had already been transferred or licensed before January 1, 1978 (the effective date of the 1976 Act). Recall that these copyrighted works traditionally were governed by the renewal term rules. With regard to this category of works, Congress enacted a separate termination provision, set forth in section 304 of the Copyright Act of 1976, which states:

(c) Termination of Transfers and Licenses Covering Extended Renewal Term.—In the case of any copyright subsisting in either its first or renewal term on January 1, 1978, other than a copyright in a work made for hire, the exclusive or nonexclusive grant of a transfer or license of the renewal copyright or any right under it, executed before January 1, 1978, by any of the persons designated by subsection (a)(1)(C) of this section, otherwise than by will, is subject to termination under the following conditions:

(1) In the case of a grant executed by a person or persons other than the author, termination of the grant may be effected by the surviving person or persons who executed it. In the case of a grant executed by one or more of the authors of the work, termination of the grant may be effected, to the extent of a particular author's share in the ownership of the renewal copyright, by the author who executed it or, if such author is dead, by the person or persons who, under clause (2) of this subsection, own and are entitled to exercise a total of more than one-half of that author's termination interest.

(2) Where an author is dead, his or her termination interest is owned, and may be exercised, as follows:

(A) The widow or widower owns the author's entire termination interest unless there are any surviving children or grandchildren of the author, in which case the widow or widower owns one-half of the author's interest.

(B) The author's surviving children, and the surviving children of any dead child of the author, own the author's entire termination interest unless there is a widow or widower, in which case the ownership of one-half of the author's interest is divided among them.

(C) The rights of the author's children and grandchildren are in all cases divided among them and exercised on a per stirpes basis according to the number of such author's children represented; the share of the children of a dead child in a termination interest can be exercised only by the action of a majority of them.

(D) In the event that the author's widow or widower, children, and grandchildren are not living, the author's executor, administrator, personal representative, or trustee shall own the author's entire termination interest.

(3) Termination of the grant may be effected at any time during a period of five years beginning at the end of fifty-six years from the date copyright was originally secured, or beginning on January 1, 1978, whichever is later.

(4) The termination shall be effected by serving an advance notice in writing upon the grantee or the grantee's successor in title. In the case of a grant executed by a person or persons other than the author, the notice shall be signed by all of those entitled to terminate the grant under clause (1) of this subsection, or by their duly authorized agents. In the case of a grant executed by one or more of the authors of the work, the notice as to any one author's share shall be signed by that author or his or her duly authorized agent or, if that author is dead, by the number and proportion of the owners of his or her termination interest required under clauses (1) and (2) of this subsection, or by their duly authorized agents.

(A) The notice shall state the effective date of the termination, which shall fall within the five-year period specified by clause (3) of this subsection, or, in the case of a termination under subsection (d), within the five-year period specified by subsection (d)(2), and the notice shall be served not less than two or more than ten years before that date. A copy of the notice shall be recorded in the Copyright Office before the effective date of termination, as a condition to its taking effect.

(B) The notice shall comply, in form, content, and manner of service, with requirements that the Register of Copyrights shall prescribe by regulation.

(5) Termination of the grant may be effected notwithstanding any agreement to the contrary, including an agreement to make a will or to make any future grant.

(6) In the case of a grant executed by a person or persons other than the author, all rights under this title that were covered by the terminated grant revert, upon the effective date of termination, to all of those entitled to terminate the grant under clause (1) of this subsection. In the case of a grant executed by one or more of the authors of the work, all of a particular author's rights under this title that were covered by the terminated grant revert, upon the effective date of termination, to that author or, if that author is dead, to the persons owning his or her termination interest under clause (2) of this subsection, including those owners who did not join in signing the notice of termination under clause (4) of this subsection. In all cases the reversion of rights is subject to the following limitations:

(A) A derivative work prepared under authority of the grant before its termination may continue to be utilized under the terms of the grant after its termination, but this privilege does not extend to the preparation after the termination of other derivative works based upon the copyrighted work covered by the terminated grant.

(B) The future rights that will revert upon termination of the grant become vested on the date the notice of termination has been served as provided by clause (4) of this subsection.

(C) Where the author's rights revert to two or more persons under clause (2) of this subsection, they shall vest in those persons in the proportionate shares provided by that clause. In such a case, and subject to the provisions of subclause (D) of this clause, a further grant, or agreement to make a further grant, of a particular author's share with respect to any right covered by a terminated grant is valid only if it is signed by the same number and proportion of the owners, in whom the right has vested under this clause, as are required to terminate the grant under clause (2) of this subsection. Such further grant or agreement is effective with respect to all of the persons in whom the right it covers has vested under this subclause, including those who did not join in signing it. If any person dies after rights under a terminated grant have vested in him or her, that person's legal representatives, legatees, or heirs at law represent him or her for purposes of this subclause.

(D) A further grant, or agreement to make a further grant, of any right covered by a terminated grant is valid only if it is made after the effective date of the termination. As an exception, however, an agreement for such a further grant may be made between the author or any of the persons provided by the first sentence of clause (6) of this subsection, or between the persons provided by subclause (C) of this clause, and the original grantee or such grantee's successor in title, after the notice of termination has been served as provided by clause (4) of this subsection.

(E) Termination of a grant under this subsection affects only those rights covered by the grant that arise under this title, and in no way affects rights arising under any other Federal, State, or foreign laws.

(F) Unless and until termination is effected under this subsection, the grant, if it does not provide otherwise, continues in effect for the remainder of the extended renewal term.

(d) Termination Rights Provided in Subsection (c) Which Have Expired on or before the Effective Date of the Sonny Bono Copyright Term Extension Act.—In the case of any copyright other than a work made for hire, subsisting in its renewal term on the effective date of the Sonny Bono Copyright Term Extension Act9 for which the termination right provided in subsection (c) has expired by such date, where the author or owner of the termination right has not previously exercised such termination right, the exclusive or nonexclusive grant of a transfer or license of the renewal copyright or any right under it, executed before January 1, 1978, by any of the persons designated in subsection (a)(1)(C) of this section, other than by will, is subject to termination under the following conditions:

(1) The conditions specified in subsections (c) (1), (2), (4), (5), and (6) of this section apply to terminations of the last 20 years of copyright term as provided by the amendments made by the Sonny Bono Copyright Term Extension Act.

(2) Termination of the grant may be effected at any time during a period of 5 years beginning at the end of 75 years from the date copyright was originally secured.

Because the Copyright Act of 1976 took effect on January 1, 1978, the five-year window during which transfers can be terminated begins thirty-five year from that date, which means many termination notices can be given beginning in 2013. Consequently, there is likely to be a considerable increase in the frequency of disputes regarding termination of transfers in the next decade.

From the author's standpoint, the termination of transfers provisions of sections 203 and 304 provide a second chance to renegotiate, at least when the work has sufficient staying power to merit renegotiation 35 years after the original transfer. The publisher, record company, or other party across the table from the author, on the other hand, faces great uncertainty as a result of this ticking contractual and legal time bomb. And it is critical to know that the termination provision *cannot be waived or disclaimed by agreement*, as specifically stated in section 203(a)(5), which states: "Termination of the grant may be effected notwithstanding any agreement to the contrary, including an agreement to make a will or to make any future grant." Precluding contractual waivers makes sense, as the waiver would otherwise simply become a standard part of any copyright assignment or license, thereby undermining the congressional policy. Whether the provision is a good idea, however, is a different question. It interferes with freedom of contract, and benefits only the small group of authors whose works actually have staying power and who are sophisticated enough to invoke the termination. Moreover, it imposes costs and uncertainties on parties seeking to obtain copyrights.

There is one general exception to the termination of transfers provision—section 203(a), quoted above, states that it does not apply to works made for hire. This obviously makes sense as the work made for hire is by definition one involving a hiring party that is presumably sophisticated and able to negotiate satisfactory deals. And the employees preparing the works do so in the course of their duties and have no claim for a second chance.

Perhaps even more importantly, the termination right does not extend to derivative works. Section 203(b)(1), which governs transfers after January 1, 1978, states: "A derivative work prepared under authority of the grant before its termination may continue to be utilized under the terms of the grant after its termination, but this privilege does not extend to the preparation after the termination of other derivative works based upon the copyrighted work covered by the terminated grant." Similarly, section 304(c)(6)(A), which governs pre–1978 transfers, states: "A derivative work prepared under authority of the grant before its termination may continue to be utilized under the terms of the grant after its termination, but this privilege does not extend to the preparation after the termination of other derivative works based upon the copyrighted work covered by the terminated grant."

Woods v. Bourne Co.[45] provides a good illustration of a termination case under the 1976 Act rules. In that case, the copyright to the song "When the Red, Red, Robin Comes Bob, Bob, Bobbin' Along" was at issue. The songwriter's heirs exercised their termination rights under section 304(c). The issue was whether this termination was effective as against various synchronization licenses issued to allow versions of this song to be used in various movies and television programs. The court held that the derivative works exception in section 304(c)(6)(A) permitted the continued use of the song in the movies and television programs, and that the termination was not effective against those derivative works. The impact of the ruling in the *Woods* case can be contrasted with *Stewart v. Abend*.[46] The termination in *Woods* does not preclude the continued use of the derivative work, in light of the savings clauses of sections 203 and 304(c), which permit the continued exploitation of the derivative work. In the *Abend* case, in contrast, the derivative work was found to infringe for the duration of the second copyright term.

One possible end run that some parties have attempted with regard to the termination rules is an agreement entered into after the work was created retroactively deeming it to be an exempt work made for hire. In *Marvel Characters, Inc. v. Simon*,[47] the court addressed the application of section 304(c)'s termination provision in this situation. As the court noted, the statute grants authors (or if deceased, their statutory heirs) an inalienable right to terminate a grant in a copyright fifty-six years after the original grant notwithstanding any agreement to the contrary. The termination provision, however, has one salient exception: copyright grants in works created for hire cannot be terminated. Accordingly, the issue in *Marvel Characters, Inc. v. Simon* was whether a settlement agreement, entered into long after a work was created and stipulating that the work was created for hire constitutes an unenforceable "agreement to the contrary" under the 1976 Act. The court reasoned as follows:

> When examining the legislative intent and purpose of § 304(c), it becomes clear that an agreement made after a work's creation stipulating that the work was created as a work for hire constitutes an "agreement to the contrary" which can be disavowed pursuant to the statute. Any other construction of

45. 60 F.3d 978 (2d Cir. 1995).   **47.** 310 F.3d 280 (2d Cir. 2002).
46. 495 U.S. 207 (1990).

§ 304(c) would thwart the clear legislative purpose and intent of the statute. If an agreement between an author and publisher that a work was created for hire were outside the purview of § 304(c)(5), the termination provision would be rendered a nullity; litigation-savvy publishers would be able to utilize their superior bargaining position to compel authors to agree that a work was created for hire in order to get their works published. In effect, such an interpretation would likely repeat the result wrought by the *Fred Fisher* decision and provide a blueprint by which publishers could effectively eliminate an author's termination right. We conclude that Congress included the "notwithstanding any agreement to the contrary" language in the termination provision precisely to avoid such a result.[48]

Therefore, the court found that Simon was not bound by the settlement agreement language stating that he created the works as an employee for hire. The court remanded the case to allow a jury to determine whether Simon was thus the author of the works in question, which would then entitle him to exercise § 304(c)'s termination right.

Several other important termination cases have been decided in the last fifteen years.[49] In *Milne v. Stephen Slesinger, Inc.*,[50] the heirs of Winnie the Pooh creator A.A. Milne attempted to terminate a 1983 renegotiated license of the original 1930 deal between the parties. The Ninth Circuit held that the heirs had already benefitted from the 1983 renegotiation, pursuant to § 304(c), and thus could not use § 304(d) to revisit the agreement. The court distinguished *Marvel Characters* as applying only to an "after-the-fact attempt to recharacterize the work." Another attempt to obtain a second renegotiation was rejected in *Penguin Group (USA) Inc. v. Steinbeck*,[51] involving John Steinbeck's heirs, who had already reached a new agreement in 1994.

---

48. *Id.* at 290–91.

49. *See* Robert J. Bernstein & Robert W. Clarida, *The Wrath of Heirs*, N.Y. L.J. (Sept. 19, 2008).

50. 430 F.3d 1036 (9th Cir. 2005).

51. 537 F.3d 193 (2d Cir. 2008).

Chapter 4

COPYRIGHT INFRINGEMENT

Table of Sections

¶ 4.01 Economic Rights of Authors

It is often said that copyright law provides the author with a series of rights analogous to a "bundle of sticks." As section 501(a) of the Copyright Act makes clear, the copyright owner has a cause of action if any of its exclusive rights are violated: "Anyone who violates any of the exclusive rights of the copyright owner as provided by sections 106 through 122 or of the author as provided in section 106A(a), or who imports copies or phonorecords into the United States in violation of section 602, is an infringer of the copyright or right of the author, as the case may be. For purposes of this chapter (other than section 506), any reference to copyright shall be deemed to include the rights conferred by section 106A(a)."

The principal "bundle of sticks" or basic set of economic rights of copyright owners are set forth in section 106 of the Copyright Act:

Subject to sections 107 through 120, the owner of copyright under this title has the exclusive rights to do and to authorize any of the following:

(1) to reproduce the copyrighted work in copies or phonorecords;

(2) to prepare derivative works based upon the copyrighted work;

(3) to distribute copies or phonorecords of the copyrighted work to the public by sale or other transfer of ownership, or by rental, lease, or lending;

(4) in the case of literary, musical, dramatic, and choreographic works, pantomimes, and motion pictures and other audiovisual works, to perform the copyrighted work publicly; and

(5) in the case of literary, musical, dramatic, and choreographic works, pantomimes, and pictorial, graphic, or sculptural works, including the individual images of a motion picture or other audiovisual work, to display the copyrighted work publicly.

In order to assess whether copyright infringement has taken place, each of the rights under section 106 of the Copyright Act must be analyzed. If any one of the copyright owner's rights in the "bundle of sticks" is violated, there is copyright infringement. Section 106 sets forth five principal rights: the right of reproduction, distribution, derivative works, public performance, and public display. Authors of "works of visual art," a very limited and precisely defined category of works identified in section 101, have additional rights of attribution and integrity, which are found in section 106A. These section 106A rights are a form of "moral rights," and are discussed in ¶ 4.03. The five rights in section 106, in contrast, are considered economic rights, and have been the touchstone of United States copyright protection for many years.

Early United States copyright law, however, provided a much narrower set of rights. The Copyright Act of 1790, for example, provided only the right of reproduction: "And be it further enacted, That any person or persons who shall print or publish and manuscript, without the consent and approbation of the author or proprietor thereof, first had and obtained as aforesaid, (if such author or proprietor be a citizen of or resident in these United States) shall be liable to suffer and pay to the said author or proprietor all damages occasioned by such injury, to be recovered by a special action on the case founded upon this act, in any court having cognizance thereof."[1]

Before addressing each right in turn, a central point should be made about the legal implications of the copyright owner's bundle of sticks. An author's sale or licensing of one or more of these rights does not necessarily mean the author has allowed the recipient to exercise other rights. Thus, for example, the sale of a copyrighted novel to a consumer does not grant the owner of the copy of that book the right to create derivative works, such as a movie version of the novel, or to make further copies of the book on a scanner or photocopying machine.

---

1. Copyright Act of 1790, Section 6,
1 Statutes At Large 124.

¶ 4.02   The Rights of Reproduction, Distribution, Derivative Works, Public Performance, and Public Display

Reproduction

The right of reproduction is probably the most straightforward of the section 106 rights, as it simply provides protection from the unauthorized reproduction of the copyrighted work. A music bootlegger who makes a few hundred copies of a popular Adele album is plainly violating the right of reproduction. Of course, an entire work need not be reproduced for a violation to occur. As long as a substantial amount of creative expression is taken, a reproduction has taken place. Accordingly, in *Horgan v. MacMillan, Inc.*,[2] the copyrighted work consisted of George Balanchine's choreographed ballet, the "Nutcracker." The defendants had taken sixty photographs of a Nutcracker performance (which they had lawfully obtained), and had placed the images in a book regarding the ballet. The court found that whether a sufficient amount of creative expression was taken via these photographs was an issue of fact and thus could not be resolved on summary judgment. Of course, the entire ballet could not be viewed by looking at the sixty photographs in the book, but perhaps substantial portions of the Nutcracker could be viewed. In contrast, had the book included only two or three photographs from the ballet, it would be highly unlikely that the book could infringe the ballet, as there would be no substantial taking from the entirety of the copyrighted ballet.

On the question of whether a prior work was infringed, consider Judge Hand's discussion in *Nichols v. Universal Pictures Corp.*:

> It is of course essential to any protection of literary property, whether at common-law or under the statute, that the right cannot be limited literally to the text, else a plagiarist would escape by immaterial variations. That has never been the law, but, as soon as literal appropriation ceases to be the test, the whole matter is necessarily at large, so that, as was recently well said by a distinguished judge, the decisions cannot help much in a new case. When plays are concerned, the plagiarist may excise a separate scene; or he may appropriate part of the dialogue. Then the question is whether the part so taken is 'substantial,' and therefore not a 'fair use' of the copyrighted work; it is the same question arises in the case of any other copyrighted work.[3]

A work can be reproduced even if it is transitory or nonpermanent. Recall that anything fixed in a tangible medium of

---

2.   789 F.2d 157 (2d Cir. 1986).   **3.**   45 F.2d 119 (2d Cir. 1930), cert. denied, 282 U.S. 902 (1931).

expression is copyrightable; thus, a work stored on a memory card or hard drive or even on a computer's random access memory (RAM) is sufficiently permanent to qualify as fixed. So too with a reproduction—when a sufficiently permanent copy is made, it can infringe the original work. For example, in *Walt Disney Productions v. Filmation Associates,*[4] the defendants were seeking to produce an unauthorized sequel to the Disney cartoon "Pinocchio." Leaving aside whether such an enterprise could have been legally created, Disney brought suit while the film was still in production, claiming that Filmation had taken copyrighted material in creating preliminary materials for its new film, including story boards, story reels, scripts, and a promotional trailer. The defendant claimed these were merely preliminary steps, and that the final version of its new film would not infringe. Nonetheless, the court held that these preliminary materials can be evaluated and can constitute an infringing reproduction of the copyrighted Disney film. In effect, the case suggests that using a preexisting copyrighted work as a "short cut" in the production of a new work can be actionable.

This point about reproduction in the form of copies is made clear by section 101's definition, which states that copies "are material objects, other than phonorecords, in which a work is fixed by any method now known or later developed, and from which the work can be perceived, reproduced, or otherwise communicated, either directly or with the aid of a machine or device." A reproduction can also be in the form of phonorecords, a rather quaint term that refers to "material objects in which sounds, other than those accompanying a motion picture or other audiovisual work, are fixed by any method now known or later developed, and from which the sounds can be perceived, reproduced, or otherwise communicated, either directly or with the aid of a machine or device." Clearly, the term phonorecord includes audio tapes, compact discs, digital storage media (such as an iPod), and "cloud" music services.

Although works cannot generally be reproduced without the consent of the copyright owner, there is a special provision in the Copyright Act allowing for a compulsory license for cover versions of a song that has been released to the general public. A compulsory license is one that anyone can obtain as long as they follow the requirements set forth in the Copyright Act and as long as they pay the appropriate licensing free—the copyright owner cannot prohibit the production of the new work. Section 115 of the Copyright Act provides for compulsory mechanical licenses for sound recordings based on musical works that have been released (i.e., cover versions of songs).[5] An example of cover versions of a song would be "Sweet Jane," a song first recorded by the Velvet Underground; a number

---

4. 628 F.Supp. 871 (C.D. Cal. 1986).   **5.** *See* 17 U.S.C. § 115.

of bands have done cover versions of this song, including the Cowboy Junkies and Mott the Hoople. The Harry Fox Agency is the easiest way to obtain and pay the statutory royalty for such a license.[6] This type of license to reproduce musical works is not available for other types of copyrightable works. Moreover, there are strict requirements in section 115 that must be complied with in order to secure the mechanical license; most significantly, the cover version cannot significantly alter the music or lyrics of the original song.

Distribution

The second right under section 106 is the right of distribution. This right involves the ability, as set forth in section 106, "to distribute copies or phonorecords of the copyrighted work to the public by sale or other transfer of ownership, or by rental, lease, or lending." The distinction between reproduction and distribution can often be important when copyright owners seek to forestall counterfeiting. The vendor of the bootleg material frequently is not the individual who made the unauthorized copies (the reproduction). Nonetheless, by selling or renting the bootleg copies, the vendor is violating the separate right of distribution. A point to keep in mind here is that direct copyright infringement does not require a showing of fault or knowledge, and therefore the vendor can be held liable for unlawful distribution even if it did not know or have reason to know that the copies were not lawfully made.

The right of distribution is limited in a very significant way by the "first sale" doctrine in section 109(a) of the Copyright Act. This provision states: "Notwithstanding the provisions of section 106(3), the owner of a particular copy or phonorecord lawfully made under this title, or any person authorized by such owner, is entitled, without the authority of the copyright owner, to sell or otherwise dispose of the possession of that copy or phonorecord." Consider the case of a consumer who purchases a new, lawful copy of a "Tin Roof Blowdown," a James Lee Burke novel involving his intriguing character, Dave Robicheaux. The consumer reads the novel and enjoys it, but then decides to sell it on eBay or at the local used bookstore. Because the consumer is selling his or her lawful copy of the book, no violation of the distribution right has taken place. And indeed, this particular copy of Tin Roof Blowdown might change hands a dozen times, as different readers enjoy the used book. Similarly, a video rental business like Blockbuster or Netflix can purchase a copy of a Harry Potter movie and rent that movie to dozens of customers.

The first sale doctrine serves as an important limit on the rights of authors, essentially allowing the market for used copies of

---

6. *See* http://www.harryfox.com/index.jsp.

works to compete with the market for new versions of the work. This tends to serve as a check on the price of copyrighted works, while at the same time the copyright owner cannot be heard to complain as it has obtained its lawful reward from the first sale of the work. The secondary market in used copies helps to alleviate the burden placed on consumers for paying a copyright "premium" on newly created works, thereby expanding access to copyrighted works.

Congress has enacted three specific exceptions to the first sale doctrine. The first concerns certain "restored works" under section 109(a):

> Notwithstanding the preceding sentence, copies or phonorecords of works subject to restored copyright under section 104A that are manufactured before the date of restoration of copyright or, with respect to reliance parties, before publication or service of notice under section 104A(e), may be sold or otherwise disposed of without the authorization of the owner of the restored copyright for purposes of direct or indirect commercial advantage only during the 12–month period beginning on—(1) the date of the publication in the Federal Register of the notice of intent filed with the Copyright Office under section 104A(d)(2)(A), or (2) the date of the receipt of actual notice served under section 104A(d)(2)(B), whichever occurs first.

The other two exceptions to the first sale doctrine are more commonly encountered—the commercial rental of computer software and of copyrighted music (quaintly known in copyright parlance as "phonorecords") is prohibited under section 109(b)(1)(A), which states:

> Notwithstanding the provisions of subsection (a), unless authorized by the owners of copyright in the sound recording or the owner of copyright in a computer program (including any tape, disk, or other medium embodying such program), and in the case of a sound recording in the musical works embodied therein, neither the owner of a particular phonorecord nor any person in possession of a particular copy of a computer program (including any tape, disk, or other medium embodying such program), may, for the purposes of direct or indirect commercial advantage, dispose of, or authorize the disposal of, the possession of that phonorecord or computer program (including any tape, disk, or other medium embodying such program) by rental, lease, or lending, or by any other act or practice in the nature of rental, lease, or lending. Nothing in the preceding sentence shall apply to the rental, lease, or lending of a phonorecord for nonprofit purposes by a nonprofit library or nonprofit educational institution. The transfer of

possession of a lawfully made copy of a computer program by a nonprofit educational institution to another nonprofit educational institution or to faculty, staff, and students does not constitute rental, lease, or lending for direct or indirect commercial purposes under this subsection.

These specific exceptions to the first sale doctrine also have special carve-outs for video games and libraries, which are found in section 109(b)(1):

(B) This subsection does not apply to—

(i) a computer program which is embodied in a machine or product and which cannot be copied during the ordinary operation or use of the machine or product; or

(ii) a computer program embodied in or used in conjunction with a limited purpose computer that is designed for playing video games and may be designed for other purposes.

(C) Nothing in this subsection affects any provision of chapter 9 of this title.

(2)(A) Nothing in this subsection shall apply to the lending of a computer program for nonprofit purposes by a nonprofit library, if each copy of a computer program which is lent by such library has affixed to the packaging containing the program a warning of copyright in accordance with requirements that the Register of Copyrights shall prescribe by regulation.

These two types of works share two characteristics—they are readily prone to copying using widely available technology and they both involve important industries with vocal lobbyists in Washington. Libraries can still lend music CDs because they are not commercial ventures, and video games available for rental at GameFly are treated differently in light of the language of section 109(b)(1)(B).

Derivative Works

The next main right is the right to create derivative works. A derivative work is defined in section 101 as "a work based upon one or more preexisting works, such as a translation, musical arrangement, dramatization, fictionalization, motion picture version, sound recording, art reproduction, abridgment, condensation, or any other form in which a work may be recast, transformed, or adapted. A work consisting of editorial revisions, annotations, elaborations, or other modifications which, as a whole, represent an original work of authorship, is a 'derivative work.'" Classic examples of derivative works emanating from the Thomas Harris novel, Hannibal, might include the movie adaption of that novel, starring Anthony Hopkins as the devious Dr. Hannibal Lecter, a condensed version of the book recorded onto CD, a Spanish language translation of the novel, and perhaps a 20–inch Hannibal Lecter action figure (were there a market for such an item). Creating these types of derivative works requires the consent of the owner of the copyright to the Hannibal book (as well as other rights in the case of the Hannibal Lecter doll, given its likely resemblance to Anthony Hopkins or to Gaspard Ulliel (if it is a "young Hannibal" doll)).

Understanding the status of derivative works provides some insight into the fundamental nature of copyright protection. The derivative work, if unauthorized, would infringe the novel even though a moviemaker adds much creative effort to the movie version of Hannibal. The reason for this is that the movie takes a substantial amount of copyrightable expression from the original novel (indeed, probably enough plot, dialogue, character, and scene development that the movie may also constitute a "reproduction" of the novel). If *authorized*, however, the movie version is itself also a separate copyrightable work, as it certainly satisfies the minimum level of creativity as required in *Feist*, given the movie producers' significant creative contributions as noted above. So the derivative work builds on the original, and often in sufficiently creative way to itself be a copyrightable work.

There are cases, however, in which the derivative work, though authorized or based on a public domain work, may not have sufficient added creative elements to merit protection as a separately copyrightable work. This problem is essentially a variation of the issue raised in the *Feist* case and discussed at length in Chapter 2, ¶ 2.03—whether a particular endeavor is sufficiently creative to satisfy the minimum standard of creativity required by the Constitution and the Copyright Act. For example, in *Alfred Bell & Co. v. Catalda Fine Arts*,[7] the court addressed whether mezzotint engravings of well known public domain paintings were copyrightable. The court stated:

> 'Original' in reference to a copyrighted work means that the particular work 'owes its origin' to the 'author.' No large measure of novelty is necessary. Said the Supreme Court in *Baker v. Selden*: 'The copyright of the book, if not pirated from other works, would be valid without regard to the novelty, or want of novelty, of its subject-matter. The novelty of the art or thing described or explained has nothing to do with the validity of the copyright. To give to the author of the book an exclusive property in the art described therein, when no examination of its novelty has ever been officially made, would be a surprise and a fraud upon the public. That is the province of letters-patent, not of copyright.' "[8]

---

7. 191 F.2d 99 (2d Cir. 1951).

8. *Id.* at 102 (quoting *Baker v. Selden*, 101 U.S. 99 (1879)).

The court went on to note "that nothing in the Constitution commands that copyrighted matter be strikingly unique or novel. Accordingly, we were not ignoring the Constitution when we stated that a 'copy of something in the public domain' will support a copyright if it is a 'distinguishable variation'.... All that is needed to satisfy both the Constitution and the statute is that the 'author' contributed something more than a 'merely trivial' variation, something recognizably 'his own.' "[9] Applying this rule to the mezzotints, the court stated:

> We consider untenable defendants' suggestion that plaintiff's mezzotints could not validly be copyrighted because they are reproductions of works in the public domain.... The mezzotints ... 'originated' with those who make them, and—on the trial judge's findings well supported by the evidence—amply met the standards imposed by the Constitution and the statute. There is evidence that they were not intended to, and did not, imitate the paintings they reproduced. But even if their substantial departures from the paintings were inadvertent, the copyrights would be valid. A copyist's bad eyesight or defective musculature, or a shock caused by a clap of thunder, may yield sufficiently distinguishable variations. Having hit upon such a variation unintentionally, the 'author' may adopt it as his and copyright it.[10]

In contrast to the outcome in *Alfred Bell & Co. v. Catalda Fine Arts*, the case of *L. Batlin & Son, Inc. v. Snyder*,[11] involved plastic reproductions of a public domain antique metal "Uncle Sam" bank. The court distinguished the earlier decision, holding that the mechanical plastic replicas were not sufficiently original to merit copyright protection. Similarly, in *Gracen v. Bradford Exchange, Inc.*, Judge Posner held that drawings and paintings taken from images in the "Wizard of Oz" were not sufficiently distinct to be protected under copyright law. In short, the variations from the public domain bank were found to be trivial. The line between trivial variations, which do not merit protection as a derivative work, and creative adaptations, which are copyrightable, is difficult to draw because it is highly fact-specific.

The issue of derivative works adapted from prior material, whether from the public domain or with authority for works still under copyright, has ramifications for considering what is in the public domain. Consider the case of Les Misérables, the famous 1862 novel written by French author Victor Hugo. Clearly the French novel is in the public domain, as the copyright on that work has long ago expired. Yet that does not mean one can run to the

---

9.   *Id.* at 102–03.

10.   *Id.* at 105 (citations omitted).

11.   536 F.2d 486 (2d Cir. 1976).

nearest bookstore and start copying any version of the book ones finds verbatim. There are, by one count, at least six different *English translations* of the novel, each of which is a derivative work and some of which are still under copyright protection. Some of these translations date back to the 1800s and are in the public domain. But at least few translations are much more recent and are certainly eligible for copyright protection, both for the creativity of the translation effort and (in some instances) the creative abridgement of the Hugo novel. Finally, the musical version of Les Misérables was composed in 1980 by the French composer Claude–Michel Schönberg, with a libretto by Alain Boublil. This work of musical theater, though based on the story in the Hugo novel, is clearly under copyright protection. The central point is that each of the recent translations and abridgements, as well as the musical theater production, involve creative effort that merits copyright protection despite the use of the Hugo original material that is squarely in the public domain.

A relatively recent Seventh Circuit case addresses an important issue concerning the requirements for securing rights to a derivative work. In *Schrock v. Learning Curve International, Inc.*, 586 F.3d 513 (7th Cir. 2009), the court dealt with a professional photographer who had permission to photograph "Thomas & Friends" toys for use in promotional materials. Although the photographer was within his rights in obtaining the photographs, he did not have express permission to obtain copyrights on the photographs. The court held that copyright protection attached as soon as the photographs were taken (i.e., were in a tangible medium of expression) and that the photographer did not need express permission to proceed to copyright those images, unless there was an agreement altering this default rule. In other words, the photographer who had permission to photograph the material did not need additional authorization to copyright his photograph of the underlying material.

Public Performance

The next major right is the right of public performance, which by the express terms of the statute only applies to a specific list of works: literary, musical, dramatic, and choreographic works, pantomimes, and motion pictures and other audiovisual works. There are two elements necessary to prove a violation of this right—it must involve a performance of the work, and it must be in public. Fortunately for many, singing copyrighted Elton John songs in the shower is not a public performance. But singing those same songs, or playing them on a CD player or karaoke machine, would be a violation of this right if it occurs in a public place when no public performance license has been obtained from the representatives of

Elton John and Bernie Taupin (the songwriters whose rights would be violated).

Therefore, to assess whether a public performance has taken places requires a close look at the definition of "performance" and "public" for purposes of copyright law. To perform a work, as defined in section 101, "means to recite, render, play, dance, or act it, either directly or by means of any device or process or, in the case of a motion picture or other audiovisual work, to show its images in any sequence or to make the sounds accompanying it audible." This definition seems rather straightforward, and rarely presents difficulties in legal analysis.

Somewhat more difficult is the term "public," which is also defined in section 101:

To perform or display a work "publicly" means—

(1) to perform or display it at a place open to the public or at any place where a substantial number of persons outside of a normal circle of a family and its social acquaintances is gathered; or

(2) to transmit or otherwise communicate a performance or display of the work to a place specified by clause (1) or to the public, by means of any device or process, whether the members of the public capable of receiving the performance or display receive it in the same place or in separate places and at the same time or at different times.

As the language of the statute makes clear, there are two ways in which a work can be publicly performed—either by being (1) performed in a public place (i.e., "a place open to the public") or semipublic place (that is, "any place where a substantial number of persons outside of a normal circle of a family and its social acquaintances is gathered") or (2) transmitted or otherwise communicated to the public or to a public place, which includes radio and television broadcasts, as well as cable and satellite transmissions.

A public place is generally a straightforward concept—any place open to the general public. Some obvious examples include airports and train stations, stadiums and arenas, and shopping centers. Most business establishments are open to the public and would thus constitute a public place. One of the more expansive readings of what constitutes a public performance is *Columbia Pictures Industries, Inc. v. Redd Horne, Inc.*[12] The case involved Maxwell's Video Showcase, which exhibited video cassettes of the plaintiffs' films, which Maxwell's called "showcasing" or "in-store rental." Each store contained a small showroom area in the front, with small, private rooms for showcasing or exhibition area in the

_____

12.   749 F.2d 154 (3d Cir. 1984).

back. There were eighty-five booths in the two stores, each of which could seat two to four people. Patrons would select a film, which would be played on a video cassette machine in the front of the store and transmitted to the booth. The viewing room is limited to people who arrived as a group (i.e., strangers were not combined in booths). The court found that because Maxwell's is open to the public and clearly movies were "performed" (i.e., played on the video cassette and television system), the showcasing constituted an unlicensed public performance:

> We find it unnecessary to examine the second part of the statutory definition because we agree with the district court's conclusion that Maxwell's was open to the public. On the composition of the audience, the district court noted that "the showcasing operation is not distinguishable in any significant manner from the exhibition of films at a conventional movie theater." Any member of the public can view a motion picture by paying the appropriate fee. The services provided by Maxwell's are essentially the same as a movie theater, with the additional feature of privacy. The relevant "place" within the meaning of section 101 is each of Maxwell's two stores, not each individual booth within each store. Simply because the cassettes can be viewed in private does not mitigate the essential fact that Maxwell's is unquestionably open to the public.[13]

In short, the court held that Maxwell's needed a license from the movie studios, just as a regular movie theater would. The found the Maxwell's showcasing system similar in substance to theater screenings:

> Maxwell's never disposed of the tapes in its showcasing operations, nor did the tapes ever leave the store. At all times, Maxwell's maintained physical dominion and control over the tapes. Its employees actually played the cassettes on its machines. The charges or fees received for viewing the cassettes at Maxwell's facilities are analytically indistinguishable from admission fees paid by patrons to gain admission to any public theater. Plainly, in their showcasing operation, the appellants do not sell, rent, or otherwise dispose of the video cassette. On the facts presented, Maxwell's "showcasing" operation is a public performance, which, as a matter of law, constitutes a copyright infringement.[14]

The court also addressed Maxwell's argument that the first sale doctrine under section 109(a) gave it the right to carry out its operations, given that it had lawfully purchased copies of the movies it showcased: "The first sale doctrine prevents the copyright

13. *Id.* at 159.   **14.** *Id.* at 160.

owner from controlling the future transfer of a particular copy once its material ownership has been transferred. The transfer of the video cassettes to the defendants, however, did not result in the forfeiture or waiver of all of the exclusive rights found in section 106. The copyright owner's exclusive right 'to perform the copyrighted work publicly' has not been affected; only its distribution right as to the transferred copy has been circumscribed."[15]

The semipublic place—"any place where a substantial number of persons outside of a normal circle of a family and its social acquaintances is gathered"—includes places that are not open to the public but are not private homes and the like. Consequently, unless exempt under section 110 (a topic addressed in Chapter 5, ¶ 5.05), many camps, clubs, college fraternities and sororities, and institutions of various types can be deemed semipublic places. Much litigation has focused what sorts of places are public or semi-public places under the Copyright Act. The American Society of Composers, Authors and Publishers (ASCAP), one of the major non-profit performance rights organizations, garnered media attention and criticism in 1996, when it threatened litigation against the Girl Scouts and Boy Scouts. The claim was that camps were having public performances (e.g., campfire sing-alongs) of copyrighted works in ASCAP's repertoire, such as "Puff the Magic Dragon" and "Happy Birthday to You." News reports indicate that the threat was dropped in light of negative publicity.[16] But leaving aside the understandable public outcry, the copyright owners' legal standing on this point is strong, as a large scout camp may well be deemed a semipublic place as defined by the statute.

Moreover, the "transmit" clause in section 101 extends public performance rights to a variety of forms of electronic dissemination, including radio, television, cable, satellite, and wire transmission of a work. The clause provides that "to perform or display a work 'publicly' means—... (2) to transmit or otherwise communicate a performance or display of the work to a place [open to the public] ... or to the public, by means of any device or process, whether the members of the public capable of receiving the performance or display receive it in the same place or in separate places and at the same time or at different times."

Thus, before HBO or a local Fox broadcast station can broadcast a movie such as "Hunger Games," the local station or the network must secure a license for that public performance. Somewhat less intuitively, consider the case of *On Command Video*

15.　*Id.* at 159–60.

16.　See William F. Patry & Richard A. Posner, Fair Use and Statutory Reform in The Wake of *Eldred*, 92 CAL. L. REV. 1639, 1657 & n.63 (2004); Carol M. Rose, The Moral Subject of Property, 48 WM. & MARY L. REV. 1897, 1909 & n.51 (2007).

Corporation v. Columbia Pictures Industries.[17] On Command developed a system for the electronic delivery of movie video tapes to hotel rooms from a bank of video cassette players centrally located in the hotel's equipment room. The video players are connected to guest rooms by wiring and a computer system. The wiring is used to carry the signal for a requested movie from the central location to the guest room, where it is displayed on the television set found in the room. The court held that this constituted a transmission:

> Plaintiff's argument that On Command's system involves not "transmissions" but "electronic rentals" similar to patrons' physical borrowing of videotapes is without merit. On Command transmits movie performances directly under the language of the definition. The system "communicates" the motion picture "images and sounds" by a "device or process"-the equipment and wiring network from a central console in a hotel to individual guest rooms, where the images and sounds are received "beyond the place from which they are sent." The fact that hotel guests initiate this transmission by turning on the television and choosing a video is immaterial.[18]

On the other hand, the Supreme Court in *Professional Real Estate Investors, Inc. v. Columbia Pictures Industries, Inc.*[19] discussed a public performance claim regarding a hotel's operation of a video rental store in its lobby, from which guests could rent videos to be viewed on televisions and video cassette players in individual hotel rooms. In this instance, the playing of movies was akin to renting a movie from Redbox or Netflix, as the hotel room (while booked to a guest) was not a public place and no "transmission" of the work took place.

Similarly, in *Cartoon Network LP v. CSC Holdings, Inc.,*[20] the Second Circuit held that digital video recorder (DVR) systems used by cable company video-on-demand services do not result in a public performance of copyrighted movies, because any copies made of the works were made by subscribers and thus no transmission "to the public" had taken place. And in *United States v. American Soc'y of Composers, Authors & Publishers,*[21] the court held that downloads of a musical work do not constitute a "public performance" of that work (of course, the download is a reproduction of the work). Finally, a lower court has held that no public performance has occurred when a cell phone company sends a ringtone to a

17. 777 F.Supp. 787 (N.D. Cal. 1991).

18. *Id.* at 789.

19. 508 U.S. 49 (1993). A full discussion of the copyright law issues can be found in the earlier Ninth Circuit opinion in this litigation, *Columbia Pictures Industries, Inc. v. Professional Real Estate Investors, Inc.*, 866 F.2d 278 (9th Cir. 1989).

20. 536 F.3d 121 (2d Cir. 2008).

21. 627 F.3d 64 (2d Cir. 2010).

customer or when the phone rings, even in a public place. *See In re Application of Cellco Partnership d/b/a Verizon Wireless.*[22] Once again, the ringtone was a licensed reproduction of the work, but the issue was whether an additional public performance license was required. In conclusion, courts have carefully interpreted the language and purpose of the Copyright Act in determining what does and what does not constitute a public performance.

Section 109(e) places a limit on public performance rights in the case of an electronic audiovisual game intended for use in coin-operated equipment. This provision states: "Notwithstanding the provisions of sections 106(4) and 106(5), in the case of an electronic audiovisual game intended for use in coin-operated equipment, the owner of a particular copy of such a game lawfully made under this title, is entitled, without the authority of the copyright owner of the game, to publicly perform or display that game in coin-operated equipment, except that this subsection shall not apply to any work of authorship embodied in the audiovisual game if the copyright owner of the electronic audiovisual game is not also the copyright owner of the work of authorship."

Public Performance Rights in Songs and Sound Recordings

One category of works that requires specific discussion is the musical work. When one considers a song found on a CD or an iTunes download, there are actually two copyrighted works embodied in the song. One is the underlying song itself—the words and the music. These are created by the songwriter or composer, and the rights to the song are typically handled by a music publishing company. The songwriter/composer and the music publishing company ordinarily share songwriter revenues. The second copyrighted work is the sound recording—the recorded version of the song made by a group of performers (i.e., the band). The rights to the sound recording are typically handled by the record company, with the band and the record company typically sharing in the revenues. Section 101 defines sound recordings as "works that result from the fixation of a series of musical, spoken, or other sounds, but not including the sounds accompanying a motion picture or other audiovisual work, regardless of the nature of the material objects, such as disks, tapes, or other phonorecords, in which they are embodied."

The scope of public performance rights in the music field is of critical importance, and is not intuitive. As mentioned earlier, songwriters such as Elton John/Bernie Taupin or Lou Reed can assert public performance rights in their *song lyrics and words.* These songwriters and their music publishing companies can collect royalties for every public performance of their songs. There are,

22. 663 F. Supp. 2d 363 (S.D.N.Y. 2009).

however, no general public performance rights in *sound recordings*, such as Elton John's recording of "Funeral for a Friend" or the various versions of the Lou Reed's song "Sweet Jane," including versions recorded by the Velvet Underground and cover versions by the Cowboy Junkies, Phish, the Kooks, and Mott the Hoople. So the record companies that own the rights to these various sound recordings do not have a copyright claim when they are played in a large concert venue.

Section 114(a) of the Copyright Act states: "The exclusive rights of the owner of copyright in a *sound recording* are limited to the rights specified by clauses (1), (2), (3) and (6) of section 106, and *do not include any right of performance under section 106(4)*." Accordingly, the songwriter has the exclusive right to make copies of the song, to perform it publicly, and to license others to make sound recordings of it. The owner of the sound recording, typically a record company, can make copies of the work and distribute it as part of its license of the work from the songwriter. The sound recording is publicly performed when it is played in a public place (such as a stadium or dance hall) or when it is broadcast or transmitted (such as by radio, television, satellite, or cable). That public performance of the sound recording necessarily includes a performance of the underlying musical work embodied in the song. Therefore, the songwriter has the right to license that performance, and is entitled to royalties for that public performance of the underlying song, collected through a performing rights society such as ASCAP or Broadcast Music Inc. (BMI). Yet the band or singer who made the CD and the record company that produced it are not entitled to public performance royalties (with one limited exception, digital transmissions, which are addressed below). As section 114(a) makes clear, this is an explicit congressional choice.

There is one exception to the general rule that there are no public performance rights in sound recordings. That exception provides such rights (and thus a potential licensing revenue stream) for digital music transmissions of sound recordings. Accordingly, when a song is played on satellite radio or on a music channel on satellite television services (such as the Dish Network), the owner of the copyright in the sound recording is entitled to royalties. Section 106(6) of the Copyright Act sets forth this specific public performance right: "Subject to sections 107 through 122, the owner of copyright under this title has the exclusive rights to do and to authorize any of the following: ... (6) in the case of sound recordings, to perform the copyrighted work publicly by means of a digital audio transmission."[23] Section 101 defines a digital transmission as

---

23. *See* Digital Performance Right in Sound Recordings Act of 1995, Pub. L. No. 104–39, § 2, 109 Stat. 336, 336 (codified at 17 U.S.C. § 106(6)). For a

"a transmission in whole or in part in a digital or other non-analog format." This provision does not apply to ordinary terrestrial radio broadcasts (i.e., local broadcast radio stations). A record company will typically own the copyright in the sound recording, and that company in turn will likely share its royalties with the recording artist under the terms of the record deal between the two parties.

There have been bills put forward to provide broader public performance rights in sound recordings, but none have been enacted thus far. In this author's view, full public performance rights should be extended to sound recordings, just as they are provided for musical compositions: "Congress should enact a version of the Performance Rights Act, which would provide full public performance rights to sound recordings. The second-class treatment given to sound recordings under current copyright law is unwarranted and is contrary to the practice in any other industrialized nation."[24] By reconfiguring public performance rights, "the size of the economic pie available to support the music industry will be significantly expanded, which will help ameliorate the decline in overall revenues from CD and download sales. This rethinking of the public performance right would also promote copyright policy as contemplated by the Constitution and Congress. It would also serve to benefit musicians and songwriters who depend upon royalties for a significant portion of their livelihood."[25] There are several versions of the Performance Rights Act.[26]

Sound recordings were not even protected under the Copyright Act until the Sound Recording Amendment of 1971.[27] Before that date, state law copyright was still the basis for copyright protection for this type of work. Indeed, state law is ordinarily still the avenue for protecting sound recordings that were fixed before the effective date of the Sound Recording Amendment to the 1909 Copyright Act–February 15, 1972.[28] These rights can survive under state law

recent case addressing how one music service should be analyzed, see *Arista Records, LLC v. Launch Media, Inc.*, 578 F.3d 148 (2d Cir. 2009), *cert. denied*, 130 S.Ct. 1290 (2010) (LAUNCHcast music service held to be eligible for statutory licensing scheme because it was deemed to not be an "interactive service," as defined in section 114 of the Copyright Act).

24. Gary Myers & George Howard, The Future of Music: Reconfiguing Public Performance Rights, 17 J. Intell. Prop. L. 1 (2010). *See also* Mary LaFrance, From Whether to How: The Challenge of Implementing a Full Public

Performance Right in Sound Recordings, 2 Harv. J. Sports & Ent. L. 221 (2011).

25. *Id.*

26. *See* H.R. 4789, 110th Cong. (1st Sess. 2007), available at http://www.opencongress.org/bill/110–h4789/text; H.R. 848, 111th Cong. (1st Sess. 2009), available at http://www.govtrack.us/congress/bill.xpd?bill=h111–848. There are similar bills in the Senate. See S. 2500, 110th Cong. (1st Sess. 2007), available at http://www.opencongress.org/bill/110–s2500/text.

27. Act of October 15, 1971 (Pub. L. 92–140, 85 Stat. 391).

28. 17 U.S.C. § 301(c).

until 2067, thereby providing 95 years of potential protection for these old sound recordings—essentially the term given to works made for hire under current copyright law.[29] The existence and scope of the relief available for these old song recordings depend on applicable state law (which can track federal copyright principles). Finally, the underlying musical composition is of course typically protected under federal copyright law. Obviously, the catalog of sound recordings of many famous performers, from the Beatles to Elvis Presley to James Brown, includes many pre–1972 works.

Public Display

The last major right is the right to display the work publicly. Section 106(5) sets forth the categories of works to which the public display right applies: "Subject to sections 107 through 122, the owner of copyright under this title has the exclusive rights to do and to authorize any of the following: . . . (5) in the case of literary, musical, dramatic, and choreographic works, pantomimes, and pictorial, graphic, or sculptural works, including the individual images of a motion picture or other audiovisual work, to display the copyrighted work publicly." As in the case of the public perform-ance right, some types of works are not amenable to a claim that the work is being publicly displayed. Two examples would be a sound recording and an architectural work—the display right would make little sense as applies to these categories of works, or would present serious issues regarding expansive application if broadly applied to those works.

Section 101 provides that to display a work "means to show a copy of it, either directly or by means of a film, slide, television image, or any other device or process or, in the case of a motion picture or other audiovisual work, to show individual images nonse-quentially." A good illustration of case involving the public display right is *Kelly v. Arriba Soft Corp.*[30] In that case, the plaintiff was a photographer whose images appeared on the defendant's website in both thumbnail (small images meant to be "clicked on" to view a larger version) form, and in full-size images by linking to Kelly's own website and framing the image on the Kelly website. The court found that Arriba did in fact display Kelly's images to the public through the website. A number of other decisions have also in-volved the public display of photographs on websites.[31]

---

29. *See generally Capitol Records, Inc. v. Naxos of America, Inc.*, 372 F.3d 471, 477–79 (2d Cir. 2004) (state law copyrights in sound recordings are not preempted for works fixed before Febru-ary 15, 1972).

30. 280 F.3d 934 (9th Cir. 2002).

31. *See, e.g., Playboy Enterprises, Inc. v. Webbworld, Inc.*, 991 F.Supp. 543 (N.D.Texas 1997) (owner of internet site infringed magazine publisher's copy-rights by displaying copyrighted images on its website); *Playboy Enterprises, Inc. v. Russ Hardenburgh, Inc.*, 982 F.Supp. 503 (N.D.Ohio 1997) (owner of electron-

The most significant limit on the public display right is the first sale doctrine. Section 109(c) states: "Notwithstanding the provisions of section 106(5), the owner of a particular copy lawfully made under this title, or any person authorized by such owner, is entitled, without the authority of the copyright owner, to display that copy publicly, either directly or by the projection of no more than one image at a time, to viewers present at the place where the copy is located." This provision essentially permits the owner of a lawful physical copy of a work to display that work, including in a public place. Consequently, a museum that owns a copyrighted painting can display that painting in its exhibition hall without violating the right of public display. Similarly, a shopping center that has purchased a sculpture can place the work in the public areas of the mall. Finally, section 109(e) states: "Notwithstanding the provisions of sections 106(4) and 106(5), in the case of an electronic audiovisual game intended for use in coin-operated equipment, the owner of a particular copy of such a game lawfully made under this title, is entitled, without the authority of the copyright owner of the game, to publicly perform or display that game in coin-operated equipment, except that this subsection shall not apply to any work of authorship embodied in the audiovisual game if the copyright owner of the electronic audiovisual game is not also the copyright owner of the work of authorship."

¶ 4.03   Moral Rights

The subject of moral rights reveals the greatest difference between current United States law and the law of many foreign nations, including Europe. In a sense, moral rights address a completely different set of rights and interests that authors might possess. Instead of focusing on the author's economic rights, which are designed to create financial incentives for creative effort, the moral rights scheme focuses on the author's personal rights to honor, reputation, artistic integrity, and attribution. Moral rights in many foreign nations, particularly France and much of the rest of Europe (and beyond), can be quite broad in scope and application. For instance, France recognizes four type of moral rights: (1) droit de divulgation, or the right of disclosure; (2) droit de repentir ou de retrait, or the right to withdraw or correct works previously disclosed to the public; (3) droit de paternite, or the right of attribution, which includes rights to publish anonymously or pseudonymously, and (4) droit au respect de l'oeuvre, the right of integrity ("the right to respect of the work").

ic bulletin board system infringed magazine publisher's copyrights by displaying images on its system; defendant encouraged subscribers to upload adult photographs, screened submitted images, and posted files so that subscribers could download them).

United States law did not expressly recognize any of these four broad rights, at least not within the confines of federal copyright law. Instead, the focus of United States law has always been on the economic rights of authors as an incentive for creativity, rather than on concerns for the personal or reputational nature of creative efforts. The Berne Convention for the Protection of Literary & Artistic Works Article, in Article 6bis, mandates that all nations adhering to the treaty offer two types of moral rights protections:

(1) Independently of the author's economic rights, and even after the transfer of the said rights, the author shall have the right to claim authorship of the work and to object to any distortion, mutilation or other modification of, or other derogatory action in relation to, the said work, which would be prejudicial to his honor or reputation.

(2) The rights granted to the author in accordance with the preceding paragraph shall, after his death, be maintained, at least until the expiry of the economic rights, and shall be exercisable by the persons or institutions authorized by the legislation of the country where protection is claimed. However, those countries whose legislation, at the moment of their ratification of or accession to this Act, does not provide for the protection after the death of the author of all the rights set out in the preceding paragraph may provide that some of these rights may, after his death, cease to be maintained.

(3) The means of redress for safeguarding the rights granted by this Article shall be governed by the legislation of the country where protection is claimed.

Recognition of an artist's "moral rights" was controversial in the American view of copyright law, and the United States did not join the Berne Convention until 1988.[32]

The Visual Artists Rights Act of 1990 (VARA)

The first specific moral rights legislation in the United States is the Visual Artists Rights Act of 1990, or VARA. Codified as section 106A of the Copyright Act, VARA provides a carefully defined group of authors with rights of attribution and integrity. Section 106A states in part:

(a) Rights of attribution and integrity.

Subject to section 107 and independent of the exclusive rights provided in section 106, the author of a work of visual art—

(1) shall have the right—

(A) to claim authorship of that work, and

32. *See* S. Rep. No. 100–352 (1988), *reprinted in* 1988 U.S.C.C.A.N. 3706.

(B) to prevent the use of his or her name as the author of any work of visual art which he or she did not create;

(2) shall have the right to prevent the use of his or her name as the author of the work of visual art in the event of a distortion, mutilation, or other modification of the work which would be prejudicial to his or her honor or reputation; and

(3) subject to the limitations set forth in section 113(d), shall have the right—

(A) to prevent any intentional distortion, mutilation, or other modification of that work which would be prejudicial to his or her honor or reputation, and any intentional distortion, mutilation, or modification of that work is a violation of that right, and

(B) to prevent any destruction of a work of recognized stature, and any intentional or grossly negligent destruction of that work is a violation of that right.

(b) Scope and exercise of rights.

Only the author of a work of visual art has the rights conferred by subsection (a) in that work, whether or not the author is the copyright owner. The authors of a joint work of visual art are co-owners of the rights conferred by subsection (a) in that work.

Thus, section 106(A)(a) provides protection for rights of attribution and integrity, as mandated by the Berne Convention. It is crucial to note, however, that VARA applies only to authors of "a work of visual art." VARA specifically identifies four categories of works to which it applies. Section 101 of the Copyright Act defines a "work of visual art" as:

(1) a painting, drawing, print, or sculpture, existing in a single copy, in a limited edition of 200 copies or fewer that are signed and consecutively numbered by the author, or, in the case of a sculpture, in multiple cast, carved, or fabricated sculptures of 200 or fewer that are consecutively numbered by the author and bear the signature or other identifying mark of the author; or

(2) a still photographic image produced for exhibition purposes only, existing in a single copy that is signed by the author, or in a limited edition of 200 copies or fewer that are signed and consecutively numbered by the author.

A work of visual art does not include—

(A)(i) any poster, map, globe, chart, technical drawing, diagram, model, applied art, motion picture or other audiovisual work, book, magazine, newspaper, periodical, data base, electronic information service, electronic publication, or similar publication;

> (ii) any merchandising item or advertising, promotional, descriptive, covering, or packaging material or container;

> (iii) any portion or part of any item described in clause (i) or (ii);

(B) any work made for hire; or

(C) any work not subject to copyright protection under this title.

Parsing this language, it is clear that VARA applies only to four types of works:

— (1) a painting, existing in a single copy or in a limited edition of 200 copies or fewer that are signed and consecutively numbered by the author

— (2) a drawing, existing in a single copy or in a limited edition of 200 copies or fewer that are signed and consecutively numbered by the author

— (3) a sculpture, existing in a single copy or in multiple cast, carved, or fabricated sculptures of 200 or fewer that are consecutively numbered by the author and bear the signature or other identifying mark of the author

— (4) a still photographic image produced for exhibition purposes only, existing in a single copy that is signed by the author, or in a limited edition of 200 copies or fewer that are signed and consecutively numbered by the author.

What these four types of works have in common is that they are typical works of fine arts, often found in museums and galleries. Although it is understandable that Congress would provide these types of works with heightened protection, particularly with regard to moral rights, it leaves aside the question of how the rights of attribution and integrity of authors of a variety of other types of works—such as books, music, sound recordings, and motion pictures—will be protected. As the Berne Convention states, "The means of redress for safeguarding the rights granted by this Article shall be governed by the legislation of the country where protection is claimed."[33] Authors of other types of works must turn to other

---

33. BERNE CONVENTION FOR THE PROTECTION OF LITERARY & ARTISTIC WORKS, Article 6bis, Part (3).

areas of federal and state law, such as the Lanham Act, the right of publicity, and other state laws for relief, as discussed below.

VARA contains a number of specific exceptions designed to permit conservation and display of works, as well as to recognize that works can be affected by the passage of time. Section 106A(c) sets forth these exceptions:

(1) The modification of a work of visual art which is a result of the passage of time or the inherent nature of the materials is not a distortion, mutilation, or other modification described in subsection (a)(3)(A).

(2) The modification of a work of visual art which is the result of conservation, or of the public presentation, including lighting and placement, of the work is not a destruction, distortion, mutilation, or other modification described in subsection (a)(3) unless the modification is caused by gross negligence.

(3) The rights described in paragraphs (1) and (2) of subsection (a) shall not apply to any reproduction, depiction, portrayal, or other use of a work in, upon, or in any connection with any item described in subparagraph (A) or (B) of the definition of "work of visual art" in section 101, and any such reproduction, depiction, portrayal, or other use of a work is not a destruction, distortion, mutilation, or other modification described in paragraph (3) of subsection (a).

More significantly, the rights of an author covered by VARA can be waived in a signed, written agreement, as set forth in section 106A(e):

(1) The rights conferred by subsection (a) may not be transferred, but those rights may be waived if the author expressly agrees to such waiver in a written instrument signed by the author. Such instrument shall specifically identify the work, and uses of that work, to which the waiver applies, and the waiver shall apply only to the work and uses so identified. In the case of a joint work prepared by two or more authors, a waiver of rights under this paragraph made by one such author waives such rights for all such authors.

(2) Ownership of the rights conferred by subsection (a) with respect to a work of visual art is distinct from ownership of any copy of that work, or of a copyright or any exclusive right under a copyright in that work. Transfer of ownership of any copy of a work of visual art, or of a copyright or any exclusive right under a copyright, shall not constitute a waiver of the rights conferred by subsection (a). Except as may otherwise be agreed by the author in a written instrument signed by the author, a waiver of the rights conferred by subsection (a) with

respect to a work of visual art shall not constitute a transfer of ownership of any copy of that work, or of ownership of a copyright or of any exclusive right under a copyright in that work.

The provision above also indicates that the VARA rights are not transferrable, and that the sale or other transfer of the physical object (i.e., the painting, drawing, sculpture, or photograph) does not by itself constitute a waiver of the rights established in VARA.

Another important limitation on the applicability of VARA can be found in the definition of a work of visual art in section 101 of the Copyright Act: "a work of visual art does not include—... (B) any work made for hire." As discussed above in Chapter 3, ¶ 3.02, when a work is created by an employee or by an agent as defined under the common law test set forth in *CCNV v. Reid*,[34] the hiring party is deemed the author of that work. Understandably, application of the personality-focused and reputational features of VARA in such situations seems inappropriate. This limitation on the scope of VARA has come into play in some of the early cases decided under the new law. In fact, this limitation on VARA was critical in the first substantive appellate case addressing VARA, *Carter v. Helmsley–Spear, Inc.*[35] This case involved a sculptural work installed in an office building lobby, which a new property manager later sought to remove. Among The VARA issues in the case included (1) whether the work qualified as a work of visual art, (2) whether the work was made for hire and therefore unprotected by VARA, and (3) whether the work was of recognized stature.

The Second Circuit ultimately resolved the case based on its determination that the sculpture in *Carter* was in fact a work made for hire. The court recognized that the plaintiffs had complete artistic freedom as to the sculpture's creation, and that the artists' conception and execution of the work required considerable skill, two factors weighing against a finding of a work made for hire. On the other hand, the court found that the defendants could (under the terms of their contract) and did in fact assign the artists several additional projects on the property. In addition, the court gave weight to the benefits provided to the plaintiffs: "the provision of employee benefits and the tax treatment of the plaintiffs weigh strongly in favor of employee status. The defendants paid payroll and social security taxes, provided employee benefits such as life, health, and liability insurance and paid vacations, and contributed to unemployment insurance and workers' compensation funds on plaintiffs' behalf."[36] Moreover, the plaintiffs were paid on a 40–hour

---

34. 490 U.S. 730 (1989).

35. 71 F.3d 77 (2d Cir. 1995).

36. *Id.* at 86. *See also Pollara v. Seymour,* 344 F.3d 265 (2d Cir. 2003) (banner ineligible for protection under VARA

work week basis, were retained for over a two-year period, and were provided with many of their supplies. Finally, two of the three sculptors filed for unemployment benefits after their positions were terminated. The court concluded that its balancing of the *CCNV v. Reid* factors weighed in favor of a finding that the sculpture was a work made for hire and thus was not protected under VARA.

Finally, VARA rights in works created after the effective date of the statute last only for the life of the author—*not the life of the author plus seventy years*—as specified in section 106A(d):

(1) With respect to works of visual art created on or after the effective date set forth in section 610(a) of the Visual Artists Rights Act of 1990, the rights conferred by subsection (a) shall endure for a term consisting of the life of the author.

(2) With respect to works of visual art created before the effective date set forth in section 610(a) of the Visual Artists Rights Act of 1990, but title to which has not, as of such effective date, been transferred from the author, the rights conferred by subsection (a) shall be coextensive with, and shall expire at the same time as, the rights conferred by section 106.

(3) In the case of a joint work prepared by two or more authors, the rights conferred by subsection (a) shall endure for a term consisting of the life of the last surviving author.

(4) All terms of the rights conferred by subsection (a) run to the end of the calendar year in which they would otherwise expire.

Although litigation involving VARA has been frequent since its enactment, there are relatively few instances in which an artist has prevailed on a VARA claim. *Martin v. City of Indianapolis*,[37] is an example of a successful VARA claim. The plaintiff, Jan Martin, was an artist who created a large (measuring twenty by forty feet) outdoor metal sculpture entitled, "Symphony #1." Some years later, the property on which the sculpture had been placed was acquired by the City of Indianapolis as part of an urban renewal project. Without notifying Martin, the City demolished the sculpture. Martin brought suit, claiming a violation of the right of integrity under VARA. In the express language of the statute, it is necessary to determine if a work is of "recognized stature" in order for it to be eligible for protection from destruction. The court noted that this involved a determination of whether the work is viewed as

because it constituted advertising or promotional material); *Kelley v. Chicago Park District,* 635 F.3d 290 (7th Cir. 2011) (rejecting VARA claim because work did not qualify as a fixed work of authorship for purposes of the Copyright Act and thus was ineligible for the protections found in VARA). The *Kelley* case is discussed in Chapter 2, ¶ 2.07.

37. 192 F.3d 608 (7th Cir. 1999).

meritorious and is therefore "recognized" by art experts, other members of the artistic community, or by a cross-section of society. In making this showing, plaintiffs generally, but not inevitably, will need to call expert witnesses who can attest to the stature of the work. The court then summarized the evidence brought forward by Martin, along with the City's objections to it:

> The City objects to the "stature" testimony that was offered by plaintiff as inadmissible hearsay. If not admitted, it would result in plaintiff's failure to sustain his burden of proof. It is true that plaintiff offered no evidence of experts or others by deposition, affidavit or interrogatories. Plaintiff's evidence of "stature" consisted of certain newspaper and magazine articles, and various letters, including a letter from an art gallery director and a letter to the editor of The Indianapolis News, all in support of the sculpture, as well as a program from the show at which a model of the sculpture won "Best of Show." After reviewing the City's objection, the district court excluded plaintiff's "programs and awards" evidence as lacking adequate foundation, but nevertheless found Martin had met his "stature" burden of proof with his other evidence.[38]

With one judge dissenting, the court in *Martin* affirmed the district court's summary judgment finding of recognized stature, and concluded that the City had indeed violated Martin's right of integrity under VARA. Martin received $20,000 in statutory damages, plus an award of attorneys' fees and costs, which was upheld on appeal.[39]

More recently, in *Massachusetts Museum of Contemporary Art Foundation, Inc. v. Büchel*,[40] the court held that VARA applied to an unfinished art installation and remanded for a determination of whether a museum's alteration of that installation without the artist's consent was a violation of his right of integrity in the football-field-sized installation, called "Training Ground for Democracy." It seems likely that VARA claims will be more frequent in the years to come, as visual artists become more aware of their rights under this federal law.

Protection for Moral Rights Under the Lanham Act and State Law

Given the narrow scope and applicability of VARA and the absence of other moral rights provisions in the Copyright Act itself, it is apparent that United States compliance with Article 6bis of the Berne Convention's moral rights mandates must be premised upon the availability of other legal theories. A prominent example of such a theory is section 43(a) of the Lanham Act, the federal trademark law. This provision states, in relevant part: "Any person who, on or

38. *Id*. at 613 (citations omitted).   **40.** 593 F.3d 38 (1st Cir. 2010).
39. *Id*. at 614.

in connection with any goods or services, . . . uses in commerce any word, term, name, symbol, or device, or any combination thereof, or any false designation of origin, false or misleading description of fact, or false or misleading representation of fact, which—(A) is likely to cause confusion, or to cause mistake, or to deceive as to the affiliation, connection, or association of such person with another person, or as to the origin, sponsorship, or approval of his or her goods, services, or commercial activities by another person. . . ."[41]

Section 43(a) of the Lanham Act is a broadly worded provision, with potential application to a wide array of situations. A leading older case in this area is *Gilliam v. American Broadcasting Co.*,[42] in which the creators of Monty Python's Flying Circus successfully sued ABC under the Lanham Act on the ground that the network had so substantially altered episodes of the plaintiff's work that placing the plaintiff's name on the copyrighted work constituted a false designation of origin. Accordingly, under this reading of the Lanham Act, it might appear possible for authors to invoke the attribution rights in the manner contemplated by the Berne Convention.

This possibility was partially eroded, however, in the Supreme Court's 2003 decision in *Dastar Corp. v. Twentieth Century Fox Film Corp.*[43] In that case, the Court considered whether section 43(a) of the Lanham Act gave rise to a claim for failure to attribute authorship when the underlying work taken had fallen into the public domain under applicable copyright rules. The Court held that no such claim can be asserted in this particular context. The ruling calls into question the extent to which section 43(a) might be used to address issues of attribution, though the case can be distinguished on the ground that the underlying work was in the public domain, whereas many attribution cases do not raise this public policy issue.

Many commentators view *Dastar* as the death knell for attribution claims under the Lanham Act. Laura A. Heymann, for example, observed: "Although a cornerstone of the European moral rights regime, a right to attribution (or, relatedly, a right to a disclaimer of nonattribution) has never had more than a toehold in United States intellectual property law. And whatever such rights federal courts had been willing to find in the Lanham Act have now largely been eviscerated following the United States Supreme Court's 2003 decision in *[Dastar]*, in which the Court rejected the

---

41. 15 U.S.C. § 1125.

42. 538 F.2d 14 (2d Cir. 1976). *See also Smith v. Montoro*, 648 F.2d 602 (9th Cir. 1981) (actor's demand for attribution in film credits and promotional materials actionable under the Lanham Act). *See generally* Joseph P. Bauer, "A Federal Law of Unfair Competition: What Should be the Reach of Section 43(a) of the Lanham Act?," 31 U.C.L.A. L. Rev. 671 (1984).

43. 539 U.S. 23 (2003).

plaintiff's attempt to use the Lanham Act to require attribution for a film in the public domain (and thus free from copyright)."[44] Howard B. Abrams commented: "After *Dastar*, the notion that the rights of attribution and integrity might be found in section 43(a) of the Lanham Act is dead."[45] Noting the international implications of the ruling, Tim Wu noted that in *Dastar*, "the Supreme Court effectively eliminated a category of moral rights protection under trademarks law without questioning whether this would put the United States in violation of its treaty obligations."[46]

Despite these broad characterizations of *Dastar*, the implications of this case for Intellectual Property law remain unclear at this point. A narrow reading of *Dastar*, focusing specifically on the extent to which its holding is based on the premise that a section 43(a) trademark claim should be asserted as to a work that is in the public domain. It can thus be argued that *Dastar* does not address section 43(a) claims involving works that are still under copyright protection, so that section 43(a)'s false advertising provision might apply in some circumstances. Rick Mortensen, for example, has observed: "While *Dastar* may have rendered those means inadequate in a few situations, it still left most of section 43(a) of the Lanham Act open to artists seeking attribution and integrity. In a majority of situations, artists outside the scope of VARA can protect their moral rights through the bundle of rights given them in the copyright act, and by insisting on moral rights protections as a term of the contract granting any of those rights to another party."[47] With regard to the analytical foundations of *Dastar*, consider this observation by Laura Heymann:

> Part of the Court's resistance in *Dastar* arose from its conclusion that the bargain inherent in U.S. copyright law requires unfettered access to the work once the copyright term ends in exchange for the benefits afforded the creator during the term. Any requirement of attribution or disclaimer would impose a restriction on the public domain that copyright law cannot tolerate; accordingly, trademark law-based claims must give way. But this view mischaracterizes both the nature of the copyright bargain and the scope of trademark law. Properly construed, the copyright bargain cedes to the public only the rights given to the creator during the copyright term: the exclusive right to control copies, distribution, display, perform-

44. Laura A. Heymann, The Trademark/Copyright Divide, 60 S.M.U. L. Rev. 55, 58–59 (2007).

45. Howard B. Abrams, The Law of Copyright § 5:408.1 (2006)

46. Tim Wu, Treaties' Domains, 93 Va. L. Rev. 571 (2007).

47. Rick Mortensen, D.I.Y. After *Dastar*: Protecting Creators' Moral Rights Through Creative Lawyering, Individual Contracts and Collectively Bargained Agreements, 8 Vand. J. Ent. & Tech. L. 335, 363–64 (2006).

ance, and derivative works. Enforcement of other interests based on other legal regimes shouldn't necessarily interfere with the public's ability to exploit any of the rights it receives as part of the copyright bargain.[48]

Finally, it should be noted that the ability of authors to assert Lanham Act claims premised on improper attribution yielded mixed results, even prior to *Dastar*.[49]

¶ 4.04　The Digital Millennium Copyright Act (DMCA)

Technological change has always presented copyright law with challenges, and indeed the printing press was the impetus for the first English copyright laws. The advent of the Internet, computer software, and other developments in digital technology have brought particularly powerful challenges to the property rights regime of copyright law. Modern technology facilitates the rapid and flawless reproduction of copyrighted works. Many copyright owners have sought to employ technological measures to reduce or eliminate this threat of infringement. These measures take the form of various types of copy-protection and encryption measures. Yet using these technological measures often results in an endless battle with hackers and others who seek to overcome these copy-protection and encryption measures.

Congress enacted the Digital Millennium Copyright Act (DMCA) in 1998 to implement the World Intellectual Property Organization Copyright Treaty (WIPO Copyright Treaty), which requires signatory countries to provide adequate legal protection and effective legal remedies against the circumvention of effective technological measures that are used by authors of copyrighted works, when the circumvention is not authorized by the author or permitted by law.[50] The purpose of the DMCA's anticircumvention provision is to establish separate and distinct causes of action for certain actions directed to technological measures used by copyright owners. The DMCA does not establish a new property right. The DMCA's text indicates that circumvention is not infringement; section 1201(c)(1) states: "Nothing in this section shall affect

---

48. Laura A. Heymann, The Trademark/Copyright Divide, 60 S.M.U. L. Rev. at 58–59.

49. *See, e.g., Leigh v. Warner Bros., Inc.*, 212 F.3d 1210 (11th Cir. 2000) (use of film and promotional materials modeled after famous photograph of "Bird Girl" statue not actionable under VARA or Lanham Act); *Batiste v. Island Records, Inc.*, 179 F.3d 217 (5th Cir. 1999) (no Lanham Act relief for alteration of song "Funky Soul"); *Boosey & Hawkes Music Publ'rs, Ltd. v. Walt Disney Co.*, 934 F.Supp. 119 (S.D.N.Y. 1996) (no Lanham Act relief for alleged lack of proper attribution and alteration of Stravinsky's "Rite of Spring," a public domain song, in "Fantasia" video); *Halicki v. United Artists*, 812 F.2d 1213 (9th Cir. 1987) (film producer lacked standing and failed to establish Lanham Act claim).

50. WIPO Treaty, Apr. 12, 1997, art. 11, S. Treaty Doc. No. 105–17 (1997), *available at* 1997 Westlaw 447232.

rights, remedies, limitations, or defenses to copyright infringement, including fair use, under this title." Accordingly, whereas copyrights establish property rights, the DMCA's prohibition on unauthorized circumvention merely creates a new cause of action under which a defendant may be liable.

Before Congress enacted the DMCA, a copyright owner would have no cause of action against someone who circumvented a technological control, but did not infringe of one of exclusive rights of the copyright owner. The DMCA rebalanced these interests to favor the copyright owner by creating circumvention liability under § 1201(a)(1) and trafficking liability under § 1201(a)(2) and § 1201(b) for facilitating infringement. These liability rules are subject to the numerous detailed limitations and exceptions outlined in the DMCA.

The DMCA contains three key provisions targeting the circumvention of technological protections.[51] The first is subsection 1201(a)(1)(A), the anticircumvention provision, which prohibits a person from circumventing a technological measure that effectively controls access to a copyrighted work. This provision states: "No person shall circumvent a technological measure that effectively controls access to a work protected under this title. The prohibition contained in the preceding sentence shall take effect at the end of the 2–year period beginning on the date of the enactment of this chapter." The statute defines the term "circumvent a technological measure" as follows: "to descramble a scrambled work, to decrypt an encrypted work, or otherwise to avoid, bypass, remove, deactivate, or impair a technological measure, without the authority of the copyright owner." A technological measure "effectively controls access to a work" when the measure "in the ordinary course of its operation, requires the application of information, or a process or a treatment, with the authority of the copyright owner, to gain access to the work."

The second and third provisions are subsections 1201(a)(2) and 1201(b)(1), the anti-trafficking provisions. Section 1201(a)(2) states: "No person shall manufacture, import, offer to the public, provide, or otherwise traffic in any technology, product, service, device,

---

51. For commentary on the DMCA, see Thomas F. Cotter, The Procompetitive Interest in Intellectual Property Law, 48 Wm. & Mary L. Rev. 483 (2006) (discussing price discrimination rationale for copyright owner's policy, and providing competition framework for misuse and other Intellectual Property doctrines); Molly Torsen, Lexmark, Watermarks, Skylink and Marketplaces: Misuse and Misperception of the Digital Millennium Copyright Act's Anticircum-vention Provision, 4 Chi.-Kent J. Intell. Prop. 117 (2004) ("The DMCA was intended to bring copyright law up to speed with technological advances. It was not meant to add a sui generis anticircumvention claim for reverse-engineering, nor was it meant to chill competition by eradicating competitors who depend on reverse-engineering."); David Nimmer, A Riff on Fair Use in the Digital Millennium Copyright Act, 148 U. Pa. L. Rev. 673 (2000).

component, or part thereof, that—(A) is primarily designed or produced for the purpose of circumventing a technological measure that effectively controls access to a work protected under this title; (B) has only limited commercially significant purpose or use other than to circumvent a technological measure that effectively controls access to a work protected under this title; or (C) is marketed by that person or another acting in concert with that person with that person's knowledge for use in circumventing a technological measure that effectively controls access to a work protected under this title." Section 1201(b)(1) states:

> No person shall manufacture, import, offer to the public, provide, or otherwise traffic in any technology, product, service, device, component, or part thereof, that—
>
> > (A) is primarily designed or produced for the purpose of circumventing protection afforded by a technological measure that effectively protects a right of a copyright owner under this title in a work or a portion thereof;
> >
> > (B) has only limited commercially significant purpose or use other than to circumvent protection afforded by a technological measure that effectively protects a right of a copyright owner under this title in a work or a portion thereof; or
> >
> > (C) is marketed by that person or another acting in concert with that person with that person's knowledge for use in circumventing protection afforded by a technological measure that effectively protects a right of a copyright owner under this title in a work or a portion thereof.
>
> (2) As used in this subsection—
>
> > (A) to "circumvent protection afforded by a technological measure" means avoiding, bypassing, removing, deactivating, or otherwise impairing a technological measure; and
> >
> > (B) a technological measure "effectively protects a right of a copyright owner under this title" if the measure, in the ordinary course of its operation, prevents, restricts, or otherwise limits the exercise of a right of a copyright owner under this title.

An early case interpreting the DMCA is *Universal City Studios, Inc. v. Reimerdes.*[52] In that case, movie studios sought an injunction under the DMCA to prohibit illegal copying of DVDs. Each motion picture DVD contained a content scrambling system (CSS), which allowed the movie to be played on DVD players, but not copied. The defendant's website allowed an individual to download DeCSS, a

---

52. 111 F. Supp. 2d 294 (S.D.N.Y. 2000), *aff'd sub nom. Universal City Stu-* *dios, Inc. v. Corley*, 273 F.3d 429 (2d Cir. 2001).

program that enabled the user to circumvent the CSS protective system and to copy or play the motion picture on any DVD player/recorder. The defendant viewed his conduct as "electronic civil disobedience." The court found that the defendant had violated section 1201(a)(2)(A), as the sole purpose of DeCSS was to decrypt the copy protection measures of CSS.

With regard to a trafficking claim, as the court stated in *Chamberlain v. Skylink*:

> A plaintiff alleging a violation of § 1201(a)(2) must prove: (1) ownership of a valid *copyright* on a work, (2) effectively controlled by a *technological measure,* which has been circumvented, (3) that third parties can now *access* (4) *without authorization,* in a manner that (5) infringes or facilitates infringing a right *protected* by the Copyright Act, because of a product that (6) the defendant either (i) *designed or produced* primarily for circumvention; (ii) made available despite only *limited commercial significance* other than circumvention; or (iii) *marketed* for use in circumvention of the controlling technological measure.[53]

Chamberlain involved replacement garage door openers that contained copyrighted software code. The court held:

> Chamberlain ... has failed to show not only the requisite lack of authorization, but also the necessary fifth element of its claim, the critical nexus between access and protection. Chamberlain neither alleged copyright infringement nor explained how the access provided by the Model 39 transmitter facilitates the infringement of any right that the Copyright Act protects. There can therefore be no reasonable relationship between the access that homeowners gain to Chamberlain's copyrighted software when using Skylink's Model 39 transmitter and the protections that the Copyright Act grants to Chamberlain. The Copyright Act authorized Chamberlain's customers to use the copy of Chamberlain's copyrighted software embedded in the GDOs that they purchased. Chamberlain's customers are therefore immune from § 1201(a)(1) circumvention liability. In the absence of allegations of either copyright infringement or § 1201(a)(1) circumvention, Skylink cannot be liable for § 1201(a)(2) trafficking. The District Court's grant of summary judgment in Skylink's favor was correct. Chamberlain failed to allege a claim under 17 U.S.C. § 1201.

Another leading case on this topic is *Lexmark Intern., Inc. v. Static Control Components, Inc.*[54] Lexmark sold toner cartridges for its printers that only Lexmark could refill. The devices contained a

53. 381 F.3d 1178, 1203 (Fed. Cir. 2004) (emphasis in the original).

54. 387 F.3d 522 (6th Cir. 2004).

microchip designed to prevent Lexmark printers from functioning with toner cartridges that Lexmark had not refilled. The defendant Static Control Components (SCC) mimicked Lexmark's computer chip and sold it to companies interested in selling refilled toner cartridges. Once again, this attempt to use the DMCA to prevent competing products from entering the market was unsuccessful.

Despite the attempt by some copyright owners to extend the DMCA beyond its original purpose, the statute does seem to fill a gap in the law and does provide copyright owners with a way to help protect their rights. In 2012, a new controversy erupted regarding the Stop On–Line Piracy Act (SOPA) and the Protect Intellectual Property Act (PIPA). These proposed bills were designed to improve enforcement of IP rights, particularly with regard to entities operating abroad. It included provisions dealing with payment processing, as well as obligations for website operators and search engines. After a massive response from Silicon Valley companies and Internet users, who argued that these bills would stifle commerce and discourse on the Internet, much of the congressional support for SOPA and PIPA dissolved. Opponents of SOPA and PIPA have proposed an alternative to address some of the concerns of copyright owners, the Online Protection and Enforcement of Digital Trade Act (OPEN Act). As of this writing, no legislation has been enacted to address these issues.

¶ 4.05　Preemption

Basic constitutional law provides the general rule that federal law preempts conflicting state and local laws under the Supremacy Clause, which states: "This Constitution, and the Laws of the United States which shall be made in Pursuance thereof; and all Treaties made, or which shall be made, under the Authority of the United States, shall be the supreme Law of the Land; and the Judges in every State shall be bound thereby, any Thing in the Constitution or Laws of any State to the Contrary notwithstanding."[55]

There are several types of preemption—express, implied, and field preemption. Express preemption deals with statutory provisions that identify the extent to which federal law governs a particular field.[56] Implied preemption occurs when there is a conflict between state and federal law, even though the federal law does not expressly preclude state regulation.[57] Field preemption involves an area in which Congress has so pervasively regulated

---

55. U.S. Const. Art. VI cl. 2.

56. *See Cipollone v. Liggett Group, Inc.*, 505 U.S. 504 (1992).

57. *See Silkwood v. Kerr–McGee Corp.*, 464 U.S. 238 (1984).

that it has "occupied the field," precluding state interference with this regulatory scheme.[58]

Section 301 of the Copyright Act provides express guidance regarding the scope of federal copyright preemption of state law. Section 301(a) states:

> On and after January 1, 1978, all legal or equitable rights that are equivalent to any of the exclusive rights within the general scope of copyright as specified by section 106 in works of authorship that are fixed in a tangible medium of expression and come within the subject matter of copyright as specified by sections 102 and 103, whether created before or after that date and whether published or unpublished, are governed exclusively by this title. Thereafter, no person is entitled to any such right or equivalent right in any such work under the common law or statutes of any State.

As this language indicates, state law claims are preempted if they are (1) equivalent to any of the exclusive rights in section 106, (2) involve works of authorship that are fixed in a tangible medium of expression, and (3) fall within the subject matter of copyright. The purpose of this provision was to set forth preemption rules "in the clearest and most unequivocal language possible, so as to foreclose any conceivable misinterpretation ... and to avoid the development of any vague borderline areas between State and Federal protection."[59]

If a state law does not fall within all three parts of these definitions, it is not preempted. Consequently, there is no preemption if the work involves subject matter that is not covered in sections 102 and 103. This would include work that are not fixed in a tangible medium of expression, even if it would be copyrightable subject matter once it was so fixed. Similarly, there is no preemption if the claim involves a right that is not equivalent to any of the exclusive rights specified by section 106. Finally, section 301(a)(4) prevents preemption of state and local landmarks, historic preservation, zoning, or building codes, as these might otherwise be called into question given copyright's protection for architectural works in section 102(a)(8).

Professor Joseph Bauer has written an excellent article discussing the lack of clarity in the copyright preemption field in spite of the enactment of section 301. He concludes:

> § 301 is intended to advance uniformity in the scope of copyright protection by bringing the vast majority of copyright law

---

58. *See Commonwealth of Pennsylvania v. Nelson*, 350 U.S. 497 (1956).

59. H.R. Rep. No. 94–1476, at 130 (1976), reprinted in 1976 U.S.C.C.A.N. 5659, 5746.

within a single, federal regime. This goal requires yielding to the judgments made by Congress about the kinds of copyright-like works for which protection will (and will not) be available; the rights available (and not available) to the owners of these forms of Intellectual Property; the actions that will (and will not) constitute an infringement of those rights; and finally, the remedies that will (and will not) be available in the event of infringement. Express invocation of a strong presumption that federal law will control, and that state law must yield in arguably close situations, should simultaneously advance the policies underlying preemption and advance the goal of certainty spoken of so fondly thirty years ago.[60]

As his article suggests, the boundaries of preemption are unclear, despite the goal of a uniform national copyright policy. Finally, it should be noted that the presence of section 301's express preemption provision does not preclude the possibility of implied preemption under the Supremacy Clause in the event a state law conflicts with the Copyright Act.[61]

---

60. Joseph P. Bauer, Addressing the Incoherency of the Preemption Provision of the Copyright Act of 1976, 10 VAND. J. OF ENT. & TECH. L. 1, 118–19 (2007).

61. *See generally Goldstein v. California*, 412 U.S. 546, 554–55 (1973).

Chapter 5

COPYRIGHT DEFENSES

Table of Sections

¶ 5.01   Overview

Defending a copyright case involves a number of strategies. First, a defendant can assert that the plaintiff's work is not copyrightable, or that the plaintiff is not the owner or author of the work. This line of defense essentially involved negating elements of the plaintiff's prima facie case. Second, a defendant can assert independent creation, which is a critical defense because copyright only prevents the *copying* of the plaintiff's work. Judge Hand expressed this point eloquently: "Borrowed the work must indeed not be, for a plagiarist is not himself pro tanto an 'author'; but if by some magic a man who had never known it were to compose anew Keats's Ode on a Grecian Urn, he would be an 'author,' and, if he copyrighted it, others might not copy that poem, though they might of course copy Keats's."[1] So if the defendant independently created the work, rather than copying it from the plaintiff's work, there is no copyright violation whatsoever.

Third, it may be possible to defend a case by showing that the two works are similar because they are based on a common source—either a public domain work or a work under copyright protection (albeit raising a possible claim by the owner of that prior

---

1. *Sheldon v. Metro–Goldwyn Pictures Corp.*, 81 F.2d 49, 54 (2d Cir. 1936)   (Hand, J.).

work). Fourth, a defendant may assert that it has been granted an express or implied license to make use of the work, or that it received rights to do so by assignment. Fifth, in the case of a defendant that is a state entity, such as a state university, there may be a defense based on Eleventh Amendment immunity.

Beyond these ways of negating the plaintiff's prima face case, a range of statutory affirmative defenses and limitations on rights can be found in sections 107 to 122 of the Copyright Act. The most far-ranging is probably the fair use defense in section 107. Section 108 provides protections for libraries and archives. Another important defense is first sale, which is codified in section 109 of the Copyright Act. Section 110 provides a panoply of defenses and limitations on claims involving public performances and displays. The remaining provisions address a variety of specific contexts. In defending a copyright case, it is important to survey the entire range of defenses and limitations on the rights of the copyright owner to assure that every possible line of defense has been identified.

¶ 5.02   The Fair Use Defense (Section 107)

The starting point in any fair use analysis is the language of the fair use statute, which is § 107 of the Copyright Act. This provision states in full:

> Notwithstanding the provisions of sections 106 and 106A, the fair use of a copyrighted work, including such use by reproduction in copies or phonorecords or by any other means specified in that section, for purposes such as criticism, comment, news reporting, teaching (including multiple copies for classroom use), scholarship, or research, is not an infringement of copyright.

> In determining whether the use made of a work in any particular case is a fair use the factors to be considered shall include—

>> the purpose and character of the use, including whether such use is of a commercial nature or is for nonprofit educational purposes;

>> the nature of the copyrighted work;

>> the amount and substantiality of the portion used in relation to the copyrighted work as a whole; and

>> the effect of the use upon the potential market for or value of the copyrighted work.

> The fact that a work is unpublished shall not itself bar a finding of fair use if such finding is made upon consideration of all the above factors.

As clearly specified in the introductory phase, "notwithstanding the provisions of § 106 and § 106A," the fair use defense applies to any claim of infringement of any of the exclusive rights of copyrights owners, including the five rights found in section 106—the rights of reproduction, distribution, creating derivative works, public performance, and public display. Section 107 fair use is also a defense of moral rights provisions in section 106A. Thus, if the plaintiff has established a prima facie moral rights violation, it is possible for the defendant to claim that the alleged violation was in some way a fair use. This much is clear from the express terms of the statute itself.

Nonetheless, there is considerable confusion regarding the application and scope of the fair use defense. Some of uncertainty arises because of the language of the first sentence in § 107. This first sentence identifies a number of particular favored purposes, including criticism, comment, news reporting, teaching, scholarship, and research. Many people assume that the fair use defense therefore is a safe harbor or absolute defense, so long as one of the *favored* purposes is implicated. But this is clearly not the law. Instead these are merely favored purposes which are considered in the multi-factor balancing analysis found in the second sentence of § 107 of Copyright Act.

The second sentence of the copyright fair use provision truly determines the manner and scope of the fair use analysis. This provision identifies four factors that are included in a case-by-case analysis of the fair use defense. As will be clear from the fair use cases discussed shortly, each factor must be analyzed in each particular case, and there are no absolute or per se fair use situations.

In considering the role of fair use, there are a number of background points that should be kept in mind. The first is the history of the fair use defense. The fair use defense originated as a judge-made equitable determination that a particular taking was not actionable under the copyright laws as they existed prior to the 1976 Copyright Act. "[S]ince the doctrine is an equitable rule of reason, no generally applicable definition is possible, and each case raising the question must be decided on its own facts."[2] Congress codified fair use when it enacted § 107 in the Copyright Act of 1976. So that is the first time that the fair use factors were specifically identified and the fair use defense itself was statutorily enacted. The legislative history indicates that Congress did not intend to narrow or broaden fair use from its common law provenance, and for it to continue to develop in a common law manner:

2. H.R. Rep. No. 1476, at 65 (1976),   5679.
reprinted in 1976 U.S.C.C.A.N. 5659,

"The bill endorses the purpose and general scope of the judicial doctrine of fair use, but there is no disposition to freeze the doctrine in the statute...."[3]

In analyzing this congressional enactment, it is useful to consider some of the legislative history, including the 1976 House Report, which gives a clear indication of some of the typical situations in which fair use can be found. These include a book review or movie review which quotes excerpts for purposes of comment or illustration. Another typical example identified in the House Report is quotation of passages from a scholarly work, such as quotes contained in a law review article, citing and quoting from earlier law review commentary. Parody is also mentioned as possible defense where some of the content of a prior work may be included. Another example is a news report which includes a summary and brief quotations from a speech or an article. In the case of a library, Congress identifies the possibility that the library might reproduce a portion of a copyrighted work to replace a damaged copy. And in the context of education settings, copying of a small part of the work to discuss a particular educational point can be a fair use. Next, the House Report identifies the possibility of reproducing a part of a work in a court or legislative proceeding or report. Finally, it identifies the possibility that a work might incidently and fortuitously appear in a news reel or a broadcast of a work. This last example involves a case in which a camera is panning across a scene in which a copyrighted work happens to appear briefly in the background, but it is not the purpose of the camera operator to depict the background copyrighted work.[4]

What is clear from these examples is that they are *very minimal uses* for very specific favored purposes of a very small amount of a prior copyrighted work. Fair use is valuable when very small segments of a copyrighted work, such as a song or a film, are used on a one-time basis for educational or other non-profit purposes. In these instances, copyright owners sometimes demand large sums ($500 to $5000 or more) for uses that very likely fall within the fair use defense.[5]

The more difficult cases involve more substantial takings of copyrighted works. In order to analyze a closer or more difficult type of case, it necessary to review the trilogy of Supreme Court

3. *Id.* at 66. *See, e.g., Triangle Publ'ns, Inc. v. Knight–Ridder Newspapers, Inc.,* 626 F.2d 1171, 1174 (5th Cir. 1980) ("Congress made clear that it in no way intended to depart from Court-created principles or to short-circuit further judicial development....").

4. H.R. Rep. No. 1476, at 65.

5. *See* R.S. Talab, Commonsense Copyright: A Guide for Educators & Librarians, at xi (McFarland 2000). On the other hand, the Los Angeles school district settled a copyright infringement claim brought by software companies; the school district paid out $300,000 to avoid the cost of litigation. *Id.*

decisions beginning with *Sony Corp. v. Universal City Studios*.[6] Considerable background information is necessary to really understand the *Sony* case. In particular the key background point relates not to fair use, but to the issue of when the manufacturer of a machine can be liable for uses to which a consumer might place the machine. In this case, the machine was the Sony Beta–Max, which is an early version a video cassette recorder. Many people used the Sony Beta–Max in order to record movies that they saw on live free broadcast television for the purpose of reviewing them at a later time. Some of these consumers would then record over the movies, effectively erasing their copy, a practice known as "time shifting." Other consumers would keep the recorded copies, a much more legally questionable practice known as "librarying." And some consumers no doubt used the Sony machine to make multiple counterfeit copies of the movies, which would clearly constitute a violation of copyright law by the individual consumer.

The central issue in this case, therefore, was whether Sony could be responsible under the Copyright Act for the actions of consumers. The Court determined that, in order to decide that issue, it was necessary to consider whether the Sony Beta–Max recorder had substantial non-infringing uses. This issue was important because any device might well be used to create an infringing copyrighted work. For example, a photocopying machine can be used to duplicate a copyrighted work, but no one would seriously suggest that the manufacturer of the photocopier should be responsible for that action, because of the substantial legitimate uses for the photocopier. And so the question the Court was trying to decide in *Sony* is whether the Beta–Max videotape recorder had substantial, non-infringing uses.

Not surprisingly, Sony argued that there were a number of non-infringing uses. One of these is the copying of public domain works which obviously would not be under copyright protection. A second use is the copying of works where the copyright owner does not object to private home taping of the work. And this in the record was found to be the case for things such as the Mr. Rogers' television show and a number of sports programs, in which the copyright owner did not object to copying as long as it was solely for personal home use. The Court did not stop here, essentially because these two particular uses were not a substantial part of the material consumers actually copied using the Beta–Max recorder.

The Court thus turned to the practice of time-shifting. Time-shifting is the copying of a broadcast movie for later viewing by the consumer at home, and it is presumed that the consumer erases or records over the copyrighted movie and reuses the blank tape.

---

6. 464 U.S. 417 (1984).

Accordingly, no permanent copy of the movie is kept by the consumer. The Court addressed whether this particular practice constitutes a fair use. The Court concluded that time-shifting is a fair use, based on an application of the four factors in section 107. In particular, the Court emphasized that the consumers were not making use of these works for any commercial purpose, but rather solely for home use. The Court also stressed that the movies that were being recorded were being broadcast free of charge and were made available to consumers for their home viewing. It was difficult to see any true harm that would injure the interest of the copyright owners because the movies were already licensed by television broadcasters for free public viewing.

In short, the consumers were simply recording the movie that they were entitled to see and viewing it at a later time. They would then destroy that copy, so there were no continuing existing copies which might be used for other purposes. In sum, the Court in analyzing the fair use factors concluded that time-shifting was a fair use and was a substantial part of how the Sony Beta–Max machine was actually used by consumers. Therefore, Sony was not liable under the Copyright Act for any other infringing uses that consumers might make of their machine—such as librarying or large-scale counterfeiting.

The second major Supreme Court case addressing fair use is *Harper & Row v. Nation Enterprises*.[7] This case involved President Gerald Ford's memoir, which was called "A Time to Heal." "A Time to Heal" was in the publication process at Harper & Row when someone stole a copy of the Ford manuscript and brought it to the attention of the editor of the Nation magazine, Victor Navasky. Navasky obtained this copy with full knowledge that it was a purloined manuscript and quickly reviewed the document, selecting interesting quotations from the book, and then rapidly returning the manuscript to the person from whom he had received it.

Navasky wrote an article which discussed some of the key elements in the Ford memoir—most importantly President Ford's impressions and thoughts in connection with Ford's pardon of former President Richard Nixon. This publication in the *Nation* magazine resulted in the cancellation of a 7,500–word authorized excerpt that *Time* magazine had licensed from Harper & Row for $25,000. In light of the *Nation*'s publication, *Time* cancelled the contract. Harper & Row then brought suit claiming copyright infringement. The *Nation* defended by saying its article was protected news reporting under the First Amendment, and that it was a fair use under section 107.

---

7. 471 U.S. 539 (1985).

The *Nation* case is a perfect illustration of the proposition that just because a particular defendant's activities fall within a favored purpose—here news reporting—does not necessarily lead to a finding of fair use. The Court engaged in a detailed analysis of each of the four fair use factors. First, the Court found that the purpose of the use was commercial in nature, because the *Nation* magazine was a profit-making venture. Secondly, the character of that use was in bad faith because the editor of the *Nation* magazine knew the manuscript had been stolen.

Second, in looking at the nature of the copyrighted work the Court focused on the fact that it was at that point an unpublished work, and therefore the *Nation* magazine had usurped Harper & Row's right of first publication. In other words, this interfered with the copyright owner's right to decide when the book makes it first published appearance.

Third, the Court found that the excerpts quoted by the *Nation* magazine did not involve a large number of words—indeed no more than about three to four hundred words were taken from the lengthy Ford memoir. This amount was not quantitatively large, which seemingly would buttress the fair use defense. Nonetheless, the Court found that those quoted excerpts were the heart of the work, the most important and significant aspects of the copyrighted book:

> In absolute terms, the words actually quoted were an insubstantial portion of "A Time to Heal." The District Court, however, found that "[T]he Nation took what was essentially the heart of the book." We believe the Court of Appeals erred in overruling the District Judge's evaluation of the qualitative nature of the taking. A Time editor described the chapters on the pardon as "the most interesting and moving parts of the entire manuscript." The portions actually quoted were selected by Mr. Navasky as among the most powerful passages in those chapters.[8]

Finally, as to the effect of the taking on the potential market for the work, the Court identified the very specific harm that resulted when *Time* magazine cancelled its contract for first publication rights of excerpts from the Ford memoir. Taken together and weighing together these factors, the Court concluded that the *Nation* magazine was not entitled to the fair use defense in spite of its news reporting purpose and the factual and the historical nature of President's Ford memoir.

8. *Id.* at 565 (citing *Roy Export Co. Establishment v. Columbia Broadcasting System, Inc.*, 503 F.Supp. 1137, 1145 (S.D.N.Y. 1980) (taking of 55 seconds out of 1 hour and 29–minute film deemed qualitatively substantial)).

The third major Supreme Court decision in fair use trilogy is *Campbell v. Acuff–Rose Music Inc.*[9] This case involves the copyrighted work "Oh Pretty Woman," which is a well-known Roy Orbison song. The defendants in the case, Two Live Crew, a well-known rap group, sought to do a parody version of "Pretty Woman." Two Live Crew's representative approached the owner of the copyright to this work, Acuff–Rose Music, seeking to license the work and offering to credit the copyright owner, but this offer was rebuffed.

Two Live Crew proceeded to record and distribute the song "Pretty Woman," which sold more than a quarter of a million copies that contained substantial elements found in the earlier Orbison work—particularly the phrase, "Oh pretty woman," and the distinctive guitar riff associated with that song. Acuff–Rose then brought suit and claimed copyright infringement. In response, Two Live Crew asserted that this was a fair use situation.

The Court analyzed the fair use question and highlighted the need for each fair use situation to be analyzed on a case-by-case, fact-specific basis. Turning to the first element, the Court found that although Two Live Crew had a commercial purpose, this was not determinative nor did it give rise to a presumption against fair use. This idea of a presumption against fair use for commercial takings was found in language in the *Sony* decision, but the *Campbell* Court specifically rejected the idea that such a presumption exists.

Accordingly, the commercial purpose of Two Live Crew's recording was simply one factor in the fair use analysis. The Court also addressed the character of the use and found that it was transformative. In other words, Two Live Crew substantially altered the Orbison song. In particular, a review of the lyrics of the Two Live Crew's song, which is found in the appendix to the Court opinion, reveals that Two Live Crew succeeded in substantially altering the words to the song, as few words overlapped between the two songs, other than the hook or phrase, "pretty woman."

As to the music, there was a greater overlap because of the repetition of the guitar riff found in the Orbison song, a point the Court later found significant. Analyzing the second factor—the nature of the copyrighted work—the Court found that Orbison's song was creative, but that nearly all parodies try to emulate creative prior works; therefore, this factor was not entitled to great weight.

The Court next considered the amount and substantiality of the taking. Here the court found that Two Live Crew mainly took

9. 510 U.S. 569 (1994).

only what was necessary to bring to mind the original Orbison song, and that this was necessary for the parody to be successful. Still, the Court remanded for consideration of whether the amount of the music taking might have been too great, but it clearly found that the lyrics were substantially changed and that this factor favored Two Live Crew.

Finally, the Court addressed the effect of the use on the potential market. It was undisputed that the Two Live Crew song was not a substitute for the Orbison song, as any music fan would recognize. But the court found that another issue on this point would be whether the Two Live Crew song had an impact on any market for derivative works based on the Orbison song. In particular, the Court was interested in the question of whether a market existed for a rap derivative version of the Orbison song, and that this theoretical market might be harmed by Two Live Crew's recording. And so the Court remanded on this issue as well. Many people read *Campbell v. Acuff–Rose* to be a blanket protection for parodies. But a careful reading of *Campbell* reveals that it simply requires a case-by-case consideration of a parody situation, just as it does for any fair use case. Indeed, as the Court stated:

> The fact that parody can claim legitimacy for some appropriation does not, of course, tell either parodist or judge much about where to draw the line. Like a book review quoting the copyrighted material criticized, parody may or may not be fair use, and petitioners' suggestion that any parodic use is presumptively fair has no more justification in law or fact than the equally hopeful claim that any use for news reporting should be presumed fair, *see Harper & Row.* The Act has no hint of an evidentiary preference for parodists over their victims, and no workable presumption for parody could take account of the fact that parody often shades into satire when society is lampooned through its creative artifacts, or that a work may contain both parodic and nonparodic elements. Accordingly, parody, like any other use, has to work its way through the relevant factors, and be judged case by case, in light of the ends of the copyright law.[10]

The Court also rejected the idea that, because the parody was commercial in nature, it should presumed to be harmful and unfair:

> No "presumption" or inference of market harm that might find support in *Sony* is applicable to a case involving something beyond mere duplication for commercial purposes. *Sony*'s discussion of a presumption contrasts a context of verbatim copying of the original in its entirety for commercial purposes, with the noncommercial context of *Sony* itself (home copying of

---

10. *Id.* at 581 (citation omitted).

television programming). In the former circumstances, what *Sony* said simply makes common sense: when a commercial use amounts to mere duplication of the entirety of an original, it clearly "supersede[s] the objects" of the original and serves as a market replacement for it, making it likely that cognizable market harm to the original will occur. But when, on the contrary, the second use is transformative, market substitution is at least less certain, and market harm may not be so readily inferred. Indeed, as to parody pure and simple, it is more likely that the new work will not affect the market for the original in a way cognizable under this factor, that is, by acting as a substitute for it ("supersed[ing] [its] objects"). This is so because the parody and the original usually serve different market functions.[11]

In this respect it reversed the lower court's decision that appeared to be weighted against commercial parodies. The Court also noted that there is a distinction between harm to copyright owners resulting from duplication of their works versus non-cognizable harm from a scathing critique or a biting parody:

> We do not, of course, suggest that a parody may not harm the market at all, but when a lethal parody, like a scathing theater review, kills demand for the original, it does not produce a harm cognizable under the Copyright Act. Because "parody may quite legitimately aim at garroting the original, destroying it commercially as well as artistically," the role of the courts is to distinguish between "[b]iting criticism [that merely] suppresses demand [and] copyright infringement[, which] usurps it." ... This distinction between potentially remediable displacement and unremediable disparagement is reflected in the rule that there is no protectible derivative market for criticism. The market for potential derivative uses includes only those that creators of original works would in general develop or license others to develop. Yet the unlikelihood that creators of imaginative works will license critical reviews or lampoons of their own productions removes such uses from the very notion of a potential licensing market.[12]

Finally, the Court was also careful to indicate that a full analysis required a complete case-by-case assessment, and the remand on the particular issues discussed above suggest that the result would be unclear. The Court concluded:

> Although 2 Live Crew submitted uncontroverted affidavits on the question of market harm to the original, neither they, nor

---

11. *Id.* at 591 (citations omitted).

12. *Id.* at 591–92 (citing Benjamin Kaplan, An Unhurried View of Copyright 69 (1967)).

Acuff–Rose, introduced evidence or affidavits addressing the
likely effect of 2 Live Crew's parodic rap song on the market
for a nonparody, rap version of "Oh, Pretty Woman." And
while Acuff–Rose would have us find evidence of a rap market
in the very facts that 2 Live Crew recorded a rap parody of
"Oh, Pretty Woman" and another rap group sought a license
to record a rap derivative, there was no evidence that a
potential rap market was harmed in any way by 2 Live Crew's
parody, rap version. The fact that 2 Live Crew's parody sold as
part of a collection of rap songs says very little about the
parody's effect on a market for a rap version of the original,
either of the music alone or of the music with its lyrics. . . . [I]t
is impossible to deal with the fourth factor except by recognizing that a silent record on an important factor bearing on fair
use disentitled the proponent of the defense, 2 Live Crew, to
summary judgment. The evidentiary hole will doubtless be
plugged on remand.[13]

Public record documents indicate that the *Campbell* case was
settled on confidential terms, so there is no further decision on the
remand issues.

The trilogy of Supreme Court fair use cases provides a temp-
late for analyzing any fair use case. Many lower court decisions
have addressed fair use scenarios, and it is useful to survey a small
selection of these cases to assess how courts have applied the case-
by-case fair use standard in some typical fact patterns. The key
take-away, however, is that it is very difficult to predict the
outcome of a fair use analysis with any degree of certainty.

An important Internet fair use case is *Kelly v. Arriba Soft
Corp.*[14] Arriba Soft developed a searchable database of photographs,
which were displayed in reduced-size form, known as thumbnails. A
user would enter a search for a photograph, such as one of a dog,
and the search engine would then display various thumbnail images
of dogs. If the user wanted to see the image in full size, Arriba's site
would permit the user to click on the thumbnail, which then
directed the user to the original website on which the image was
displayed. In a photographer's copyright suit against Arriba, the
Ninth Circuit held that the use of thumbnails was fair use. Although Arriba's site was commercial in nature and did reproduce
entire photographs, it did so in reduced thumbnail form, which the
court found was transformative and was not exploitative in purpose
or effect. With regard to the second fair use factor, the photographer's works were creative, but were also published. Even though
the entire work was copied, no more was taken than necessary

13. *Id.* at 593–94.   14.   336 F.3d 811 (9th Cir. 2003).

given the goal of Arriba's site. Finally, with regard to the market impact of the use, the court found that Arriba's site would not supplant the market for the originals, and indeed the site would direct users to the photographer's site, on which the photograph was displayed in its original form. Moreover, it was unlikely that the thumbnails could be used to make printed copies of the photographs, given the very low resolution quality of the thumbnail image.

The widely used search engine provider, Google, has been the subject of a number of copyright cases. In *Field v. Google*,[15] the court held that Google's practice of having an archived or "cached" copy of articles found on the Internet was fair use. Even though the articles could be found in full text, the court held that having an archived copy available was beneficial given that the original work was often no longer accessible. Moreover, the copyright owner had made his works available on the Internet, even though he had then removed them (apparently in part to prevent Google from merely linking to his site, which would clearly have been permissible).

A second Google-related case is *Perfect 10, Inc. v. Amazon.com, Inc.*[16] The Ninth Circuit reaffirmed its favorable view of search engines, noting that "a search engine may be more transformative than a parody, ... because a search engine provides an entirely new use of the original work, while a parody typically has the same entertainment purpose as the original work."[17] Finally, Google is currently in protracted litigation regarding its Google Library Project, which has provoked litigation as it involves Google's attempt to digitally scan books into a searchable database without the consent of the copyright owners.

The use of a copyrighted work for compatibility purposes can constitute a fair use. For example, as the court held in *Sega Enterprises Ltd. v. Accolade, Inc.*,[18] when a defendant needed to make a copy of the copyrighted source code for compatibility/reverse engineering purposes, "intermediate copying" of the operating system constituted a fair use.

One important ruling that is a post-script to the *Sony* case is the Audio Home Recording Act of 1992 ("AHRA"). This law specifically allows home audio taping, required device makers to incorporate some copy controls, and imposed a royalty on device manufacturers to compensate copyright owners. Although this law might

---

15. 412 F. Supp. 2d 1106, 1114–23 (D. Nev. 2006).

16. 487 F.3d 701 (9th Cir. 2007).

17. *Id.* at 721.

18. 977 F.2d 1510, 1520–28 (9th Cir. 1992). *See also Sony Computer Entertainment, Inc. v. Connectix Corp.*, 203 F.3d 596, 602–08 (9th Cir. 2000); *Bateman v. Mnemonics, Inc.*, 79 F.3d 1532, 1539–40 n. 18 (11th Cir. 1996); *Atari Games Corp. v. Nintendo of America, Inc.*, 975 F.2d 832, 842–44 (Fed.Cir. 1992).

appear to be of present importance, it is virtually obsolete because the technology addressed in the AHRA, digital audio tapes, has basically disappeared from the marketplace and has been supplanted by newer technologies that are not covered by the AHRA.

In sum, fair use is one of the most complicated, unpredictable, and enigmatic doctrines in the copyright field. It has been viewed by commentators and by the Supreme Court as one of the bulwarks of free expression and as an important accommodation of the public's right to gain access to limited amounts of material in copyrighted works. Because it involves a multi-factor balancing test that is to be applied on a case-by-case basis with no apparent presumptions for or against any particular types of uses, the fair use analysis is inherently unpredictable in all but the most clear-cut cases. It is essentially a test of reasonableness in the circumstances. Probably one of the few guides that might help predict the likely outcome of a fair use case is the concept that fair use is designed to protect uses of copyrighted material that generally do not supplant the market for a particular work. Consequently, if the defendant has taken so much that it allows a reader or viewer to forgo the original work completely, it is likely that no fair use will be found. Similarly, courts consider derivative markets for a work, so that a translation of a popular copyrighted work from English to French would supplant a likely derivative market for that work.

¶ 5.03   Libraries & Archives (Section 108)

Libraries and archives have particularly strong arguments for special protections from copyright infringement liability, given their critical role as repositories and disseminators of information and their non-profit status. Section 108 of the Copyright Act contains very specific protections for these institutions.

Section 108(a) allows the making of *a single copy* of a work, for example for library or archival use:

> Except as otherwise provided in this title and notwithstanding the provisions of section 106, it is not an infringement of copyright for a library or archives, or any of its employees acting within the scope of their employment, to reproduce no more than one copy or phonorecord of a work, except as provided in subsections (b) and (c), or to distribute such copy or phonorecord, under the conditions specified by this section, if—
>
> (1) the reproduction or distribution is made without any purpose of direct or indirect commercial advantage;
>
> (2) the collections of the library or archives are (i) open to the public, or (ii) available not only to researchers affiliated with the library or archives or with the institution of which it is a

part, but also to other persons doing research in a specialized field; and

(3) the reproduction or distribution of the work includes a notice of copyright that appears on the copy or phonorecord that is reproduced under the provisions of this section, or includes a legend stating that the work may be protected by copyright if no such notice can be found on the copy or phonorecord that is reproduced under the provisions of this section.

Section 108(b) and (c) allow copying for preservation and replacement purposes:

(b) The rights of reproduction and distribution under this section apply to three copies or phonorecords of an unpublished work duplicated solely for purposes of preservation and security or for deposit for research use in another library or archives of the type described by clause (2) of subsection (a), if—

(1) the copy or phonorecord reproduced is currently in the collections of the library or archives; and

(2) any such copy or phonorecord that is reproduced in digital format is not otherwise distributed in that format and is not made available to the public in that format outside the premises of the library or archives.

(c) The right of reproduction under this section applies to three copies or phonorecords of a published work duplicated solely for the purpose of replacement of a copy or phonorecord that is damaged, deteriorating, lost, or stolen, or if the existing format in which the work is stored has become obsolete, if—

(1) the library or archives has, after a reasonable effort, determined that an unused replacement cannot be obtained at a fair price; and

(2) any such copy or phonorecord that is reproduced in digital format is not made available to the public in that format outside the premises of the library or archives in lawful possession of such copy.

For purposes of this subsection, a format shall be considered obsolete if the machine or device necessary to render perceptible a work stored in that format is no longer manufactured or is no longer reasonably available in the commercial marketplace.

Additional reproduction and distribution privileges are provided in section 108(d)–(e):

(d) The rights of reproduction and distribution under this section apply to a copy, made from the collection of a library or archives where the user makes his or her request or from that of another library or archives, of no more than one article or other contribution to a copyrighted collection or periodical issue, or to a copy or phonorecord of a small part of any other copyrighted work, if—

(1) the copy or phonorecord becomes the property of the user, and the library or archives has had no notice that the copy or phonorecord would be used for any purpose other than private study, scholarship, or research; and

(2) the library or archives displays prominently, at the place where orders are accepted, and includes on its order form, a warning of copyright in accordance with requirements that the Register of Copyrights shall prescribe by regulation.

(e) The rights of reproduction and distribution under this section apply to the entire work, or to a substantial part of it, made from the collection of a library or archives where the user makes his or her request or from that of another library or archives, if the library or archives has first determined, on the basis of a reasonable investigation, that a copy or phonorecord of the copyrighted work cannot be obtained at a fair price, if—

(1) the copy or phonorecord becomes the property of the user, and the library or archives has had no notice that the copy or phonorecord would be used for any purpose other than private study, scholarship, or research; and

(2) the library or archives displays prominently, at the place where orders are accepted, and includes on its order form, a warning of copyright in accordance with requirements that the Register of Copyrights shall prescribe by regulation.

Section 108(f) addresses the use of photocopying equipment by patrons, indicating that the patron but not the library or archive can be liable for these activities taking place if certain conditions are met:

Nothing in this section—

(1) shall be construed to impose liability for copyright infringement upon a library or archives or its employees for the unsupervised use of reproducing equipment located on its premises: Provided, That such equipment displays a notice that the making of a copy may be subject to the copyright law;

(2) excuses a person who uses such reproducing equipment or who requests a copy or phonorecord under subsection (d) from liability for copyright infringement for any such

act, or for any later use of such copy or phonorecord, if it exceeds fair use as provided by section 107. . . .

Under this provision, libraries regularly post notices in photocopying areas so as to invoke this safe harbor. Section 108(g) addresses repeated copying of the same work:

The rights of reproduction and distribution under this section extend to the isolated and unrelated reproduction or distribution of a single copy or phonorecord of the same material on separate occasions, but do not extend to cases where the library or archives, or its employee—

(1) is aware or has substantial reason to believe that it is engaging in the related or concerted reproduction or distribution of multiple copies or phonorecords of the same material, whether made on one occasion or over a period of time, and whether intended for aggregate use by one or more individuals or for separate use by the individual members of a group; or

(2) engages in the systematic reproduction or distribution of single or multiple copies or phonorecords of material described in subsection (d): Provided, That nothing in this clause prevents a library or archives from participating in interlibrary arrangements that do not have, as their purpose or effect, that the library or archives receiving such copies or phonorecords for distribution does so in such aggregate quantities as to substitute for a subscription to or purchase of such work.

In the last twenty years of a published work's copyright term, if copies of the work are not available at a reasonable price, section 108(h)(1) permits libraries and archives to make, distribute, display, and perform copies of the work for purposes of preservation, scholarship, or research:

For purposes of this section, during the last 20 years of any term of copyright of a published work, a library or archives, including a nonprofit educational institution that functions as such, may reproduce, distribute, display, or perform in facsimile or digital form a copy or phonorecord of such work, or portions thereof, for purposes of preservation, scholarship, or research, if such library or archives has first determined, on the basis of a reasonable investigation, that none of the conditions set forth in subparagraphs (A), (B), and (C) of paragraph (2) apply.

(2) No reproduction, distribution, display, or performance is authorized under this subsection if—(A) the work is subject to normal commercial exploitation; (B) a copy or

phonorecord of the work can be obtained at a reasonable price; or (C) the copyright owner or its agent provides notice pursuant to regulations promulgated by the Register of Copyrights that either of the conditions set forth in subparagraphs (A) and (B) applies.

(3) The exemption provided in this subsection does not apply to any subsequent uses by users other than such library or archives.

This provision reflects Congress' attempt to ameliorate the effect of the Sonny Bono Amendment's twenty-year extension of copyright terms.

Finally, section 108(i) precludes library and archival reproduction of certain specified types of works under this exemption: "The rights of reproduction and distribution under this section do not apply to a musical work, a pictorial, graphic or sculptural work, or a motion picture or other audiovisual work other than an audiovisual work dealing with news, except that no such limitation shall apply with respect to rights granted by subsections (b), (c), and (h), or with respect to pictorial or graphic works published as illustrations, diagrams, or similar adjuncts to works of which copies are reproduced or distributed in accordance with subsections (d) and (e)."

¶ 5.04   The First Sale Doctrine (Section 109)

As noted in the discussion of copyright owner rights under section 106, these rights are limited in a very significant regard by the "first sale" doctrine in section 109 of the Copyright Act. Section 109(a) states: "Notwithstanding the provisions of section 106(3), the owner of a particular copy or phonorecord lawfully made under this title, or any person authorized by such owner, is entitled, without the authority of the copyright owner, to sell or otherwise dispose of the possession of that copy or phonorecord." The first sale doctrine, in effect, allows the market for used copies of works to compete with the market for new versions of the work. This tends to serve as a check on the price of copyrighted works, while at the same time the copyright owner cannot be heard to complain as it has obtained its lawful reward from the first sale of the work. This provision limits the right of public distribution in a very significant way and is discussed in Chapter 4, ¶ 4.02.

Section 109(b) contains industry-specific exceptions to the first sale doctrine—the commercial rental of computer software and of copyrighted music (known in copyright parlance as "phonorecords"). These industry exceptions, along with the even more specific carve-outs for libraries and video game rentals, are also discussed in Chapter 4, ¶ 4.02.

Section 109(c) states: "Notwithstanding the provisions of section 106(5), the owner of a particular copy lawfully made under this title, or any person authorized by such owner, is entitled, without the authority of the copyright owner, to display that copy publicly, either directly or by the projection of no more than one image at a time, to viewers present at the place where the copy is located." This provision places a logical limit on the right of public display, and is discussed in Chapter 4, ¶ 4.02.

Section 109(d) indicates that the first sale privileges set forth in sections 109(a)–(c) do not apply "to any person who has acquired possession of the copy or phonorecord from the copyright owner, by rental, lease, loan, or otherwise, without acquiring ownership of it," unless authorized by the copyright owner. Section 109(e) applies to certain public performances or displays of an electronic audiovisual game intended for use in coin-operated equipment.

The importation of copyrighted works presents a challenging question regarding the scope of the first sale doctrine. Courts have thus far held that the first sale doctrine does not apply to these imported works, because they were not lawfully made under the United States Copyright Act.[19] If an authorized sale of the imported work has been made in the United States, then the first sale doctrine will clearly apply.[20]

Finally, it should be noted that the court in *Vernor v. Autodesk, Inc.*, 621 F.3d 1102 (9th Cir. 2010), held that when copyrighted software is licensed, rather than sold outright, the first sale doctrine (as well as some specific rights granted to software purchasers) may not apply: "We hold today that a software user is a licensee rather than an owner of a copy where the copyright owner (1) specifies that the user is granted a license; (2) significantly restricts the user's ability to transfer the software; and (3) imposes notable use restrictions. Applying our holding to Autodesk's SLA, we conclude that CTA was a licensee rather than an owner of copies of Release 14 and accordingly was not entitled to invoke the first sale doctrine or the essential step defense." In order for a restriction to be binding, however, it must be the result of an agreement between the parties. Thus, in a case involving the resale of promotional CDs distributed with a label stating that the CD is "the property of the record company and is licensed to the intended recipient for personal use only," the label does not preclude a first

---

19. *See John Wiley & Sons, Inc. v. Kirtsaeng*, 654 F.3d 210 (2d Cir. 2011); *Costco Wholesale Corp. v. Omega, S.A.*, 541 F.3d 982 (9th Cir. 2008), *aff'd by an equally divided court*, 131 S.Ct. 565 (2010).

20. *See Denbicare U.S.A., Inc. v. Toys R Us, Inc.*, 84 F.3d 1143 (9th Cir. 1996).

sale defense asserted by someone who obtained the CDs and sold them on Ebay.[21]

¶ 5.05 Limitations of the Rights of Public Performance and Display (Section 110)

Without carefully drawn limits, the rights of public performance and public display would seem to cover a vast array of ordinary situations in which requiring a license and possible payment of royalties seems unwarranted on public policy grounds. Section 110 contains eleven specific exceptions to the public performance and display rights. Each is briefly summarized here.

Section 110(1)'s classroom exception permits "performance or display of a work by instructors or pupils in the course of face-to-face teaching activities of a nonprofit educational institution, in a classroom or similar place devoted to instruction." This exception, in short, allows movies, music, and other works to be played in classroom settings. Absent this exception, showing a movie in class could constitute a public performance. There is one caveat to this exception: with regard to movies and other audiovisual works, the exemption does not apply if the person responsible for the performance knew or had reason to believe the copy of the work was not lawfully made. Consequently, a teacher who shows a bootleg copy of a movie to his or her class would not be exempt from the public performance claim.

Section 110(2) is a counterpart to the classroom exception, providing an exemption for some public performances and displays in the context of distance education. The distance education exemption is designed to provide these educational programs with some of the rights found in traditional classroom settings, while also protecting the legitimate concerns of copyright owners regarding potential infringements that could occur if their works are disseminated via the Internet or other similar technologies. The distance education exception does not apply to works "produced or marketed primarily for performance or display as part of mediated instructional activities transmitted via digital networks." Like the classroom exemption, it also does not apply if the educational program knew or had reason to believe the copy of the work was not lawfully made or acquired. The exemption is also more limited and more difficult to satisfy that the classroom exemption. It only applies in the following detailed requirements are met:

> the performance of a nondramatic literary or musical work or reasonable and limited portions of any other work, or display of a work in an amount comparable to that which is typically

21. *See UMG Recordings, Inc. v. Augusto,* 628 F.3d 1175 (9th Cir. 2011).

displayed in the course of a live classroom session, by or in the course of a transmission, if—

(A) the performance or display is made by, at the direction of, or under the actual supervision of an instructor as an integral part of a class session offered as a regular part of the systematic mediated instructional activities of a governmental body or an accredited nonprofit educational institution;

(B) the performance or display is directly related and of material assistance to the teaching content of the transmission;

(C) the transmission is made solely for, and, to the extent technologically feasible, the reception of such transmission is limited to—

(i) students officially enrolled in the course for which the transmission is made; or

(ii) officers or employees of governmental bodies as a part of their official duties or employment; and

(D) the transmitting body or institution—

(i) institutes policies regarding copyright, provides informational materials to faculty, students, and relevant staff members that accurately describe, and promote compliance with, the laws of the United States relating to copyright, and provides notice to students that materials used in connection with the course may be subject to copyright protection; and

(ii) in the case of digital transmissions—

(I) applies technological measures that reasonably prevent—

(aa) retention of the work in accessible form by recipients of the transmission from the transmitting body or institution for longer than the class session; and

(bb) unauthorized further dissemination of the work in accessible form by such recipients to others; and

(II) does not engage in conduct that could reasonably be expected to interfere with technological measures used by copyright owners to prevent such retention or unauthorized further dissemination. . . .

Section 110(3) is a straightforward exemption for the performance of a nondramatic literary or musical works or of dramatico-musical works of a religious nature, or display of a work, in the course of services at a place of worship or other religious assembly.

Section 110(4) exempts certain non-profit performances of non-dramatic literary or musical works. It is not a general exemption for all such performances. Instead, three requirements must be met: (1) there must be no transmission to the public of the work, (2) there is no purpose of direct or indirect commercial advantage and no payment of any fee or other compensation for the performance to any of its performers, promoters, or organizers, and (3) there is either no direct or indirect admission charge or else the proceeds, after deducting the reasonable costs of producing the performance, are used exclusively for educational, religious, or charitable purposes and not for private financial gain. Moreover, section 110(4) permits the copyright owner to prevent this performance by providing written, signed notice of its objection to the performance to the person responsible for the performance at least seven days before the date of the performance. The notice must state the reasons for the objection and must comply with requirements set forth in regulations promulgated by the Register of Copyrights.

Section 110(5) is perhaps the most important and widely publicized exemption, frequently known as the "home-style" or *Aiken* exception, because it is allows certain home-style performances of works, akin to the factual scenario (under the 1909 Act) in *Twentieth Century Music Corp. v. Aiken*.[22]

> (5)(A) except as provided in subparagraph (B), communication of a transmission embodying a performance or display of a work by the public reception of the transmission on a single receiving apparatus of a kind commonly used in private homes, unless—
>
>> (i) a direct charge is made to see or hear the transmission; or
>>
>> (ii) the transmission thus received is further transmitted to the public;
>
> (B) communication by an establishment of a transmission or retransmission embodying a performance or display of a nondramatic musical work intended to be received by the general public, originated by a radio or television broadcast station licensed as such by the Federal Communications Commission, or, if an audiovisual transmission, by a cable system or satellite carrier, if—

22. 422 U.S. 151 (1975).

(i) in the case of an establishment other than a food service or drinking establishment, either the establishment in which the communication occurs has less than 2,000 gross square feet of space (excluding space used for customer parking and for no other purpose), or the establishment in which the communication occurs has 2,000 or more gross square feet of space (excluding space used for customer parking and for no other purpose) and—

(I) if the performance is by audio means only, the performance is communicated by means of a total of not more than 6 loudspeakers, of which not more than 4 loudspeakers are located in any 1 room or adjoining outdoor space; or

(II) if the performance or display is by audiovisual means, any visual portion of the performance or display is communicated by means of a total of not more than 4 audiovisual devices, of which not more than 1 audiovisual device is located in any 1 room, and no such audiovisual device has a diagonal screen size greater than 55 inches, and any audio portion of the performance or display is communicated by means of a total of not more than 6 loudspeakers, of which not more than 4 loudspeakers are located in any 1 room or adjoining outdoor space;

(ii) in the case of a food service or drinking establishment, either the establishment in which the communication occurs has less than 3,750 gross square feet of space (excluding space used for customer parking and for no other purpose), or the establishment in which the communication occurs has 3,750 gross square feet of space or more (excluding space used for customer parking and for no other purpose) and—

(I) if the performance is by audio means only, the performance is communicated by means of a total of not more than 6 loudspeakers, of which not more than 4 loudspeakers are located in any 1 room or adjoining outdoor space; or

(II) if the performance or display is by audiovisual means, any visual portion of the performance or display is communicated by means of a total of not more than 4 audiovisual devices, of which not more than 1 audiovisual device is located in any 1 room, and no such audiovisual device has a diagonal screen size greater than 55 inches, and any audio portion of the performance or display is communicated by means of a total of not more than 6 loudspeakers, of which not more than 4 loudspeakers are located in any 1 room or adjoining outdoor space;

(iii) no direct charge is made to see or hear the transmission or retransmission;

(iv) the transmission or retransmission is not further transmitted beyond the establishment where it is received; and

(v) the transmission or retransmission is licensed by the copyright owner of the work so publicly performed or displayed.

This exemption includes two terms—which are treated separately—that are defined in section 101 of the Copyright Act:

An "establishment" is a store, shop, or any similar place of business open to the general public for the primary purpose of selling goods or services in which the majority of the gross square feet of space that is nonresidential is used for that purpose, and in which nondramatic musical works are performed publicly.

A "food service or drinking establishment" is a restaurant, inn, bar, tavern, or any other similar place of business in which the public or patrons assemble for the primary purpose of being served food or drink, in which the majority of the gross square feet of space that is nonresidential is used for that purpose, and in which nondramatic musical works are performed publicly.

Clearly, the food service or drinking establishment received more favorable treatment than other ordinary establishments under this provision. Section 101 also indicates that the gross square feet of space of an establishment "means the entire interior space of that establishment, and any adjoining outdoor space used to serve patrons, whether on a seasonal basis or otherwise." This exemption was broadened in the Fairness in Music Licensing Act of 1998, which added section 110(5)(B) to the prior version of the exemption (which is now section 110(5)(A)).

In 2000, the World Trade Organization (WTO) Dispute Panel has found that this broadened exemption violated United States treaty obligations to protect public performance rights. These obligations are found in Articles 9.1 and 13 of the Trade Related Aspects of Intellectual Property (TRIPS) provisions of the WTO Agreement. The exemption has thus far not been amended, and the

United States consequently remains out of compliance with this treaty obligation, despite the passage of more than a dozen years.

International Intellectual Property always involves a delicate balance. One goal is to offer a sufficient level of Intellectual Property protection to enable and protect investment in innovation and creativity. There is also a public interest goal in access to creative works. The foundational treaty, as mentioned, is TRIPS, which provides minimum standards for international protection in the areas of copyright, trademarks, geographical indications, and integrated circuits. This author has written an article contending that the expanded exemption adopted in the Fairness in Music Licensing Act should be abolished and the United States should be brought back into compliance with international agreements protecting basic public performance rights.[23]

Section 110(6) permits the performance of a nondramatic musical work by a governmental body or a nonprofit agricultural or horticultural organization, in the course of an annual agricultural or horticultural fair or exhibition. The exemption specifically extends to any liability for copyright infringement under doctrines of vicarious or other secondary liability resulting from the conduct of a concessionaire, business establishment, or other persons at the fair or exhibition, but does not excuse these direct infringers from liability for the performance.

Section 110(7) permits the performance of a nondramatic musical work by certain retail stores that are promoting and selling copyrighted works, such as record stores, as long as the store is open to the public and imposes no direct or indirect admission charge. The store must not transmit the performance beyond its location and can only play the work within the immediate area where the sale is occurring. Consequently, a large retail store like Wal–Mart or Best Buy can have a song playing in a stereo or a movie playing on television, so long as it is within the area of the store in which movies are sold.

Section 110(8) permits the performance of a nondramatic literary work in the course of a transmission specifically designed for and primarily directed to blind, deaf, or other disabled persons. This provision would allow the broadcast of a program for the hearing or visually impaired, as long as there is no "purpose of direct or indirect commercial advantage and its transmission is made through the facilities of: (i) a governmental body; or (ii) a noncommercial educational broadcast station (as defined in section 397 of title 47); or (iii) a radio subcarrier authorization (as defined

---

23. *See* Gary Myers & George Howard, The Future of Music: Reconfiguring Public Performance Rights, 17 J. Intell. Prop. L. 207 (2010).

in 47 CFR 73.293–73.295 and 73.593–73.595); or (iv) a cable system (as defined in section 111 (f))."[24]

Section 110(9) allows the "performance *on a single occasion* of a dramatic literary work published at least ten years before the date of the performance, by or in the course of a transmission specifically designed for and primarily directed to blind or other handicapped persons who are unable to read normal printed material as a result of their handicap, if the performance is made without any purpose of direct or indirect commercial advantage and its transmission is made through the facilities of a radio subcarrier authorization referred to in clause (8)(iii)."[25] This exemption does not apply to more than one performance of the same work by the same performers or under the auspices of the same organization.

Section 110(10) expands on the exemption found in section 110(4) in the case of a nonprofit veterans' or fraternal organization, such as the Elks Club, Lions Club, or Veterans of Foreign Wars. It provides that "the following is not an infringement of copyright: performance of a nondramatic literary or musical work in the course of a social function which is organized and promoted by a nonprofit veterans' organization or a nonprofit fraternal organization to which the general public is not invited, but not including the invitees of the organizations, if the proceeds from the performance, after deducting the reasonable costs of producing the performance, are used exclusively for charitable purposes and not for financial gain."[26] For purposes of this section, the social functions of any college or university fraternity or sorority are not exempt, unless the social function is held solely to raise funds for a specific charitable purpose.

Section 110(11) was added to the copyright laws in the "Family Entertainment and Copyright Act of 2005." It allows the skipping or silencing of limited portions of a movie, typically by a parent seeking to supervise and prevent viewing or listening to the objectionable content of movies being viewed by their children. The exemption was brought on in response to copyright infringement suits against ClearPlay, a software company that provided parental movie editing services. Although the purpose of the exemption is to allow parental supervision, by its terms the statute could extend to other methods of editing or suppressing some content from a lawful copy of a film.[27] The exemption does not allow the addition of audio or video content that is performed or displayed over or in place of existing content in a motion picture. The exemption also allows the marketing of software to achieve these goals, as long as no fixed

---

24. 17 U.S.C. § 110(8).

25. 17 U.S.C. § 110(9) (emphasis added).

26. 17 U.S.C. § 110(10).

27. 17 U.S.C. § 110(11).

copy of the altered version of the motion picture is created by the computer program.

¶ 5.06   Other Statutory Defenses (Sections 111–122)

Copyright law includes a number of other detailed statutory defenses applicable to particular types of uses. Section 111 regulates secondary transmissions by cable systems, which involve public performances or displays of television broadcasts. A cable system is defined in section 111(f) as "a facility, located in any State, Territory, Trust Territory, or Possession, that in whole or in part receives signals transmitted or programs broadcast by one or more television broadcast stations licensed by the Federal Communications Commission, and makes secondary transmissions of such signals or programs by wires, cables, microwave, or other communications channels to subscribing members of the public who pay for such service."

Section 112 limits exclusive rights with regard to ephemeral recordings. Ephemeral recordings are copies created for the purpose of facilitating a transmission of a public performance of a sound recording under the limitations on exclusive rights specified by section 114(d)(1)(C)(iv) or under a statutory license under section 114(f), and subject to the limitations specified in section 112(e).

Section 113 addresses the scope of exclusive rights in pictorial, graphic, and sculptural works incorporated into useful articles. Among other things sections 113(a) and (b) indicate that the rights of copyright owners in such works are generally neither greater nor less than the rights of owners of copyrighted works. Section 113(c) permits such works to be photographed for certain purposes: "In the case of a work lawfully reproduced in useful articles that have been offered for sale or other distribution to the public, copyright does not include any right to prevent the making, distribution, or display of pictures or photographs of such articles in connection with advertisements or commentaries related to the distribution or display of such articles, or in connection with news reports." Finally, section 113(d) addresses the case of a work of visual art that has been incorporated in or made part of a building.

Section 114 is a complex provision addressing the scope of exclusive rights in sound recordings. Section 114(a), which was discussed in Chapter 6, ¶ 4.06, indicates that there are no general public performance rights in sound recordings: "The exclusive rights of the owner of copyright in a sound recording are limited to the rights specified by clauses (1), (2), (3) and (6) of section 106, and do not include any right of performance under section 106(4)." Section 106(4) is the public performance rights provision. Section

114(b) includes other limitations on the rights of owners of sound recordings:

> The exclusive right of the owner of copyright in a sound recording under clause (1) of section 106 is limited to the right to duplicate the sound recording in the form of phonorecords or copies that directly or indirectly recapture the actual sounds fixed in the recording. The exclusive right of the owner of copyright in a sound recording under clause (2) of section 106 is limited to the right to prepare a derivative work in which the actual sounds fixed in the sound recording are rearranged, remixed, or otherwise altered in sequence or quality. The exclusive rights of the owner of copyright in a sound recording under clauses (1) and (2) of section 106 do not extend to the making or duplication of another sound recording that consists entirely of an independent fixation of other sounds, even though such sounds imitate or simulate those in the copyrighted sound recording. The exclusive rights of the owner of copyright in a sound recording under clauses (1), (2), and (3) of section 106 do not apply to sound recordings included in educational television and radio programs (as defined in section 397 of title 47) distributed or transmitted by or through public broadcasting entities (as defined by section 118(g)): Provided, That copies or phonorecords of said programs are not commercially distributed by or through public broadcasting entities to the general public.

Most of the remaining sections of section 114 address the scope of digital transmission rights in sound recordings, which are recognized by section 106(6) of the Copyright Act, as well as statutory licenses for such works.

Section 115 provides for compulsory licenses for making and distributing phonorecords (i.e., copies) of musical works. This provision permits the creation and distribution of certain specified "cover" versions of songs once the song has been published or distributed to the public by authority of the copyright owner. A compulsory license, as the term implies, can be obtained by following the procedures set forth in this statute and paying the statutorily determined royalties, regardless of whether the copyright owner in the underlying song desires to grant a license or not. The provision authorizes the establishment of a schedule of reasonable rates and terms to be determined by Copyright Royalty Judges.

Section 116 addresses licenses for public performances "by means of coin-operated phonorecord players," better known as jukeboxes.

Section 117 sets forth limitations on exclusive rights in computer programs, including provisions for limited copying and transfer of copies:

(a) Making of Additional Copy or Adaptation by Owner of Copy.—Notwithstanding the provisions of section 106, it is not an infringement for the owner of a copy of a computer program to make or authorize the making of another copy or adaptation of that computer program provided:

(1) that such a new copy or adaptation is created as an essential step in the utilization of the computer program in conjunction with a machine and that it is used in no other manner, or

(2) that such new copy or adaptation is for archival purposes only and that all archival copies are destroyed in the event that continued possession of the computer program should cease to be rightful.

(b) Lease, Sale, or Other Transfer of Additional Copy or Adaptation.—Any exact copies prepared in accordance with the provisions of this section may be leased, sold, or otherwise transferred, along with the copy from which such copies were prepared, only as part of the lease, sale, or other transfer of all rights in the program. Adaptations so prepared may be transferred only with the authorization of the copyright owner.

(c) Machine Maintenance or Repair.—Notwithstanding the provisions of section 106, it is not an infringement for the owner or lessee of a machine to make or authorize the making of a copy of a computer program if such copy is made solely by virtue of the activation of a machine that lawfully contains an authorized copy of the computer program, for purposes only of maintenance or repair of that machine, if—

(1) such new copy is used in no other manner and is destroyed immediately after the maintenance or repair is completed; and

(2) with respect to any computer program or part thereof that is not necessary for that machine to be activated, such program or part thereof is not accessed or used other than to make such new copy by virtue of the activation of the machine.

Section 117(d) defines maintenance of a machine as "the servicing of the machine in order to make it work in accordance with its original specifications and any changes to those specifications authorized for that machine." It defines repair as "the restoring of the machine to the state of working in accordance with its original specifications and any changes to those specifications authorized for that machine."

Computer software presents a variety of important challenges, some of which are addressed by other areas of law, and by contracts in particular. The Uniform Computer Information Transactions Act, or UCITA, a proposed model statute designed to address the enforceability of software licenses, can be found through the website of the National Conference of Commissioners on Uniform State Laws. It has thus far been adopted by only two states, Virginia and Maryland. Much has been written about UCITA, and much of the writing has criticized the statute as being overly protective of copyright interests at the expense of consumers. No additional states have adopted UCITA in recent years. Nonetheless, some restrictions on the use of software may be principally designed to prevent copyright infringement.[28]

For a software company's amusing way to suggest compliance with its copyright registration policy, consider this quote from Alchemy Mindworks, which inspired the title of a law review article, written by Lydia Pallas Loren: "if a user fails to register software downloaded through their web pages 'a leather-winged demon of the night will tear itself, shrieking blood and fury, from the endless caverns of the nether world, hurl itself into the darkness with a thirst for blood on its slavering fangs and search the very threads of time for the throbbing of your heartbeat. Just thought you'd want to know that.' "[29] Loren goes on to suggest that "a rebuttable presumption of misuse should be recognized anytime copyright owners seek, by contract, to avoid the express statutory limitations on their rights. This rebuttable presumption should also arise when the contract attempts to restrict activity that courts have generally recognized to be fair use. To rebut the presumption of misuse, the copyright owner would be required to prove that encouraging the type of contracting behavior at issue is not likely to lead to a reduction of the external benefits the Copyright Act seeks to ensure through the limitation the copyright owner is contractually attempting to avoid."[30]

Section 118 addresses the scope of exclusive rights with regard to the use of certain works in connection with noncommercial

28. *See generally* Theodore Dorenkamp, Copyright Misuse or a Right to Compete?: A Critique of Alcatel USA v. DGI Technologies, 9 TEX. INTELL. PROP. L.J. 269 (2001) (suggesting need for "guidance to copyright holders over the extent to which a license agreement can prevent or refuse third-party access to its software, [given] ... that copyright holders have the freedom to control and restrict access through imposing a cost on the right to use the copyrighted work").

29. Lydia Pallas Loren, Slaying the Leather-Winged Demons in the Night: Reforming Copyright Owner Contracting with Clickwrap Misuse, 30 OHIO N.U. L. REV. 495, 496 (2004) (quoting company's policy).

30. *Id.* at 501.

broadcasting. The provision applies to a public broadcasting entity, which is defined as "a noncommercial educational broadcast station as defined in section 397 of title 47 and any nonprofit institution or organization engaged in the activities described in paragraph (2) of subsection (c)."

Section 119 governs secondary transmissions by superstations, satellite carriers, and network stations for private home viewing.

Section 120 governs the scope of exclusive rights in architectural works:

(a) Pictorial Representations Permitted.—The copyright in an architectural work that has been constructed does not include the right to prevent the making, distributing, or public display of pictures, paintings, photographs, or other pictorial representations of the work, if the building in which the work is embodied is located in or ordinarily visible from a public place.

(b) Alterations to and Destruction of Buildings.—Notwithstanding the provisions of section 106(2), the owners of a building embodying an architectural work may, without the consent of the author or copyright owner of the architectural work, make or authorize the making of alterations to such building, and destroy or authorize the destruction of such building.

Section 121 sets for limitations on exclusive rights in the case of reproduction for blind persons or other persons with disabilities.

Finally, section 122 addresses secondary transmissions by satellite carriers within local markets.

¶ 5.07   Copyright Misuse

The misuse doctrine, which is part of both patent and copyright law, plays a fundamental role in delineating the boundaries of Intellectual Property rights. Often Intellectual Property owners seek to obtain rights or otherwise seek benefits that are not within the scope of the rights granted to them by Congress. The misuse doctrine covers behavior in which a patent or copyright owner attempts to extend its power beyond the boundaries of the lawful rights under the patent or copyright.[31]

One of the central questions still left unclear in the case law is whether misuse rules extend to substantive conduct that is not condemned under antitrust principles, and if so, how to give definition to the misuse doctrine. Thus, the scope of the misuse doctrine is unclear, but the following cases provide some illustrations of typical scenarios. In *PRC Realty Sys., Inc. v. National Ass'n of*

---

31. *Zenith Radio Corp. v. Hazeltine Research, Inc.*, 395 U.S. 100, 140 (1969).

Realtors,[32] the court found misuse where copyright license required defendant to use "best efforts" to persuade customers to use plaintiff's publishing services, effectively precluding defendant from offering its own publishing services. In *F.E.L. Publications Ltd. v. Catholic Bishops*,[33] the court noted that "it is copyright misuse to exact a fee for the use of a musical work which is already in the public domain," and observed that misuse question turns on whether copyright owner "has extended its copyright beyond the strict boundaries of the conferring statute." Similarly, in *Qad. Inc. v. ALN Associates*,[34] the plaintiff had failed to acknowledge on its copyright registration form that its copyrighted software was a derivative work. The court held that pursuit of an infringement claim that encompassed noncopyrightable portion of the work constituted copyright misuse under *Lasercomb*. In *Tempo Music, Inc. v. Myers*,[35] the court found unclean hands/equitable estoppel where the plaintiff's agent ASCAP violated an antitrust consent decree by refusing to provide a list of music in its repertory to defendant, who then inadvertently infringed music in that repertory.

For examples of failed efforts to prove misuse, consider *Supermarket of Homes, Inc. v. San Fernando Valley Bd. of Realtors*.[36] In that case, the court held there was no copyright misuse when the copyright owner offered better terms to some licensees than others. In *Mitchell Bros. Film Group v. Cinema Adult Theater*,[37] the court rejected an unclean hands/copyright misuse defense based on claim of general "public injury" arising from plaintiff's "obscene" subject matter, but noted that such a defense might be based on fraudulent registration or tying arrangements. Because misuse is an equitable defense, the party asserting misuse may be precluded in some circumstances from asserting the defense if it acted with unclean hands. On somewhat unusual facts, *Atari Games Corp. v. Nintendo, Inc.*,[38] the court focused on the equitable nature of copyright misuse. It found the misuse defense to be unavailable in light of the plaintiff's showing of "unclean hands," because the defendant had committed fraud on Copyright Office to obtain copy of plaintiff's software which it later reproduced.

One point that appears to be settled is the proposition that patent and copyright owners are not categorically exempt from standard antitrust analysis. As the Federal Circuit succinctly stated

32. Copyr. L. Rep. (CCH) ¶ 26,961 (4th Cir. 1992).

33. Copyr. L. Rep. (CCH) ¶ 25,376 (7th Cir. 1982) (citing *Mercoid Corp. v. Mid–Continent Investment Co.*, 320 U.S. 661 (1944)).

34. 770 F.Supp. 1261, 1266–67 (N.D. Ill. 1991), *aff'd in part, dismissed in part*, 974 F.2d 834 (7th Cir. 1992).

35. 407 F.2d 503 (4th Cir. 1969).

36. 786 F.2d 1400, 1408 (9th Cir. 1986).

37. 604 F.2d 852, 865 (5th Cir. 1979), *cert. denied*, 445 U.S. 917 (1980).

38. 975 F.2d 832, 846 (Fed. Cir. 1992).

in *In re Indep. Serv. Orgs. Antitrust Litigation*: "Intellectual property rights do not confer a privilege to violate the antitrust laws."[39] Consequently, a copyright or patent holder cannot argue, "we have a copyright or patent; therefore, we can do as we please." On June 28, 2001, the Court of Appeals for the District of Columbia effectively dispatched this approach in *United States v. Microsoft Corporation*:

> Microsoft argues that the license restrictions are legally justified because, in imposing them, Microsoft is simply "exercising its rights as the holder of valid copyrights.".... Microsoft's primary copyright argument borders on the frivolous. The company claims an absolute and unfettered right to use its Intellectual Property as it wishes: "[I]f Intellectual Property rights have been lawfully acquired," it says, then "their subsequent exercise cannot give rise to antitrust liability.".... That is no more correct than the proposition that use of one's personal property, such as a baseball bat, cannot give rise to tort liability."[40]

One of the most significant features of misuse law is the rule that defendants in Intellectual Property cases can raise the misuse defense even though they were not bound by the contractual provisions found to constitute copyright or patent misuse. The rationale, which originates in patent law, is that the courts should not enforce patent rights which are being exercised in violation of public policy.[41] The same rule, based on similar policy concerns, was extended to copyright misuse in *Lasercomb America, Inc. v. Reynolds*.[42] In this manner, the misuse doctrine can be invoked defensively by an alleged infringer even if that infringer does not have formal antitrust standing—it may not have been the direct target of the conduct claimed to be misuse. The misuse doctrine is thus grounded in principles of equity, as well as Intellectual Property policy.[43]

---

39. 203 F.3d 1322, 1325 (Fed. Cir. 2000).

40. 253 F.3d 34, 63 (D.C. Cir. 2001).

41. *See Morton Salt Co. v. G.S. Suppiger*, 314 U.S. 488 (1942); *Compton v. Metal Products, Inc.*, 453 F.2d 38 (4th Cir. 1971), *cert. denied*, 406 U.S. 968 (1972).

42. 911 F.2d 970 (4th Cir. 1990).

43. *See Broadcast Music, Inc. v. Hearst/ABC Viacom Entertainment Servs.*, 746 F.Supp. 320, 329–30 (S.D.N.Y. 1990) (noting that unclean hands defense is recognized "rarely" in copyright law, and only when the copyright owner's transgression is serious and relates directly to the subject matter of the infringement action); *Vogue Ring Creations, Inc. v. Hardman*, 410 F.Supp. 609, 616 (D. R.I. 1976) (failure to disclose derivative nature of work on copyright registration form, combined with "suspect" testimony at trial and misleading copyright warning, rendered copyright unenforceable due to unclean hands/copyright misuse). *Cf. Reed–Union Corp. v. Turtle Wax, Inc.*, 77 F.3d 909, 913 (7th Cir. 1996) ("Misuse of copyrights in pursuit of an anticompetitive end may be a defense to a suit for infringement, along the lines of the patent-misuse doctrine in antitrust.... We do not say that it is (an open issue in

Examples of typical misuse questions include: whether the doctrine of misuse differs in content from antitrust law, when tying is anticompetitive, what rules govern an Intellectual Property holder's refusal to deal with competitors, what licensing provisions are impermissible, the standard of proof for when a copyright is fraudulently obtained, the possible use of litigation as a predatory practice, prohibitions on cartels and other anticompetitive agreements among competitors, blanket copyright licensing, rules governing standard-setting, resale and other vertical restrictions, and remedies for a finding of misuse.

A full-blown analysis of the misuse doctrine is beyond the scope of this book.[44] The overarching theme of the misuse doctrine is that appropriate limits should be placed on Intellectual Property rights. The misuse doctrine is an integral part of both patent and copyright law, offering an affirmative defense to infringers when the Intellectual Property owner has overstepped its rights. Similarly, the antitrust laws place limits on the exercise of Intellectual Property rights. These issues have been the subject of public debate, for example, in studies and hearings about competition in Intellectual Property conducted by the Federal Trade Commission and Justice Department. Strikingly, despite the importance of the interaction between antitrust and Intellectual Property policy, there is no general framework or paradigm to analyze potential conflicts between these two fields. The balance between Intellectual Property and antitrust policy must be struck by reference to the policies and analytical framework inherent in patent and copyright law, and from the teachings of antitrust law and economics. In other words, by examining the policy choices made in antitrust and Intellectual Property law, it is possible to determine the role patents and copyrights play in the analysis of competitive practices in the marketplace.

The balance between these two fields can lead to varying results. For example, if it is found that Intellectual Property law

this court); copyrights do not exclude independent expression and therefore create less market power than patents."); *Data Gen. Corp. v. Grumman Sys. Support Corp.,* 36 F.3d 1147, 1170 (1st Cir. 1994) (concluding that it "would be a poor reason to refrain entirely from recognizing copyright misuse defense," court acknowledged "that it is often more difficult to prove an antitrust violation when the claim rests on the questionable market power associated with a copyright").

44. The author of this book has written a casebook on this topic. *See* GARY MYERS, THE INTERSECTION OF ANTITRUST & INTELLECTUAL PROPERTY LAW (Thomson West 2007). Some other useful sources on the issue of copyright misuse include: 2 PAUL GOLDSTEIN, COPYRIGHT § 9.6.1–.2 (1998); HERBERT HOVENKAMP ET AL., IP AND ANTITRUST (Aspen 2011); MELVILLE NIMMER, NIMMER ON COPYRIGHT § 13.09; Ramsey Hanna, Note, Misusing Antitrust: The Search for Functional Copyright Misuse Standards, 46 STAN L. REV. 361 (1994); Note, Clarifying the Copyright Misuse Defense: The Role of Antitrust Standards and First Amendment Values, 104 HARV. L. REV. 1289 (1991).

expressly or implicitly permits or reserves certain rights to owners of patents or copyrights, then the exercise of those rights is likely to raise fewer antitrust concerns. On the other hand, when Intellectual Property doctrine is expressly designed to constrain the exercise of particular rights, then there is likely to be heightened scrutiny of conduct that is designed to circumvent these limits. Finally, if Intellectual Property law is silent on the particular practice in question, then the standard analytical methods of antitrust law and economics are most likely to be applied. These at least are my overall conclusions about the scope of misuse, a topic on which commentators and courts have not reached a consensus.

¶ 5.08   Internet Service Providers

Over the last twenty years, there has been dramatic improvement and expansion in the ability of people to communicate and to do business over the Internet. The information services now available to people represent an extraordinary advance in the availability of avenues of communication, of commerce, and of educational and informational resources. Moreover, users of these services have substantial control over the information that they receive and distribute to others. The Internet provides a forum for a wide diversity of political, cultural, economic, and intellectual discourse.

The Internet is also a tremendously effective vehicle for copyright infringement. Copyrighted works can be reproduced in perfect digital form, distributed to millions of other users, turned into derivative works with a variety of software tools, and of course publicly displayed or performed on the Internet. One issue which arose early on is the extent to which internet service providers (ISPs) can be liable for the infringing activities of its users. Examples of ISPs include AOL and other early "dial up" Internet services, as well as more modern cable and DSL Internet providers, universities and other large entities.

The question is not entirely novel in copyright law, as case law certainly addresses parties who serve as mere conduits for infringing material. Consider the case of a telephone company or package delivery service, either of which can be used for the transmission of infringing material, such as a faxed version of a copyrighted work sent over telephone lines or a set of infringing music CDs sent via FedEx. No one would seriously contend that these delivery services should be responsible for the infringing activities of their customers. Importantly, these service providers do not have knowledge or control over the vast amount of information conveyed through their systems.

During the early development of the Internet, a number of cases addressed ISP liability, applying common law rules which logically focused on whether the ISP was a mere conduit for infringing material or whether it had knowledge or control over the information. In the Digital Millenium Copyright Act, Congress specifically addressed this important question. The Act, codified in 17 U.S.C.A. § 512, establishes various safe harbors for ISPs. For purposes of most of these safe harbors, an ISP (or "service provider") is defined in section 512(k) as follows:

(1) Service provider.—(A) As used in subsection (a), the term "service provider" means an entity offering the transmission, routing, or providing of connections for digital online communications, between or among points specified by a user, of material of the user's choosing, without modification to the content of the material as sent or received.

(B) As used in this section, other than subsection (a), the term "service provider" means a provider of online services or network access, or the operator of facilities therefor, and includes an entity described in subparagraph (A).

The protections in section 512 apply to ISPs only if they have adopted, propounded to subscribers or account holders, and reasonably implemented "a policy that provides for the termination in appropriate circumstances of subscribers and account holders of the service provider's system or network who are repeat infringers" and have accommodated and do not interfere with standard technical measures against copying used by copyright owners.[45]

Section 512(a) establishes limitations on liability for transitory digital network communications. This involves the actual routing and temporary storage of information through the ISP's system. Recall that copyright liability can attach whenever a work is fixed in a tangible medium of expression, and that this fixation can readily be achieved in digital or electronic form, as discussed in Chapter 2, ¶ 2.07. Section 512(a) states that "[a] service provider shall not be liable for monetary relief, or, except as provided in subsection (j), for injunctive or other equitable relief, for infringement of copyright by reason of the provider's transmitting, routing, or providing connections for, material through a system or network controlled or operated by or for the service provider, or by reason of the intermediate and transient storage of that material in the course of such transmitting, routing, or providing connections." This provision requires that the material was not modified, initiated, or selected by the ISP, and that the ISP not keep a copy of the material after it is transmitted.

Similarly, section 512(b) limits liability for system caching, defined as "the intermediate and temporary storage of material on

---

45. 17 U.S.C.§ 512(i).

a system or network controlled or operated by or for the service provider." To come within the safe harbor in this section, the ISP must comply with the detailed conditions set forth in section 512(b)(2), including no modification of the material and compliance with the "notice and takedown" rules of section 512(c)(3).

The most important part of this safe harbor statute is section 512(c), which addresses material stored on systems or networks at the direction of ISP users. This section states:

> A service provider shall not be liable for monetary relief, or, except as provided in subsection (j), for injunctive or other equitable relief, for infringement of copyright by reason of the storage at the direction of a user of material that resides on a system or network controlled or operated by or for the service provider, if the service provider—
>
> (A)(i) does not have actual knowledge that the material or an activity using the material on the system or network is infringing;
>
> > (ii) in the absence of such actual knowledge, is not aware of facts or circumstances from which infringing activity is apparent; or
> >
> > (iii) upon obtaining such knowledge or awareness, acts expeditiously to remove, or disable access to, the material;
>
> (B) does not receive a financial benefit directly attributable to the infringing activity, in a case in which the service provider has the right and ability to control such activity; and
>
> (C) upon notification of claimed infringement as described in paragraph (3), responds expeditiously to remove, or disable access to, the material that is claimed to be infringing or to be the subject of infringing activity.

In essence, this provision immunizes ISPs from liability for actions of users who place infringing material on the ISP's system, as long as the ISP is unaware of the action, promptly removes the material upon notice, and does not financially benefit from the infringing activity. The ISP must also register with the Copyright Office and provide a designated agent to receive take-down notices.

The "notice and take-down" provision provides an important mechanism by which copyright owners can inform ISPs of the presence of infringing material. To put the ISP on effective notice of infringing activity, the take-down notice—

must be a written communication provided to the designated agent of a service provider that includes substantially the following:

(i) A physical or electronic signature of a person authorized to act on behalf of the owner of an exclusive right that is allegedly infringed.

(ii) Identification of the copyrighted work claimed to have been infringed, or, if multiple copyrighted works at a single online site are covered by a single notification, a representative list of such works at that site.

(iii) Identification of the material that is claimed to be infringing or to be the subject of infringing activity and that is to be removed or access to which is to be disabled, and information reasonably sufficient to permit the service provider to locate the material.

(iv) Information reasonably sufficient to permit the service provider to contact the complaining party, such as an address, telephone number, and, if available, an electronic mail address at which the complaining party may be contacted.

(v) A statement that the complaining party has a good faith belief that use of the material in the manner complained of is not authorized by the copyright owner, its agent, or the law.

(vi) A statement that the information in the notification is accurate, and under penalty of perjury, that the complaining party is authorized to act on behalf of the owner of an exclusive right that is allegedly infringed.[46]

Section 512(d) allows the ISP to allow searches and linking to websites that may contain infringing material:

Information location tools.—A service provider shall not be liable for monetary relief, or, except as provided in subsection (j), for injunctive or other equitable relief, for infringement of copyright by reason of the provider referring or linking users to an online location containing infringing material or infringing activity, by using information location tools, including a directory, index, reference, pointer, or hypertext link, if the service provider—

(1)(A) does not have actual knowledge that the material or activity is infringing;

46. 17 U.S.C.§ 512(c).

(B) in the absence of such actual knowledge, is not aware of facts or circumstances from which infringing activity is apparent; or

(C) upon obtaining such knowledge or awareness, acts expeditiously to remove, or disable access to, the material;

(2) does not receive a financial benefit directly attributable to the infringing activity, in a case in which the service provider has the right and ability to control such activity; and

(3) upon notification of claimed infringement as described in subsection (c)(3), responds expeditiously to remove, or disable access to, the material that is claimed to be infringing or to be the subject of infringing activity, except that, for purposes of this paragraph, the information described in subsection (c)(3)(A)(iii) shall be identification of the reference or link, to material or activity claimed to be infringing, that is to be removed or access to which is to be disabled, and information reasonably sufficient to permit the service provider to locate that reference or link.

Finally, section 512(e) provides a safe harbor for nonprofit educational institutions:

(1) When a public or other nonprofit institution of higher education is a service provider, and when a faculty member or graduate student who is an employee of such institution is performing a teaching or research function, for the purposes of subsections (a) and (b) such faculty member or graduate student shall be considered to be a person other than the institution, and for the purposes of subsections (c) and (d) such faculty member's or graduate student's knowledge or awareness of his or her infringing activities shall not be attributed to the institution, if—

(A) such faculty member's or graduate student's infringing activities do not involve the provision of online access to instructional materials that are or were required or recommended, within the preceding 3–year period, for a course taught at the institution by such faculty member or graduate student;

(B) the institution has not, within the preceding 3–year period, received more than two notifications described in subsection (c)(3) of claimed infringement by such faculty member or graduate student, and such notifications of claimed infringement were not actionable under subsection (f); and

(C) the institution provides to all users of its system or network informational materials that accurately describe, and promote compliance with, the laws of the United States relating to copyright.

(2) For the purposes of this subsection, the limitations on injunctive relief contained in subsections (j)(2) and (j)(3), but not those in (j)(1), shall apply.

Although these provisions are controversial to some because they essentially permit copyright owners to take down sites containing infringing material, the statute does provide remedies for knowing misrepresentations that material is (or is not) infringing:

Any person who knowingly materially misrepresents under this section—

(1) that material or activity is infringing, or

(2) that material or activity was removed or disabled by mistake or misidentification, shall be liable for any damages, including costs and attorneys' fees, incurred by the alleged infringer, by any copyright owner or copyright owner's authorized licensee, or by a service provider, who is injured by such misrepresentation, as the result of the service provider relying upon such misrepresentation in removing or disabling access to the material or activity claimed to be infringing, or in replacing the removed material or ceasing to disable access to it.[47]

Section 512(g) immunizes ISPs from liability for removed or disabled material in most circumstances, and provides procedures for counter-notices that the take-down was mistaken. Finally, section 512(j) establishes detailed rules for injunctive relief against ISPs.

In short, these provisions have enabled ISPs to operate effectively and without undue restriction on open discourse on the Internet. At the same time, the notice-and-takedown provisions allow copyright owners to place ISPs on notice of infringing material, at which time the ISP is obligated to "take down" the alleged infringing material. This system seems to provide a reasonable balance between the interests of ISPs, Internet users, and copyright owners. In 2012, an effort in Congress to enact stronger enforcement mechanisms for copyright owners, particularly as to foreign websites and payment processors, met strong public resistance. These proposed laws, known as SOPA and PIPA, are discussed above in Chapter 4, ¶ 4.04.

¶ 5.09   Other Defenses

Statute of Limitations

The statute of limitations for civil copyright infringement actions is three years from the date the infringement occurred: "No

---

47.   15 U.S.C.§ 512(f).

civil action shall be maintained under the provisions of this title unless it is commenced within three years after the claim accrued.''[48]

Manufacturing Clause

The Manufacturing Clause, section 601(a) of the Copyright Act, was a defense available for works that were imported into the United States before a U.S.-made version of the work had been registered. Essentially this provision mandated that works be printed in the United States. Because this mandate was eliminated for works imported on or after July 1, 1986, the defense will rarely be invoked.

Eleventh Amendment Immunity

A state entity may be entitled to assert Eleventh Amendment immunity from liability for copyright infringement, as illustrated by the Fifth Circuit decision in *Chavez v. Arte Publico Press*.[49] The plaintiff in that case asserted that the University of Houston, a state law school, infringed her copyright by continuing to publish her book without her consent. The court accepted the University of Houston's argument that it has immunity from suit in federal court under the Eleventh Amendment.

---

48. 17 U.S.C. § 507.

49. 204 F.3d 601 (5th Cir. 2000); *see also Richard Anderson Photography v. Brown*, 852 F.2d 114 (4th Cir. 1988). These decisions are interpretations of the Supreme Court's more general rulings in the area of Eleventh Amendment immunity. *See generally College Savings Bank v. Florida Prepaid Postsecondary Educ. Expense Bd.*, 527 U.S. 666 (1999); *Florida Prepaid Postsecondary Educ. Expense Bd. v. College Savings Bank*, 527 U.S. 627 (1999).

Chapter 6

COPYRIGHT REMEDIES

Table of Sections

¶ 6.01 Injunctions

Section 502(a) of the Copyright Act authorizes courts to issue injunctive relief: "Any court having jurisdiction of a civil action arising under this title may, subject to the provisions of section 1498 of title 28, grant temporary and final injunctions on such terms as it may deem reasonable to prevent or restrain infringement of a copyright." By its express terms, this provision is permissive, and thus injunctions are not mandatory and are within the sound discretion of the court. Relief available includes temporary restraining orders (TROs), preliminary injunctions, and permanent injunctions.

To obtain a preliminary injunction, a plaintiff must prove: (1) the plaintiff has a likelihood of success on the merits; (2) irreparable harm to the plaintiff; (3) that less harm will result to the defendant if the preliminary injunction issues than to the plaintiff if the preliminary injunction does not issue (i.e., the balancing of harms favors the plaintiff); and (4) that the public interest, if any, weighs in favor of the plaintiff.

In many successful copyright cases, the court will issue a permanent injunction barring the reproduction, distribution, or other infringing use of the defendant's work. But injunctive relief is not automatic. A prominent statement on this point can be found in the Supreme Court's *Campbell v. Acuff–Rose*[1] decision:

> Because the fair use enquiry often requires close questions of judgment as to the extent of permissible borrowing in cases involving parodies (or other critical works), courts may also wish to bear in mind that the goals of the copyright law, "to stimulate the creation and publication of edifying matter," are

---

1. 510 U.S. 569, 578 n.10 (1994).

not always best served by automatically granting injunctive relief when parodists are found to have gone beyond the bounds of fair use. See 17 U.S.C. § 502(a) (court "may . . . grant . . . injunctions on such terms as it may deem reasonable to prevent or restrain infringement") (emphasis added); Leval 1132 (while in the "vast majority of cases, [an injunctive] remedy is justified because most infringements are simple piracy," such cases are "worlds apart from many of those raising reasonable contentions of fair use" where "there may be a strong public interest in the publication of the secondary work [and] the copyright owner's interest may be adequately protected by an award of damages for whatever infringement is found"). . . .

Similarly, in *New York Times v. Tasini*,[2] after holding that the defendant did not have the right to include freelance print articles in its electronic databases, Justice Ginsburg stated:

Notwithstanding the dire predictions from some quarters, it hardly follows from today's decision that an injunction against the inclusion of these Articles in the Databases (much less all freelance articles in any databases) must issue. The parties (Authors and Publishers) may enter into an agreement allowing continued electronic reproduction of the Authors' works; they, and if necessary the courts and Congress, may draw on numerous models for distributing copyrighted works and remunerating authors for their distribution. In any event, speculation about future harms is no basis for this Court to shrink authorial rights Congress established in § 201(c). Agreeing with the Court of Appeals that the Publishers are liable for infringement, we leave remedial issues open for initial airing and decision in the District Court.

The Supreme Court issued an important decision involving injunctive relief, *eBay, Inc. v. Merc Exchange, LLC.*,[3] which addressed the standard for issuing injunctions in patent cases. The Court held that a patent holder must make the traditional showing in order to receive equitable relief: "(1) that it has suffered an irreparable injury; (2) that remedies available at law, such as monetary damages, are inadequate to compensate for that injury; (3) that, considering the balance of hardships between the plaintiff and defendant, a remedy in equity is warranted; and (4) that the public interest would not be disserved by a permanent injunction." The Court rejected the Federal Circuit's presumption that injunc-

---

2. 533 U.S. 483, 505–06 (2001) (citations omitted). *See also Abend v. MCA, Inc.*, 863 F.2d 1465, 1479 (9th Cir. 1988) (finding special circumstances that would cause great injustice to defendants and public injury were injunction to issue), *aff'd sub nom. Stewart v. Abend*, 495 U.S. 207 (1990).

3. 547 U.S. 388, 393–94 (2006).

tions should be routinely granted in patent cases. The Court's decision makes it clear that injunctions are only granted when the four-part showing is made. In practical effect, the patent owner is likely to be able to make this showing in most (but not all) cases. Although not directly applicable to copyright litigation, the ruling reaffirms the principle (reflected in the copyright cases cited above) that a plaintiff asserting Intellectual Property rights has the burden of proving the four-part test for injunctive relief on the specific facts of each individual case.

In addition to injunctive relief, section 503 provides for the impounding and disposition of infringing articles:

(a) At any time while an action under this title is pending, the court may order the impounding, on such terms as it may deem reasonable, of all copies or phonorecords claimed to have been made or used in violation of the copyright owner's exclusive rights, and of all plates, molds, matrices, masters, tapes, film negatives, or other articles by means of which such copies or phonorecords may be reproduced.

(b) As part of a final judgment or decree, the court may order the destruction or other reasonable disposition of all copies or phonorecords found to have been made or used in violation of the copyright owner's exclusive rights, and of all plates, molds, matrices, masters, tapes, film negatives, or other articles by means of which such copies or phonorecords may be reproduced.

This remedy is critical for copyright owners seeking to remove infringing material from the marketplace.

¶ 6.02 Compensatory Damages—Actual Damages and Profits

Section 504 sets forth monetary remedies for copyright infringement. In general, an infringer of copyright is liable for either (1) the copyright owner's actual damages and any additional profits of the infringer or (2) statutory damages, as provided in section 504(c). The first of these options is a typical remedy in the Intellectual Property field, and indeed in many other areas of the law as well. In essence, this option allows the copyright owner to recover compensatory damages for the loss it suffered or the gain the defendant obtained. The second option, statutory damages, is a much more unusual provision, as discussed below.

With regard to actual damage and profits, section 504(b) states:

The copyright owner is entitled to recover the actual damages suffered by him or her as a result of the infringement, and any profits of the infringer that are attributable to the infringement and are not taken into account in computing the actual damages. In establishing the infringer's profits, the copyright owner is required to present proof only of the infringer's gross revenue, and the infringer is required to prove his or her deductible expenses and the elements of profit attributable to factors other than the copyrighted work.

Often damages in copyright cases are difficult to prove or to quantify, and Congress has provided for a relatively unique alternative method for allowing copyright owners to obtain monetary relief—the statutory damage claim. This remedy is not found in most other areas of Intellectual Property law, and indeed is quite unusual in the law more generally. Section 504(c) establishes the general range for statutory damage awards: "the copyright owner may elect, at any time before final judgment is rendered, to recover, instead of actual damages and profits, an award of statutory damages for all infringements involved in the action, with respect to any one work, for which any one infringer is liable individually, or for which any two or more infringers are liable jointly and severally, in a sum of not less than $750 or more than $30,000 as the court considers just." Accordingly, the factfinder can award statutory damages in an amount ranging from $750 to $30,000 per copyrighted work. For the purposes of the statutory damage rule, all parts of a compilation or derivative work constitute one work, and so only one award can be collected for that type of work.

The statutory damage range can be modified by a showing of either bad faith or good faith on the part of the defendant. If the copyright owner proves that defendant committed infringement willfully, the court in its discretion can increase the award of statutory damages up to $150,000. Conversely, if the infringer proves that it "was not aware and had no reason to believe that his or her acts constituted an infringement of copyright, the court in its discretion may reduce the award of statutory damages to a sum of not less than $200."[4]

The statute also provides dispensation of statutory damages in some cases "where an infringer believed and had reasonable grounds for believing that his or her use of the copyrighted work was a fair use under section 107," but only if the infringer is an employee or agent of a public broadcasting entity or a nonprofit educational institution, library, or archives acting within the scope of his or her employment.[5]

Finally, the statute specifically addresses defendants who are proprietors of an establishment claiming a defense under section 110(5)'s small business exemption. If the defendant did not have

---

4. 17 U.S.C. § 504(c).   **5.** 17 U.S.C. § 504(c).

reasonable grounds to believe that its use of a copyrighted work was exempt under section 110(5), the plaintiff is entitled to recover an additional award of two times the license fee that the proprietors would have paid the plaintiff for public performance royalties during the preceding three years, in addition to the statutory damages awarded under this section.[6]

Section 505 provides for a discretionary award of costs and attorneys fees: "In any civil action under this title, the court in its discretion may allow the recovery of full costs by or against any party other than the United States or an officer thereof. Except as otherwise provided by this title, the court may also award a reasonable attorney's fee to the prevailing party as part of the costs."

There is one important caveat regarding the ability to collect statutory damages and attorneys' fees—the copyright owner cannot recover statutory damages and attorneys' fees when the acts of infringement precede the date of registration (except when registration takes place within 3 months of publication). Section 412 states:

> In any action under this title, other than an action brought for a violation of the rights of the author under section 106A(a), an action for infringement of the copyright of a work that has been preregistered under section 408(f) before the commencement of the infringement and that has an effective date of registration not later than the earlier of 3 months after the first publication of the work or 1 month after the copyright owner has learned of the infringement, or an action instituted under section 411(b), no award of statutory damages or of attorney's fees, as provided by sections 504 and 505, shall be made for—
>
> (1) any infringement of copyright in an unpublished work commenced before the effective date of its registration; or
>
> (2) any infringement of copyright commenced after first publication of the work and before the effective date of its registration, unless such registration is made within three months after the first publication of the work.

¶ 6.03   Criminal Penalties

Section 506(a) sets forth criminal penalties for copyright infringement:

> (1) In general.—Any person who willfully infringes a copyright shall be punished as provided under section 2319 of title 18, if the infringement was committed—

---

6.   17 U.S.C. § 504(d).

(A) for purposes of commercial advantage or private financial gain;

(B) by the reproduction or distribution, including by electronic means, during any 180–day period, of 1 or more copies or phonorecords of 1 or more copyrighted works, which have a total retail value of more than $1,000; or

(C) by the distribution of a work being prepared for commercial distribution, by making it available on a computer network accessible to members of the public, if such person knew or should have known that the work was intended for commercial distribution.

(2) Evidence.—For purposes of this subsection, evidence of reproduction or distribution of a copyrighted work, by itself, shall not be sufficient to establish willful infringement of a copyright.

(3) Definition.—In this subsection, the term "work being prepared for commercial distribution" means—

(A) a computer program, a musical work, a motion picture or other audiovisual work, or a sound recording, if, at the time of unauthorized distribution—

(i) the copyright owner has a reasonable expectation of commercial distribution; and

(ii) the copies or phonorecords of the work have not been commercially distributed; or

(B) a motion picture, if, at the time of unauthorized distribution, the motion picture—

(i) has been made available for viewing in a motion picture exhibition facility; and

(ii) has not been made available in copies for sale to the general public in the United States in a format intended to permit viewing outside a motion picture exhibition facility.

Section 507 specifies that criminal proceedings must be commenced within five years after the cause of action arose. Criminal penalties are generally invoked only when large-scale counterfeiting or other harmful infringement has taken place.

Chapter 7

TRADEMARK VALIDITY

Table of Contents

TRADEMARK AND UNFAIR COMPETITION LAW

"A brand for a company is like a reputation for a person. You earn reputation by trying to do hard things well."

—Jeff Bezos, Entrepreneur, April 2012, at 14.

"The Lanham Act is the embodiment of the purpose to secure to every businessman the advantage which public preference for his goods gives to him and to protect him in the exclusive right to the names and marks which perpetuate the good will which merit earns."

—Edward S. Rogers, "Introduction," Daphne Robert, the New Trade-mark Manual: A Handbook on Protection of Trade-marks in Interstate Commerce, at xx–xxi (1947).

¶ 7.01 Introduction

Trademark law involves the protection of good will—for example, brand names such as "Coca–Cola" or "Mercedes–Benz"—from improper usurpation by competitors or others who might mislead or confuse consumers. The garden variety trademark claim would involve an imitator who is trying to sell a carbonated beverage using the Coca–Cola brand name. A trademark can include "any word, name, symbol, or device or any combination thereof" used by

178

any person "to identify and distinguish his or her goods, including a unique product, from those manufactured or sold by others and to indicate the source of the goods, even if that source is unknown."[1] Trademarks are protected under both state and federal law. Trademark law has three principal objectives: (1) protecting the good will and reputation of sellers; (2) preventing consumer confusion or deception about who produced the goods or services they have purchased (this is sometimes described as a signaling or informational role for trademarks); and (3) promoting competition in the market by allowing non-misleading advertising by competitors.

More specifically, trademark and unfair competition law promote important interests of both sellers of goods and services and of consumers. These legal claims protect the good will that is—for many businesses—their most valuable asset. As the Jeff Bezos quote above illustrates, a company's brand is much like an individual's reputation, and a brand's reputation must be earned. Sellers of goods and services develop good will through lengthy and reliable production, extensive advertising and marketing, and other expenditures of time, money, and resources. Trademark and unfair competition laws protect prior investments in good will and provide an incentive for further investments. Trademark law also prevents counterfeiters, pirates, and other imitators from benefitting from the good will of others; in other words, the law prevents unjust enrichment by those who try to reap where they have not sown. Moreover, trademark law protects consumers from deception or confusion as to the source or origin of goods and services. Permitting an imitator to sell its goods or services as those of a recognized producer works a fraud upon the consuming public.

Although these are good reasons to provide protection for trademarks, there is a balance of interests in this field, just as in other areas of Intellectual Property law. For example, no one is entitled to a monopoly on the name of a product—such as "cola" or "automobile." These words are necessary to identify the product being sold, and permitting any one producer to monopolize these terms would give that firm an unfair advantage in the market. Similarly, if a firm chooses a highly descriptive word as its trademark (such as "green"), it will be entitled to less protection that if it selects a more distinctive name. Other firms may, in good faith, seek to use the descriptive term to refer to the product—not to usurp good will or confuse consumers. Thus, a balance must be struck in trademark law between the rights of trademark owners and the rights of those who wish to compete in an honest manner.

The origins of trademark law can be traced back to the state law claim of unfair competition. Unfair competition can also be

---

1. 15 U.S.C. § 1127.

known as palming off, passing off, and deceit. The RESTATEMENT (THIRD) OF UNFAIR COMPETITION § 4 states: "One is subject to liability to another ... if, in connection with the marketing of goods or services, the actor makes a representation likely to deceive or mislead prospective purchasers by causing the mistaken belief that the actor's business is the business of the other, or that the actor is the agent, affiliate, or associate of the other, or that the goods or services that the actor markets are produced, sponsored, or approved by the other."

Trademark law rewards diligent effort—which could be called "sweat of the brow" or "superior skill, foresight, and industry" to borrow a term from antitrust law. This is the point of the Jeff Bezos quote at the start of this chapter: that a company's brand is akin to its reputation, and that reputation is earned "by trying to do hard things well." The Supreme Court, in *Feist Publications, Inc. v. Rural Telephone Service Co.*,[2] has repudiated the "sweat of the brow" doctrine in the copyright field. But copyright and trademark law are fundamentally different in their foundational premises. Copyright law protects authors of creative works, and the keystone of protection in that field is that the author must have engaged in at least a minimally creative effort in order to receive protection. Consequently, mere "sweat of the brow" effort, such as the diligent collection of factual data, is not enough. So the Court held in determining that a white-pages telephone directory is not copyrightable.

In trademark law, on the other hand, a firm must decide to provide a desirable product or service and must then select brand names and other marks to promote that product or service and to identify itself to consumers. Over time, the firm can develop significant brand recognition through sustained and creative marketing and promotion. Maintaining the brand image of such a mark is a constant battle, involving regular advertising and promotion, maintenance of consistent quality, and rapid response to technological changes and consumer preferences. The firms that manufacture famous brand-name products have spent considerable resources to develop a high-quality product, which is what consumers now come to expect when they purchase a soft drink or a car bearing those brand names. The firms have also invested considerable resources in marketing their products and increasing the recognition of their brands.

The essence of trademark ownership is use of that mark in commerce. With market success and consistent quality, the firm's marks can become so well known that they develop selling power and serve a valuable informational role for consumers. As Judge

2. 499 U.S. 340 (1991). This case is discussed in Chapter 2, ¶ 2.03.

Easterbrook has suggested in *Scandia Down Corp. v. Euroquilt, Inc.,*[3] "[t]rademarks help consumers to select goods. This level of brand recognition is the reward for entrepreneurial effort."

William R. Warner & Co. v. Eli Lilly & Co.[4] is an example of a classic decision based on state unfair competition law. The case highlights the nature of trademark infringement and the extent of the relief available. The court held that the plaintiff was entitled to prevent the defendant from marketing a chocolate and quinine tonic under a name that was confusingly similar to the plaintiff's brand, and to prevent the defendant from inducing druggists to substitute the defendant's product for that of the plaintiff. Trademark owners can assert harm to their own commercial interests, but they have a more compelling case when they can show that consumers have been defrauded or deceived in some way. Has a consumer who enters a druggist's shop and asked for the plaintiff's Coco–Quinine been harmed if he or she is unwittingly given a bottle of the defendant's Quin–Coco instead? The products appear to be identical in taste, ingredients, and other characteristics, but the consumer has certainly been deprived of his or her sovereignty— the right to choose the preferred brand. Consider cost differences as well—the druggist might substitute the defendant's inexpensive product but charge the higher price applicable to the name brand product. If one substitutes modern-day products and brand names, this action would be equivalent to ordering a Coca–Cola and getting a private-label or store-brand cola. A comparison can also be made to brand-name prescription drugs, many of which have inexpensive generic substitutes once the patent on the drug has expired.

The plaintiff was unable, however, to obtain an injunction barring the defendant from selling the product at all. Trademark law does not prevent competitors from advertising and competing honestly. *Warner v. Lilly* thus highlights the difference between trademark rights as distinguished from patent protection, which does provide an exclusive right to make, use, sell, or offer to sell the product itself. In other words, trademark law focuses on deceptive marketing, but does not provide exclusive rights to sell the product itself. The injunction accordingly barred use of a confusingly similar name, but did not prevent the defendant from truthfully marketing the product under a different brand name. Although the plaintiff sought this broader relief, to provide it would have given the plaintiff a patent-like monopoly under the guise of trademark law. Trademark law does not offer exclusivity with regard to selling the product itself. It only protects the brand or trademark.

3. 772 F.2d 1423, 1429–30 (7th Cir. 1985), *cert. denied*, 475 U.S. 1147 (1986).   **4.** 265 U.S. 526 (1924).

Beyond these traditional common law claims, which can still be asserted today, a panoply of statutory causes of action are now available. These claims include federal trademark law, state trademark statutes, and state deceptive trade practices statutes. Often these statutes incorporate common law concepts and standards, which makes it important to have an understanding of unfair competition despite the existence of these state and federal statutory schemes. The current version of federal trademark law was enacted in the Lanham Act of 1946.[5] The Lanham Act has been amended a number of times since then. Together with state common law claims and state trademark statutes, the Lanham Act today provides extensive protection for trademark owners.

The Lanham Act has two general purposes, according to the Senate Report: "One is to protect the public so it may be confident that, in purchasing a product bearing a particular trade-mark which it favorably knows, it will get the product which it asks for and wants to get. Secondly, where the owner of a trade-mark has spent energy, time, and money in presenting to the public the product, he is protected in his investment from its misappropriation by pirates and cheats. This is the well-established rule of law protecting both the public and the trade-mark owner."[6] The Report indicated that the Act would further serve "to protect the public from deceit, to foster fair competition, and to secure to the business community the advantages of reputation and good will by preventing their diversion from those who have created them to those who have not. This is the end to which this bill is directed."[7] The House Report indicates that an important goal of the Act was to provide uniform nationwide relief for trademarks, which were increasingly used on a national if not global scale. Finally, Texas Congressman Fritz Garland Lanham, the bill's namesake and sponsor, stated: "The purpose of [the Act] is to protect legitimate business and the consumers of the country."[8] In summary, the legislative history identifies three principal goals for federal trademark law: prevention of consumer confusion and deception, protection of good will against free riding, and providing a nationwide system of rights for all marks.

Many states have statutes recognizing an even broader claim for "dilution" of distinctive trademarks. These dilution claims do not require the showing of consumer confusion traditionally made in trademark infringement cases. In 1995, Congress enacted legislation providing for a federal claim for dilution of widely recognized trademarks. Congress modified the federal dilution statute in 2006,

---

5. 15 U.S.C. §§ 1051–1127.

6. S. Rep. No. 1333, 79th Cong., 2d Sess., 3 (1946).

7. *Id.* at 4.

8. 92 Cong. Rec. 7524 (1946).

in a law known as the Trademark Dilution Revision Act ("TDRA"). These claims of state and federal trademark infringement, unfair competition, and dilution offer overlapping protection. Often, several claims can be asserted on one set of facts. Consequently, parties seeking to protect their trademarks have a variety of available options in terms of registration and enforcement of their rights.

¶ 7.02   Generic Terms

For a brand name to serve as a trademark, it must be capable of identifying a particular producer or source of the goods in question. As a result, a generic term cannot qualify as a trademark, because it is associated in the consuming public's mind with a product or service itself. In other words, the term identifies the product itself, rather than serving as a brand name (identifying a particular source or producer of that product). A term can be generic because it has always been a product name or category, such as grapes, light beer, or thin-crust pizza. If trademark law allowed one producer to usurp these terms as brand names, it would place competitors at a considerable disadvantage. Consider, for example, how competitors could market a product such as a laptop computer if they were precluded from using the term "laptop computer" in advertisements, on the internet, or on the product packaging.

Companies and entities sometimes try to adopt a generic name as its trademark, but this enterprise is frequently not a fruitful one. For instance, in *Self–Realization Fellowship Church v. Ananda Church of Self–Realization*,[9] the court held that the term "self-realization" is generic as to Hindu or yoga spiritual organizations. Similarly, in an appeal from a trademark office denial of registration, the court in *In re K–T Zoe Furniture, Inc.*,[10] affirmed the refusal to register "the sofa & chair company" for a furniture store. The court held that the term was generic.

Sometimes, however, a term starts out as a brand name but the brand becomes so successful that it eventually comes to be known to the consuming public as the product name itself. There are many historic examples of this phenomenon, including "Aspirin," "Kleenex" "Cellophane," and "Thermos." All of these terms began as brand names but were so successful that consumers eventually came to use them as generic product names. This is sometimes called "genericide." The reader can readily conjure up examples of well known current brands that have become so

9. 59 F.3d 902 (9th Cir. 1995); *see also Society of Financial Examiners v. National Association of Certified Fraud Examiners, Inc.*, 41 F.3d 223 (5th Cir. 1995) (fact issues presented regarding whether the term "CFE" is generic), *cert. denied*, 515 U.S. 1103 (1995).

10. 16 F.3d 390 (Fed. Cir. 1994).

successful that the term is often used to refer to the product or service itself.

Determining whether a term is generic requires some rigor, primarily through the use of consumer surveys, as well as reviewing trade publications, media reports, and other sources. Although finding that a very successful trademark has become generic seems like a harsh result, it is consistent with the general policies of trademarks: (1) protecting the good will and reputation of sellers; (2) preventing consumer confusion or deception; and (3) promoting competition in the market. Can a firm really show good will if it markets its product under a generic name that consumers do not view primarily as a brand? Is there any consumer deception if consumers themselves use the generic term to signify the product itself? Finally, there is harm to competition if one firm is allowed to monopolize the use of a generic term. Accordingly, the doctrine that no one can monopolize a generic name is arguably consistent with all three trademark policies. On the other hand, if a well-known and highly successful brand is deemed generic, the trademark owner does suffer a substantial loss of its investment in the brand name. Still, success alone does not render most trademarks generic. The problem only arises when consumers cease using alternative generic terms and begin to adopt the trademark to identify the entire product category.

Although consumer perceptions of a trademark can be affected by the trademark owner's efforts, those efforts—or the lack thereof—are not controlling. As the court stated in *King–Seeley Thermos Co. v. Aladdin Industries, Inc.*:

> We are not convinced that the trademark's loss of distinctiveness was the result of some failure on plaintiff's part. Substantial efforts to preserve the trademark significance of the word were made by plaintiff, especially with respect to members of the trade. However, there was little they could do to prevent the public from using "thermos" in a generic rather than a trademark sense. And whether the appropriation by the public was due to highly successful educational and advertising campaigns or to lack of diligence in policing or not is of no consequence; the fact is that the word "thermos" had entered the public domain beyond recall. Even as early as 1910 plaintiff itself asserted that "Thermos had become a household word."[11]

Nonetheless, trademark owners frequently influence public perceptions in a number of ways: advertising to inform consumers and others about the brand name and of the proper generic name for the product; efforts to make the media and trade publications aware of the brand name; use of the brand name on other products

---

11.   321 F.2d 577 (2d Cir. 1963).

to heighten brand recognition; and vigorous enforcement of trademark rights against infringers. Companies such as Xerox, Tabasco, and Apple (iPod or iPad) employ a variety of measures to protect their brands by encouraging use of the terms photocopy, hot sauce, Mp3 player, and tablet. Consider the following list of well known brands and the accompanying product names.

Crisco—shortening, cooking oil
Formica—laminated plastic
Jacuzzi—whirlpool bath
Jet Ski—personal watercraft
Kleenex—tissues
Rolodex—card file
Scotch tape—adhesive plastic tape
Tabasco—hot pepper sauce
Xerox—photocopier

Dixie cup—paper cup
Ipod–Mp3 player
Jell–O—gelatin dessert
Jockey shorts—men's briefs
Muzak—background music
Saran wrap—clear plastic wrap
Spam—canned meat products
Weed Eater—lawn trimmer
FedEx—overnight delivery service

Each of these brand names has had so much success that they are nearly all—as perceived by many consumers—synonymous with the product itself. Yet whether they fall in the category of a generic term is a complex question requiring detailed market analysis.

A finding of that a formerly well-known trademark has come to be a generic term for the product itself can engender some residual confusion because some consumers do recognize the brand name, but courts can balance the equities nicely by requiring that new market entrants use the generic term in a manner that reduces the likelihood of confusion—perhaps in lower case, preceded by the new entrant's own brand name, and without reference to claims of being the "original" or the "genuine" product.[12]

¶ 7.03   The Spectrum of Distinctiveness

The "spectrum of distinctiveness" refers to the degree to which a mark is distinctive and can thereby serve a source-indicating trademark function. The spectrum extends from unprotectable generic names at one end of the spectrum to descriptive names (which can serve as a trademark, but only upon a showing of secondary meaning or consumer recognition, as discussed below) to suggestive, arbitrary, and fanciful marks at the other end of the spectrum. These last three categories of marks are eligible for trademark protection upon adoption as they are each considered inherently distinctive—the suggestive, arbitrary, and fanciful marks. Courts still distinguish between suggestive, arbitrary, and fanciful marks, even though all of them are analyzed in the same manner for purposes of trademark validity (*i.e.*, each is treated as inherently distinctive). These categories are terms of art used to categorize

12. *See King–Seeley Thermos Co. v.*   (2d Cir. 1963).
Aladdin Industries, Inc., 321 F.2d 577

marks in the trademark field, and they are also pertinent to the "strength of the mark" factor in the likelihood of confusion test (where a mark's arbitrary or fanciful status would arguably indicate a stronger mark than one that was suggestive). In other words, the stronger a trademark is on the spectrum of distinctiveness, the greater the scope of protection it is likely to receive against confusingly similar uses of the same or a similar mark.

A frequently cited decision addressing the spectrum of distinctiveness is *Abercrombie & Fitch Co. v. Hunting World, Inc.*[13] In that case, the court held that the term "safari" is generic for purposes of the sale of hats and jackets, as the term represents a type of product. In contrast, when used to market boots, the court concluded the term is descriptive, as there is no particular category of boots identified by that name. The court provided useful definitions of each type of mark in the spectrum of distinctiveness.

A *generic* term, the court noted, "is one that refers, or has come to be understood as referring, to the genus of which the particular product is a species." A *descriptive* term identifies a significant characteristic of the article. As the court expressed it, "[a] term is descriptive if it forthwith conveys an immediate idea of the ingredients, qualities or characteristics of the goods." A *suggestive* term "requires imagination, thought and perception to reach a conclusion as to the nature of goods." *Arbitrary* marks involve the use of a common word applied in an unfamiliar way. Finally, a *fanciful* term "is usually applied to words invented solely for their use as trademarks." In other words, fanciful marks are words that have been coined or made up to serve as a mark.[14]

The same word can be in various parts of the spectrum when applied to different products. The word "ivory" is generic when used to describe a product made from the tusks of elephants, but is suggestive or perhaps arbitrary as applied to soap. The word "apple" is generic when used to identify the fruit, but is arbitrary as applied to computers.

The process by which Steve Jobs developed the idea for the naming of Apple is highly illustrative:

> Now that they had decided to start a business, they needed a name.... Finally Jobs proposed Apple Computer. "I was on one of my fruitarian diets," he explained. "I had just come back from the apple farm. It sounded fun, spirited, and not intimidating. Apple took the edge off the word 'computer.' Plus, it would put us ahead of Atari in the phone book.
>
>   . . .

---

13.   537 F.2d 4 (2d Cir. 1976).   **14.**   *Id.* at 10–11.

Apple. It was a smart choice. .... And the two words together—Apple Computer—provided an amusing disjuncture. "it doesn't quite make sense," said Mike Markkula, who soon thereafter became the first chairman of the new company.... "Apple and computers, that doesn't go together! So it helped us grow brand awareness."[15]

These categories of marks are best understood by seeing illustrations of each type of mark:

Mark	*Product*	*Category*
Best Buy	electronics	descriptive
Food Fair	supermarkets	descriptive
Beef & Brew	restaurants	descriptive
America's Best Popcorn!	popcorn snacks	descriptive
Easyload	tape recorders	descriptive[16]
Citibank	banking services	suggestive
At–A–Glance	calendars	suggestive
Gobble Gobble	turkey meat	suggestive
Hula hoop	toys	suggestive[17]
Amazon	books and retailing	arbitrary
Apple	computers	arbitrary
Mustang	motel	arbitrary
Nova	television series	arbitrary[18]
Google	search engines	arbitrary
Kodak	film/supplies	fanciful
Exxon	petroleum	fanciful[19]

Consider several other examples drawn from LANGE, LAFRANCE, MYERS & LOCKRIDGE, INTELLECTUAL PROPERTY: CASES & MATERIALS: "Precision Cuts" barber shops, "Steelbuildings.com" metal buildings, and "Brick Oven" pizza were found to be generic. "Yellow

---

15. WALTER ISAACSON, STEVE JOBS, at 63 (Simon & Shuster 2011).

16. *See Food Fair Stores, Inc. v. Lakeland Grocery Corp.*, 301 F.2d 156 (4th Cir.1962) ("Food Fair"); *beef & brew, inc. v. Beef & Brew, Inc.*, 389 F.Supp. 179, 184–85 (D. Or.1974) ("Beef & Brew"); *In re Wileswood, Inc.*, 201 U.S.P.Q. 400, 402–04 (T.T.A.B. 1978) ("America's Best Popcorn!"); *In re Sony Corp.*, 176 U.S.P.Q. 61 (T.T.A.B. 1972) ("Easyload").

17. *See Citibank, N.A. v. Citibanc Group, Inc.*, 724 F.2d 1540, 1545 (11th Cir.1984) (Citibank); *Cullman Ventures, Inc. v. Columbian Art Works, Inc.*, 717 F.Supp. 96, 119–20 (S.D.N.Y.1989) ("At–A–Glance"); *Louis Rich, Inc. v. Horace W. Longacre, Inc.*, 423 F.Supp. 1327, 1337–38 (E.D. Pa.1976) ("Gobble Gob-

ble"); *In re Wham–O Mfg. Co.*, 134 U.S.P.Q. 447, 449 (T.T.A.B. 1962) ("Hula hoop").

18. *See Fleischmann Distilling Corp. v. Maier Brewing Co.*, 314 F.2d 149, 153–54 (9th Cir.1963) ("Black & White"), *cert. denied*, 374 U.S. 830 (1963); *Mustang Motels, Inc. v. Patel*, 226 U.S.P.Q. 526, 527–28 (C.D. Cal. 1985) (Mustang); *WGBH Educational Foundation, Inc. v. Penthouse Int'l Ltd.*, 453 F.Supp. 1347, 1350 (S.D.N.Y.1978) (Nova), *aff'd*, 598 F.2d 610 (2d Cir. 1979).

19. *See Eastman Kodak Co. v. Rakow*, 739 F.Supp. 116, 117–18 (W.D.N.Y. 1989) (Kodak); *Exxon Corp. v. XOIL Energy Resources, Inc.*, 552 F.Supp. 1008, 1014 (S.D.N.Y.1981) (Exxon).

cab" was found to present fact issues as to whether the term is generic or descriptive.[20] "Coppertone" sun tan lotion and "Wrangler" jeans have been held to be suggestive; "Chicken of the Sea" canned tuna is arguably suggestive as well, although it has been held to be descriptive (though with acquired distinctiveness).[21] "Arm & Hammer" baking soda, "Camel" cigarettes, "Shell" gasoline, and "Sun" bank are likely to be arbitrary.[22] Finally, "Polaroid" cameras, "Sanka" coffee and "Yuban" coffee have been found to be fanciful.[23]

Categorizing marks along the spectrum can sometimes be challenging, particularly when a mark seems to be arguably in more than one category. Generally this problem will occur when a term is arguably either generic or descriptive, or descriptive or suggestive. (It is usually rather clear, on the other hand, that a mark is arbitrary as it has no connection to the product, or fanciful as it is a coined term and thus had no prior meaning at all.)

In assessing a mark that is on the borderline between descriptive and suggestive, there are three possible ways to analyze the problem: (1) whether imagination is required in order to see a connection between the mark and the product, (2) whether other producers need to use the term in order to compete effectively (competitive need), and (3) whether the mark has been used extensively by competitors other than the purported trademark owner (third-party use).

The competitive need and third-party use tests are discussed in *Zobmondo Entertainment, LLC v. Falls Media, LLC*, 602 F.3d 1108 (9th Cir. 2010), which involved the use of the mark "WOULD YOU RATHER. . . ." on board games and books. The court found there was no competitive need to use the phrase, given the alternative terms available for use in games, such as "would you rather" or "would you most like." The court found that the numerous prof-

---

20. See In re Precision Cuts, 131 Fed. Appx. 288 (Fed Cir. 2005); In re Steelbuilding.com, 415 F.3d 1293 (Fed Cir. 2005); Schwan's IP, LLC v. Kraft Pizza Co., 460 F.3d 971 (8th Cir. 2006); Yellow Cab Co. of Sacramento v. Yellow Cab of Elk Grove, Inc., 419 F.3d 925 (9th Cir. 2005).

21. See Van Camp Sea Food Co. v. A.B. Stewart Organizations, 50 F.2d 976 (C.C.P.A. 1931) (Chicken of the Sea); *Douglas Laboratories Corp. v. Copper Tan, Inc.*, 210 F.2d 453 (2d Cir. 1954) (Coppertone), cert. denied, 347 U.S. 968 (1954); *Blue Bell, Inc. v. Ruesman*, 335 F.Supp. 236 (N.D. Ga. 1971). *But see Van Camp Sea Food Co. v. Packman Brothers*, 4 F.Supp. 522 (D.N.J. 1933)

(holding that "Chicken of the Sea" is descriptive and has attained secondary meaning), *aff'd*, 79 F.2d 511 (3d Cir. 1935).

22. See Sun Banks of Florida, Inc. v. Sun Federal Savings & Loan Association, 200 U.S.P.Q. 758 (N.D. Fla. 1978) (Sun), *aff'd in relevant part and rev'd in part on other grounds*, 651 F.2d 311 (5th Cir. 1981); *Sara Lee Corp. v. Kaiser–Roth Corp.*, 81 F.3d 455 (4th Cir. 1996) (Apple and Camel).

23. See Polaroid Corp. v. Polaraid, *Inc.*, 319 F.2d 830 (7th Cir. 1963) (Polaroid); *McDonald's Corp. v. McBagel's Inc.*, 649 F.Supp. 1268 (S.D.N.Y. 1986) (Sanka).

erred third-party uses were relevant to a factual determination of whether a mark was distinctive or descriptive. Ultimately, the court held that there were fact issues regarding whether the term was suggestive or descriptive.

¶ 7.04   Descriptive Marks and Secondary Meaning

Companies often seek to adopt descriptive terms as trademarks. This strategy is often seen as desirable from a marketing standpoint because the descriptive term "says something about the product" or is connected to the product. Courts have held that "Holiday Inn," "Raisin Bran," and "Rich 'n Chips" have been found to be descriptive.[24] A descriptive term can be protected as a trademark if it has secondary meaning (i.e., acquired distinctiveness). Secondary meaning is established when a mark has come through use to be uniquely associated with a specific source. "To establish secondary meaning, a manufacturer must show that, in the minds of the public, the primary significance of a product feature or term is to identify the source of the product rather than the product itself."[25] The Holiday Inn brand is a good example of a mark that is descriptive, but which has attained strong consumer recognition in the marketplace as a brand. This recognition is the essence of secondary meaning. The issue of whether secondary meaning is present is separate from the question of whether a mark is descriptive.

International Kennel Club of Chicago, Inc. v. Mighty Star, Inc.[26] involved as plaintiff a Chicago-area dog show known as the International Kennel Club. The plaintiff did not have a particularly strong mark but it nonetheless prevailed. Although it had used the mark for some time, it lacked any visibility outside of its particular field. On the other hand, dog fanciers were much more likely to recognize the name. If the plaintiff's mark is not particularly strong, there is some question whether those in other fields should be barred from using it. The defendant produced a line of dog toys to which it affixed the "International Kennel Club" name. The defendant's attorney had conducted a trademark search and learned of the plaintiff's mark, but assumed that it operated a dog kennel, as opposed to a dog fancier's show.

This case deals with a range of issues, including protection for descriptive marks, secondary meaning, the likelihood of confusion

---

24. *See Zimmerman v. Holiday Inns of America, Inc.*, 438 Pa. 528, 266 A.2d 87 (1970) (Holiday Inn), *cert. denied*, 400 U.S. 992 (1971); *Skinner Manufacturing Co. v. Kellogg Sales Co.*, 143 F.2d 895 (8th Cir. 1944) (Raisin Bran), *cert. denied*, 323 U.S. 766 (1944); *Application*

of Keebler Co., 479 F.2d 1405 (C.C.P.A. 1973) (Rich 'N Chips).

25. *Inwood Laboratories, Inc. v. Ives Laboratories, Inc.*, 456 U.S. 844, 851, n. 11 (1982). *See* Restatement (Third) of Unfair Competition § 13, Comment e.

26. 846 F.2d 1079 (7th Cir. 1988).

test, evidence of "actual confusion," disclaimers, and the scope of injunctive relief. Consequently, the case raises most of the issues that typically arise in trademark litigation and serves as a useful introduction to concepts that will be discussed further in later portions of the trademark material.

There is some danger that a term that is already descriptive can become generic, but so can a mark that is arbitrary, fanciful, or suggestive. The acquisition of secondary meaning (i.e., acquired distinctiveness) through use and successful marketing can lead to protection for a descriptive (or otherwise weak) mark, but even that strong de facto consumer recognition does not lead to legal protection in the case of generic marks. For example, "corn flakes" is a generic term and cannot be protected. Yet most consumers probably think of Kellogg's when they think of corn flakes. Kellogg's has strong de facto recognition in the term "corn flakes," but possesses no right to exclude others from its use in the market. The term remains the generic name for the cereal product, despite its associations with Kellogg.

Often a proposed brand will be highly descriptive of the product itself. Consider the cases of "brick oven" for pizza, or "yellow cab" for taxicab services. Ordinarily, these types of marks receive very little or no protection. First it must be determined whether these marks are generic terms for the product itself. Even if they are descriptive rather than generic, they are still not entitled to trademark protection unless they have developed secondary meaning in the market, in which case the mark can be protected to the extent that it is distinctive and there is a likelihood of confusion.

In *Schwan's IP, LLC v. Kraft Pizza Co.*,[27] the court held that the term "brick oven" is generic for purposes of the sale of frozen pizza. In *Yellow Cab Co. of Sacramento v. Yellow Cab of Elk Grove, Inc.*,[28] the court held that the term "yellow cab" presented fact issues as to whether it was descriptive or generic for purposes of the taxicab services. In the case of *In re Rath*,[29] the court found that a showing of secondary meaning in the United States market was necessary before the mark could be placed on the principal register (for federally registered trademarks). The case contains a good discussion of the issue of foreign trademark registrations. In *In re Steelbuilding.com*,[30] the court found that this term (steelbuilding.com) was highly descriptive and lacked secondary meaning, rejecting evidence from an Internet poll that was deemed unreliable.

27.   460 F.3d 971 (8th Cir. 2006).

28.   419 F.3d 925 (9th Cir. 2005).

29.   402 F.3d 1207 (Fed Cir. 2005).

30.   415 F.3d 1293 (Fed. Cir. 2005).

The central point of this line of cases is that it is often difficult to establish that a highly descriptive term is entitled to trademark protection, because it may be deemed generic and because it may be difficult to prove that it has attained sufficient recognition as a brand to have secondary meaning (i.e., acquired distinctiveness). A number of factors go into determining of whether a mark has sufficient recognition that warrants a finding of secondary meaning, including "[t]he amount and manner of advertising, volume of sales, the length and manner of use, direct consumer testimony, and consumer surveys."[31]

¶ 7.05   Surnames

A surname or personal name is considered to be a descriptive term, and is protected as a trademark only upon a showing of secondary meaning (i.e., acquired distinctiveness). So if someone named Jones opens a taco restaurant, the Jones Taco brand can be protected once it has consumer recognition in the marketplace, just as in the case of a descriptive term. In order for a mark to be considered a personal name, it must be understood as such by ordinary consumers. Consider the case of "Niles," a first name used for a toy camel. In *Peaceable Planet, Inc. v. Ty, Inc.*,[32] the court found the "Niles" toy camel to be protectable mark despite the absence of secondary meaning (i.e., acquired distinctiveness). In this entertaining opinion by Judge Posner, the court found that the name "Niles" is unlikely to be understood to be a personal name by the relevant consumer market.

Cases such as *David B. Findlay, Inc. v. Findlay*[33] raise the issue of trademark protection for surnames and the ability of others to use their own names in marketing when there are prior users who have developed recognition in the market:

> In the present case Wally knew that David had conducted his business and built a reputation under the names "Findlay Galleries" and "Findlay's on 57th St." and that many years of effort and expenses had gone into promoting the name of "Findlay" in the art business on 57th Street. He also knew that people would come into his gallery looking for "Findlay Galleries" and even instructed his employees on this matter before he opened. Nonetheless he opened his gallery next door to David dealing in substantially similar works and using the name Findlay. The *bona fides* of Wally's intentions do not change the applicable principles. The objective facts of this unfair competition and injury to plaintiff's business are deter-

---

31. *Union Carbide Corp. v. Ever-Ready Inc.*, 531 F.2d 366, 380 (7th Cir.), cert. denied, 429 U.S. 830 (1976).

32. 362 F.3d 986 (7th Cir. 2004).

33. 18 N.Y.2d 12, 271 N.Y.S.2d 652, 218 N.E.2d 531 (1966).

minative, not the defendant's subjective state of mind. Wally's conduct constituted unfair competition and an unfair trade practice, and it is most inequitable to permit Wally to profit from his brother's many years of effort in promoting the name of "Findlay" on 57th Street. Wally should use any name other than "Findlay" in the operation of his business next door to his brother.[34]

Imagine the case of an individual whose last name is McDonald and who aspires to open a fast-food restaurant using that family name. The right to use one's own name for trade purposes is often said to be a "sacred right," but the case law demonstrates that this right can be limited to dispel consumer confusion.

The *Sullivan v. Ed Sullivan Radio & T.V., Inc.*[35] and *E. & J. Gallo Winery v. Gallo Cattle Co.*[36] cases provide examples in which the courts have given very wide protection to a senior user of a trademark (i.e., the first user in commerce), at the expense of parties who are operating in markets that are not particularly proximate but at the same time not completely removed from that of the senior user. For example, Ed Sullivan, the host of a well-known television show, was successfully able to enjoin Ed Sullivan Radio & TV from engaging in the business of selling and repairing radio and television sets in Buffalo, New York. The court reached this conclusion despite the fact that the local store was owned primarily by an individual named Edward J. Sullivan.

The *Sullivan* court noted that the plaintiff had "no objection to use of the name 'Sullivan' as such nor even 'E. J. Sullivan', nor the full name 'Edward J. Sullivan', since he feels that such forms of the name would not induce or result in any confusion in the public mind. The objection here stems from the use of the diminutive form 'Ed' in conjunction with the surname 'Sullivan' in the combined name 'Ed Sullivan' which appellant has continuously used throughout his entire career. In this regard it is to be noted that our courts have, on a number of occasions, enjoined the use even of variants of a name where such use threatened confusion in the public mind." The court held that even though the defendant currently operated only one isolated store in Buffalo, "nevertheless the state of facts may so change as to encompass a situation wherein there may be a series or a chain of similar stores throughout the country, in which case indeed, unless appellant had taken this present, prompt action, he might at a later date encounter great difficulty in obtaining an injunction because of his own laches. Also, at this stage the corpo-

34. 18 N.Y.2d 12, 271 N.Y.S.2d 652, 218 N.E.2d 531 (1966).

35. 1 A.D.2d 609, 152 N.Y.S.2d 227 (1956).

36. 967 F.2d 1280 (9th Cir. 1992).

rate enterprise would suffer minimal inconvenience in dropping the diminutive prefix, a situation which might not hold true at some future time."[37]

In *Gallo*, the Gallo winery has operated for many years and is owned by brothers Ernest and Julio Gallo. Their younger brother, Joseph Gallo, who does not have rights to the Gallo winery name, sought to use the Gallo name in the sale of meats and cheeses. Applying the principles of *Findlay* and *Sullivan*, it would seem that relief might be granted if there is a finding of consumer confusion. The court in *Gallo* found such confusion, based partly on a consumer survey that found forty percent of the sample assumed the cheese was produced or sponsored by the winery. Perhaps today it is conceivable that a television personality would endorse or sponsor a television retailer—or more likely, a restaurant—and that a winery would sell cheese and meat. These cases are much more far-reaching than the *Findlay* decision, which provided the plaintiff senior user with only modest relief.

Even when courts enjoin the use of a family name, courts often fashion relief that recognizes the legitimate interests of junior users seeking to employ their personal names. In *David B. Findlay, Inc. v. Findlay*, the court framed a very narrow injunctive remedy:

> In framing its injunction the trial court went no farther than was necessary to avoid the harm threatened. It prevented the use of the name Findlay but limited this to the particular area in which its use would cause confusion and diversion—East 57th Street. It resolved the conflict with as little injury as possible to Wally. The proof showed and the trial court found that many, if not most of the leading art galleries, are now located on Madison Avenue and in the area of the 60's, 70's and 80's in New York City. Wally could probably have found an appropriate place for his New York gallery other than at 17 East 57th Street and can now either find such another location or remain where he is under some name such as "W. C. F. Galleries."[38]

Litigation over the use of family names seems to occur rather frequently. Courts will allow the use of family names despite prior uses by others if confusion is unlikely. For example, *Brennan's, Inc. v. Brennan's Rest., LLC*[39] involved litigation between a branch of

---

37. 1 A.D.2d 609, 152 N.Y.S.2d 227 (1956).

38. 18 N.Y.2d 12, 271 N.Y.S.2d 652, 218 N.E.2d 531 (1966).

39. 360 F.3d 125 (2d Cir. 2004). For more litigation involving various Brennan family restaurants, *see Brennan's Inc. v. Dickie Brennan & Co.*, 376 F.3d 356 (5th Cir. 2004). In this case, the court allowed a family member to use the Brennan family name within New Orleans, because the new restaurant (Dickie Brennan's Steak House) clearly differentiated itself from the original Brennan's.

the Brennan family in New Orleans, owners of a long-established New Orleans restaurant called "Brennan's." They sought to enjoin a new Manhattan restaurant called "Terrance Brennan's Seafood & Chop House," to be named after a New York celebrity chef Terrance Brennan. The court found that the Brennan name is widely used by family members, that the geographic markets were disparate, and that Terrance Brennan's use of his own full name avoided potential confusion. The court denied the New Orleans Brennan's restaurant owners any relief as there was no likelihood of success on the merits. This case is consistent with the other personal names cases above, which often allow use of one's full name despite a prior use under the same last name.

Section 2(c) of the Lanham Act prohibits the registration of, among others, the name, picture, or signature of a living person as a trademark without that person's consent. Consequently, this provision prevents the appropriation of someone's "right of publicity" in a registered trademark without their consent. It does not address questions of conflicts between two or more persons seeking to use their own names. The right of publicity is discussed in Chapter 12.

When an individual has operated a business under his or her own name, and he or she then sells the business as a going concern, including any trademarks and associated good will, there is certainly an argument that the individual should be precluded from then reestablishing a competing business under the individual's name. *Levitt Corp. v. Levitt*,[40] presents this scenario. William Levitt was the controlling shareholder of Levitt and Sons, the builders of residential communities in New York and Pennsylvania, known as "Levittown." In 1968, his company merged with another firm (a subsidiary of ITT) and became known as Levitt & Sons, Inc. The new company obtained all assets of the old New York corporation, including its goodwill and service marks, including the registered names "Levitt," "Levitt and Sons," and the common law trademark for "Levittown." Levitt received more than $60 million dollars in ITT common stock, and ITT agreed to employ Levitt for at least five years at a minimum annual salary of $175,000. The company's assets were eventually sold to Levitt Corporation, which continued to utilize the "Levitt" marks on housing developments in Florida. Levitt signed a contract allowing him to become a developer after June 1977, but barring him from using the "Levitt" name in a trademark sense, although he was allowed to use his name in identifying himself as the officer of a development. In 1978, Levitt announced and advertised plans to build "a new Levittown" in Florida, and he identified himself as the founder of the company

---

40.   593 F.2d 463 (2d Cir. 1979).

that had built the Levittown in New York. The court found that a two-year injunction barring Levitt from publicizing his involvement in the new development was not an abuse of discretion:

> Where, as here, however, the infringing party has previously sold his business, including use of his name and its goodwill, to the plaintiff, sweeping injunctive relief is more tolerable. Goodwill is a valuable property right derived from a business's reputation for quality and service. When a business purchases trademarks and goodwill, the essence of what it pays for is the right to inform the public that it is in possession of the special experience and skill symbolized by the name of the original concern, and of the sole authority to market its products. The value of goodwill obviously becomes diluted and sales lost if confusion arises in the mind of the public over the source of the reputable goods or services. To protect the property interest of the purchaser, then, the courts will be especially alert to foreclose attempts by the seller to "keep for himself the essential thing he sold, and also keep the price he got for it." And if the district court finds that the seller has attempted to arrogate to himself the trade reputation for which he received valuable consideration, broad remedies may be effected to restore to the plaintiff the value of his purchase.[41]

Compare *Levitt*, however, with *Holiday Inns, Inc. v. Trump*,[42] allowing Donald Trump to use his name in connection with his Atlantic City Hotel & Casino, despite an earlier license allowing Holiday Inn to use his name in connection with their casinos, and despite evidence of actual confusion. The license did not clearly grant exclusivity; the court also observed that Trump typically used his name in connection with his own major projects, and indeed he has continued to do in the years since this case.

In general, the buyer of an on-going business concern can protect itself from the problem in *Levitt* or *Trump* by obtaining a covenant not to compete (*i.e.*, a non-competition agreement) from the seller. This type of agreement not only prevents the seller from using his or her name but more generally from competing under *any name* and often in any capacity (*e.g.*, owner, partner, employee, consultant) with the buyer. The buyer of any on-going concern should always consider inclusion of such an agreement as an essential part of the sale transaction. Covenants not to compete are discussed in Chapter 18, ¶ 18.02. Although covenants not to compete are often disfavored when they are imposed by an employer onto an employes, courts view this covenants more favorably when

---

41.   *Id.* at 468 (citations omitted).   **42.**   617 F.Supp. 1443 (D. N.J. 1985).

they are part of an arm's length negotiation for the sale of an on-going business.

¶ 7.06   Colors, Sounds, Scents, and Other Marks

In *Qualitex Co. v. Jacobson Products Co.*,[43] the Supreme Court resolved a split among the circuits concerning whether a color alone can be registered as a trademark under the Lanham Act. It had long been established that a color scheme could be a component of a registered trademark, such as the red and white colors of the Coca–Cola trademark. This issue of whether a color—by itself—was protectable, was a more difficult one. In *Qualitex*, the manufacturer of dry cleaning and laundry press pads sued a competitor, alleging that the defendant's imitation of the green-gold color of the plaintiff's pads constituted trademark infringement and unfair competition. The plaintiff had used the color scheme since the 1950s and had obtained a federal trademark registration for the color. The Ninth Circuit overturned a judgment for the plaintiff on the ground that the green-gold color of the plaintiff's press pad was not subject to trademark protection and registration.

The *Qualitex* Court thus had an opportunity to resolve a split among the circuits concerning whether a color alone can be registered as a trademark under the Lanham Act. Perhaps the two most prominent prior decisions were *NutraSweet Co. v. Stadt Corp.*,[44] which involved the blue color of NutraSweet packages and which held that color alone could not be trademarked, and *In re Owens–Corning Fiberglas Corp.*,[45] which held that Owens–Corning was entitled to register the color pink for its fiberglass insulation products. The Owens–Corning pink trademark is recognizable partly because of that company's use of the Pink Panther advertisements, which highlighted its distinctive pink product.

The Supreme Court unanimously decided that a color was not precluded from registration, as long as it satisfied the requisites of trademark law:

> The language of the Lanham Act describes that universe in the broadest of terms. It says that trademarks "includ[e] any word, name, symbol, or device, or any combination thereof." Since human beings might use as a "symbol" or "device" almost anything at all that is capable of carrying meaning, this language, read literally, is not restrictive. The courts and the Patent and Trademark Office have authorized for use as a mark a particular shape (of a Coca–Cola bottle), a particular sound (of NBC's three chimes), and even a particular scent (of

---

43.   514 U.S. 159 (1995).

44.   917 F.2d 1024, 1028 (7th Cir. 1990).

45.   774 F.2d 1116, 1128 (Fed. Cir. 1985).

plumeria blossoms on sewing thread). If a shape, a sound, and a fragrance can act as symbols why, one might ask, can a color not do the same?

Justice Breyer concluded that no special legal rule precludes color alone from serving as trademark and that the green-gold color of a manufacturer of dry cleaning press pads could in itself be registered as a source-indicating trademark. Significantly, the court required that the trademark owner establish secondary meaning (i.e., acquired distinctiveness), in effect treating the color trademark in the same manner as other descriptive marks.

It is also important that the color not serve any functional purpose. This requirement has generated a considerable amount of litigation. For example, in *Sunbeam Products, Inc. v. West Bend Co.*,[46] the court found that color combinations for mixers are clearly not functional. In *Brunswick Corp. v. British Seagull Ltd.*,[47] on the other hand, the color black when used on outboard motors was found to be aesthetically functional. Similarly, in *Polaris Pool Systems, Inc. v. Letro Products, Inc.*,[48] the court held that blue and white colors are functional in the swimming pool industry.

In light of *Qualitex*, the range of marks that can be registered is probably limited only by the imagination of trademark lawyers and owners, as long as the symbol is capable of distinguishing a source, has inherent or acquired distinctiveness, is not already used or registered by others, and is not functional. The Lanham Act (primarily in section 2) also restricts the registrability of certain marks—though it does not affirmatively bar their use or recognition at the state level. Courts generally hold today that any "word, name, phrase, symbol or device" that is capable of distinguishing goods or services in the marketplace can be recognized as a mark. This includes sounds, scents, colors—in short, virtually anything distinctive. When the reach of trademark law extends to marks for which it is difficult to assess distinctiveness in a given setting, the threshold requirement of secondary meaning (as in *Qualitex*) is helpful in limiting protection to marks that truly serve as source indicators.

Categorizing marks that involve shapes, sounds, colors, scents, trade dress (e.g., packaging or ambience), or product design can often be challenging. In *Seabrook Foods, Inc. v. Bar–Well Foods*,[49] which involved a stylized leaf design serving as a mark for frozen vegetables, the court analyzed inherent distinctiveness by considering four issues: "whether it was a 'common' basic shape or design,

46. 123 F.3d 246, 256 n.19 (5th Cir. 1997).

47. 35 F.3d 1527 (Fed. Cir. 1994).

48. 886 F.Supp. 1513 (C.D. Cal. 1995).

49. 568 F.2d 1342 (C.C.P.A. 1977).

whether it was unique or unusual in a particular field, whether it was a mere refinement of a commonly-adopted and well-known form of ornamentation for a particular class of goods viewed by the public as a dress or ornamentation for the goods, or whether it was capable of creating a commercial impression distinct from the accompanying words."[50] The court found that the design did not function as a source indicator. Similarly, in *Amazing Spaces, Inc. v. Metro Mini Storage*,[51] the court found that a five-pointed star was descriptive and lacked secondary meaning.

In re Clarke[52] illustrates the Lanham Act's broad scope with regard to the sorts of marks that can be protected. The mark in that case was a "high impact, fresh, floral fragrance reminiscent of Plumeria blossoms." It was used in connection with sewing thread and embroidery yarn, and the court found that it was eligible for trademark registration. Other examples include trademarks registered for the distinctive shape of the old-fashioned Coca–Cola bottle, Registration No. 696,147 (April 12, 1960); and NBC's chimes, Registration No. 523,616 (April 4, 1950) and Registration No. 916,522 (July 13, 1971). A lemon scent for dishwashing detergent, on the other hand, would clearly be barred on the ground that it is functional, as language in *Clarke* makes clear.

In each instance when a color or other feature is proposed for trademark protection, it is essential to assess the issues of functionality, distinctiveness, and confusion. In *Wal–Mart Stores v. Samara Bros.*,[53] the Court followed *Qualitex* in requiring secondary meaning (i.e., acquired distinctiveness) before recognizing a trademark in the design of a product. In doing so, it limited the effect of *Two Pesos, Inc. v. Taco Cabana, Inc.*,[54] which had treated the "trade dress" (decor or ambience) of a restaurant chain as inherently distinctive, as against claims by the defendant that the decor had not acquired secondary meaning. Both cases are discussed below in Chapter 7, ¶ 7.07 and 7.09.

¶ 7.07 Trade Dress

In the landmark case of *Two Pesos, Inc. v. Taco Cabana, Inc.*,[55] the Supreme Court addressed whether the trade dress of a restaurant is protected under section 43(a) of the Lanham Act if it is inherently distinctive, given the absence of proof of secondary meaning (i.e., acquired distinctiveness) on the record at trial. Taco Cabana operated Mexican fast-food restaurants in Texas. Its trade dress consisted of "a festive eating atmosphere having interior

---

50. *Id.* at 1344.

51. 608 F.3d 225 (5th Cir. 2010).

52. 17 U.S.P.Q.2d 1238 (T.T.A.B. 1990).

53. 529 U.S. 205 (2000).

54. 505 U.S. 763 (1992).

55. 505 U.S. 763 (1992).

dining and patio areas decorated with artifacts, bright colors, paintings and murals. The patio includes interior and exterior areas with the interior patio capable of being sealed off from the outside patio by overhead garage doors. The stepped exterior of the building is a festive and vivid color scheme using top border paint and neon stripes. Bright awnings and umbrellas continue the theme."[56] Two Pesos entered the Texas market later, opening restaurants that were deliberately and strikingly similar to the overall appearance of a Taco Cabana location. Taco Cabana brought suit. The jury addressed five specific issues and found that Taco Cabana had ownership of trade dress in its restaurants, that the trade dress was not functional, that it was inherently distinctive, that it lacked secondary meaning, and that the defendant had caused a likelihood of consumer confusion as to the source or association of the restaurants' goods and services.

Thus, the issue was framed for the Supreme Court because the jury below had found that the plaintiff had rights to trade dress which was inherently distinctive, and that no secondary meaning (i.e., acquired distinctiveness) had been established. The Court held that no textual basis existed in the Lanham Act for treating trade dress in a manner different from other types of trademarks. Consequently, trade dress is to be analyzed under the *Abercrombie* spectrum of distinctiveness, as would any mark, and is protectable if it has inherent or (in the case of descriptive trade dress) acquired distinctiveness. The Court observed that marks are often classified in categories of generally increasing distinctiveness. As set forth by Judge Friendly in *Abercrombie & Fitch Co. v. Hunting World, Inc.*,[57] marks may be (1) generic; (2) descriptive; (3) suggestive; (4) arbitrary; or (5) fanciful. The Court reaffirmed, however, that only nonfunctional trade dress features are eligible for trademark protection.

The Court defined trade dress as follows: "The 'trade dress' of a product is essentially its total image and overall appearance. It involves the total image of a product and may include features such as size, shape, color or color combinations, texture, graphics, or even particular sales techniques."[58] A second definition discussed by Court indicates that trade dress is "the total image of the business. Taco Cabana's trade dress may include the shape and general appearance of the exterior of the restaurant, the identifying sign, the interior kitchen floor plan, the decor, the menu, the equipment used to serve food, the servers' uniforms and other features reflecting on the total image of the restaurant."[59]

---

56. *Id.* at 765 (quoting *Taco Cabana Intern., Inc. v. Two Pesos, Inc.*, 932 F.2d 1113, 1117 (5th Cir. 1991)).

57. 537 F.2d 4 (2d Cir. 1976).

58. *Id.* at 764 n.1.

59. *Id.* at 764 n.1.

Litigation concerning the subject matter and extent of protection available for trade dress has increased considerably in recent years, particularly as trademark owners have become aware of the broad range of features that can be protected as trade dress and of the generous protections the Supreme Court accorded to trade dress in *Two Pesos*. Particularly since the Supreme Court's decision in *Two Pesos*, a wide and growing variety of trade dress cases have been brought, covering an array of different product packaging, as well as products and product features. At least until *Two Pesos*, there had been some question concerning whether trade dress can be registered on the principal register, or whether it is protected solely under section 43(a) and any state law counterparts. This issue seems to have been resolved by implication in *Two Pesos*'s holding that trade dress questions are analyzed in the same manner as other trademarks under the Lanham Act.[60]

The product packaging cases, of which there are many, are relatively uncontroversial. This lack of controversy may reflect the fact that there are many packaging choices available to competitors and ordinarily no plausible claim that the packaging serves functional purposes. Product packaging is largely an extension of ordinary trademarks found on products such as logos and brand names. Accordingly, not only is the name Coca–Cola protectable, but so is the red-and-white swirl packaging of its producer's cans and the distinctive shape of the old-fashioned Coke bottle.

The following is a sampling of product packaging trade dress discussed in post-*Two Pesos* cases: plastic fruit juice bottles, vodka bottles, mail order company's catalog, packaging of reusable diapers, packaging of hand lotion, spice containers, "Ouzo" liqueur packaging, packaging for metal polishing cleaners, packaging of tortillas, and paint packaging trade dress.[61]

---

60. *Compare Aromatique, Inc. v. Gold Seal, Inc.*, 28 F.3d 863, 868 (8th Cir. 1994) (plurality opinion) ("[T]rade dress may now be registered on the Principal Register of the PTO. The trade dress at issue in this case was so registered."); *Kohler Co. v. Moen Inc.*, 12 F.3d 632 (7th Cir. 1993) (faucet's shape registerable as a trademark); *Application of Mogen David Wine Corp.*, 328 F.2d 925 (C.C.P.A. 1964) (shape of bottle registrable as trademark) *with Vornado Air Circulation Systems, Inc. v. Duracraft Corp.*, 58 F.3d 1498, 1499 n.1 (10th Cir. 1995) ("One does not register a product's trade dress—its overall look or image—but trade dress is protected under section 43(a) of the Lanham Act.") (citation omitted); *Vision Sports, Inc. v. Melville Corp.*, 888 F.2d 609, 613 (9th Cir. 1989) (trade dress protection provides broader protection for aspects of packaging and product design that are not registerable as trademarks).

61. *Continental Plastic Containers v. Owens Brockway Plastic Products, Inc.*, 141 F.3d 1073 (Fed. Cir. 1998) (plastic fruit juice bottles); *Carillon Importers, Ltd. v. Frank Pesce International Group, Ltd.*, 112 F.3d 1125 (11th Cir. 1997) (upholding injunction involving trade dress infringement of vodka bottles); *Tools USA & Equipment Co. v. Champ Frame Straightening Equipment, Inc.*, 87 F.3d 654 (4th Cir. 1996) (successful claim for infringement of mail order company's catalog trade dress); *Denbicare U.S.A. Inc. v. Toys "R" Us, Inc.*, 84 F.3d 1143 (9th Cir. 1996) (unsuccessful

Trade dress may be protected under section 43(a) of the Lanham Act whether it is registered or not, as in *Two Pesos*. In practical terms, this means that a section 43(a) action for unregistered trade dress will be tested for distinctiveness only by a jury or a finder of fact, with whatever appellate review is permitted in the case. A section 32 action for registered trade dress will be evaluated (for distinctiveness) first by an examiner in the PTO, whose approval is necessary for registrability. As a practical matter, this distinction makes it possible that trade dress may get protection more readily under section 43(a) than under section 32.

The scope of trade dress claims can present challenging issues, sometimes overlapping with claims sounding in copyright law. For example, *Romm Art Creations Ltd. v. Simcha International, Inc.*,[62] presented the issue of whether an artist's unique and distinctive style, embodied in a line of fine art posters (the "Tarkay" posters), could be considered trade dress and be protected from imitation by competing artists. *Romm Art* would appear at first glance to be a copyright case, but it is a trade dress suit. Both the plaintiff and the defendant artists were engaged in making fine art posters. The defendant's posters resembled those of the plaintiff. The court found that the plaintiff Tarkay's "Women and Cafes" series entered the market prior to the defendant Govezensky, and that the posters' overall appearance was distinctive. The court then quickly determined that the trade dress was not functional, though with surprisingly little analysis, and then found a likelihood of confusion. The potential ramifications of this decision for artists and others are startling, as the court seems to grant exclusive rights to an artistic style, something the copyright laws would not provide.

But the question of imitation is a serious one. Are the festive colors and overall appearance of a Taco Cabana or the style and content of "Women and Cafes" completely unavailable to competitors? If not, when does the competitor cross over the line and create a likelihood of confusion? Are some elements of the plaintiffs' trade dress in *Taco Cabana* and *Romm Art* functional? The likelihood of

claim involving packaging of reusable diapers); *Conopco, Inc. v. May Department Stores Co.*, 46 F.3d 1556 (Fed. Cir. 1994) (no likelihood of confusion in packaging of hand lotion); *Tone Brothers, Inc. v. Sysco Corp.*, 28 F.3d 1192 (Fed. Cir. 1994) (holding that fact issues were presented regarding distinctiveness of spice containers); *Paddington Corp. v. Attiki Importers & Distributors, Inc.*, 996 F.2d 577 (2d Cir. 1993) (trade dress claim for "Ouzo" packaging); *George Basch Co. v. Blue Coral, Inc.*, 968 F.2d 1532 (2d Cir. 1992) (trade dress of metal polishing cleaners was infringed); *Mexican Food*

Specialties, Inc. v. Festida Foods, Ltd., 953 F.Supp. 846 (E.D. Mich. 1997) (packaging of tortillas protected as trade dress); *Benjamin Moore & Co. v. Talon Paints Products, Inc.*, 917 F.Supp. 331 (D.N.J. 1996) (paint packaging trade dress may be infringed by competitor); *see also Stephen W. Boney, Inc. v. Boney Services, Inc.*, 127 F.3d 821 (9th Cir. 1997) (no infringement of grocery store trade dress).

62. 786 F.Supp. 1126 (E.D.N.Y. 1992).

confusion and functionality tests provide little guidance in this area. Trade dress cases are being heavily litigated today, and courts are struggling to resolve these questions. The volume of litigation (measured by reported decisions on Westlaw "Allfeds" database) is illustrated by the following table:

	Trade dress claims	Dilution claims
2010s	94 (as of Sept. 24, 2012)	95 (as of Sept. 24, 2012)
2000s	273	341
1990s	320	182
1980s	103	96
1970s	7	31
1960s	2	11

¶ 7.08 The Functionality Doctrine

An aspect of a product or trade dress is legally functional, and thus unprotected under trademark law, if it is one of a limited number of efficient options available to competitors and free competition would be unduly hindered by according the design trademark protection.[63] This doctrine helps to assure that competition will not be stifled by the exhaustion of a limited number of options for product packaging or design. As the Court noted in *Qualitex*:

> The functionality doctrine prevents trademark law, which seeks to promote competition by protecting a firm's reputation, from instead inhibiting legitimate competition by allowing a producer to control a useful product feature. It is the province of patent law, not trademark law, to encourage invention by granting inventors a monopoly over new product designs or functions for a limited time, after which competitors are free to use the innovation. If a product's functional features could be used as trademarks, however, a monopoly over such features could be obtained without regard to whether they qualify as patents and could be extended forever (because trademarks may be renewed in perpetuity).[64]

To carry out this policy, a product feature is deemed functional and cannot serve as a trademark, "if it is essential to the use or purpose of the article or if it affects the cost or quality of the article."[65]

Codified in the 1998 Trademark Amendments, the doctrine of functionality also has a long history in the common law of trademarks. The statute now provides that "[i]n a civil action for trade dress infringement . . . for trade dress not registered on the principal register, the person who asserts trade dress protection has the

63. *See Sicilia Di R. Biebow & Co. v. Cox*, 732 F.2d 417, 426 (5th Cir. 1984).

64. 514 U.S. at 164–65 (citing *Kellogg Co. v. National Biscuit Co.*, 305 U.S. 111 (1938)).

65. *Inwood Laboratories, Inc.*, 456 U.S. at 850.

burden of proving that the matter sought to be protected is not functional."[66] As the Supreme Court indicated in *Two Pesos, Inc. v. Taco Cabana, Inc.*, in order for trademarks or trade dress to be protected under the Lanham Act, it must not be functional.[67] The Court in *Qualitex* recognized that "[t]he functionality doctrine prevents trademark law, which seeks to promote competition by protecting a firm's reputation, from instead inhibiting legitimate competition by allowing a producer to control a useful product feature."[68] Hence, as a matter of accepted trademark doctrine, "the functionality doctrine marks the boundaries of trade dress protection."

The functionality doctrine serves as an important bulwark against undue expansion of trademark protection, particularly in the trade dress area. A commonly raised scenario involves a functional feature that has attained secondary meaning (i.e., acquired distinctiveness) through the success of the product—and perhaps by virtue of a patent monopoly. The functionality doctrine would suggest that, despite the recognition of origin and other indicia of secondary meaning with regard to the product, the functional elements of that product cannot be trademarked.[69] For example, suppose the trademark owner is the first to invent and market a particular shape of faucet or stove. The seller may even possess patents on some aspects of the product configuration. Given the monopoly the firm has on the faucet or stove design, it is likely that consumers will come to recognize many product features of the faucet or stove as having originated with the firm. Nonetheless, the firm is not entitled to perpetual trademark or trade dress protection for the functional features in the product design.

Thus, once the patent expires, competitors are free to imitate all functional features of the product, so long as they do not also imitate the non-functional trademark features.[70] This is precisely the result the Supreme Court reached in *TrafFix Devices, Inc. v.*

---

66. Pub. L. 105–330 (codified at 15 U.S.C. § 1125(a)(3)) expressly incorporated the functionality doctrine in the Lanham Act.

67. *See Two Pesos, Inc. v. Taco Cabana, Inc.*, 505 U.S. 763, 775 (1992). The Court did not adopt a definition of functionality, but noted that the Fifth Circuit views a design as functional "if it is one of a limited number of equally efficient options available to competitors and free competition would be unduly hindered by according the design trademark protection." *Id.* at 775 (citing *Sicilia Di R. Biebow & Co. v. Cox*, 732 F.2d 417, 426 (5th Cir. 1984)).

68. *Qualitex*, 514 U.S. at 164,

69. *See I.P. Lund*, 163 F.3d at 38–39 (citing *Fisher Stoves, Inc. v. All Nighter Stove Works, Inc.*, 626 F.2d 193 (1st Cir. 1980)). *See generally* McCarthy, *supra* note 152, at § 7:66.

70. Bonito Boats, Inc. v. Thunder Craft Boats, Inc., 489 U.S. 141, 165 (1989) ("For almost one hundred years, it has been well established that in the case of an expired patent, federal patent laws do create a federal right to 'copy and use.'").

Marketing Displays, Inc.[71] In that case, a patent on a hinge design had expired, and the plaintiff sought to assert trade dress rights in the design instead. The Court noted that the plaintiff must meet a heavy burden of proof that the hinge design was not functional (plaintiffs are always required to prove non-functionality under section 43(a) trade dress actions). This burden cannot be met when the feature claimed under the utility patent is also the feature claimed for trade dress purposes. In an earlier case, the Federal Circuit, in *Elmer v. ICC Fabricating, Inc.*,[72] held that the plaintiff's vehicle-mounted advertising signs, which were also the subject of utility and design patents, consisted of primarily functional and unprotectable elements. The alleged trade dress features of the signs made it aerodynamic, allowed drivers to see through them, and maximized visibility to the public.

These cases illustrate some of the issues that arise at the intersection between patent and trademark law and suggest that a patent holder cannot have two bites at the apple—broad utility patent protection followed by potentially perpetual trademark protection upon expiration of the patent. Consider the extent to which this rule would apply if the functional features of a product are distinct from its source-indicating features.

The functionality doctrine can apply to "aesthetic" as well as utilitarian features. Two recent cases illustrate this intricate problem. In *E.R.B.E. Elektromedizin GmbH v. Canady Tech. LLC*,[73] the court held that the color blue was functional for purposes of use on certain medical devices, because the color was commonly used and because it made the device more readily visible. The case involved blue-tipped endoscopic probes used in medical procedures.

In a widely publicized recent case, a federal district court held that red soles are functional when used on high fashion shoes. The court invalidated a well-known trademark registration obtained by Christian Louboutin in 2008, allowing Yves Saint Laurent to sell shoes that were also adorned with red soles. *See Christian Louboutin S.A. v. Yves Saint Laurent America, Inc.*, 778 F. Supp. 2d 445 (S.D.N.Y. 2011). In September 2012, the Second Circuit ruled that Louboutin is entitled to protection for his distinctive red-soled shoe, except that he cannot have exclusive rights to red soles when the entire shoe is red in color. The ruling effectively allows YSL to sell its monochrome red shoes, while allowing Louboutin to protect its distinctive red sole mark in other situations.

---

71. 532 U.S. 23 (2001).

72. 67 F.3d 1571, 1578–81 (Fed. Cir. 1995). *See also* Vornado Air Circulation Systems, Inc. v. Duracraft Corp., 58 F.3d 1498 (10th Cir. 1995) (patent law prohibits trade dress protection on product configuration that involves a "significant inventive aspect" and that is subject of a utility patent).

73. 629 F.3d 1278, 1289 (Fed Cir. 2010).

¶ 7.09   Product Configurations

The Supreme Court addressed trademark protection for product configurations (the actual appearance of the product itself) in *Wal–Mart Stores, Inc. v. Samara, Inc.*[74] The plaintiff Samara manufactured seersucker children's garments. Wal–Mart contracted with a supplier for a large quantity of children's seersucker garments to be sold under Wal–Mart's house brand, "Small Steps." Wal–Mart based its design on samples of Samara's garments, making some alterations. Samara brought suit under both copyright and trade dress theories, and prevailed at trial on both claims. Wal–Mart appealed the judgment on the ground that Samara's clothing designs were not distinctive for purposes of the Lanham Act and there was insufficient evidence of consumer confusion.[75] The plaintiff did not claim secondary meaning (i.e., acquired distinctiveness) in its clothing line, and hence the validity of its trade dress claim hinged on whether its clothing could qualify as inherently distinctive.

Justice Scalia began his analysis by noting the broad scope of marks that are protectable under the Lanham Act, based either upon inherent distinctiveness or upon a showing of secondary meaning, a distinction that has clear support in the language of the statute.[76] He then noted that *Qualitex* indicates that color-only marks are eligible for trademark protection only upon a showing of secondary meaning (i.e., acquired distinctiveness), and found that a similar approach must be followed with regard to product configurations:

> It seems to us that design, like color, is not inherently distinctive. The attribution of inherent distinctiveness to certain categories of word marks and product packaging derives from the fact that the very purpose of attaching a particular word to a product, or encasing it in a distinctive packaging, is most often to identify the source of the product. Although the words and packaging can serve subsidiary functions—a suggestive word mark (such as "Tide" for laundry detergent), for instance, may invoke positive connotations in the consumer's mind, and a garish form of packaging (such as Tide's squat, brightly decorated plastic bottles for its liquid laundry detergent) may attract an otherwise indifferent consumer's attention on a crowded store shelf—their predominant function remains source identification. Consumers are therefore predisposed to regard those symbols as indication of the producer, which is why such symbols "almost automatically tell a cus-

74. 529 U.S. 205 (2000).

75. 165 F.3d 120, 123–24 (2d Cir. 1998), *rev'd*, 529 U.S. 205 (2000). The court also affirmed the copyright award. *Id.* at 132.

76. 529 U.S. 205 (2000).

tomer that they refer to a brand," and "immediately ... signal a brand or a product 'source.' " And where it is not reasonable to assume consumer predisposition to take an affixed word or packaging as indication of source—where, for example, the affixed word is descriptive of the product ("Tasty" bread) or of a geographic origin ("Georgia" peaches)—inherent distinctiveness will not be found. ... In the case of product design, as in the case of color, we think consumer predisposition to equate the feature with the source does not exist. Consumers are aware of the reality that, almost invariably, even the most unusual of product designs—such as a cocktail shaker shaped like a penguin—is intended not to identify the source, but to render the product itself more useful or more appealing. The fact that product design almost invariably serves purposes other than source identification not only renders inherent distinctiveness problematic; it also renders application of an inherent-distinctiveness principle more harmful to other consumer interests. Consumers should not be deprived of the benefits of competition with regard to the utilitarian and esthetic purposes that product design ordinarily serves by a rule of law that facilitates plausible threats of suit against new entrants based upon alleged inherent distinctiveness.[77]

The Court was clearly concerned with the potentially anticompetitive consequences of allowing protection for trade dress based on inherent distinctiveness. Justice Scalia then distinguished *Two Pesos*, noting that it addressed trade dress but not product configurations. He acknowledged that the distinction between these two can be unclear. Indeed the restaurant décor in *Two Pesos* itself cannot neatly be characterized as trade dress; Justice Scalia acknowledged that the décor might constitute "some tertium quid that is akin to product packaging."[78]

In *Wal–Mart Stores v. Samara Brothers,* the Supreme Court thus held that a product design (here, children's clothing designs) cannot be inherently distinctive, and therefore could be protected (whether under section 32 or section 43(a)) only upon a showing of secondary meaning (i.e., acquired distinctiveness). The Court attempted to distinguish *Two Pesos* on the supposed differences between product design and trade dress (i.e., packaging), rather than overruling *Two Pesos* on the inherent distinctiveness point. Nonetheless, the Court succeeds in slowing the movement toward increased trademark protection for ephemeral symbols. On the other hand, it leaves the actual application of the law more complex than it was before, particularly as to the difference between trade dress and product configurations.

77. *Id.* at 213–14.   **78.** *Id.* at 215.

A large number of decisions have addressed the nature and extent of protection available for product configurations. For instance, claims have been asserted for such things as the design and appearance of stand mixers, faucets, speakers, gumball machines, knives, the design of a golf course hole, and plastic planters— though not always successfully.[79]

¶ 7.10   Marks Precluded From Registration

Section 1052 of the Lanham Act identifies marks that are ineligible for registration. For example, section 1052(a) states:

> No trademark by which the goods of the applicant may be distinguished from the goods of others shall be refused registration on the principal register on account of its nature unless it—(a) [c]onsists of or comprises immoral, deceptive, or scandalous matter; or matter which may disparage or falsely suggest a connection with persons, living or dead, institutions, beliefs, or national symbols, or bring them into contempt, or disrepute.

In re Old Glory Condom Corp.[80] discusses at some length the Lanham Act's absolute prohibition on the registration of "scandalous" or "immoral" marks. The case provides considerable historical and policy background on this rule, as well as a good illustration of the modern trend towards permitting registration of marks that some might find offensive. The case includes citations to most of the major decisions in this area. There have been only a few recent reported cases. *In re Wilcher Corp.*,[81] affirmed the refusal to register the mark "Dick Heads" and the accompanying logo for restaurant and bar services. *In re Hines*[82] reversed the refusal to register the "Buddha beachware" mark and logo. The Federal Circuit's *In re Mavety Media Group, Ltd.*,[83] decision sets forth the standard for

79. Many of these cases predate *Wal–Mart v. Samara*, but still present useful fact scenarios. *See Sunbeam Products, Inc. v. West Bend Co.*, 123 F.3d 246 (5th Cir. 1997) (successful claim for infringement of plaintiff's stand mixer); *Kohler Co. v. Moen Inc.*, 12 F.3d 632 (7th Cir. 1993) (faucet design entitled to protection); *International Jensen, Inc. v. Metrosound U.S.A., Inc.*, 4 F.3d 819 (9th Cir. 1993) (no likelihood of confusion as to appearance of audio speakers); *Big Top USA, Inc. v. Wittern Group*, 998 F.Supp. 30 (D. Mass. 1998) (no likelihood of confusion as to giant-sized vending machines that dispense gumballs); *Pebble Beach Co. v. Tour 18 I, Ltd.*, 942 F.Supp. 1513 (S.D. Tex. 1996) (defendant liable for infringement of the appearance of one hole of golf course); *Forschner Group, Inc. v. Arrow Trading Co.*, 124 F.3d 402 (2d Cir. 1997) (use of red color on "Swiss Army" knives was not protectable); *Duraco Products, Inc. v. Joy Plastic Enterprises, Ltd.*, 40 F.3d 1431 (3d Cir. 1994) (Grecian-style plastic planters not distinctive and lacking in secondary meaning).

80. 26 U.S.P.Q.2d 1216 (T.T.A.B. 1993).

81. 40 U.S.P.Q.2d 1929 (T.T.A.B. 1996).

82. 32 U.S.P.Q.2d 1376 (T.T.A.B. 1994).

83. 33 F.3d 1367 (Fed. Cir. 1994).

refusals to register marks on the ground that they are immoral or scandalous.

These decisions ultimately turn on cultural imperatives and taboos, as sensed by the decision-makers (judges, the Trademark Trial & Appeal Board, and initially the examiner). The lasting principle to be discerned from these cases is the one with which they all begin: (1) that trademarks may not be registered under section 2 if they are scandalous or immoral (whatever that may mean from time to time); and (2) that they may be cancelled when they have become offensive.

Trademarks can be precluded from registration on grounds of offensiveness. Recent and still on-going litigation involving the Washington Redskins marks addresses whether the registrations for those marks should be cancelled as disparaging toward Native Americans.[84]

The court in *In re Budge Manufacturing Co.*[85] discusses and analyzes another section 1052 bar to registration under the Lanham Act, this one prohibiting the registration of "deceptive" marks. The case includes a three-part test for assessing whether a mark is deceptive under the Lanham Act—

(1) Is the term misdescriptive of the character, quality, function, composition or use of the goods?

(2) If so, are prospective purchasers likely to believe that the misdescription actually describes the goods?

(3) If so, is the misdescription likely to affect the decision to purchase?

Essentially the three-part test focuses on the extent to which the trademark falsely implies some fact about the product that would plausibly lead consumers to be more likely to purchase the product or more willing to pay a higher price for it. Unlike a case of fraud, intent to defraud or scienter is not required to establish deceptiveness. Instead of intent, the focus is on consumer perception and on the impact of the mark itself. Essentially, intent is not

---

84. *See Harjo v. Pro Football, Inc.*, 30 U.S.P.Q.2d 1828 (T.T.A.B.1994) (denying motion to dismiss suit to cancel registration of Washington Redskins trademark on the ground that it disparages Native Americans and striking defenses based on secondary meaning and equitable considerations), *later proceeding*, 50 U.S.P.Q.2d 1705 (T.T.A.B.1999) (finding certain marks to be disparaging and may bring Native Americans into contempt or disrepute). The trademark owner has appealed these determinations. Litigation concerning the Wash-ington Redskins marks continues to proceed through the courts. *See Pro–Football, Inc. v. Harjo*, 415 F.3d 44 (D.C. Cir. 2005) (reversing grant of summary judgment to team based on laches defense and remanding for further consideration). *See also* Catherine M. Clayton, *Supreme Court Denies Certiorari in Trademark Challenge to Washington Redskins Name*, Gibbons IP Law Alert (Jan. 12, 2010).

85. 857 F.2d 773, 775 (Fed. Cir. 1988).

required under the test set forth in *Budge*—a mark can be deceptive even though merely carelessly marketed, if in its context it is likely to mislead consumers into reliance to their detriment. The older case of *In re House of Windsor, Inc.*,[86] provides another illustration of a deceptive mark, here focusing on a geographic characteristic, rather than a quality of the product itself. One might consider whether cigar afficionados would be more likely to purchase a cigar if they thought it came from Bahia.

The issue of geographic misdescription is more fully addressed in *In re California Innovations, Inc.*[87] This case addresses recent developments related to geographically misdescriptive marks in light of the North American Free Trade Agreement (NAFTA) Implementation Act of 1993. In particular, the Lanham Act has been amended so that geographically misdescriptive marks are treated in the same manner as deceptive marks, and therefore are barred from registration regardless of the level of acquired distinctiveness (i.e., secondary meaning or consumer recognition of the name as a brand). This case applies that standard and requires a three-part showing to prove that a mark is geographically misdescriptive:

> Thus, due to the NAFTA changes in the Lanham Act, the PTO must deny registration under § 1052(e)(3) if (1) the primary significance of the mark is a generally known geographic location, (2) the consuming public is likely to believe the place identified by the mark indicates the origin of the goods bearing the mark, when in fact the goods do not come from that place, and (3) the misrepresentation was a material factor in the consumer's decision.

Section 1052(b) precludes registration of marks that consist of "the flag or coat of arms or other insignia of the United States, or of any State or municipality, or of any foreign nation, or any simulation thereof." Section 1052(c) prohibits registration of marks that consist of "a name, portrait, or signature identifying a particular living individual except by his written consent, or the name, signature, or portrait of a deceased President of the United States during the life of his widow, if any, except by the written consent of the widow." Section 1052(d) prohibits registration of marks that are confusingly similar to a mark that is already registered in the Patent and Trademark Office, or a mark previously used in the United States by another that has not been abandoned.[88]

---

86. 221 U.S.P.Q. 53 (T.T.A.B. 1983).

87. 329 F.3d 1334 (Fed. Cir. 2003).

88. *See, e.g., Marshall Field & Co. v. Mrs. Fields Cookies*, 25 U.S.P.Q.2d 1321 (T.T.A.B. 1992) (cookie company's brand found not confusingly similar to department store's mark).

Section 1052(e) precludes registration of marks that consist of "a mark which (1) when used on or in connection with the goods of the applicant is merely descriptive or deceptively misdescriptive of them, (2) when used on or in connection with the goods of the applicant is primarily geographically descriptive of them, except as indications of regional origin may be registrable under section 4 [15 U.S.C. § 1054], (3) when used on or in connection with the goods of the applicant is primarily geographically deceptively misdescriptive of them, (4) is primarily merely a surname, or (5) comprises any matter that, as a whole, is functional."

Finally, section 1052(f) allows certain marks to be registered if they have attained secondary meaning (i.e., acquired distinctiveness)—specifically (1) descriptive marks, (2) geographically descriptive terms, and (3) surnames. These are three types of marks that, as has been discussed, can obtain trademark status upon sufficient use and consumer recognition. Section 1052(f) states that the trademark office "may accept as prima facie evidence that the mark has become distinctive, as used on or in connection with the applicant's goods in commerce, proof of substantially exclusive and continuous use thereof as a mark by the applicant in commerce for the five years before the date on which the claim of distinctiveness is made."

¶ 7.11   Service Marks

Section 1053 of the Lanham Act provides in pertinent part: "Subject to the provisions relating to the registration of trademarks, so far as they are applicable, service marks used in commerce shall be registrable, in the same manner and with the same effect as are trade-marks, and when registered they shall be entitled to the protection provided in this chapter in the case of trademarks...." A service mark is defined in section 1127 as "a mark used in the sale or advertising of services to identify and distinguish the services of one person, including a unique service, from the services of others and to indicate the source of services, even if that source is unknown." The case of *In re Dr. Pepper Co.*[89] discusses the concept of the service mark and the requirement that trademark owners make bona fide use of a mark to sell a service before being eligible for additional service mark protection. The policy behind this requirement is that owners of trademarks on goods not be permitted to expand the scope of their rights beyond their actual use of the mark to market a particular category of product or service. To permit multiple registrations without bona fide use (or intent to use) would potentially permit a well-heeled party to proliferate its trademark registrations and thereby expand

89.   836 F.2d 508 (Fed. Cir. 1987).

its trademark rights beyond the field in which it truly has good will and conducts business. For example, most trademark owners engage in marketing of the product, but this does not entitle them to a separate service mark for the "marketing" activities. Those marketing efforts are simply ways in which their product trademark is strengthened, as opposed to being a separate, bona fide line of commerce.

Despite the point of *In re Dr. Pepper Co.*, many companies do use a mark in a bona fide way in more than one product or service market, or both. The Lanham Act expressly makes service marks registrable and protectable in the same manner and to the same extent as trademarks. *In re Dr. Pepper Co.* does not in any way prohibit a service mark or trademark owner from registering its mark for each and every such bona fide use. Accordingly, for example, General Electric can register its GE name as a trademark for light bulbs and other electronic products, while also registering a service mark for GE Commercial Finance (formerly known as GE Capital), which offers commercial lending services.

¶ 7.12   Certification and Collective Marks

In addition to the typical trademarks and service marks, there are two other categories of trademarks that are protected under the Lanham Act—certification marks and collective marks. Section 1127 defines a certification mark as a mark "used upon or in connection with the products or services of one or more persons other than the owner of the mark to certify regional or other origin, material, mode of manufacture, quality, accuracy or other characteristics of such goods or services...." *Midwest Plastic Fabricators, Inc. v. Underwriters Laboratories, Inc.*[90] discusses certification marks and the unique concerns associated with this type of mark. It is helpful to become familiar with the distinctions between this type of mark, collective marks, and the typical trademarks and service marks.

Understanding the difference between certification and collective marks can be aided by reviewing some illustrations. Some common examples of certification marks are suggested by J. Thomas McCarthy:

(1) The "Good Housekeeping Seal"—type certification of quality of goods or services. Similar is the Underwriters Laboratories standards and testing type of mark.

(2) The "Roquefort Cheese"—type of certification of regional origin; and

---

90.   906 F.2d 1568 (Fed. Cir. 1990).

(3) The "Union Label"—type certification that goods were made or services performed by union labor.[91]

Each of these marks indicate and certify some fact about the products or services that bear the mark. The Good Housekeeping Seal of Approval certifies that the standards of that organization have been met. McCarthy notes that Good Housekeeping claims that eight out of ten women are more likely to purchase a product that bears its seal. The Roquefort certification mark indicates that the cheese has been made using goat's milk and that it has been aged in caves in the Roquefort region of France.[92] Another example of a certification mark is "Certified Angus Beef," by which the American Angus Association certifies the quality of a type of beef product.

In addition to certification marks, the Lanham Act provides trademark protection for "collective marks," which are used by members of a cooperative, association, or other collective group to show membership in the group or association. Collective marks indicate that a seller of goods or services is a member of the cooperative or association that owns the mark. Examples cited by McCarthy include an agricultural cooperative, the Sebastian hair salons, and the Professional Golfers Association.[93]

The distinction between certification marks and collective marks is somewhat unclear. McCarthy notes that "where sellers are a member of an organization with standards of membership, there is a collective trademark, while if there is no membership, but products are certified, there is a certification mark"[94] Commentators have noted that some parties might seek to avoid the more rigorous burdens of a certification mark by opting to register a collective mark.[95]

91. J. Thomas McCarthy, McCarthy on Trademarks § 19.32[1] (3d ed. 1995).

92. *Community of Roquefort v. William Faehndrich, Inc.*, 303 F.2d 494 (2d Cir. 1962).

93. J. Thomas McCarthy, McCarthy on Trademarks § 19.32[1] (3d ed. 1995) (citing *Professional Golfers Association v. Bankers Life & Casualty Co.*, 514 F.2d 665 (5th Cir. 1975) (PGA mark used by members in tournaments, golfing stores, and elsewhere); *Sebastian International, Inc. v. Longs Drug Stores Corp.*, 29 U.S.P.Q.2d 1710 (C.D. Cal. 1993) ("Sebastian Collective Salon Member" collective mark identifies seller as being qualified to advise buyers of hair care products)). *See also National Pork Board v. Supreme Lobster & Seafood Co.*, 96 U.S.P.Q.2d 1479 (T.T.A.B. 2010) (involving the collective mark, "The Other White Meat," for promoting pork production).

94. *Id.* (citing *Opticians Association of America v. Independent Opticians of America*, 920 F.2d 187 (3d Cir. 1990)).

95. *Id.* (citing Breitenfeld, "Collective Marks: Should They Be Abolished?" 47 Trademark Rep. 1 (1957)).

Chapter 8

TRADEMARK OWNERSHIP

Table of Sections

¶ 8.01 Common Law Trademark Use

Trademark rights are traditionally developed through use in commerce. The landmark case of *Dawn Donut Company, Inc. v. Hart's Food Stores, Inc.,*[1] illustrates the basic concept. The plaintiff in that case was a wholesale distributor of doughnuts and other baked goods under its federally registered "Dawn Donut" trademark. It sought to enjoin the defendant from using the Dawn mark in connection with the retail sale of doughnuts and baked goods in a six-county area surrounding Rochester, New York. The plaintiff licensed purchasers of its doughnut mixes to use its trademarks at the retail level, but it had not licensed or otherwise used the mark at the retail level in the Rochester market area in over thirty years. The court held that no likelihood of consumer confusion would arise from the concurrent use of the Dawn mark by the two parties in separate trading areas. Because there was no likelihood that the plaintiff will expand its retail use of the mark into defendant's market area, plaintiff was not entitled to any relief under the Lanham Act at that time. The court proceeded to note that if the plaintiff later expanded its retail activities into the Rochester area, it would be entitled to enjoin the defendant's use of the mark because of its longstanding prior federal registration of the mark. This statutory right is discussed in ¶ 8.03 below.

Galt House, Inc. v. Home Supply, Co.[2] also illustrates the concept of trademark use and distinguishes trademarks from registered corporate names. The plaintiff had registered a corporate name, "Galt House," in 1964 but had not made any use of that name. In 1971, the defendant sought to open a hotel in Louisville

---

1. 267 F.2d 358 (2d Cir. 1959).

2. 483 S.W.2d 107 (Ky. App. 1972).

213

under the name "Galt House," which resulted in litigation between the parties. The court held that "the plaintiff possessed neither good will nor a reasonable prospect to acquire it. Its right to preempt the name by the mere act of incorporation had expired because a reasonable period in which to allow business to begin had passed and the plaintiff neither alleged nor could show reasonable prospect to acquire good will through actively engaging in business." In modern practice, a well-advised company will seek early registration of its trademarks under the federal Lanham Act, as well as any necessary registration of corporate names under state law. The firm might also seek a distinctive toll-free number, such as 1–800–ENTERGY, a distinctive domain name on the World Wide Web, such as www.entergy.com, and a Twitter handle, such as @Entergy.

Blue Bell, Inc. v. Farah Manufacturing Co. provides a useful illustration of the concept of trademark ownership under the common law and traditional state law. Often, two or more entities will be seeking protection for the same or similar mark. *Blue Bell v. Farah* illustrates the concept of "trademark use" as the lynchpin of trademark ownership. The first-to-use principle of *Blue Bell v. Farah* remains in place when neither party has sought federal registration for the trademarks. Under federal law, changes in the ownership rules have been wrought by the later addition of the "intent to use" (or "ITU") provisions of the Lanham Act. This provision is discussed in ¶ 8.02 below.

Finally as to the nature of trademark use, the case of *Department of Parks & Recreation for the State of California v. Bazaar del Mundo, Inc.*[3] involved a trademark priority dispute involving a state park concession operations in Old Town San Diego State Historical Park and a nearby restaurant. The court found that the State had not made sufficient commercial and public use of the mark to establish priority, as it had only licensed a concession stand for a period of time in the park.

¶ 8.02   The Intent to Use (ITU) Trademark Application

Traditionally, trademark rights depend upon use in commerce, and specifically use in interstate commerce in the case of federally registered trademarks. Nonetheless, the Lanham Act has been amended to provide an alternative method by which ownership rights to a trademark can be secured. The "intent to use" (or ITU) provisions of the Lanham Act essentially enable a party to obtain temporary preemptive rights to a mark that it intends in good faith to use in commerce in the reasonably foreseeable future. 15 U.S.C. § 1051(b) states as follows:

3.   448 F.3d 1118 (9th Cir. 2006).

(1) A person who has a bona fide intention, under circumstances showing the good faith of such person, to use a trademark in commerce may request registration of its trademark on the principal register hereby established by paying the prescribed fee and filing in the Patent and Trademark Office an application and a verified statement, in such form as may be prescribed by the Director.

(2) The application shall include specification of the applicant's domicile and citizenship, the goods in connection with which the applicant has a bona fide intention to use the mark, and a drawing of the mark.

(3) The statement shall be verified by the applicant and specify—

(A) that the person making the verification believes that he or she, or the juristic person in whose behalf he or she makes the verification, to be entitled to use the mark in commerce;

(B) the applicant's bona fide intention to use the mark in commerce;

(C) that, to the best of the verifier's knowledge and belief, the facts recited in the application are accurate; and

(D) that, to the best of the verifier's knowledge and belief, no other person has the right to use such mark in commerce either in the identical form thereof or in such near resemblance thereto as to be likely, when used on or in connection with the goods of such other person, to cause confusion, or to cause mistake, or to deceive.

Except for applications filed pursuant to section 1126 of this title, no mark shall be registered until the applicant has met the requirements of subsections (c) and (d) of this section.

(4) The applicant shall comply with such rules or regulations as may be prescribed by the Director. The Director shall promulgate rules prescribing the requirements for the application and for obtaining a filing date herein.

There is an elaborate process for filing an intent-to-use application. Of particular importance are the time periods—specified in section 1051(d)—within which trademark use in commerce must begin. The applicant must file a statement of use of the mark within six months of the issuance of a notice of allowance from the PTO; a six-month extension is available on timely written request; and up to a twenty-four month window may be granted upon timely request if the applicant has good cause. At any time during examination of the ITU trademark application, an applicant who has made use of the mark in commerce can claim the benefits of trademark registration by amending the application to bring it into conformity with the requirements of subsection § 1051(a). 15 U.S.C. § 1051(d) requires a verified statement that the trademark is used in commerce:

(1) Within six months after the date on which the notice of allowance with respect to a mark is issued under section 1063 (b)(2) of this title to an applicant under subsection (b) of this section, the applicant shall file in the Patent and Trademark Office, together with such number of specimens or facsimiles of the mark as used in commerce as may be required by the Director and payment of the prescribed fee, a verified statement that the mark is in use in commerce and specifying the date of the applicant's first use of the mark in commerce and those goods or services specified in the notice of allowance on or in connection with which the mark is used in commerce. Subject to examination and acceptance of the statement of use, the mark shall be registered in the Patent and Trademark Office, a certificate of registration shall be issued for those goods or services recited in the statement of use for which the mark is entitled to registration, and notice of registration shall be published in the Official Gazette of the Patent and Trademark Office. Such examination may include an examination of the factors set forth in subsections (a) through (e) of section 1052 of this title. The notice of registration shall specify the goods or services for which the mark is registered.

(2) The Director shall extend, for one additional 6–month period, the time for filing the statement of use under paragraph (1), upon written request of the applicant before the expiration of the 6–month period provided in paragraph (1). In addition to an extension under the preceding sentence, the Director may, upon a showing of good cause by the applicant, further extend the time for filing the statement of use under paragraph (1) for periods aggregating not more than 24 months, pursuant to written request of the applicant made before the expiration of the last extension granted under this paragraph. Any request for an extension under this paragraph shall be accompanied by a verified statement that the applicant has a continued bona fide intention to use the mark in commerce and specifying those goods or services identified in the notice of allowance on or in connection with which the applicant has a continued bona fide intention to use the mark in commerce. Any request for an extension under this paragraph shall be accompanied by payment of the prescribed fee. The Director shall issue regulations setting forth guidelines for

determining what constitutes good cause for purposes of this paragraph.

(3) The Director shall notify any applicant who files a statement of use of the acceptance or refusal thereof and, if the statement of use is refused, the reasons for the refusal. An applicant may amend the statement of use.

(4) The failure to timely file a verified statement of use under paragraph (1) or an extension request under paragraph (2) shall result in abandonment of the application, unless it can be shown to the satisfaction of the Director that the delay in responding was unintentional, in which case the time for filing may be extended, but for a period not to exceed the period specified in paragraphs (1) and (2) for filing a statement of use.

The intent-to-use application process is certainly a valuable one, as it gives some assurance to a trademark applicant that the resources it plans to expend to develop a mark will likely result in securing full ownership and PTO approval of a mark. It avoids the kind of "race to prove use" found in *Blue Bell v. Farah*, discussed in ¶ 8.01 above. Nonetheless, the ITU application process may present other complications, which are discussed below. Under current law and in today's marketplace, large companies such as the ones involved in *Blue Bell v. Farah* will have trademark counsel, and the trademark race between them is more likely to be a race "to the courthouse" to file an intent-to-use application with the PTO. Once the PTO issues a notice of allowance, the party receiving this notice will have some assurance (subject to court challenge) that it will have trademark priority. The intent-to-use system avoids instances of wasted resources, which Blue Bell, for instance, suffered in its losing attempt to secure the trademark.

In *Eastman Kodak Co. v. Bell & Howell Document Management Products Co.*,[4] the court considered the interaction between the "intent to use" provision of the Lanham Act and the substantive requirements for trademark eligibility (particularly the rules regarding descriptive marks). In other words, the issue was how to evaluate a trademark for its descriptiveness or secondary meaning before it has actually been used in the marketplace. The court found that in this instance the evaluation of distinctiveness should occur after the trademark applicant has had an opportunity to introduce the mark in commerce. To the extent that a mark describes some characteristic of a product, the PTO could assess its descriptiveness at the outset, as in the case of a "slow-cooker" Dutch oven, an example given in *Kodak v. Bell & Howell*. The term "Washington apples" is likely to be generic and thus could not be protected. Similarly, the PTO would bar a new potential user of

---

4. 994 F.2d 1569 (Fed. Cir. 1993).

"McDonald's Restaurant" on the ground that it is already registered (i.e., confusingly similar to a previously registered mark). A state flag would not be registrable in light of the bar in section 1052(b). These examples that show that the PTO can frequently make a prima facie determination at the point when the intent-to-use application is filed.

Eastman Kodak Co. v. Bell & Howell is a useful springboard for consideration of the purpose of the ITU provision. Importantly, this provision is an example of the trend toward international harmonization in Intellectual Property law. Many foreign nations premise the acquisition of trademark rights upon the filing of applications akin to the ITU application, while American law required a showing of actual use in trade, as illustrated by *Galt House* and *Farah v. Blue Bell*. The American law placed U.S. firms at some disadvantage in obtaining rights against foreign competitors. The intent to use provision eliminates this problem and conforms United States law to that of foreign states. An additional consideration, which the court identifies in *Kodak v. Bell & Howell*, is the assurance given by the intent to use provision that a firm (which has received a notice of allowance from the Trademark Office) can proceed to invest in a new mark and will generally be able to secure rights to that mark. Consequently, the ITU provision avoids situations like that in *Farah v. Blue Bell*, discussed in ¶ 8.01 above, where two firms invested in the same mark, but only one firm was able to obtain rights to the mark.

It is possible that trademark owners, particularly wealthy ones, can take advantage of the ITU provision to tie up brand names that they have not used and potentially may never use. Is this as much of a problem as Kodak claimed in *Eastman Kodak Co. v. Bell & Howell*, or a minor one as the court concluded? The court noted the extensive procedural requirements that an intent-to-use applicant must meet. A review of the steps in this process, which are discussed in the case and the statute itself, are helpful in addressing the issue.

Some marks will be set aside for substantial periods (up to twenty-four months in the aggregate) without ever actually being used in commerce. It is therefore possible that someone who might have used the mark will be deterred from using that particular mark, and will turn to another mark as a result. This unfortunate outcome can occur even if no fraud is involved. But whether this is as much of a problem as Kodak claimed is debatable. The marks that most likely fall into this intent-to-use limbo are likely to be weak marks drawn from the public domain—descriptive words, phrases, color combinations and the like. On the other hand, arbitrary or fanciful (and in all likelihood even suggestive) marks are unlikely to be a real problem, as the available universe of such marks is limited only by the imagination of the potential user.

Despite the development of the intent-to-use application process, the common law and state statutory concepts of trademark ownership based on appropriation and use in trade are not obsolete. These ways of securing trademark rights are still commonly used by small businesses that do not have the resources or the legal sophistication to file "intent to use" applications or that operate on such a localized scale that they do not need (and perhaps could not obtain) federal trademark registration. Accordingly, the traditional doctrines governing trademark ownership and priority continue to be important in determining the rights of participants in the marketplace. Nonetheless, a trademark lawyer can clearly provide helpful advice regarding the intent-to-use process, which enables a potential trademark owner to proceed in developing a brand with much greater certainty that it will ultimately be able to secure full ownership rights.

¶ 8.03   Statutory Trademark Rights—Constructive Notice & Incontestability

Enterprises that successfully register and maintain their trademarks with the U.S. Patent & Trademark Office receive significant benefits. The most important of these rights are constructive notice under section 22 (15 U.S.C. § 1072) and incontestability under section 15 of the Lanham Act (15 U.S.C. § 1065). In effect, this pair of provisions permits a federal registrant to obtain preemptive rights over any post-registration users of confusingly similar trademarks.

Section 22 simply states: "Registration of a mark on the principal register provided by this Act or under the Act of March 3, 1981, or the Act of February 20, 1905, shall be constructive notice of the registrant's claim of ownership thereof." Section 15 states:

> Except on a ground for which application to cancel may be filed at any time under paragraphs (3) and (5) of section 14 of this Act [15 USC 1064(3), (5)], and except to the extent, if any, to which the use of a mark registered on the principal register infringes a valid right acquired under the law of any State or Territory by use of a mark or trade name continuing from a date prior to the date of registration under this Act of such registered mark, the right of the registrant to use such registered mark in commerce for the goods or services on or in connection with which such registered mark has been in continuous use for five consecutive years subsequent to the date of such registration and is still in use in commerce, shall be incontestable.

The importance of these provisions is highlighted by several examples. To illustrate the extent of the preemptive effect, consider the case in which Acme Corp. federally registered the trademark "Acme" for dynamite products. Acme registered its mark in 1995. In 1997, a newcomer into the dynamite industry opens its doors ("Acme II"), calling itself Acme as well. The newcomer is unaware of the existence of Acme Corp. and is unaware of its federal registration. Nonetheless, section 22 of the Lanham Act (15 U.S.C. § 1072) places Acme II on constructive notice of Acme Corp.'s prior use and registration. Acme Corp. can successfully bring suit and will (barring some other defense) obtain an injunction precluding Acme II from using the Acme name *anywhere* in the United States for the sale of dynamite. This will be the result even if Acme II was unaware of the senior user. As the junior user, Acme II will be deemed to have been on constructive notice of the prior use. Of course, a well-advised company today would have conducted a trademark search and discovered the existence of the senior user. Accordingly, it would have actual (as well as constructive) knowledge of the senior user.

Thrifty Rent–A–Car System, Inc. v. Thrift Cars, Inc.[5] further illustrates the statutory rights available to parties who register trademarks. The *Thrifty* case presents a different fact scenario than the Acme hypothetical. In *Thrifty*, the defendant (Thrift Cars) had already begun its operations in good faith and without knowledge of Thrifty's prior use. *After* Thrift Cars began its operations, Thrifty obtained its federal registration. In this situation, section 33(b) of the Lanham Act, the "limited area" exception, comes into play. This provision states:

> To the extent that the right to use the registered mark has become incontestable under section 15, the registration shall be conclusive evidence of the validity of the registered mark and of the registration of the mark, of the registrant's ownership of the mark, and of the registrant's exclusive right to use the registered mark in commerce. ...Such conclusive evidence of the right to use the registered mark shall be subject to proof of infringement as defined in section 32, and shall be subject to the following defenses or defects:
>
> . . .
>
> That the mark whose use by a party is charged as an infringement was adopted without knowledge of the registrant's prior use and has been continuously used by such party or those in privity with him from a date prior to (A) the date of constructive use of the mark established pursuant to section 7(c), (B) the registration of the mark under this Act if the application

5. 831 F.2d 1177 (1st Cir. 1987).

for registration is filed before the effective date of the Trademark Law Revision Act of 1988, or (C) publication of the registered mark under subsection (c) of section 12 of this Act: Provided, however, That this defense or defect shall apply only for the area in which such continuous prior use is proved....

The limited-area exception permits Thrift Cars to continue to conduct business in the market area that it had staked out at the time of Thrifty's registration, but does not permit Thrift Cars to expand beyond that area. To avoid confusion, Thrifty was barred from conducting business in Thrift Cars' market area, but of course it is free to operate anywhere else in the United States. Of course, Thrifty wanted to shut its competitor down completely from any operation using the name "Thrift." It did not achieve this objective because Thrift Cars successfully established its rights under the "limited area" exception. Similarly, Thrift Cars was able to continue advertising in some local publications (including some that were distributed *beyond* Thrift Cars' strictly defined market area), because it had already begun doing so by the time of Thrifty's registration. On the other hand, Thrifty was able to thwart Thrift Cars' attempt to gain a foothold in the lucrative Nantucket resort market (including the Nantucket airport). This plum area was found to be outside of Thrift Cars' market area as of the time of Thrifty's federal registration.

This case highlights the importance of federal registration and the effect of that action on other parties who use confusingly similar names. Despite not achieving complete victory, Thrifty was able to "freeze" Thrift Cars into the geographic market of Taunton, Massachusetts. There may well be consumer confusion in this limited area, but the statute appears to contemplate that such confusion is a necessary consequence of the division of rights. Trademark courts often must make just this sort of equitable determination—akin to splitting the baby—but for sound policy and legal reasons.

Burger King v. Hoots[6] addresses the issue of trademark priority and the geographic scope of trademark rights in the case of a nationally known company with federal trademark registration and a good-faith local trademark owner who has registered under state law. In light of the Supremacy Clause, it is not surprising that primacy is given to federal law in this area. But once again, the court acknowledges and protects the right of good faith local trademark owners to continue their use of a mark in their market area as it existed at the time the other party obtained federal trademark registration. But the scope of the smaller restaurants rights are once again limited to the area in which it actually had

---

6. 403 F.2d 904 (7th Cir. 1968).

operations when the national Burger King obtained its federal registration—the area around Mattoon, Illinois. Despite having registered its mark under the Illinois statute, the local restaurant did not thereby obtain rights to the entire state of Illinois.

In both *Thrifty* and *Hoots,* this result could lead to some lingering consumer confusion—a visitor to the defendant's "Burger King" in Mattoon, Illinois, might wonder whether it was associated with the plaintiff's national company. Or someone searching the Internet for a Burger King chain restaurant in that city would drive to a restaurant that turns out to be unaffiliated with the national chain. Once again, this type of concurrent or parallel use of the same mark is often necessary to protect the established good will of two good faith parties. Consumer confusion in this setting realistically will be limited, as presumably the defendant's restaurant will not have the same trade dress that accompanies any of the plaintiff's "Burger King" restaurants—*i.e.*, the color schemes, restaurant format, menus, employee uniforms, and exterior building design will differ.

It is useful to consider how the *Hoots* case would have been decided had the defendant burger restaurant not begun its use of the mark until after the plaintiff's federal registration. In this scenario, the defendant would have been on constructive notice of the plaintiff's registration and could be barred from any use of the mark anywhere in which the plaintiff is likely to do business. This result would be reached regardless of whether the defendant sought or obtained state trademark registration for its mark. In short, the state registration would have no bearing on the outcome.

The decision in *Hoots* presents an occasion to discuss the extent of federal preemption of state trademark law. In general, the Lanham Act contemplates that the concurrent systems of federal and state (statutory and common law) trademark law can peacefully coexist. Nonetheless, as indicated by the discussion in *Hoots*, the Lanham Act's "protection of federally registered marks used in interstate commerce[] 'may not be defeated or obstructed by State law' and that if state law conflicts with the [federal] policy it 'must yield to the superior federal law.' "[7] The Seventh Circuit interpreted the Illinois Trademark Act in a manner that avoided any conflict with federal law by holding that the state law did not give statewide rights based simply on state registration; rather, state-wide rights would require actual use throughout Illinois by the state registrant.

The most important benefit of trademark registration is the establishment of nationwide rights in the mark, as effectuated by the constructive notice imputed to all later users under section

---

7. *Id.* at 907 (citation omitted).

1072 (i.e., section 22 of the Lanham Act). Consequently, the federal registrant secures rights to its mark throughout the country, enabling it to bar any later users, as well as to "freeze" any prior users in their then-existing markets. As illustrated by the *Thrifty* and *Hoots* decisions, these benefits undoubtedly outweigh the relatively low cost of trademark registration for any trademark owner expecting to operate outside of a very small geographic area or seeking to expand its operations in the future. Nearly all large national chains began as small businesses operating in one local market, including such international behemoths as McDonald's and Wal–Mart.

Section 15 of the Lanham Act defines the circumstances in which a mark qualifies for "incontestability" under federal trademark law. Section 1065 the Lanham Act states:

> Except on a ground for which application to cancel may be filed at any time under paragraphs (3) and (5) of section 14 of this Act, and except to the extent, if any, to which the use of a mark registered on the principal register infringes a valid right acquired under the law of any State or Territory by use of a mark or trade name continuing from a date prior to the date of registration under this Act of such registered mark, the right of the registrant to use such registered mark in commerce for the goods or services on or in connection with which such registered mark has been in continuous use for five consecutive years subsequent to the date of such registration and is still in use in commerce, shall be incontestable: Provided, That—
>
> (1) there has been no final decision adverse to registrant's claim of ownership of such mark for such goods or services, or to registrant's right to register the same or to keep the same on the register; and
>
> (2) there is no proceeding involving said rights pending in the Patent and Trademark Office or in a court and not finally disposed of; and
>
> (3) an affidavit is filed with the Director within one year after the expiration of any such five-year period setting forth those goods or services stated in the registration on or in connection with which such mark has been in continuous use for such five consecutive years and is still in use in commerce, and the other matters specified in paragraphs (1) and (2) of this section; and
>
> (4) no incontestable right shall be acquired in a mark which is the generic name for the goods or services or a portion thereof, for which it is registered.

Subject to the conditions above specified in this section, the incontestable right with reference to a mark registered under this shall apply to a mark registered under the Act of March 3, 1881, or the Act of February 20, 1905, upon the filing of the required affidavit with the Director within one year after the expiration of any period of five consecutive years after the date of publication of a mark under the provisions of subsection (c) of section 12 of this Act.

This provision is somewhat akin to a statute of limitations or an action to quiet title. In other words, after some period of time, the owner of a registered trademark is entitled to assume that its rights are secure, unless the mark has become generic or has run afoul of one of the specifically enumerated grounds that can still be asserted against an incontestable mark. Third parties who wish to challenge the mark must therefore proceed within five years of registration or else be barred by operation of law when this incontestability period has run.

The benefits of incontestability for the trademark owner are substantial: (1) ownership of the mark is established as a matter of law; (2) validity of the mark is established as a matter of law, subject to specifically enumerated exceptions; and (3) the mark cannot be attacked simply for being descriptive or for lack of sufficient secondary meaning. Section 1115(b) sets forth the limited range of defenses that can be asserted in the case of an incontestable mark:

To the extent that the right to use the registered mark has become incontestable under section 15, the registration shall be conclusive evidence of the validity of the registered mark and of the registration of the mark, of the registrant's ownership of the mark, and of the registrant's exclusive right to use the registered mark in commerce. Such conclusive evidence shall relate to the exclusive right to use the mark on or in connection with the goods or services specified in the affidavit filed under the provisions of section 15, or in the renewal application filed under the provisions of section 9 if the goods or services specified in the renewal are fewer in number, subject to any conditions or limitations in the registration or in such affidavit or renewal application. Such conclusive evidence of the right to use the registered mark shall be subject to proof of infringement as defined in section 32, and shall be subject to the following defenses or defects:

(1) That the registration or the incontestable right to use the mark was obtained fraudulently; or

(2) That the mark has been abandoned by the registrant; or

(3) That the registered mark is being used, by or with the permission of the registrant or a person in privity with the

registrant, so as to misrepresent the source of the goods or services on or in connection with which the mark is used; or

(4) That the use of the name, term, or device charged to be an infringement is a use, otherwise than as a mark, of the party's individual name in his own business, or of the individual name of anyone in privity with such party, or of a term or device which is descriptive of and used fairly and in good faith only to describe the goods or services of such party, or their geographic origin; or

(5) That the mark whose use by a party is charged as an infringement was adopted without knowledge of the registrant's prior use and has been continuously used by such party or those in privity with him from a date prior to (A) the date of constructive use of the mark established pursuant to section 7(c), (B) the registration of the mark under this Act if the application for registration is filed before the effective date of the Trademark Law Revision Act of 1988, or (C) publication of the registered mark under subsection (c) of section 12 of this Act: Provided, however, That this defense or defect shall apply only for the area in which such continuous prior use is proved; or

(6) That the mark whose use is charged as an infringement was registered and used prior to the registration under this Act or publication under subsection (c) of section 12 of this Act of the registered mark of the registrant, and not abandoned: Provided, however, That this defense or defect shall apply only for the area in which the mark was used prior to such registration or such publication of the registrant's mark; or

(7) That the mark has been or is being used to violate the antitrust laws of the United States; or

(8) That the mark is functional; or

(9) That equitable principles, including laches, estoppel, and acquiescence, are applicable.

The Supreme Court addressed this provision in *Park 'N Fly, Inc. v. Dollar Park and Fly, Inc.*[8] In that case, the plaintiff operated long-term airport parking lots under the "Park 'N Fly" name. It had registered the mark in 1969 and had sought and obtained "incontestable" status upon five years of continuous use and unchallenged (or unsuccessfully challenged) registration. The defendant opened a long-term airport parking service in Portland, Oregon, using the name "Dollar Park and Fly." The plaintiff brought suit, seeking an injunction barring the defendant's use of that name, and the defendant counterclaimed, seeking to cancel the

8.   469 U.S. 189 (1985).

plaintiff's mark on the ground that it is generic or alternatively descriptive and unenforceable.[9]

Starting with the language of the Lanham Act, the Court noted that the statute distinguishes generic marks (which are never entitled to protection) from descriptive ones, which are entitled to protection upon a showing of secondary meaning. Although the statute allows a mark to be challenged on the ground that it is or has become generic at any time, or if certain other enumerated grounds can be shown, descriptiveness is not one of those grounds.[10]

> One searches the language of the Lanham Act in vain to find any support for the offensive/defensive distinction applied by the Court of Appeals. The statute nowhere distinguishes between a registrant's offensive and defensive use of an incontestable mark. On the contrary, § 33(b)'s declaration that the registrant has an "exclusive right" to use the mark indicates that incontestable status may be used to enjoin infringement by others. A conclusion that such infringement cannot be enjoined renders meaningless the "exclusive right" recognized by the statute. Moreover, the language in three of the defenses enumerated in § 33(b) clearly contemplates the use of incontestability in infringement actions by plaintiffs.[11]

Turning to the policies underpinning the trademark law, Justice O'Connor found no reason to depart from the plain meaning of the statute. "The incontestability provisions, as the proponents of the Lanham Act emphasized, provide a means for the registrant to quiet title in the ownership of his mark. The opportunity to obtain incontestable status by satisfying the requirements of § 15 thus encourages producers to cultivate the goodwill associated with a particular mark."[12] Justice O'Connor rejected the argument that allowing descriptive marks to become incontestable would allow monopolization of descriptive words. If a term becomes generic (as opposed to being descriptive), it can be cancelled at any time on that ground. Moreover, the fair use defense allows non-trademark use of descriptive terminology; and even incontestable marks can be challenged if they are used in an anti-competitive way.[13]

Clearly the Lanham Act provides an array of defenses enumerated in section 33(b). Moreover, the trademark owner must still prove a likelihood of confusion in order to prevail. The incontest-

---

9. *Park N' Fly*, 469 U.S. at 192.

10. *Id.* at 194–96.

11. *Id.* at 196 (citing 15 U.S.C.§§ 1052, 1064).

12. *Id.* at 198 (citing Hearings on H.R. 82 before the Subcommittee of the Senate Committee on Patents, 78th Cong., 2d Sess., 21 (1944) (remarks of Rep. Lanham); *id.*, at 21, 113 (testimony of Daphne Robert, ABA Committee on Trade Mark Legislation); Hearings on H.R. 102 et al. before the Subcommittee on Trade–Marks of the House Committee on Patents, 77th Cong., 1st Sess., 73 (1941) (remarks of Rep. Lanham)).

13. *Id.* at 201–02.

ability doctrine serves several purposes. First, it provides a reward to established registered trademark owners, assuring them of the security of their investments in good will. Second, it provides some certainty and guidance, which enables the courts, the trademark owner, and potential competitors (or other later users) to predict the outcome on issues of ownership and validity of a trademark. Third, it eliminates several issues from litigation regarding established trademarks. Consequently, the owner of an incontestable mark need not repeatedly prove the mark's validity or its ownership of it, and courts need not repeatedly resolve these questions. The only remaining issues would be infringement, remedies, and any defenses still available under section 33(b) of the Lanham Act.

Chapter 9

TRADEMARK INFRINGEMENT

Table of Sections

¶ 9.01 The Likelihood of Confusion Standard

To establish a classic claim of unfair competition or trademark infringement, the trademark owner must show a likelihood that ordinary purchasers will be confused regarding the source, sponsorship, affiliation, or origin of the goods or services in question. This standard is expressly part of the language of the Lanham Act, both with regard to proof of infringement of registered trademarks (under section 32 of the Lanham Act) and of unregistered trademarks, which are protected under section 43(a) of the Lanham Act. The likelihood of confusion standard is also frequently applied in cases of unfair competition and other state trademark law doctrines. The likelihood of confusion standard can be likened to the lens or fulcrum by which the scope of the trademark owner's rights are determined, at least under traditional trademark law principles. The dilution theory expands those rights, and is discussed below in ¶ 9.03.

In short, the likelihood of confusion showing establishes that the owner of a valid trademark has demonstrated that its trademark rights have been infringed by the defendant. Despite its central role in trademark law, there is no agreement on precisely how a court should define the factors relevant to the test for a likelihood of confusion. The specific formulation of the likelihood of confusion test therefore varies from circuit to circuit under federal law, and indeed each state may have its own delineation of the factors relevant to the likelihood of confusion for purposes of state law claims. The Supreme Court has not definitively addressed the factors that are relevant to proof of a likelihood of confusion.

A starting point for discussing the relevant factors for likelihood of confusion is the Second Circuit decision in *Polaroid Corp. v. Polarad Electronics Corp.*[1] This case set forth a balancing test for determining the likelihood of confusion, consisting of the following factors: (1) the strength of the mark; (2) the degree of similarity between the two marks; (3) the marketplace proximity of the two marks; (4) the likelihood that the senior user of the mark will bridge the gap; (5) evidence of actual confusion; (6) the junior user's bad faith in adopting the mark; (7) the quality of the junior user's mark; and (8) the sophistication of the relevant consumer group.

The Ninth Circuit's list of factors, as established in *AMF Inc. v. Sleekcraft Boats,*[2] include: the strength of the mark, relatedness of the goods, similarity between the marks, actual confusion, marketing channels used, the degree of purchaser care, the defendant's intent, and likelihood of expansion of product lines. The Eighth Circuit, in *SquirtCo v. Seven–Up Co.,*[3] considers the strength of the mark, the similarity between the marks, the degree of competition between the goods, intent, the degree of care exercised by consumers, and actual confusion. The Third Circuit, in *Scott Paper Co. v. Scott's Liquid Gold, Inc.,*[4] evaluates the similarity between the marks, strength of the mark, customer care, the length of time the defendant has used the mark without actual confusion, intent, actual confusion, marketing channels, the targets of sales efforts, the relationship between the goods, and the likelihood of bridging the gap.

Because it is a multi-factor balancing test, the likelihood of confusion standard is malleable—there is often an argument to be made for both the trademark owner and the defendant with regard to several of the confusion factors. It can be difficult to predict the outcome of a particular case. Indeed, the courts do not even agree whether the ultimate issue of a likelihood of confusion is itself an issue of fact or whether is it is a mixed question of law and fact—in which each of the individual confusion factors are fact issues, while the final weighing or balancing of the factors is an issue of law.[5]

If the likelihood of confusion test is entirely a factual issue, then it would be a matter for the fact-finder to determine—either

---

1. 287 F.2d 492, 495 (2d Cir.), *cert. denied,* 368 U.S. 820 (1961).

2. 599 F.2d 341, 348–49 (9th Cir. 1979).

3. 628 F.2d 1086, 1091 (8th Cir. 1980).

4. 589 F.2d 1225, 1229 (3d Cir. 1978).

5. *Compare, e.g., In re Hearst Corp.,* 982 F.2d 493, 494 (Fed. Cir. 1992) (holding that likelihood of confusion finding is reviewed under de novo standard of review) *with Ocean Garden, Inc. v. Marktrade Co.,* 953 F.2d 500, 506 (9th Cir. 1991) (holding likelihood of confusion finding is reviewed under clearly erroneous standard of review).

the jury or a judge in a bench trial. On the other hand, if the issue is a mixed question of law and fact, then the final determination of confusing similarity would be resolved by the judge. Moreover, the standard of review for appeals of likelihood of confusion determinations is also affected by this issue. If it is an entirely factual issue, then the district court's determination will be entitled to considerable weight and will be overturned only if it is clearly erroneous. On the other hand, if it is a mixed question of law and fact, then the appellate court would review the legal determination de novo, with no deference given to the lower court's judgment of the ultimate issue of law. Regardless of the standard of review, it is clear that a careful weighing of the likelihood of confusion factors is both necessary and desirable.

Although there may be some value to allowing the lower courts to develop the law in this area, it would seem that the Supreme Court should definitively resolve the factors that are useful in resolving the likelihood of confusion test, as well as the standard of review for such determinations. Establishing national uniformity would further the fundamental policies of trademark law, which is designed to permit trademark owners to operate throughout the country in interstate commerce under a set of uniform federal rules. To date, however, the Supreme Court has yet to take this step.

It is important to work through a variety of fact settings in order to develop a "feel" for the likelihood of confusion analysis. The following examples help illustrate the point: Is there confusion in the use of "Beauty Sleep" and "Beauty–Rest" for mattresses? "Roach Inn" and "Roach Motel" for insect traps? "Blue Lightning" and "Blue Thunder" for audio speakers? In each of these cases, a likelihood of consumer confusion was found.[6] Next, consider whether "Healthy Choice" and "Healthy Selections" for low-calorie foods are confusingly similar. "Holiday Inn" motels and "Holiday Out" trailer parks? "Mister Clean" cleansers and "Master Kleen" dry cleaners? Courts found no likelihood of confusion in these three cases.[7] If the outcome in some of these cases seems unpredictable, it shows how trademark law works in practice.

The following series of cases are excerpted in LANGE, LAFRANCE, MYERS, & LOCKRIDGE, INTELLECTUAL PROPERTY: CASES & MATERIALS and provide further examples of the confusion analysis. *CBS, Inc. v.*

---

6. *See Simmons Co. v. Royal Bedding Co.*, 5 F.Supp. 946 (E.D. Pa. 1933); *American Home Products Corp. v. Johnson Chemical Co.*, 589 F.2d 103 (2d Cir. 1978); *Mitek Corp. v. Pyramid Sound Corp.*, 20 U.S.P.Q.2d 1389 (N.D. Ill. 1991).

7. *See ConAgra Inc. v. George A. Hormel, & Co.*, 990 F.2d 368 (8th Cir. 1993); *Holiday Inns, Inc. v. Holiday Out in America, Inc.*, 481 F.2d 445 (5th Cir. 1973); *Procter & Gamble Co. v. Master Kleens of America, Inc.*, 487 F.2d 550 (C.C.P.A. 1973).

Liederman[8] applies the Second Circuit's well-known *Polaroid* formulation of the "likelihood of confusion" test for trademark infringement. The plaintiff operated the CBS "Television City" studio in the Los Angeles area and sought to enjoin the defendant from opening a restaurant called "Television City" in New York. Despite the similarity of the marks, the court found that the mark was not strong outside its limited field, there was no likelihood that CBS would bridge the gap, and there was no evidence of bad faith, inferior quality, or actual confusion. This case illustrates that trademark owners are not always successful at preventing uses of their marks in disparate markets, even when there might be some indication that the defendant is in fact seeking to benefit from the plaintiff's good will. The case seems correctly decided, but is probably closer than the court indicates. Although the parties' product markets are disparate, there is some proximity and it did appear that CBS was at least considering bridging the gap by opening a television theme restaurant. Certainly today the possibility that a television studio might do so is not a remote one. The plaintiff might have been able to bolster its case with a consumer survey, although it perhaps recognized the danger that a survey might not have shown any significant actual confusion.

Whether the defendant could open a "Television City" restaurant in the Los Angeles area (as opposed to New York) highlights why this is a close case. The only change in the analysis is that there would be greater geographic proximity between the parties, but the primary focus of the "proximity" factor is on the proximity of the product markets, not *geographic* proximity. Moreover, the plaintiff certainly operated on a nationwide basis (i.e., its "Television City" programming appeared nationwide). Hence, there would be little change in the likelihood of confusion analysis, even though a court might be more troubled by the opening of such a restaurant in in the Los Angeles area, particularly if it was very close to the location of the CBS Television City studio. Recall the importance of geographic proximity in the *Findlay* case, discussed in Chapter 7, ¶ 7.05, in which two art galleries were opened on the same street in Manhattan.

Perhaps a consumer survey would reveal a greater likelihood of confusion if the restaurant opened in the Los Angeles area, where the plaintiff's physical operations are located. Consider also whether the defendant can engage in merchandise marketing, given that the plaintiff already operated a retail store selling "Television City" memorabilia. Accordingly, the defendant arguably should not be permitted to enter that market. Yet the defendant might wish to

---

8. 866 F.Supp. 763 (S.D.N.Y. 1994),   1995).
aff'd per curiam, 44 F.3d 174 (2d Cir.

sell merchandise related to its restaurant. As long as the defendant's merchandise clearly originates from the restaurant, it might have an argument that it should be permitted to make such sales.

Marks that are particularly strong can receive protection from a wider range of conflicting uses. In *Blockbuster Entertainment Group, Inc. v. Laylco, Inc.,*[9] the court applied the likelihood of confusion test in the case of a well-known mark, Blockbuster. The defendants were not using the identical mark, however, which makes the case somewhat difficult. They called their less wholesome video rental store Video Busters. An important issue is how dissimilar the defendants' mark must be before it ceases to infringe on the plaintiff's mark. This case provides a good analysis of the "strength of the mark" factor, evaluating both the mark's inherent distinctiveness (i.e., where the mark falls in the spectrum from generic to fanciful marks) and its actual recognition and success in the marketplace. The case also presents evidence of "actual confusion" in the form of a survey. It is worth considering the value of this type of evidence, as well as the manner in which survey evidence might be manipulated through the use of leading questions. Finally, the case provides another common formulation of the "likelihood of confusion" test, this version drawn from the Sixth Circuit. This formulation is very similar to the Second Circuit test, except for the addition of the "marketing channels" factor. The court found confusion was likely.

Foxworthy v. Custom Tees, Inc.[10] provides a somewhat humorous illustration of a successful trademark infringement case involving some element of deliberateness on the defendant's part, a strong mark, and identical or closely related markets. The plaintiff, Jeff Foxworthy, is a comedian known for his "redneck" humor, particularly his "you might be a redneck if . . ." jokes. In addition to many jokes with this lead-in, he marketed a comedy album entitled "You Might be a Redneck If . . .," as well as calendars, t-shirts, and concerts. The defendant began marketing t-shirts bearing exact replications of plaintiff's jokes.

A wide array of subject matter can qualify as a protectable mark, as illustrated by the "you might be a redneck" slogan in this case. Not every slogan is used as extensively in a trademark manner as this phrase, and most comedians probably do not have protectable trademarks in the texts of their jokes. The court in *Foxworthy* correctly notes that the plaintiff probably would not have a protectable trademark in his slogan if he had not marketed it extensively or if he had used a variety of phrases and slogans. Here, the same "you might be a redneck" phrase appeared promi-

9. 869 F.Supp. 505 (E.D. Mich.1994).   **10.** 879 F.Supp. 1200 (N.D. Ga. 1995).

nently on books, comedy tours, albums, television specials, videos, and calendars. There are certainly other entertainers with whom certain phrases are closely linked, such as Bob Hope's "Thanks for the memories," and Rodney Dangerfield's "Take my wife please" and "I don't get no respect." Foxworthy has successfully obtained Intellectual Property protection for most of his act: his introductory slogan is protected as a trademark and the actual text or expression of his jokes is arguably protected under copyright law. Of course, Foxworthy's name and image are protected under the right of publicity and possibly other theories as well (this right is discussed in Chapter 12). This case thus illustrates the many Intellectual Property weapons in a successful marketer's arsenal.

In *International Kennel Club of Chicago, Inc. v. Mighty Star, Inc.*,[11] discussed above in Chapter 7, ¶ 7.04, the plaintiff, the International Kennel Club, ran a dog fancier's show in Chicago. The plaintiff did not have a particularly strong mark, but had used the mark for some time. Although not widely known, it had recognition among dog fanciers. The defendant produced a line of dog toys under the name "International Kennel Club." The defendant's attorney had conducted a trademark search and learned of the plaintiff's mark, but assumed that it operated a dog kennel, as opposed to a dog show.

On the issue of likelihood of confusion, the plaintiff in *International Kennel Club* made a strong showing of actual confusion— there were consumers and others who in fact believed that the plaintiff was selling, sponsoring, or endorsing the defendant's toy dogs. The plaintiff had received calls and letters from people interested in purchasing the toy dogs, as well as some complaints about its sale of the toys. This evidence of actual confusion is a significant factor in the likelihood of confusion test. If there is actual confusion among a substantial number of consumers, there would almost certainly be a *likelihood* of confusion.

Yet as Judge Cudahy notes in dissent in *International Kennel Club*, the likelihood of confusion, considered against all of the countervailing circumstances in this case, is less than overwhelming. If confusion is not the motivation for the court's decision, what might that motivation be instead? The majority may be moved by the simple fact that the plaintiff was first in time to use the mark. The key to trademark ownership is use, and the dog show was the first to use this particular mark in commerce, and indeed had been doing so for many years. So the dog show certainly had priority, as it was the first to use the mark.

Survey evidence plays an important role in trademark litigation. Along with direct consumer testimony, a survey is one of the

___
11.   846 F.2d 1079 (7th Cir. 1988).

few ways to assess whether a reasonable consumer would in fact be confused by the defendant's actions. One concern that courts frequently have is whether the survey is leading in that it suggests that there might be some association or connection between the defendant's stores and the plaintiff's stores. *See, e.g., American Footwear Corp. v. General Footwear Co.*, 609 F.2d 655 (2d Cir. 1979) (noting that question "With whom or what do you associate a product labeled Bionic?" was improperly leading), *cert. denied*, 445 U.S. 951 (1980).

It is somewhat uncertain what percentage of consumers must be confused about source or sponsorship to warrant a finding of actual confusion. Some courts have found relatively low percentages to be sufficient to show actual confusion, including percentages as low as 11, 15, 16, and 20 percent.[12] A survey showing less than ten percent confusion has generally been deemed insufficient to show actual confusion.[13] Valid surveys showing more than twenty-five percent confusion are given great weight.[14]

Consider, for instance, the strength of the plaintiff's evidence of actual confusion in *Foxworthy*. There was no consumer survey, and the court's assessment of actual confusion is somewhat problematic. First, it consisted at most of an isolated case of actual confusion. It is well established that a single, isolated case of actual confusion is not sufficient to prove this factor. For example, in *Daddy's Junky Music Stores, Inc. v. Big Daddy's Family Music Center*,[15] the court found that isolated instances of confusion after

---

12. *See RJR Foods, Inc. v. White Rock Corp.*, 603 F.2d 1058 (2d Cir. 1979) (15 to 20 percent confusion); *James Burrough Ltd. v. Sign of Beefeater, Inc.*, 540 F.2d 266 (7th Cir. 1976) (15 percent sufficient to establish likelihood of confusion); *Humble Oil & Refining Co. v. American Oil Co.*, 405 F.2d 803 (8th Cir. 1969) (11 percent confusion found to be sufficient), *cert. denied*, 395 U.S. 905 (1969); *Quality Inns International, Inc. v. McDonald's Corp.*, 695 F.Supp. 198 (D. Md. 1988) (16.3 percent confusion found to be sufficient).

13. *See Henri's Food Products Co. v. Kraft, Inc.*, 717 F.2d 352 (7th Cir. 1983) (7.6 percent confusion found in defendant's survey; plaintiff adduced no survey evidence); *Weight Watchers International, Inc. v. Stouffer Corp.*, 744 F.Supp. 1259 (S.D.N.Y. 1990) (9.2 percent confusion found insufficient); *G. Heileman Brewing Co. v. Anheuser-Busch Inc.*, 676 F.Supp. 1436 (E.D. Wis. 1987) (survey showing 4.5 percent actual confusion tends to weigh against finding likelihood of confusion), *aff'd*, 873 F.2d 985 (7th

Cir. 1989); *Wuv's International, Inc. v. Love's Enterprises, Inc.*, 208 U.S.P.Q. 736 (D. Colo. 1980) (9 percent confusion insufficient).

14. *See Piper Aircraft Corp. v. Wag Aero, Inc.*, 741 F.2d 925 (7th Cir. 1984) (45 percent confusion strong evidence of actual confusion); *Union Carbide Corp. v. Ever-Ready, Inc.*, 531 F.2d 366 (7th Cir. 1976) (over 50 percent confusion), *cert. denied*, 429 U.S. 830 (1976); *A.T. Cross Co. v. TPM Distributing, Inc.*, 226 U.S.P.Q. 521 (D. Minn. 1985) (34–43 percent strong evidence of actual confusion); *McDonald's Corp. v. McBagel's, Inc.*, 649 F.Supp. 1268 (S.D.N.Y. 1986) (25 percent confusion shows actual confusion).

15. 109 F.3d 275 (6th Cir. 1997); *see also Aero-Motive Co. v. U.S. Aeromotive, Inc.*, 922 F.Supp. 29 (W.D. Mich. 1996) (isolated instances of confusion over extended period of time may indicate absence of likelihood of confusion).

extensive sales and advertising were not indicative of confusion and may weigh against such a finding. In *Duluth News–Tribune v. Mesabi Publishing Co.*,[16] the court held that isolated instances of confusion were insufficient to establish a fact issue as to likelihood of confusion. In *Universal Money Centers, Inc. v. American Telephone & Telegraph Co.*,[17] the court found that the isolated instances of confusion shown by the plaintiff were de minimus.

Second, anecdotal evidence of confusion, particularly when it is attested to by people connected to the trademark owner, would seem to be of little or no value. For instance, in *Heartsprings, Inc. v. Heartspring, Inc.*,[18] the court held that anecdotal evidence of actual confusion by acquaintances of the company president did not support a finding of a likelihood of confusion. Third, the plaintiff's evidence of actual confusion in *Foxworthy* is drawn from a witness who himself was not confused or misled, but who overheard someone else express confusion. Although the *Foxworthy* court notes that this evidence would be hearsay if offered to show the fact of confusion, the court seems nonetheless to rely on it to prove that very fact. A number of courts have rejected similar types of hearsay evidence. In *Versa Products Co. v. Bifold Co.*,[19] the court held that the plaintiff's employee's statement that a sales manager heard statements showing confusion at trade shows is hearsay. Similarly, in *Vitek Systems, Inc. v. Abbott Laboratories, Inc.*,[20] the court held that the testimony of the plaintiff's employees regarding customer confusion is unreliable and is essentially hearsay. On the other hand, the court in *Programmed Tax Systems, Inc. v. Raytheon Co.*,[21] admitted evidence of phone calls under the "state of mind" exception to the hearsay rule.

Another case involving a comedian's signature phrase is *Carson v. Here's Johnny Portable Toilets, Inc.*[22] The facts can almost be inferred from the style of the case: the defendant produced a portable toilet under the name "Here's Johnny." The plaintiff, Johnny Carson, brought suit, claiming that this phrase is associated with him. The court found that the defendant had improperly appropriated Carson's identity by using the phrase by which Carson was regularly introduced (by Ed McMahon) at the beginning of each show.

---

16. 84 F.3d 1093 (8th Cir. 1996).

17. 22 F.3d 1527 (10th Cir. 1994); *see also Atlantic Richfield Co. v. Arco Globus International Co.*, 43 U.S.P.Q.2d 1574 (S.D.N.Y. 1997) (isolated instances of confusion by unidentified persons insufficient to show likelihood of confusion), *aff'd*, 150 F.3d 189 (2d Cir. 1998); *Sweet v. City of Chicago*, 953 F.Supp. 225 (N.D. Ill. 1996) (same).

18. 143 F.3d 550 (10th Cir. 1998).

19. 50 F.3d 189 (3d Cir. 1995).

20. 675 F.2d 190 (8th Cir. 1982).

21. 439 F.Supp. 1128 (S.D.N.Y. 1977).

22. 698 F.2d 831 (6th Cir. 1983).

More generally, phrases are widely used to market products and are protectable and registrable as trademarks. Slogans protected as trademarks include:

— "You're in good hands with Allstate"

— Nike's "Just Do It"

— American Express' "Don't leave home without it"

— McDonald's "Two all beef patties special sauce lettuce cheese pickles onion on a sesame seed bun"

— A moving company's slogan, "From Maine's Cool Breeze to the Florida Keys."[23]

As in the case of any trademark, the key is establishing that the slogan serves a source-identifying function. Consider the following series of cases:[24]

— *Norm Thompson Outfitters, Inc. v. General Motors Corp.*: "Escape from the ordinary," slogan used in catalogs for imported exotic clothing and goods, held to be descriptive of clothing and lacking in secondary meaning

— *Application of Sun Oil Co.*: "Custom-blended" mark for gasoline found to be descriptive and lacking in secondary meaning; concurrence argued that this mark was so common and descriptive that it could never establish sufficient secondary meaning to be registrable

— *In re Wileswood, Inc.*: "America's Best Popcorn!" held to be descriptive

— *In re Carvel Corp.*: "America's Freshest Ice Cream" found to be a common descriptive and self-laudatory phrase lacking in distinctiveness

— *Taylor Brothers, Inc. v. Pinkerton Tobacco Co.*, 231 U.S.P.Q. 412 (T.T.A.B. 1986) ("America's Best Chew" sufficiently distinctive to be registrable).

In light of the cases discussed thus far, a fairly clear picture of the scope of trademark rights should emerge. The scope of trademark rights is bounded and defined by the likelihood of confusion test. *CBS v. Liederman* involved a moderately strong mark that

23. *See Allstate Insurance Co. v. Allstate Inc.*, 307 F.Supp. 1161 (N.D. Tex. 1969); *In re McDonald's Corp.*, 199 U.S.P.Q. 490 (T.T.A.B. 1978); *In re Lincoln Park Van Lines*, 149 U.S.P.Q. 313 (T.T.A.B. 1966).

24. *See Norm Thompson Outfitters, Inc. v. General Motors Corp.*, 448 F.2d 1293 (9th Cir. 1971) ("Escape from the ordinary"); Application of Sun Oil Co., 426 F.2d 401 (C.C.P.A. 1970) ("Custom-blended"); *In re Wileswood, Inc.*, 201 U.S.P.Q. 400 (T.T.A.B. 1978) ("America's Best Popcorn!"); *In re Carvel Corp.*, 223 U.S.P.Q. 65 (T.T.A.B. 1984) ("America's Freshest Ice Cream"). *Compare Taylor Brothers, Inc. v. Pinkerton Tobacco Co.*, 231 U.S.P.Q. 412 (T.T.A.B. 1986) ("America's Best Chew").

was not infringed by use in a rather disparate and unrelated market. *Foxworthy* involved a well-known (though unorthodox) mark that was blatantly infringed. *Blockbuster v. Laylco* involved a household name trademark, but the defendants used a somewhat different mark (though one that was nonetheless found to infringe). In sum, the likelihood of confusion standard (in its various formulations) is applied in cases of infringement of (1) registered marks under section 32, (2) registered or unregistered marks under section 43(a), and (3) state statutory trademark and common law unfair competition claims. The test is also applied by the PTO in determining whether to allow registration of a particular mark, as the proposed mark must not be confusingly similar to a previously registered mark.

The Internet has posed some challenges for trademark analysis. Early cases often involved a practice that came to be known as cybersquatting, in which an unrelated party would attempt to register a domain name consisting of a well-known trademark. This practice is discussed in Chapter 20, ¶ 20.01. More recent cases involve more complicated issues regarding the use of brands for advertising and other legitimate purposes on the Internet. In *Network Automation, Inc. v. Adanced Systems Concepts, Inc.*, 638 F.3d 1137 (9th Cir. 2011), the Ninth Circuit addressed the extent to which a competitor could use another firm's trademark term in "keyword" advertising on Google and Microsoft Bing. On the facts, the court found that there was no likelihood of confusion when a competitor makes use of such terms, noting the following analogy based on a consumer shopping in person at Macy's: "if a shopper en route to the Calvin Klein section is diverted by a prominently displayed Charter Club (Macy's own brand) collection and never reaches the Calvin Klein collection, it could not be said that Macy's had infringed on Calvin Klein's trademark by diverting the customer to it with a clearly labeled, but more prominent display. Therefore, it would be wrong to expand the initial interest confusion theory of infringement beyond the realm of the misleading and deceptive to the context of legitimate comparative and contextual advertising." Here, the appearance and context of the sponsored links dispelled any likelihood of confusion, in the court's view.

Similarly, Judge Kozinkski in the Ninth Circuit applied a nominative fair use analysis in concluding that auto brokers specializing in Lexus automobiles are entitled to make some use of the Lexus brand despite the objections of Toyota, the trademark owner. In *Toyota Motor Sales, U.S.A., Inc. v. Tabari*,[25] the court applied the following test to determine whether the nominative fair use defense can be invoked to make reference to a third party's brand name:

25.   610 F.3d 1171 (9th Cir. 2010).

"whether (1) the product was 'readily identifiable' without use of the mark; (2) defendant used more of the mark than necessary; or (3) defendant falsely suggested he was sponsored or endorsed by the trademark holder." The court provided a number of illustrations of ways in which marks may be used as part of a domain name in non-misleading ways:

> You can preen about your Mercedes at mercedesforum.com and mercedestalk.net, read the latest about your double-skim-no-whip latte at starbucksgossip.com and find out what goodies the world's greatest electronics store has on sale this week at fryselectronics-ads.com. Consumers who use the internet for shopping are generally quite sophisticated about such matters and won't be fooled into thinking that the prestigious German car manufacturer sells boots at mercedesboots.com, or homes at mercedeshomes.com, or that comcastsucks.org is sponsored or endorsed by the TV cable company just because the string of letters making up its trademark appears in the domain.

The court remanded for a determination of an appropriate balance between preventing confusion and permitting the defendants to market their Lexus vehicle brokerage business on the Internet, which required making some reference to the brand name.

The most recent decision addressing the use of trademarked terms in search is *Rosetta Stone Ltd. v. Google, Inc.*[26] Rosetta Stone had claimed that Google accepted paid key-word advertising from various third parties, making use of various versions of its trademark, Rosetta Stone. The lower court had rejected Rosetta Stone's trademark claims, but the Fourth Circuit held that the plaintiff presented fact issues on its direct infringement, contributory infringement, and dilution claims. As to the confusion analysis, the court found fact issues on (1) intent, (2) actual confusion, and (3) consumer sophistication, and remanded for consideration of all relevant factors.[27]

¶ 9.02　Infringement Analysis Cases of Parody, Satire, and Other Expressive Uses

Courts sometimes employ the standard likelihood-of-confusion analysis in situations involving satire and parody. For example, *Mutual of Omaha Insurance Co. v. Novak*[28] involves claims of trademark infringement in the context of claims involving commentary making use of a well-known trademark. The defendant sold t-shirts highlighting the threat of nuclear war, and the shirts were imprinted with a satirical "Mutant of Omaha" mark and a stylized

---

26.　2012 Westlaw 1155143 (4th Cir. 2012).

27.　*Id.* at 11.

28.　836 F.2d 397 (8th Cir. 1987).

logo reminiscent of the plaintiff company's Indian-head logo. The district court found in favor of Mutual of Omaha; the Eighth Circuit, viewing the "likelihood of confusion" finding as a fact issue, held that the lower court's ruling was not clearly erroneous. This case may present a situation in which the standard of review played an important role, as did Mutual of Omaha's showing of "actual confusion" through its survey evidence. Another significant factor that explains the result is the court's adoption of a "property" approach to trademarks, drawing an analogy to the rule that real property cannot generally be used for a message because alternative avenues exist for expressing the message.

One can question, however, whether any reasonably sensible consumer is truly likely to be confused as to whether the defendant's anti-nuclear t-shirts were produced or endorsed by the insurance company. Indeed, the court's analysis of several factors can be criticized. In particular, it is not clear that the defendant's parody terms and logo were as similar to Mutual of Omaha's as the court suggests. It is worthwhile to review an illustration of the parody mark and logo in question; these illustrations can be found in the lower court's opinion.[29]

The court's analysis of competitive proximity is questionable because the court viewed the parties as competitors in the market for t-shirts and coffee mugs. Although the record evidence indicated that Mutual of Omaha distributed these items as promotional materials, it is quite obvious that Mutual of Omaha's principal business is the sale of various forms of insurance (and that it sold mugs and t-shirts to promote the insurance business, not as a second line of business). Recall the case of *In re Dr Pepper Co.*,[30] discussed in Chapter 7, ¶ 7.11, in which the court held that a mark used simply to promote a product cannot be registered as a service mark. Here the Mutual of Omaha products in question, such as mugs and t-shirts, are likely to be promotional items used to support sales of Mutual of Omaha's insurance services. So, in effect, the case is a converse counterpart to *In re Dr. Pepper Co.*, with the products being promotional while the services are bona fide.

The likelihood of confusion test focuses in part on the proximity between the plaintiff's product market and that of the defendant, as well as the likelihood that the plaintiff will "bridge the gap" by entering the defendant's product market. If the plaintiff has entered a number of different product markets (and registered its mark in those markets), it may be able to lay claim to exclusivity in a wider range of markets.

29. 648 F.Supp. 905, 905–08 (D. Neb. 1986), *aff'd*, 836 F.2d 397 (8th Cir. 1987).

30. 836 F.2d 508 (Fed. Cir. 1987).

The court's analysis of the survey evidence is also open to criticism. As suggested by the dissent, the central question was leading—it suggested to the survey audience that a connection might be found. Moreover, one might question whether the ten percent showing of confusion was sufficient; when only ten percent of those surveyed thought that Mutual of Omaha "goes along" with the message on the parody t-shirt, ninety percent therefore *did not* believe so.

Some courts are more favorably disposed to parody than the *Mutual of Omaha* court, although the procedural posture, survey evidence, and particular types of parodies all play a role in each decision. In *Anheuser–Busch, Inc. v. L & L Wings, Inc.*,[31] a t-shirt maker was also hailed into court by the proprietor of a highly successful and well-known trademark owner. The humorous logo quite clearly imitates the trademarked Budweiser beer can design (as can be seen in an appendix to the court opinion). As in *Mutual of Omaha*, the defendant was a for-profit t-shirt peddler. Unlike that case, the defendant here had no particular political message. Ironically, the defendant in *Mutual of Omaha* thus had an arguably greater First Amendment right to express its political message than the defendant in the beer case, given that Novak's anti-nuclear speech went to the heart of traditionally protected speech. Nonetheless, the defendant in *L & L Wings* prevailed, while Novak lost his case.

It may be possible to reconcile the two cases. One way to do so is to note that both appellate panels deferred to the trier of fact—in *Mutual of Omaha* ruling that the finding of a likelihood of confusion was not clearly erroneous, and in *L & L Wings* finding that the jury's verdict (finding no likelihood of confusion) was also not clearly erroneous. This purely factual approach allows for some flexibility, but provides little guidance.[32] Consider how a lawyer should advise a potential parodist as to its liability in light of this standard, as well as the parodist's likely response if it were not interested in defending against protracted and unpredictable litigation involving a large, well financed opponent. Another important factor was the weight the *Mutual of Omaha* court gave to the plaintiff's survey evidence and the apparent absence of such evidence in *L & L Wings*. In light of the outcomes in these cases, it seems likely that a well advised and wealthy trademark owner would foot the bill for a survey to bolster its claim of confusion.

More recently, the court in *Louis Vuitton Malletier S.A. v. Haute Diggity Dog, LLC.*, 507 F.3d 252 (4th Cir. 2007), addressed a

31. 962 F.2d 316 (4th Cir. 1992).

32. *See also Elvis Presley Enterprises, Inc. v. Capece*, 141 F.3d 188 (5th Cir. 1998).

claim by the famous Louis Vuitton handbag maker that the defendant's line of "Chewy Vuitton" dog toys infringed its marks. Applying a likelihood of confusion analysis, the court held that there was no showing of trademark infringement given the obvious nature of the parody.

Even though cases of obvious parody do seem to be result in rulings for the defendants, it appears that the likelihood of confusion test is sometimes ill suited to parody cases, or at a minimum that it must be weighed carefully and differently in parody cases. This author has suggested as much in a law review article:

> The treatment of parodies in trademark law is one of the more serious areas of difficulty, particularly because the Lanham Act does not appear to contemplate or address the issue. The "likelihood of confusion" test provides a conceptual approach that works well enough in garden variety trademark cases, but it provides an uncomfortable fit in parody cases. The Supreme Court's recent copyright decision in *Campbell v. Acuff–Rose Music, Inc.*, provides some guidance for the treatment of parodies in copyright cases. Although *Campbell* focused on copyright parodies, the case may also provide some important principles for the analysis of parody in trademark law....
>
> To accomplish this task [of balancing conflicting interests] in trademark law, a careful assessment of the likelihood of confusion test is required. The analysis must be attuned to the realities of parody cases. If mechanically applied, some factors in the likelihood of confusion test are likely always to favor the plaintiff because of the parodist's need to conjure up the original and the need to parody a strong mark. If these factors are nearly always weighed in the plaintiff's favor, the deck will be stacked against parody. It was this approach that the Supreme Court repudiated in copyright law when it decided *Campbell*. Yet courts have used a similar approach in trademark law, where the likelihood of confusion test is much more unsuitable for parody cases than copyright's fair use analysis.[33]

The Eleventh Circuit recently addressed the balance between trademark and First Amendment rights, in *University of Alabama Board of Trustees v. New Life Art, Inc.*, 683 F.3d 1266 (11th Cir. 2012). Daniel A. Moore was a long-time painter of famous football scenes involving the University of Alabama, featuring realistic portrayals of past games, along with various trademarks (insignia and colors) belonging to the school. The court summarized the school's main claim as follows: "The University's claim is that Moore's unlicensed paintings, prints, and calendars infringe on the

---

33. Gary Myers, "Trademark Parody: Lessons from the Copyright Decision in *Campbell v. Acuff–Rose Music, Inc.*," 59 LAW & CONTEMP. PROBS. 181 (1996).

University's trademarks because the inclusion in these products of the University's football uniforms (showing the University's crimson and white colors) creates a likelihood of confusion on the part of buyers that the University sponsored or endorsed the product." The court applied the *Rogers* test and rejected the University's main trademark claim:

> In this case, we readily conclude that Moore's paintings, prints, and calendars are protected under the Rogers test. The depiction of the University's uniforms in the content of these items is artistically relevant to the expressive underlying works because the uniforms' colors and designs are needed for a realistic portrayal of famous scenes from Alabama football history. Also there is no evidence that Moore ever marketed an unlicensed item as "endorsed" or "sponsored" by the University, or otherwise explicitly stated that such items were affiliated with the University. Moore's paintings, prints, and calendars very clearly are embodiments of artistic expression, and are entitled to full First Amendment protection.

The court held that any slight harm from isolated instances of consumer confusion was outweighed by Moore's right of free expression.

¶ 9.03 Dilution

Under standard trademark law principles, trademark owners were required to prove a likelihood of confusion to obtain relief under federal or state trademark law. In other words, the plaintiff was required to prove that the defendant's use of a mark was "likely to cause confusion, or to cause mistake, or to deceive as to the affiliation, connection, or association of such person.[34] In practical effect, the requirement of proof of confusion meant that weak trademarks were given limited protection, dissimilar marks were not barred from use even in the same product or service market, and that the trademark claim was less likely to succeed if a similar mark was being used in a particular product or service market that was far removed from the plaintiff's product or service market. In the large majority of cases, this standard worked a desirable balance between the rights of trademark owners and the rights of those who wished to use non-confusingly similar marks.

There were some instances, however, in which the result under this standard might be undesirable. The classic hypothetical examples are "DuPont shoes, Buick aspirin tablets, Schlitz varnish, Kodak pianos, [and] Bulova gowns."[35] In each of these instances,

---

34. 15 U.S.C. § 1125(a)(1)(A)(1994).

35. *Mead Data Central, Inc. v. Toyota Motor Sales, U.S.A., Inc.*, 875 F.2d

even though the ordinary consumer would not be confused—i.e., would probably not believe that the plaintiff trademark owner was the source or sponsor of the defendant's goods or services—there was still some damage done to the distinctive quality of the plaintiff's brand name. Over time, if these uses were allowed to proceed unabated, the term "Kodak" would no longer automatically bring to mind the maker of film and other photographic products. To address this problem, many states enacted trademark dilution statutes, which allowed relief when a distinctive or famous trademark was blurred or tarnished by the use of a substantially similar or identical mark, even in the absence of a showing of consumer confusion or direct competition in the plaintiff's market. In late 1995, Congress enacted the federal Trademark Dilution Act, which made the dilution doctrine a matter of federal trademark law.

The development of dilution law begins with state law, given the lack of a federal dilution statute until 1995. The most frequently discussed state law dilution claim is *Mead Data Central, Inc. v. Toyota Motor Sales, U.S.A., Inc.*[36] Mead operated the LEXIS legal research service, and Toyota was just introducing its LEXUS line of luxury automobiles. Given the wide disparity in the markets at issue, consumer confusion was unlikely. But Mead brought suit under section 368–d of New York's General Business Law, the New York dilution statute, which states:

> Likelihood of injury to business reputation or of dilution of the distinctive quality of a mark or trade name shall be a ground for injunctive relief in cases of infringement of a mark registered or not registered or in cases of unfair competition, notwithstanding the absence of competition between the parties or the absence of confusion as to the source of goods or services.

This case essentially involves a "blurring" claim—dilution of the distinctive quality of a mark. The case makes note of several hypothetical examples, such as "DuPont shoes, Buick aspirin tablets, Schlitz varnish, Kodak pianos, Bulova gowns." The court noted that the LEXIS mark does not have this type of selling power, and thus cannot suffer from dilution of the type cognizable under the state dilution statute:

> The strength and distinctiveness of LEXIS is limited to the market for its services—attorneys and accountants. Outside that market, LEXIS has very little selling power. Because only one percent of the general population associates LEXIS with the attributes of Mead's service, it cannot be said that LEXIS identifies that service to the general public and distinguishes it

1026, 1031 (2d Cir. 1989) (quoting 1954　　**36.**　875 F.2d 1026 (2d Cir. 1989).
N.Y. Legis. Ann. 49–50).

from others. Moreover, the bulk of Mead's advertising budget is devoted to reaching attorneys through professional journals.[37]

The court noted that the type of mental association that would give rise to a dilution claim requires a famous and distinctive mark. On the other hand, when a mark is recognizable only in a limited market, such as the attorneys and accountants in this case, "LEXIS has no distinctive quality that LEXUS will dilute."[38]

Finally, the court recognized that Toyota's LEXUS brand was likely to become a household name, essentially swamping the Mead brand. But this does not change the analysis of whether Mead can prevent the junior user from making use of its mark. Even though LEXUS is now a famous mark, Mead, as the senior user of the LEXIS mark, will of course be entitled to continue to make use of its LEXIS mark in its market, as long as that mark is continuously used.[39] Trademark law generally protects the first to arrive and participate in the marketplace.

In *Coca–Cola Co. v. Gemini Rising, Inc.*,[40] the court addressed a claim involving the other theory of liability for dilution—tarnishment or injury to business reputation. The court found the defendant's "Enjoy Cocaine" poster, which also made use of the Coca–Cola color scheme, did tarnish the Coca–Cola mark. It is worth considering the circumstances in which another's use of a well-known name would tarnish the mark. The ultimate question is whether a defendant should be permitted to use the well-known imagery of a trademark to highlight, strengthen, or make more humorous its message. Those who view Intellectual Property rights as somewhat akin to tangible property rights would say "of course

---

37. *Id.* at 1031.

38. *Id.* at 1031.

39. *See, e.g.,* 15 U.S.C. § 1125(c) (1) (permitting dilution action against defendant only when "such use begins after the mark has become famous").

40. 346 F.Supp. 1183, 1186–87 (E.D.N.Y.1972). For other of claims involving tarnishment, *see Jews For Jesus v. Brodsky*, 993 F.Supp. 282 (D. N.J.) (granting preliminary injunction in case involving *inter alia* dilution by blurring and tarnishment claims by religious organization against operator of "jewsforjesus.org" website), *aff'd*, 159 F.3d 1351 (3rd Cir. 1998); *Playboy Enterprises, Inc. v. Webbworld, Inc.*, 991 F.Supp. 543 (N.D. Tex. 1997) (dilution by tarnishment claim by adult magazine against provider of Internet site selling photographs), *aff'd*, 168 F.3d 486 (5th Cir. 1999); *Guess?, Inc. v. Tres Hermanos*, 993 F.Supp. 1277 (C.D. Cal. 1997) (discussing tarnishment claim in case involving Guess jeans maker's suit against maker of jeans with "yield" logo); *Haas Outdoors, Inc. v. Oak Country Camo, Inc.*, 957 F.Supp. 835 (N.D. Miss. 1997) (discussing tarnishment claim involving camouflage clothing); *Sports Authority, Inc. v. Abercrombie & Fitch, Inc.*, 965 F.Supp. 925 (E.D. Mich. 1997) (discussing tarnishment in connection with dilution claim involving term "authority"). *See also* 141 Cong. Rec. 19310 (Dec. 29, 1995) (statement of Sen. Hatch regarding purpose of bill, namely to prevent blurring or tarnishment of famous marks). The recent Federal Trademark Dilution Revision Act of 2006 expressly includes claims for tarnishment when the reputation of a famous mark is harmed.

not, just as they would have no right to take my microphone or billboard or hillside and print their message on it." Others would distinguish Intellectual Property from tangible property and would argue that there should be more room for creative expression that makes some use of or evokes trademark imagery. Ultimately, the question is where to draw the line. Trademark law seems to offer at least some guidance under the "likelihood of confusion" test, but dilution theory presents more serious dangers of chilling creative expression.

Generally, tarnishment cases involve humorous (satiric or parodic) uses of a well-known mark; indeed, if the mark is not well known, then it is usually not suited to the efforts of the second (junior) user. Sometimes the tarnishing use is meant as an unkind commentary on the original mark. In the late 1960s, the Disney characters were often subject to such appropriations. Sometimes, as was arguably the case in *Coca–Cola Co. v. Gemini Rising* and apparently as the defendant itself argued, the use was not actually meant to disparage the original mark, but rather to permit the junior user to offer a commentary in which the role assigned to the senior mark is that of a supporting actor rather than an antagonist.

Courts have not always been receptive to dilution claims as a general matter, but tarnishment claims (even in the absence of a dilution statute, so that the plaintiff had to recast the complaint in terms of confusion) have long found greater favor. Section 25(2) of the Restatement (3d) of Unfair Competition accepts the concept of dilution, including tarnishment, but suggests that in tarnishment cases amounting to an attack upon the senior mark (or a related product or service) the plaintiff should prevail only upon proof of a prima facie tort action (such as defamation, invasion of privacy or injurious falsehood). The Restatement comments also note that First Amendment issues may arise in these and similar cases.

Perhaps this case would have had a different outcome if the defendant had not deliberately made use of so much of the plaintiff's trademark, such as the script lettering and the color scheme. In other words, had the defendant simply designed a poster bearing the slogan, "Enjoy Cocaine," the plaintiff would have had a weaker case. Even so, it could argue that the defendant's poster made use of a substantially similar version of its registered trademark in its slogan. But too much can be made of refinements like these: no self-respecting satirist would have contented itself with anything but an outright appropriation. The whole point of the defendant's poster is to be outrageous.

Dilution claims are, of course, even more important now in light of Congress's enactment of a federal dilution statute; about half the states also have dilution statutes, which are generally similar to the New York statute quoted above. Even after enactment of the federal dilution statute, a number of significant dilution cases have been decided under state law.[41] Courts struggled with defining the scope of the new federal dilution statute. In *Moseley v. V Secret Catalogue, Inc.*,[42] the Supreme Court had an opportunity to determine the standard for trademark dilution under federal law. After this ruling, Congress amended the dilution law, essentially overruling the main holding of the case. To understand the current state of federal dilution law, however, a review of the *Moseley* case is beneficial.

In *Moseley*, the famous lingerie company, "Victoria's Secret," brought suit against a small retail store called "Victor's Little Secret." The defendant store, located in a strip mall in Elizabethtown, Kentucky, sold a variety of items including: "Intimate Lingerie for every woman," "Romantic Lighting," "Lycra Dresses," "Pagers," and "Adult Novelties/Gifts." The plaintiff operated over 750 Victoria's Secret stores, two of which were in nearby Louisville, Kentucky, spent over $55 million advertising, distributed 400 million copies of its Victoria's Secret catalog annually (including 39,-000 in Elizabethtown), and had sales exceeding $1.5 billion in 1998. The Supreme Court took the case to determine the proper standard for trademark dilution under federal law. Interpreting the statutory language in effect at the time, the Court concluded that *actual dilution*, rather than a likelihood of dilution, must be proven. This ruling was based on the following language under the dilution statute in effect at the time: "The owner of a famous mark shall be entitled ... to an injunction against another person's commercial use in commerce of a mark or trade name, if such use begins after the mark has become famous and *causes dilution of the distinctive quality of the mark*, and to obtain such other relief as is provided in this subsection."[43]

The Trademark Dilution Revision Act of 2006 (TDRA) revised section 43(c) in several crucial ways: (1) reversing the *Moseley* case's actual dilution standard, and putting into place a likelihood of dilution standard somewhat akin to the *Mead Data Central* approach under the New York dilution statute; (2) expressly recognizing a dilution by tarnishment claim; (3) more precisely defining a famous mark, which must be famous to general consumer audiences in the United States; and (4) setting forth factors for determining whether a mark is famous and whether it has been blurred

---

41. *See, e.g., Exxon Corp. v. Oxxford Clothes, Inc.*, 109 F.3d 1070 (5th Cir. 1997) (addressing claim by Exxon that Oxxford diluted its trademark, and counterclaim by Oxxford that Exxon tarnished its trademark as a result of that company's allegedly poor environmental record).

42. 537 U.S. 418 (2003).

43. 15 U.S.C.§ 1125(c)(1) (pre–2006 version of the FTDA) (emphasis added).

by the defendant's mark. The revised language of section 43(c) states: "Subject to the principles of equity, the owner of a famous mark that is distinctive, inherently or through acquired distinctiveness, shall be entitled to an injunction against another person who, at any time after the owner's mark has become famous, commences use of a mark or trade name in commerce that is *likely to cause dilution by blurring or dilution by tarnishment of the famous mark*, regardless of the presence or absence of actual or likely confusion, of competition, or of actual economic injury."[44] Consequently, by its plain language, the new statute rejects the actual dilution standard and establishes instead a likelihood of dilution standard similar to the New York dilution law analyzed in *Mead Data Central*.

To understand dilution law, it is important to be aware of two fundamental concepts. The first is fame and distinctness. The mark should be both a household name and one that is readily recognizable. Accordingly, Exxon, duPont, and Kodak are famous and unique marks. Mead Data Central's LEXIS brand would not qualify, as it remains a niche brand. Section 43(c)(2)(A) sets forth factors for determining whether a mark is famous:

> For purposes of paragraph (1), a mark is famous if it is widely recognized by the general consuming public of the United States as a designation of source of the goods or services of the mark's owner. In determining whether a mark possesses the requisite degree of recognition, the court may consider all relevant factors, including the following:
>
> (i) The duration, extent, and geographic reach of advertising and publicity of the mark, whether advertised or publicized by the owner or third parties.
>
> (ii) The amount, volume, and geographic extent of sales of goods or services offered under the mark.
>
> (iii) The extent of actual recognition of the mark.
>
> (iv) Whether the mark was registered under the Act of March 3, 1881, or the Act of February 20, 1905, or on the principal register.

A number of cases have applied the TDRA's narrowing of the types of marks eligible for protection under federal dilution law. In *Cosi, Inc. v. WK Holdings, LLC.*,[45] the court held that the Cosi mark for restaurants was not eligible for protection under federal dilution law because it was not a nationwide, household name.

---

44. 15 U.S.C.§ 1125(c)(1) (emphasis added). For further discussion of dilution claims involving "blurring" and "tarnishment," see 3 J. THOMAS McCAR-THY, TRADEMARKS AND UNFAIR COMPETITION §§ 24.13 to 24.20 (3d ed. 1995); RESTATE-MENT (THIRD) OF UNFAIR COMPETITION § 25 (1995).

45. 2007 WL 1288028 (D. Minn. 2007).

Although well known in some parts of the U.S., the Cosi brand has not had nationwide market penetration. With regard to the degree of fame, consider the recent case of *Milbank Tweed Hadley & McCloy LLP v. Milbank Holding Corp.*,[46] which involved the Milbank Tweed law firm's Milbank mark. The defendant offered real estate services in the Los Angeles market. The law firm, which is large and which operated with offices in cities across the U.S. was still somewhat unknown to general consumer audiences, and thus the court held it was not widely known by the general consuming public in the U.S.

The famous mark need not be a coined term that has no other use in the language; it need only be substantially exclusive. For example, in *Nike, Inc. v. Nikepal International, Inc.*,[47] the court found that the Nike shoe brand was indeed a famous mark for dilution purposes. The court rejected the defendant's argument that Nike was not sufficiently exclusive because of the presence in the U.S. market of a rather obscure Nike Hydraulics brand. The court also rejected the argument that Nike was not sufficiently exclusive because it is the name of a deity in Greek mythology and a missile system used by the U.S. Department of Defense in the 1950s. These uses, the court noted, are not commercial in nature.

Second, it is critical to understand that dilution does not require a likelihood of consumer confusion or deception. Instead, the focus is on dilution of the distinctiveness of the brand, or tarnishment of that mark. Section 43(c)(2)(B) delineates the factors relevant to a blurring claim:

(B) For purposes of paragraph (1), "dilution by blurring" is association arising from the similarity between a mark or trade name and a famous mark that impairs the distinctiveness of the famous mark. In determining whether a mark or trade name is likely to cause dilution by blurring, the court may consider all relevant factors, including the following:

(i) The degree of similarity between the mark or trade name and the famous mark.

(ii) The degree of inherent or acquired distinctiveness of the famous mark.

(iii) The extent to which the owner of the famous mark is engaging in substantially exclusive use of the mark.

(iv) The degree of recognition of the famous mark.

(v) Whether the user of the mark or trade name intended to create an association with the famous mark.

46. 82 U.S.P.Q.2d 1583 (C.D. Cal. 2007).

47. 84 U.S.P.Q.2d 1820 (E.D. Cal. 2007).

(vi) Any actual association between the mark or trade name and the famous mark.

Section 43(c)(2)(C) defines a tarnishment claim: "For purposes of paragraph (1), 'dilution by tarnishment' is association arising from the similarity between a mark or trade name and a famous mark that harms the reputation of the famous mark." Tarnishment cases ordinarily involve use of the famous mark in settings involving pornography and other unsavory material. The tarnishment claim can involve other types of unfavorable associations. In *Dan–Foam A/S v. Brand Named Beds, LLC,*[48] the court held that the use of the famous mark in connection with a materially different "gray market" (i.e., imported without authority) product is cognizable as a tarnishment claim.

Finally, section 43(c)(3) identifies activities that do not constitute dilution:

> The following shall not be actionable as dilution by blurring or dilution by tarnishment under this subsection:
>
> (A) Any fair use, including a nominative or descriptive fair use, or facilitation of such fair use, of a famous mark by another person other than as a designation of source for the person's own goods or services, including use in connection with—
>
>> (i) advertising or promotion that permits consumers to compare goods or services; or
>>
>> (ii) identifying and parodying, criticizing, or commenting upon the famous mark owner or the goods or services of the famous mark owner.
>
> (B) All forms of news reporting and news commentary.
>
> (C) Any noncommercial use of a mark.

¶ 9.04 Attribution & False Advertising Claims Under Section 43(a)

Section 43(a) of the Lanham Act states, in relevant part: "Any person who, on or in connection with any goods or services, . . . uses in commerce any word, term, name, symbol, or device, or any combination thereof, or any false designation of origin, false or misleading description of fact, or false or misleading representation of fact, which—(A) is likely to cause confusion, or to cause mistake, or to deceive as to the affiliation, connection, or association of such person with another person, or as to the origin, sponsorship, or approval of his or her goods, services, or commercial activities by

---

48. 500 F.Supp.2d 296, 317 (S.D.N.Y. 2007).

another person...."[49] As this quotation shows, section 43(a) is a broadly worded provision, with potential application to a wide array of situations.

A leading older case in this area is *Gilliam v. American Broadcasting Co.*,[50] in which the creators of Monty Python's Flying Circus successfully sued ABC under the Lanham Act on the ground that the network had so substantially altered episodes of the plaintiff's work that placing the plaintiff's name on the copyrighted work constituted a false designation of origin. In *Choe v. Fordham University School of Law*,[51] the court applied the *Gilliam* decision to a case involving a law review comment that allegedly contained errors introduced by the law review. The court concludes that the errors do not rise to the level of substantial alteration, as was found in *Gilliam*, and that the work that the defendant published was basically that of the plaintiff (i.e., its general thesis and substantive content were intact).

The applicability and scope of section 43(a) in the attribution context was seriously undermined, however, in the Supreme Court's 2003 decision in *Dastar Corp. v. Twentieth Century Fox Film Corp.*[52] In that case, the Court considered whether section 43(a) gave rise to a claim for failure to attribute authorship when the underlying work had fallen into the public domain under applicable copyright rules. The Court held that no such claim can be asserted in this particular context. The ruling calls into question the extent to which section 43(a) might be used to address issues of attribution, though the case can be distinguished on the ground that the underlying work was in the public domain, whereas many attribution cases do not raise this public policy issue. The applicability of section 43(a) to attribution cases is also discussed in Chapter 4, ¶ 4.03, with particular emphasis on its potential role in safeguarding moral rights.

Section 43(a) has been applied in a variety of contexts. One type of attribution claim involved a party who alleges that he or she contributed to, played a role in, or created a work but was not given credit for it. There have only been a relatively few cases litigated under this theory, but it certainly appeared to be a viable claim under section 43(a) until *Dastar* (and may continue to be if that case can be distinguished). One case involving this claim is *Schatt v.*

---

49. 15 U.S.C. § 1125.

50. 538 F.2d 14 (2d Cir. 1976). *See also Smith v. Montoro*, 648 F.2d 602 (9th Cir. 1981) (actor's demand for attribution in film credits and promotional materials actionable under the Lanham Act). *See generally* Joseph P. Bauer, "A Federal Law of Unfair Competition:

What Should be the Reach of Section 43(a) of the Lanham Act?," 31 U.C.L.A. L. Rev. 671 (1984).

51. 920 F.Supp. 44 (S.D.N.Y. 1995), *aff'd*, 81 F.3d 319 (2d Cir. 1996).

52. 539 U.S. 23 (2003).

Curtis Management Group, Inc.,[53] where a section 43(a) claim was premised on defendants' failure to provide photo credit and copyright credit to the plaintiff. The viability of this line of cases after *Dastar* should continue to be an interesting question. The mere use of an idea without attribution has been held to not be actionable under the Lanham Act. In *Brown v. Armstrong*,[54] the plaintiff alleged that the defendants misappropriated his golf techniques in their instructional videos and commercials. The court held that the Lanham Act neither "proscribes the misappropriation of ideas nor affords protection to the purported use of an idea as a trademark or other design of origin."

Section 43(a) has also been applied in cases where the plaintiff did not wish to have his or her name used in connection with the material in question. In *King v. Allied Vision, Ltd.*,[55] Stephen King had assigned the rights to a short story called "The Lawnmower Man" to the defendant film company. He brought a claim under section 43(a) when a film bearing little resemblance to his story was marketed as "Stephen King's The Lawnmower Man." The court found that the direct attribution to King violated section 43(a) because it was facially untrue, but also found that the defendant could market—and in fact was obligated under the contract to market—the film as being "based upon" King's short story. In *Follett v. Arbor House Publishing Co.*,[56] the plaintiff was named as the lead author of a book when in fact he had merely reworked the story "to make [it] more palatable and comprehensible to the intended audience." The court held that the representation that the plaintiff was the principal author of the book was literally false and a violation of section 43(a), because his "contributions display[ed] none of the special creative attributes which are associated with authorship."[57]

False advertising is yet another type of activity prohibited by section 43(a). The false advertising prong of this section states: "Any person who, on or in connection with any goods or services, or any container for goods, uses in commerce any word, term, name,

---

53. 764 F.Supp. 902, 913 (S.D.N.Y. 1991). *See also Smith v. Montoro*, 648 F.2d 602, 606–07 (9th Cir. 1981) (allowing claim under section 43(a) where defendants removed actor's name from all credits and advertising, and substituted name of their own choosing); *Dodd v. Forth Smith Special School District No. 100*, 666 F.Supp. 1278, 1284–85 (W.D. Ark. 1987) (section 43(a) claim based on school district's publication of book without giving any credit to teacher and students who had authored manuscript on which book was based).

54. 957 F.Supp. 1293, 1301 (D. Mass. 1997), *aff'd*, 129 F.3d 1252 (1st Cir. 1997).

55. 976 F.2d 824 (2d Cir. 1992).

56. 497 F.Supp. 304, 305 (S.D.N.Y. 1980).

57. *Id.* at 312. *Compare Lish v. Harper's Magazine Foundation*, 807 F.Supp. 1090, 1093 (S.D.N.Y. 1992) (rejecting Lanham Act claim based on defendant's publication of an edited version of plaintiff's letter because there was no substantial distortion of plaintiff's original work).

symbol, or device, or any combination thereof, or any false designation of origin, false or misleading description of fact, or false or misleading representation of fact, which—. . . in commercial advertising or promotion, misrepresents the nature, characteristics, qualities, or geographic origin of his or her or another person's goods, services, or commercial activities, shall be liable in a civil action by any person who believes that he or she is or is likely to be damaged by such act."[58]

In *Castrol, Inc. v. Quaker State Corp.*,[59] the court addressed a claim of false advertising involving an advertising campaign focusing on test-proven results for motor oil. The court found the assertion of such claims without sufficient supporting evidence to be grounds for false advertising. Ordinary claims of product quality, on the other hand, often fall into the category of "puffing" under the common law and under section 43(a) of the Lanham Act. For instance, in *United Industries Corp. v. Clorox Co.*,[60] the court held that a roach bait maker failed to establish that its competitor, which claimed its product killed roaches in 24 hours, made any literally or implicitly false statements. Finally, in *Proctor & Gamble Co. v. Haugen*,[61] the court found that a competitor's message alleging Proctor & Gamble's connection with Satan is actionable under Section 43(a). Although the message sent to other Amway distributors on the company's communication system contained no misrepresentations about the competitor's goods and services, the court ruled that the allegations of affiliation with Satan and of the use of company profits to fund Satanic causes were actionable.

---

58.   15 U.S.C. § 1125(a).

59.   977 F.2d 57 (2d Cir. 1992); *see also Castrol Inc. v. Pennzoil Co.*, 987 F.2d 939 (3d Cir. 1993) (although general claims regarding a product being "better" are not actionable, defendant's claims of product superiority and less viscosity breakdown were proved to be literally false statements of fact).

60.   140 F.3d 1175 (8th Cir. 1998).

61.   222 F.3d 1262 (10th Cir. 2000).

Chapter 10

TRADEMARK DEFENSES

Table of Sections

¶ 10.01 Abandonment and Equitable Defenses

The essence of trademark ownership is use of the mark in commerce. Accordingly, when the owner of a mark ceases to make use of it or otherwise fails to take steps to control the mark that ordinary care would require, the mark may be challenged on abandonment grounds. Once a mark is abandoned, it reverts back to the public domain and can be appropriated by anyone who adopts the mark for his or her own use. Thus a party that is found to have abandoned its mark is deprived of any claim to priority in the mark before the date of abandonment and may regain rights in the mark only through subsequent use after the time of abandonment.

Under the Lanham Act, a mark is deemed to be abandoned if either of the following occurs:

(1) When its use has been discontinued with intent not to resume such use. Intent not to resume may be inferred from circumstances. Nonuse for 3 consecutive years shall be prima facie evidence of abandonment. "Use" of a mark means the bona fide use of such mark made in the ordinary course of trade, and not made merely to reserve a right in a mark.

(2) When any course of conduct of the owner, including acts of omission as well as commission, causes the mark to become the generic name for the goods or services on or in connection with which it is used or otherwise to lose its significance as a mark.

253

Purchaser motivation shall not be a test for determining abandonment under this paragraph.[1]

As the statute indicates, two elements must be shown to prove abandonment by non-use: (1) non-use and (2) intent not to resume use. Intent not to resume use can be inferred from circumstances, and involves an intent not to resume within the reasonably foreseeable future. Intent to abandon has been refuted when the owner of the mark made other efforts to maintain the commercial value of the mark during the period of non-use. Abandonment issues frequently arise in trademark litigation, although the defense is rarely successful except in cases in which the trademark owner has ceased any substantial use of the mark. The Lanham Act makes abandonment a ground for challenging or defending against any mark, including ones that have attained incontestable status. Section 1115(b), addressing incontestable marks, states: "Such conclusive evidence of the right to use the registered mark shall be subject to proof of infringement as defined in section 32, and shall be subject to the following defenses or defects: ... (2) That the mark has been abandoned by the registrant." Under section 1064, abandonment is also a ground for cancelling a federally registered mark.[2]

A number of cases have addressed the abandonment defense, albeit usually reaching the conclusion that abandonment did not occur. For example, in *General Cigar Co. v. G.D.M., Inc.*,[3] the court rejected various defense arguments that plaintiff had abandoned the "Cohiba" trademark for cigars. Several cases involving well known names in sports also provide useful illustrations. First, in *Major League Baseball Properties, Inc. v. Sed Non Olet Denarius, Ltd.*,[4] the court addressed the issue of whether the Los Angeles Dodgers abandoned the trademark "Brooklyn Dodgers." If there ever was a good case for finding abandonment, surely this was it, and the court so held (though the parties later settled the case and the court vacated its judgment). Not surprisingly, the plaintiff eventually learned its lesson and reestablished limited rights to the Brooklyn Dodgers name in 1981, but these rights did not "relate back" to the earlier Dodger days. The court thus found the rights were not sufficiently extensive to preclude the defendant's operation of the "Brooklyn Dodger" restaurant. A second sports case is *Indianapolis Colts, Inc. v. Metropolitan Baltimore Football Club*

---

1. 15 U.S.C. § 1127.

2. *See* 15 U.S.C. § 1064(3).

3. 988 F.Supp. 647 (S.D.N.Y. 1997). *See also STX, Inc. v. Bauer USA, Inc.*, 43 U.S.P.Q.2d 1492 (N.D. Cal. 1997) (denying defendant's motion for summary judgment on its abandonment defense based on alleged widespread third-party use); *Warner–Lambert Co. v. Schick U.S.A., Inc.*, 935 F.Supp. 130 (D. Conn. 1996) (rejecting abandonment defense); *cf. Rust Environment & Infrastructure, Inc. v. Teunissen*, 131 F.3d 1210 (7th Cir. 1997) (competitor's use of abandoned mark did not create confusion).

4. 817 F.Supp. 1103 (S.D.N.Y. 1993), *vacated pursuant to settlement*, 859 F.Supp. 80 (S.D.N.Y. 1994).

Ltd. Partnership, 34 F.3d 410 (7th Cir. 1994), which involved the issue of whether the Baltimore Colts mark had been abandoned when the Colts moved to Indiana. Third, a court rejected the abandonment defense in a case involving Kareem Abdul–Jabbar's given name, Lew Alcindor, in *Abdul–Jabbar v. General Motors Corp.*[5]

In addition to the Brooklyn Dodgers case, *Freed v. Farag*[6] is another example of a case in which the court decided that the mark had been abandoned after 44 years of non-use. *Rivard v. Linville*,[7] involved a Canadian trademark owner who failed to establish intent to resume use of the "Ultracuts" name for hair salons. The trademark owner had not opened any salons in the United States, and the court thus upheld the cancellation of the mark.

Finally, *Sands, Taylor & Wood Co. v. The Quaker Oats Co.*[8] involved an unusual but instructive fact pattern. The plaintiff (and its predecessors) had a once-successful but now nearly dormant trademark in "Thirst Aid." The defendant, a highly successful producer of consumer products, adopted an advertising campaign stressing that "Gatorade is Thirst Aid." In the ensuing litigation, the court set forth the standards for fair use (or descriptive use) and for trademark abandonment. The defendant lost on both of these issues, because its advertising campaign stressed the "Thirst Aid" name in a non-descriptive or trademark manner, rather than simply to describe the product. Further, the plaintiff's halting efforts to license the "Thirst Aid" brand were found sufficient to evidence its intent to resume use, thus precluding a finding of abandonment.

A trademark owner can theoretically lose or abandon its trademark rights through naked licensing, though such cases are rare.[9] Naked licensing involves a failure to exercise control over the licensing of a mark. In addition, a trademark can only be assigned with the good will associated with the mark. The assignment of a mark without its associated goodwill is prohibited as an "assignment in gross."[10] These doctrines vindicate the trademark law policy protecting consumers against confusion and deception. For trademark lawyers, this doctrine highlights the importance of being certain that the proper contractual language is used in all documen-

---

5. 85 F.3d 407 (9th Cir. 1996).

6. 994 F.Supp. 887 (N.D. Ohio 1997).

7. 133 F.3d 1446 (Fed. Cir. 1998).

8. 978 F.2d 947 (7th Cir. 1992).

9. *See TMT North America, Inc. v. Magic Touch GmbH*, 124 F.3d 876, 885–86 (7th Cir. 1997) (rejecting claim of abandonment through naked licensing and discussing inconsistent statements

of standard for this form of abandonment); *Exxon Corp. v. Oxxford Clothes, Inc.*, 109 F.3d 1070 (5th Cir. 1997) (rejecting claim that Exxon abandoned its trademark through naked licensing). *See generally* McCarthy on Trademarks §§ 18:42, 18:48 (1995).

10. *See Sugar Busters LLC v. Brennan*, 177 F.3d 258 (5th Cir. 1999).

tation of transfers of trademark rights. Finally, as in other areas of Intellectual Property, courts will entertain a variety of equitable defenses, such as acquiescence and laches.[11]

¶ 10.02 Generic Terms

A trademark can always be attacked on the ground that it is or has become generic. Section 1065 the Lanham Act states that "the right of the registrant to use such registered mark in commerce for the goods or services on or in connection with which such registered mark has been in continuous use for five consecutive years subsequent to the date of such registration and is still in use in commerce, shall be incontestable: Provided, That—. . . (4) no incontestable right shall be acquired in a mark which is the generic name for the goods or services or a portion thereof, for which it is registered."

In *Jeffrey Milstein, Inc. v. Greger, Lawlor, Roth, Inc.*,[12] the Second Circuit held that greeting card trade dress, which consisted of common and functional elements, including die-cutting, photographs, and blank white interiors, was generic. In other words, no one is entitled to a monopoly on greeting cards consisting of cut-out shapes and photographs of people, animals, and objects. The idea that industry-wide use of a product design can render it generic was reaffirmed in *Indonesian Imports, Inc. v. Old Navy, Inc.*,[13] in which the court held that the plaintiff's claimed trade dress in a handbag known as "The Sak" was generic. The Sak's claimed trade dress was an ambiguous combination of woven nylon cord in various colors and a specific bag shape. In *Sunrise Jewelry Manufacturing Corp. v. Fred S.A.*,[14] the Federal Circuit held that registered trade dress consisting of a "metallic nautical rope design" for clocks, watches, and jewelry could be cancelled on the ground that it was generic. Competitors can freely use trade dress that is or has become generic.[15]

Similarly, a grape leaf design was held to be generic as an emblem in the wine industry.[16] Packaging lemon-lime soda in green

---

11. *See TMT North America, Inc. v. Magic Touch GmbH*, 124 F.3d 876, 885–86 (7th Cir. 1997) (discussing acquiescence defense); *STX, Inc. v. Bauer USA, Inc.*, 43 U.S.P.Q.2d 1492 (N.D. Cal. 1997) (discussing laches defense); *Warner–Lambert Co. v. Schick U.S.A., Inc.*, 935 F.Supp. 130 (D. Conn. 1996) (rejecting laches defense).

12. 58 F.3d 27, 33–34 (2d Cir. 1995).

13. 1999 WL 179680, at *5–6 (N.D. Cal. 1999).

14. 175 F.3d 1322, 1325–26 (Fed. Cir. 1999).

15. Nora Beverages, Inc. v. Perrier Group of America, Inc., 164 F.3d 736, 744 (2d Cir. 1998) (product packing trade dress case).

16. Kendall–Jackson Winery, Ltd. v. E. & J. Gallo Winery, 150 F.3d 1042, 1048–49 (9th Cir. 1998). *See also* Bell-South Corp. v. DataNational Corp., 60 F.3d 1565, 1570–71 (Fed. Cir. 1995) ("walking fingers" are generic for purposes of telephone directories).

cans or bottles has also been found to be common and generic.[17] Red covers are generic for dictionaries.[18] And finally, no one has a monopoly on the idea of a colonial-style candle store, as the overall appearance and features of such a store are in part generic.[19] The issue of generic terms is more fully addressed in Chapter 7, ¶ 7.02.

¶ 10.03   Fair Use

Section 1115(b) of the Lanham Act provides the trademark fair use defense. It states:

> Such conclusive evidence of the right to use the registered mark shall be subject to proof of infringement as defined in section 1114 of this title, and shall be subject to the following defenses or defects:
>
> . . .
>
> (4) That the use of the name, term, or device charged to be an infringement is a use, otherwise than as a mark, of the party's individual name in his own business, or of the individual name of anyone in privity with such party, or of a term or device which is descriptive of and used fairly and in good faith only to describe the goods or services of such party, or their geographic origin. . . .

The Supreme Court addressed this defense in *KP Permanent Make–Up, Inc. v. Lasting Impression I, Inc.*,[20] a case involving two competitors in the market for permanent makeup, both using the term "micro color" in marketing and selling their products. The Court addressed the interplay between the trademark fair use defense and the likelihood of confusion standard. The Court concluded that a defendant asserting trademark fair use is not required to negate or disprove that its actions cause a likelihood of confusion. Some likelihood of confusion is likely to arise in many such instances, and the Court refused to require that such confusion be negated once the defendant has met the requisite elements of the fair use defense.

The defendant has the burden of proving the elements of the fair use defense: use of the term other than as a mark, good faith, and use of the term descriptively. In *Sands, Taylor & Wood Co. v. The Quaker Oats Co.*,[21] for example, the plaintiff (and its predeces-

---

17. Paddington Corp. v. Attiki Importers & Distributors, Inc., 996 F.2d 577, 583 (2d Cir. 1993).

18. Merriam–Webster, Inc. v. Random House, Inc., 35 F.3d 65 (2d Cir. 1994).

19. The Yankee Candle Co. v. New England Candle Co., 14 F. Supp. 2d 154 (D. Mass. 1998) (finding some features to be generic and others to be functional in appearance of colonial-style candle stores).

20. 543 U.S. 111 (2004).

21. 978 F.2d 947 (7th Cir. 1992).

sors) had a once-successful but now nearly dormant trademark in "Thirst Aid." The defendant, a highly successful producer of consumer products, adopted an advertising campaign stressing that "Gatorade is Thirst Aid." The defendant failed to prove fair use, because its advertising campaign stressed the "Thirst Aid" name in a non-descriptive or trademark manner, rather than simply to describe the product. The decision in *Abercrombie & Fitch Co. v. Hunting World, Inc.*[22] also discusses the "fair use" defense. The court held that the defendant's use of the word "safari" in marketing boots as "Camel Safari," "Hippo Safari," and "Chukka Safari" was found to be descriptive; had the defendant simply referred to its products as "Safari boots," its fair use defense would likely fail. The federal dilution statute, section 43(c)(3) of the Lanham Act, also expressly permits fair use and bars claims of dilution on that basis.

¶ 10.04   Comparative Advertising

One of the fundamental purposes of trademark law is to promote legitimate competition in the marketplace. In order for a new or small competitor to sell its product in competition with large well known branded products, it is often helpful to mention the famous brand name. Thus, the ability of competitors to make reference to the trademarks of others for purposes of comparative advertising is helpful to competition and consumers. Competition in the marketplace requires that a firm be able to make truthful statements about its competitor's product, including claims of equivalence. In *R.G. Smith v. Chanel, Inc.*,[23] the defendant advertised a fragrance called "Second Chance" as being comparable to the plaintiff's well known "Chanel No. 5" fragrance. Another case addressing the comparative advertising or nominative use defense is *Pebble Beach Co. v. Tour 18 I Limited.*[24] In that case, the court held that a golf course that copied the design of particular holes from other famous golf courses could not rely upon defense of nominative use because it not only made the lawful comparison but also suggested or implied that the golf courses were affiliated, sponsored, or approved.

There are two ways in which a firm can exceed the bounds of the comparative advertising safe harbor. First, if the comparative advertising reference creates a likelihood of confusion, for example by making reference to the plaintiff's trademark in larger and bolder letters than that of the defendant advertiser or by otherwise

---

22.   537 F.2d 4 (2d Cir. 1976).

23.   402 F.2d 562 (9th Cir. 1968). *See also Calvin Klein Cosmetics Corp. v. Lenox Laboratories, Inc.*, 815 F.2d 500 (8th Cir. 1987) (in case involving "Obses-sion" perfume, discussing ability to imitate products of others and to make truthful comparisons).

24.   155 F.3d 526 (5th Cir. 1998).

suggesting affiliation or sponsorship. Second, if the statement is not true, the plaintiff can obtain relief under section 43(a) of the Lanham Act—as well as perhaps state law—for false advertising.

¶ 10.05   Used or Reconditioned Goods

One of the strongest forms of competition faced by branded products comes from the secondary market—used versions of the branded product that are resold by competitors. Long before eBay came on the scene, the used Mercedes Benz offered consumers a lower priced alternative avenue for obtaining one of these fine automobiles. The classic case of *Champion Spark Plug Co. v. Sanders*[25] addressed the extent to which repaired or reconditioned products can continue to be sold under the trademark of the original seller, even though someone else has done the repair. The key here, as in comparative advertising, is in truthful disclosure. As long as the identity of the repairer is made very clear, the fact that the product is used is well marked, and the repair was not so extensive as to make any reference to the original manufacturer misleading, the Lanham Act provides no relief. Repackaging a product in a way that generates confusion, on the other hand, is actionable.[26]

The question of reconditioned goods also arises in the patent law context, where the issue is whether the sale of a reconditioned product infringes on the patent holder's exclusive right to make, use, sell, offer to sell, or import the product. In patent law, the answer to this question depends on the extent of the reconditioning.

¶ 10.06   Eleventh Amendment Immunity

A state entity may be entitled to assert Eleventh Amendment immunity from liability for trademark infringement, in light of the Court's ruling in *College Savings Bank v. Florida Prepaid Postsecondary Educ. Expense Bd.*[27]

¶ 10.07   First Amendment

As noted in previously, the Eleventh Circuit recently addressed the balance between trademark and First Amendment rights, in

---

25. 331 U.S. 125 (1947). *See also Brandtjen & Kluge, Inc. v. Prudhomme,* 765 F.Supp. 1551 (N.D. Tex. 1991) (sale of rebuilt printing presses not actionable).

26. *See Eastman Kodak Co. v. Photaz Imports Ltd.,* 853 F.Supp. 667 (W.D.N.Y. 1993) (misleading repackaging of film); *Intel Corp. v. Terabyte International, Inc.,* 6 F.3d 614 (9th Cir. 1993) (remarking and modification of slower computer chips to make them function as faster chips found to infringe Intel trademark); *Neles–Jamesbury, Inc. v. Valve Dynamics, Inc.,* 974 F.Supp. 964 (S.D. Tex. 1997) (fact issues presented regarding reconditioning and resale of valves).

27. 527 U.S. 666 (1999).

University of Alabama Board of Trustees v. New Life Art, Inc., 683 F.3d 1266 (11th Cir. 2012). Daniel A. Moore was a long-time painter of famous football scenes involving the University of Alabama, featuring realistic portrayals of past games, along with various trademarks (insignia and colors) belonging to the school. The court summarized the school's main claim as follows: "The University's claim is that Moore's unlicensed paintings, prints, and calendars infringe on the University's trademarks because the inclusion in these products of the University's football uniforms (showing the University's crimson and white colors) creates a likelihood of confusion on the part of buyers that the University sponsored or endorsed the product." The court applied the *Rogers* test and rejected the University's main trademark claim:

> In this case, we readily conclude that Moore's paintings, prints, and calendars are protected under the Rogers test. The depiction of the University's uniforms in the content of these items is artistically relevant to the expressive underlying works because the uniforms' colors and designs are needed for a realistic portrayal of famous scenes from Alabama football history. Also there is no evidence that Moore ever marketed an unlicensed item as "endorsed" or "sponsored" by the University, or otherwise explicitly stated that such items were affiliated with the University. Moore's paintings, prints, and calendars very clearly are embodiments of artistic expression, and are entitled to full First Amendment protection.

The court held that any slight harm from isolated instances of consumer confusion was outweighed by Moore's right of free expression.

Chapter 11

TRADEMARK REMEDIES

Table of Sections

¶ 11.01 Overview

Trademark owners often wish to bring infringement actions not only against those who directly infringed their trademarks, but also against others involved in or assisting in the distribution of those counterfeit products to consumers. This type of secondary liability for the actions of others can be based on theories of contributory infringement or inducement. No provision of the Lanham Act expressly provides for contributory infringement or secondary liability. The Patent Act, in contrast, contains an express provision.[1] Thus, there is some question whether courts should impose secondary liability at all in the absence of statutory mandate, but it is well established as a matter of common law and precedent.

The Supreme Court established the necessary showing for secondary liability in *Inwood Laboratories, Inc. v. Ives Laboratories, Inc.*[2] The standard can be met in either of two ways. The first is fairly straightforward: one who "intentionally induces another to infringe a trademark" is secondarily liable for infringement. Under the second prong, one who "continues to supply its product to one whom it knows or has reason to know is engaging in trademark infringement" is also secondarily liable. This second theory of liability is more difficult to interpret and apply, as is illustrated in the *Hard Rock Café Licensing Corp. v. Concession Services, Inc.*[3] This case applies the *Inwood* doctrine in a situation involving trademark infringers at a flea market. The Seventh Circuit tried to tread a fine line: on the one hand placing some potential liability on flea market operators, while not making them responsible for

---

1. 35 U.S.C. § 271.
2. 456 U.S. 844 (1982).

3. 955 F.2d 1143 (7th Cir. 1992).

continuously policing the actions of independent vendors. The court adopted a standard that requires a showing of "willful blindness" in order to impose secondary liability—"a person must suspect wrongdoing and deliberately fail to investigate." Mere negligence is not sufficient. It is worthwhile to consider what types of conduct would satisfy this standard, which essentially seems to require a showing of reckless disregard by the defendant. In the case of a flea market operator, there may well be situations in which the vendor deliberately ignores suspicious behavior. In the case of an ordinary landlord, instances of secondary liability would be rare. Given its lack of daily involvement in the business, perhaps the landlord would and should be liable only situations in which the landlord somehow knowingly, or at least recklessly, participated in the infringement.

A recent Second Circuit case applied the "willful blindness" test in the context of counterfeit merchandise being sold by vendors on Ebay. In *Tiffany (N.J.), Inc. v. Ebay, Inc.*,[4] the court held that Ebay was not willfully blind to the counterfeiting. Although it had knowledge that some counterfeit goods were listed and sold on its site, Ebay took steps to remove offending listings, suspend repeat offenders, and compensate misled buyers.

Drawing on the RESTATEMENT (SECOND) OF AGENCY, some circuits have adopted an even broader standard of secondary liability, at least in certain contexts. For example, in *AT & T v. Winback & Conserve Program,*[5] the court stated: "when a principal authorizes its independent contractor agent to conduct and conclude a transaction with third parties on the principal's own behalf, and the principal benefits financially from the contracts, the principal will be liable in an action brought pursuant to section 43(a) of the Lanham Act based on the agents' *foreseeable* infringing actions upon which it would be reasonable for the third party to rely, provided the third party has no notice that the representations are unauthorized."

¶ 11.02 Injunctive Relief

The most common form of relief in trademark cases is injunctive relief, which is provided in section 34 of the Lanham Act, 15 U.S.C. § 1116(a). This section provides: "The several courts vested with jurisdiction of civil actions arising under this chapter shall have power to grant injunctions, according to the principles of equity and upon such terms as the court may deem reasonable, to prevent the violation of any right of the registrant of a mark registered in the Patent and Trademark Office or to prevent a

---

4. 600 F.3d 93 (2d Cir. 2010).

5. 42 F.3d 1421, 1438 (3d Cir. 1994) (emphasis in the original).

violation under subsection (a), (c), or (d) of section 1125 of this title."

Injunctive relief is not the norm in most areas of the law, and the showing typically required to obtain such relief is difficult to make outside of Intellectual Property and a few other fields. Injunctions are frequently granted in the Intellectual Property field, although the decision whether to issue an injunction is always decided on a case-by-case basis. In trademark law, the injunctive relief enables the trademark owner to maintain control over its marks and prevents consumer confusion or deception. The payment of a license fee—a type of compulsory license, in effect—would prevent the trademark owner from retaining control over its brand name and good will. A disclaimer may be helpful in some instances, but is often inadequate to dispel confusion, particularly if the disclaimer is commonly (and easily) removed, or is not very prominent. Thus, courts frequently issue injunctive remedies in trademark cases, as long as the plaintiff satisfies the standard requisites under principles of equity.

¶ 11.03　Monetary Relief

Monetary relief is provided in section 1117(a), under which the plaintiff is entitled to the following remedies:

> When a violation of any right of the registrant of a mark registered in the Patent and Trademark Office, or a violation under section 1125(a) of this title, shall have been established in any civil action arising under this chapter, the plaintiff shall be entitled, subject to the provisions of sections 1111 and 1114 of this title, and subject to the principles of equity, to recover (1) defendant's profits, (2) any damages sustained by the plaintiff, and (3) the costs of the action. The court shall assess such profits and damages or cause the same to be assessed under its direction. In assessing profits the plaintiff shall be required to prove defendant's sales only; defendant must prove all elements of cost or deduction claimed. In assessing damages the court may enter judgment, according to the circumstances of the case, for any sum above the amount found as actual damages, not exceeding three times such amount. If the court shall find that the amount of the recovery based on profits is either inadequate or excessive the court may in its discretion enter judgment for such sum as the court shall find to be just, according to the circumstances of the case. Such sum in either of the above circumstances shall constitute compensation and not a penalty. The court in exceptional cases may award reasonable attorney fees to the prevailing party.

A number of factors play a role in damage assessments under the Lanham Act, including the defendant's intent or bad faith, proven losses suffered by the plaintiff (in the form of lost sales or injury to its reputation and good will), profits earned by the defendant as a result of its actions, and evidence of actual confusion or deception of consumers. The district court has considerable discretion in assessing damage awards.[6]

Defendant's Profits. An important measure of recovery in Lanham Act cases is the profit gained by the defendant as a result of its unlawful acts. Particularly when the parties are competitors, courts have noted that "[t]he defendant's profits . . . are a rough measure of the plaintiff's damages. Indeed, they are probably the best possible measure of damages available."[7] An award of the defendant's profits can serve one or more of three functions: as a measure of the plaintiff's damages, to prevent unjust enrichment of the defendant, and to deter a willful or intentional infringer from repeating its actions.[8]

Courts have awarded an accounting of the defendant's profits, but this form of relief is not automatically awarded; rather it must be based on a showing of the plaintiff's entitlement on the particular facts of the case.[9] When the defendant acts knowingly, it is generally answerable for any profits earned as a result of its infringing activity. As stated by the Eleventh Circuit in *Burger King Corp. v. Mason*, "[a]n accounting for profits has been determined by this Court to further the congressional purpose by making infringement unprofitable and is justified because it deprives the defendant of unjust enrichment and provides a deterrent to similar activity in the future."[10] The court further noted that the plaintiff need not show that it suffered actual damages in order to receive an accounting of the defendant's profits.

6. *See* McCarthy on Trademarks § 30.24[2] (1995). *See also Playboy Enterprises, Inc. v. Baccarat Clothing Co.,* 692 F.2d 1272, 1275 (9th Cir. 1982); *Holiday Inns, Inc. v. Alberding,* 683 F.2d 931, 935 (5th Cir. 1982).

7. *Polo Fashions, Inc. v. Craftex, Inc.,* 816 F.2d 145, 149 (4th Cir. 1987) (state unfair competition claim).

8. *See George Basch Co. v. Blue Coral, Inc.,* 968 F.2d 1532, 1537 (2d Cir. 1992), *cert. denied,* 506 U.S. 991 (1992); *Frisch's Restaurant, Inc. v. Elby's Big Boy, Inc.,* 661 F.Supp. 971, 989 (S.D. Ohio 1987), *aff'd,* 849 F.2d 1012 (6th Cir. 1988).

9. *See Lindy Pen Co. v. Bic Pen Corp.,* 982 F.2d 1400, 1405 (9th Cir. 1993) (citing *Champion Spark Plug Co.*

v. Sanders, 331 U.S. 125 (1947)), *cert. denied,* 510 U.S. 815 (1993); *Foxtrap, Inc. v. Foxtrap, Inc.,* 671 F.2d 636, 641 (D.C. Cir. 1982) (accounting granted upon showing of bad faith or willful infringement); *Monsanto Chemical Co. v. Perfect Fit Products Manufacturing Co.,* 349 F.2d 389, 391–92 (2d Cir. 1965), *cert. denied,* 383 U.S. 942 (1966). *See also George Basch Co. v. Blue Coral, Inc.,* 968 F.2d 1532, 1537 (2d Cir. 1992) (requiring a showing of willfulness in order to recover defendant's profits), *cert. denied,* 506 U.S. 991 (1992).

10. 855 F.2d 779, 781 (11th Cir. 1988) (awarding profits in case of purposeful violation); *see also Wolfe v. National Lead Co.,* 272 F.2d 867, 871 (9th Cir. 1959), *cert. denied,* 362 U.S. 950 (1960).

The basic approach for determining the defendant's profits is set forth in the Lanham Act itself: "In assessing profits the plaintiff shall be required to prove defendant's sales only; defendant must prove all elements of cost or deduction claimed.... If the court shall find that the amount of recovery based on profits is either inadequate or excessive the court may in its discretion enter judgment for such sum as the court shall find to be just, according to the circumstances of the case. Such sum ... shall constitute compensation and not a penalty."[11]

As the Supreme Court noted in interpreting similar language in a prior version of the trademark statute, "[t]he burden is the infringer's to prove that his infringement had no cash value in sales made by him. If he does not do so, the profits made on sales of goods bearing the infringing mark properly belong to the owner of the mark. There may well be a windfall to the trademark owner where it is impossible to isolate the profits which are attributable to the use of the infringing mark. But to hold otherwise would give the windfall to the wrongdoer."[12]

Once the plaintiff has proven the defendant's gross revenues, the defendant has the burden of showing any deductions, whether for sales not attributable to its infringing acts or for any deductible costs and expenses related to its sales. If the defendant fails to satisfy its burden, a number of decisions have awarded the full sum of the defendant's gross revenue.[13] Some decisions have also allowed the plaintiff to recover a flat percentage of the defendant's gross revenue when the defendant has lost money because of its inefficiency or because it sold infringing goods at cost.[14] There is some disagreement regarding whether overhead should be taken into account (and allocated in proportion to gross sales).[15]

---

11. 15 U.S.C.§ 1117(a).

12. *Mishawaka Rubber & Woolen Manufacturing Co. v. S.S. Kresge Co.*, 316 U.S. 203, 206–07 (1942) (citations omitted). *See also Wynn Oil Co. v. American Way Service Corp.*, 943 F.2d 595, 606 (6th Cir. 1991) (noting that burden of proof is placed on infringer to apportion profits and that defendant must bear the loss that may result in cases of confusion or doubt).

13. *See Aris Isotoner Inc. v. Dong Jin Trading Co.*, 17 U.S.P.Q.2d 1017, 1022–23 (S.D.N.Y. 1989); *Pillsbury Co. v. Southard*, 682 F.Supp. 497, 5 U.S.P.Q.2d 1298, 1300 (E.D. Okla. 1986); *Tassy Brand v. NCC Corp.*, 540 F.Supp. 562, 565 (E.D. Pa. 1982).

14. *See Otis Clapp & Son, Inc. v. Filmore Vitamin Co.*, 754 F.2d 738, 744–45 (7th Cir. 1985) (upholding award of 15 percent of defendant's sales revenue, because defendant operated inefficiently); *Polo Fashions, Inc. v. Dick Bruhn, Inc.*, 793 F.2d 1132, 1134–35 (9th Cir. 1986) (awarding 100 percent of sales of counterfeit shirts sold at defendant's cost).

15. *See Wolfe*, 272 F.2d at 871–72 (allowing partial allocation of overhead); *see also American Honda Motor Co. v. Two Wheel Corp.*, 918 F.2d 1060, 1064 (2d Cir. 1990) (apportion expenses in relation to ratio of net profit to total sales); *Polo Fashions, Inc. v. Craftex, Inc.*, 816 F.2d 145, 149 (4th Cir. 1987) (in state law unfair competition case, allowing deduction of allocable overhead but noting that the monetary award was then trebled); *Winterland Concessions Co. v. Fenton*, 835 F.Supp. 529, 533 (N.D. Cal. 1993) (citing *Wolfe* and hold-

Upon appropriate proof, the defendant can usually deduct the cost of any goods sold and related operating expenses from its total revenue during the time of the infringement. *Manhattan Industries, Inc. v. Sweater Bee By Banff, Ltd.*[16] provides an extensive discussion of the calculation. The court in that case calculated profits based first on the defendant's gross sales during the relevant time period, less discounts, which were $2,165,074; the court then deducted the costs and expenses for goods sold of $786,298 and commissions, returns, samples, markdowns, shipping, interest, and taxes of $619,341, and finally $19,758 of overhead (which had been conceded by the plaintiff), for a net profit of $147,199 plus interest from the day the trial court entered judgment. The court rejected the defendant's claim for an additional deduction of $281,730 for overhead.

Plaintiff's Damages. The second measure of damages specified by the Lanham Act is the plaintiff's damages. Section 1117(a) states: "In assessing damages the court may enter judgment, according to the circumstances of the case, for any sum above the amount found as actual damages, not exceeding three times such amount." Damages suffered by the plaintiff can include lost profits, injury to good will and reputation, and corrective advertising. The plaintiff cannot recover both damages (for its lost sales) and the defendant's profits (for sales by the defendant), as this would amount to a double recovery.[17] The plaintiff can, however, recover both forms of damages to the extent that they are not based on the same lost sales, for example when the defendant has made profits and the plaintiff also shows harm to its good will. As the RESTATEMENT (THIRD) OF UNFAIR COMPETITION section 36(c) states:

> In some cases courts have permitted recovery of both damages . . . and an accounting of the defendant's profits . . ., with the caveat that the plaintiff may not recover twice for the same loss. The prohibition against double recovery most clearly applies when the goods of the parties directly compete and the plaintiff seeks to recover both damages for losses attributable to diverted sales and the profits earned on sales made by the

---

ing that defendant is allowed to deduct overhead expenses to the extent they contributed to production and sale of infringing product). *Compare Manhattan Industries,* 885 F.2d at 7–8 (requiring defendant to show nexus between overhead and sale of infringing goods before deduction will be allowed); McCARTHY ON TRADEMARKS § 30.26[2][b] (citing cases and arguing that income taxes should not be deducted).

16. 885 F.2d 1, 7–8 (2d Cir. 1989), *cert. denied,* 494 U.S. 1029 (1990); *see*

also Wolfe v. National Lead Co., 272 F.2d 867, 871 (9th Cir. 1959), *cert. denied,* 362 U.S. 950 (1960); *W.E. Bassett Co. v. Revlon, Inc.,* 435 F.2d 656 (2d Cir. 1970) (allowing broad deductions).

17. *See Polo Fashions, Inc. v. Extra Special Products, Inc.,* 208 U.S.P.Q. 421, 427 (S.D.N.Y. 1980); RESTATEMENT (THIRD) OF UNFAIR COMPETITION section 36, comment c; McCARTHY ON TRADEMARKS § 30.27[1][a].

defendant. Although the two sums are not necessarily identical since the parties may have different profit margins and not all of the defendant's sales may represent sales diverted from the plaintiff, in the absence of contrary evidence the court may conclude that the defendant's profits adequately reflect the sales lost by the plaintiff.... Recovery of both profits and damages is most clearly appropriate when the profits of the defendant are used as a measure of the loss attributable to sales diverted from the plaintiff, and the plaintiff in addition proves other losses such as harm to reputation.

Courts are more exacting in requiring proof of the fact of damage, but once proved will give the plaintiff greater leeway to establish the amount of damages. As the court noted in *Porous Media Corp. v. Pall Corp.*,[18] "[w]hen assessing these actual damages, the district court may take into account the difficulty of proving an exact amount of damages from false advertising, as well as the maxim that 'the wrongdoer shall bear the risk of the uncertainty which his own wrong has created.'"

Harm to Good Will and Reputation. A number of trademark decisions have allowed recovery for injury to the plaintiff's good will and reputation. As noted in the RESTATEMENT (THIRD) OF UNFAIR COMPETITION section 36(d): "The threat to reputation may be direct, as when the defendant misrepresents the quality of plaintiff's goods in comparative advertising.... [T]he plaintiff may lose future sales because of the misrepresentation even after the defendant's conduct has ceased. Such reputational injury, if proved with sufficient certainty, is a recoverable loss...."[19]

Corrective Advertising. The courts have taken a number of approaches in assessing whether the plaintiff is entitled to recover damages for corrective advertising, i.e., damages to correct any false and misleading impression created by the defendant's false advertising or other violations of the Lanham Act. A leading case is *U–*

---

18. 110 F.3d 1329, 1336 (8th Cir. 1997). *See also Broan Manufacturing Co. v. Associated Distributors, Inc.*, 923 F.2d 1232, 1235 (6th Cir. 1991); *Otis Clapp & Sons, Inc. v. Filmore Vitamin Co.*, 754 F.2d 738, 745 (7th Cir. 1985) (wrongdoer bears the risk of uncertainty regarding amount of damages, though the plaintiff must prove that defendant in fact caused harm).

19. *See Heaton Distributing Co. v. Union Tank Car Co.*, 387 F.2d 477, 486 (8th Cir. 1967) (awarding $7500 for harm to plaintiff's good will and reputation); *Aladdin Manufacturing Co. v. Mantle Lamp Co.*, 116 F.2d 708, 716–18 (7th Cir. 1941) (allowing recovery of damages for harm to reputation and good will of plaintiff, as well as for defendant's profits); *Singer Manufacturing Co. v. Redlich*, 109 F.Supp. 623 (S.D. Cal. 1952) (awarding $12,000 total, or $1500 for each of the defendant's eight outlets, for harm to the plaintiff's good will and reputation); *see also Bangor Punta Operations, Inc. v. Universal Marine Co.*, 543 F.2d 1107, 1109–11 (5th Cir. 1976) (awarding plaintiff damages for lost sales and damage to business reputation); *ALPO Petfoods, Inc. v. Ralston Purina Co.*, 997 F.2d 949, 953 (D.C. Cir. 1993) (noting that harm to good will and reputation is a possible measure of damages).

Haul International, Inc. v. Jartran, Inc.[20] In that case, the plaintiff was allowed to recover the full amount it had spent in corrective advertising—a total of $13.6 million—which far exceeded the original $6 million expended by the defendant in its false advertising campaign. The court noted that the large expenditure was necessary in order to correct harm done to the U–Haul trademark. Similarly, in *ALPO Petfoods, Inc. v. Ralston Purina Co.*,[21] the court upheld the award of $3.6 million for responsive advertising (less deductions for the plaintiff's own false advertising), which also exceeded the defendant's original false advertising expenditures. The court noted that the Lanham Act allows parties injured by false advertising to recover the cost of its own advertising when they reasonably responded to the defendant's offending advertisements.

When the plaintiff has not engaged in corrective advertising, the courts have generally followed the approach used by the Federal Trade Commission (FTC) in its false advertising cases. In *Big O Tire Dealers, Inc. v. Goodyear Tire & Rubber Co.*,[22] the plaintiff successfully brought suit against Goodyear for infringement of its "Bigfoot" trademark and for falsely stating that "Bigfoot" was only available through Goodyear. The plaintiff claimed that the only way to remedy Goodyear's actions was to engage in a corrective advertising campaign to dispel the impression created by Goodyear's $10 million advertising campaign. The lower court had awarded $2.8 million for this purpose. The appellate court held that the award was excessive and reduced it to twenty-five percent of $2.8 million, or $678,302, concluding that this amount was sufficient to place the plaintiff in the position it was in prior to Goodyear's advertising campaign, and that a dollar-for-dollar award based on the defendant's total advertising expenditure was unnecessary to dispel consumer confusion.[23]

Increased Damage Awards. The Lanham Act specifically provides for increases in the award of damages and profits in the court's discretion. 15 U.S.C. section 1117(a) states: "If the court shall find that the amount of the recovery based on profits is either inadequate or excessive the court may in its discretion enter judgment for such sum as the court shall find to be just, according

---

20. 793 F.2d 1034 (9th Cir. 1986). *See also Otis Clapp & Son, Inc. v. Filmore Vitamin Co.*, 754 F.2d 738, 744–45 (7th Cir. 1985) (allowing full reimbursement of the plaintiff's actual expenditures for corrective advertising).

21. 997 F.2d 949 (D.C. Cir. 1993).

22. 408 F.Supp. 1219 (D. Colo. 1976), *modified*, 561 F.2d 1365 (10th Cir. 1977), *cert. dismissed*, 434 U.S. 1052 (1978).

23. *Id.* at 1375–76. Other courts follow the *Big O* approach. *See also West Des Moines State Bank v. Hawkeye Bancorporation*, 722 F.2d 411, 414 (8th Cir. 1983); *Durbin Brass Works, Inc. v. Schuler*, 532 F.Supp. 41, 44 (E.D. Mo. 1982) (awarding $10,000 for corrective advertising to remedy consumer confusion).

to the circumstances of the case. Such sum in either of the above circumstances shall constitute compensation and not a penalty." Increases have generally been awarded when the plaintiff has established a knowing, willful, or intentional violation of the Lanham Act.[24]

Pre-judgment interest. The Seventh Circuit, in *Gorenstein Enterprises, Inc. v. Quality Care–USA, Inc.*,[25] noted that pre-judgment interest is often awarded by federal courts when granting relief under federal law. The court established a presumption that pre-judgment interest should be awarded in a trademark case.

Costs & Attorneys' Fees. The Lanham Act specifically provides the award of costs and allows for the recovery of reasonable attorneys' fees "in exceptional cases." 15 U.S.C. section 1117(a) states in part: "When a violation of any right of the registrant of a mark registered in the Patent and Trademark Office, or a violation under section 1125(a) of this title, shall have been established in any civil action arising under this chapter, the plaintiff shall be entitled ... to recover ... (3) the costs of the action.... The court in exceptional cases may award reasonable attorney fees to the prevailing party." Attorneys fee awards are ordinarily granted in cases of intentional or willful conduct or fraud.[26]

---

24. *See Taco Cabana International, Inc. v. Two Pesos, Inc.*, 932 F.2d 1113, 1127 (5th Cir. 1991) (awarding double damages for intentional copying of trade dress), *aff'd*, 505 U.S. 763 (1992); *Gorenstein Enterprises, Inc. v. Quality Care–USA, Inc.*, 874 F.2d 431, 435–36 (7th Cir. 1989) (trebling of damages allowed when knowing or deliberate violation occurs); *U–Haul*, 793 F.2d at 1042–43 (upholding award of double damages, plus profits and attorneys' fees); *American Express Co. v. Lipscomb*, 210 U.S.P.Q. 827, 834–35 (E.D. Mich. 1981) (treble damages for knowing and willful violation), *aff'd*, 663 F.2d 1070 (6th Cir. 1981), *cert. denied*, 454 U.S. 901 (1981).

25. 874 F.2d 431, 436 (7th Cir. 1989) (citing other decisions).

26. *See Taco Cabana International, Inc. v. Two Pesos, Inc.*, 932 F.2d 1113, 1127–28 (5th Cir. 1991) (awarding $940,000 in attorneys' fees for intentional copying of trade dress), *aff'd*, 505 U.S. 763 (1992).

Chapter 12

THE RIGHT OF PUBLICITY

Table of Section

¶ 12.01   Scope of the Right of Publicity

The right of publicity is one of the four "privacy" torts identified by Samuel Warren and Louis Brandeis[1] in a widely cited 1890 law review article. The four privacy torts protect the right to prevent publication of embarrassing private facts, the right to prevent being portrayed in a false light, the right to be free from intrusion into one's personal space, and the right of publicity. The right of publicity generally focuses on the right to prevent one's name or likeness from being used for commercial purposes. Although it originated as a personal right, akin to defamation, the modern reality is that it is generally commercial in nature. Many athletes and celebrities, such as Tiger Woods and Maria Sharapova, derive significant revenue from product endorsements, merchandising, and event appearances. Tiger Woods has had a large number of endorsement deals, including Nike (shoes), Buick (cars), American Express (financial services), and Tag Heuer (watches). One estimate indicated he earned $70 million in endorsements in 2002,[2] but the number and amount of his endorsement deals has declined since his divorce. Other celebrities earning large amounts of endorsement income include David Beckham, George Foreman, and LeBron James.

States vary considerably on the conceptual question regarding the nature of the right of publicity (i.e., whether it is a personal or commercial right), as well as having some disagreement on its doctrinal limits. The RESTATEMENT (THIRD) OF UNFAIR COMPETITION

---

1. *See* Samuel D. Warren & Louis D. Brandeis, "The Right to Privacy," 4 HARV. L. REV. 193 (1890).

2. *See* John McMillen & Rebecca Atkinson, Artists and Athletes: Balancing the First Amendment and the Right of Publicity in Sport Celebrity Portraits, 14 J. LEGAL ASPECTS SPORT. 117 (2004).

§ 46 succinctly summarizes the gist of the tort: "One who appropriates the commercial value of a person's identity by using without
consent the person's name, likeness, or other indicia of identity for
purposes of trade is subject to liability for the relief appropriate
under the rules stated in §§ 48 and 49." Section § 47 indicates that
uses are made for purposes of trade "if they are used in advertising
the user's goods or services, or are placed on merchandise marketed
by the user, or are used in connection with services rendered by the
user. However, use 'for purposes of trade' does not ordinarily
include the use of a person's identity in news reporting, commentary, entertainment, works of fiction or nonfiction, or in advertising
that is incidental to such uses."

It should be noted that the right of publicity extends not only
to celebrities, but also to ordinary, unknown persons whose identity
is appropriated for commercial gain. For example, in *Flake v.
Greensboro News Co.*,[3] the court addressed a right of publicity claim
based on use of photograph of the plaintiff in a bathing suit in an
advertisement for bread. The plaintiff, Nancy Flake, was not a
celebrity. The court concluded:

> We are of the opinion ... that the unauthorized use of one's
> photograph in connection with an advertisement or other com-
> mercial enterprise gives rise to a cause of action which would
> entitle the plaintiff, without the allegation and proof of special
> damages, to a judgment for nominal damages, and to injunctive
> relief, if and when the wrong is persisted in by the offending
> parties.

> One of the accepted and popular methods of advertising in the
> present day is to procure and publish the indorsement of the
> article being advertised by some well-known person whose
> name supposedly will lend force to the advertisement. If it be
> conceded that the name of a person is a valuable asset in
> connection with an advertising enterprise, then it must like-
> wise be conceded that his face or features are likewise of value.
> Neither can be used for such a purpose without the consent of
> the owner without giving rise to a cause of action.[4]

A more recent example of using ordinary people in commercial
advertisement was the series of (pre-Gecko) Geico insurance commercials, in which celebrities are paired with various "real people."
The celebrities undoubtedly received larger payments than the
ordinary persons who appeared in the advertisement, but both
groups of people must give their consent to the use of their images
and names.

3. 212 N.C. 780, 195 S.E. 55 (1938).   4. *Id.* at 63.

The scope of the right of publicity has been tested and often expanded in a number of cases in the last several decades, particularly under California law (the state in which many celebrities reside). A relatively early case illustrating the growth of the right of publicity is *Midler v. Ford Motor Co.*[5] At he time singer Bette Midler apparently made it a practice to refuse to be involved in commercial advertisements (though she has since appeared in a recent commercial for Acura). In the 1980s, she rejected an offer to participate in a Ford Lincoln Mercury television commercial, which was part of the company's "Yuppie Campaign." Ford's advertising agency then hired Ula Hedwig, who had been a backup singer for Midler, to sing "Do You Want To Dance" (a song Midler had recorded) in the commercial. Hedwig was asked to "sound as much as possible like the Bette Midler record." Although neither Midler's name nor a picture of Midler was used in the commercial, the court held that "when a distinctive voice of a professional singer is widely known and is deliberately imitated in order to sell a product, the sellers have appropriated what is not theirs and have committed a tort in California."[6]

Midler expands the scope of the right of publicity beyond its traditional protection of name and images and even its broader coverage of name, voice, likeness, or other identifying characteristics associated with the plaintiff. The court allows the plaintiff to obtain relief for the use of a "sound-alike" imitator of her voice in a commercial. The outcome of the case can be explained by two facts. The first is the defendants' bad faith in using an imitator after Midler declined to participate in the advertisement and instructing the imitator to make her voice and style sound as similar as possible to Midler in voice and style. Second, the sound-alike was perhaps too successful-listeners could reasonably believe that the voice was in fact Midler's, and no apparent effort was made to dispel this notion.

If the *Midler* decision is viewed as an understandable expansion of the right of publicity on somewhat unique facts, *White v. Samsung Electronics America, Inc.*[7] tests the outer reaches of the claim. The defendant's advertisement consisted of an image of a robot with a blonde wig and evening dress, turning the letters in a futuristic game similar to "Wheel of Fortune." The court's finding of potential liability in Vanna White's suit against Samsung seems to leave little room for parody in product advertising, as it would be difficult to conjure up the image of any well-known celebrity without doing at least as much as was done in this case. Many commentators find the outcome and reasoning of this decision to be

---

5. 849 F.2d 460 (9th Cir. 1988).

6. *Id.* at 463.

7. 971 F.2d 1395 (9th Cir. 1992).

troubling, as it expands the right of publicity beyond the *Midler* context, where some viewers or listeners might well have believed Midler's voice was actually incorporated into the advertisement. Samsung's parody advertisement did not use the plaintiff's image, name, voice, or any other traditionally protected attribute. Judge Kozinski's eloquent dissent from the denial of en banc rehearing persuasively addresses some of the broader problems with the panel opinion.[8] Significantly, the panel did not actually hold that the plaintiff was entitled to relief, but only that she was entitled to go to trial on her claims.

The White case has spawned further litigation in this area. *Wendt v. Host International, Inc.*,[9] involved robotic figures resembling characters from television series "Cheers" placed in airport bars, including Cliff and Norm. George Wendt, who portrayed Norm in the series, and John Ratzenberger (Cliff) brought suit. Once again, the Ninth Circuit held that the plaintiffs had raised fact issues on their right of publicity claim. In that case, the robotic figures more closely resembled the physical features of Cliff and Norm that the Samsung robot, which merely evoked the image of a blonde game show host. In *Carson v. Here's Johnny Portable Toilets, Inc.*,[10] the court found a violation of Johnny Carson's right of publicity by the defendant, who sold "Here's Johnny" portable toilets. A number of cases involve look-alike celebrity impersonators. In *Brimley v. Hardee's Food Systems, Inc.*,[11] actor Wilford Brimley sued a restaurant chain and advertising agency for use of a look-alike in advertisements. *Apple Corps Ltd. v. A.D.P.R., Inc.*,[12] involved Beatles imitators, and the court found that fact issues existed regarding a look-alike and sound-alike group. Two reported cases have involved movie director Woody Allen. In *Allen v. Men's World Outlet, Inc.*,[13] the court held that the use of a Woody Allen look-alike in clothing advertisements violated the Lanham Act, but not the New York publicity statute. In *Allen v. National Video, Inc.*,[14] the court found that the use of a Woody Allen look-alike in advertisements, without disclaimers, violated both the Lanham Act and the New York publicity statute.

In addition to serving as an additional ground for relief in some of these cases, the Lanham Act, in section 2(c), prohibits the registration of the name, picture, or signature of a living person as a trademark without that person's consent. Thus, this provision

---

8. *White v. Samsung Electronics America, Inc.*, 989 F.2d 1512 (9th Cir. 1993) (Kozinski, J., dissenting from denial of rehearing en banc).

9. 125 F.3d 806 (9th Cir. 1997).

10. 698 F.2d 831 (6th Cir. 1983).

11. 1995 WL 51177 (S.D.N.Y. 1995).

12. 843 F.Supp. 342 (M.D. Tenn. 1993).

13. 679 F.Supp. 360 (S.D.N.Y. 1988).

14. 610 F.Supp. 612 (S.D.N.Y. 1985).

prevents the appropriation of someone's "right of publicity" in a registered trademark without their consent.

Because of its variation from state to state, some commentators have endorsed the concept of a uniform federal statute addressing the right of publicity. There are a number of reasons why such a statute might be desirable, such as national uniformity, predictability, and simplification of the law, as well accommodation of First Amendment concerns. But it can be questioned whether the right of publicity is much different from any number of other areas of tort law in which widely varying state laws are tolerated. Finally, it should be noted that in some instances the right of publicity can be preempted by federal copyright law.[15] This question depends upon the interplay between the right of publicity and section 301 of the Copyright Act. For further discussion of copyright preemption, see the copyright discussion in Chapter 4, ¶ 4.05.

¶ 12.02   First Amendment Considerations

The broad scope of the right of publicity frequently raises First Amendment concerns. The Restatement indicates that use of one's image " 'for purposes of trade' does not *ordinarily* include the use of a person's identity in news reporting...."[16] In *Zacchini v. Scripps–Howard Broadcasting Co.,*[17] however, the Supreme Court addressed a right of publicity claim brought by the performer of a "human cannonball" act against a television broadcasting company when, against his wishes, the broadcaster taped his entire 15–second performance and played it on a news program. The Court held that the First Amendment does not immunize a broadcaster from liability when it taped and broadcast the entire performance: "Wherever the line in particular situations is to be drawn between media reports that are protected and those that are not, we are quite sure that the First and Fourteenth Amendments do not immunize the media when they broadcast a performer's entire act without his consent."[18] Moreover, it can be argued that because the defendant in *Zacchini* broadcast the plaintiff's entire performance, the plaintiff could certainly argue that the defendant's actions exceeded the bounds of routine news reporting and thus could be actionable under the Restatement's formulation of the right of publicity tort.

---

15.   *See, e.g., Baltimore Orioles, Inc. v. Major League Baseball Players Association,* 805 F.2d 663 (7th Cir. 1986) (in suit claiming that broadcast of baseball games violated baseball players' right of publicity, court held that plaintiffs' state law right of publicity claims were preempted by the Copyright Act of 1976).

16.   Restatement (Third) of Unfair Competition § 47 (1995) (emphasis added).

17.   433 U.S. 562 (1977).

18.   *Id.* at 574–75.

A number of cases have held that the use of a person's name and other identifying characteristics in a movie or play is not actionable. *Joplin Enterprises v. Allen*,[19] involved a play making use of Janis Joplin's voice and name. The court held that the play did not infringe on her right of publicity. Similarly, in *Rogers v. Grimaldi*,[20] Ginger Rogers brought suit against the makers of the movie "Ginger and Fred." The court found that Rogers did not prove a violation of the right of publicity under Oregon law.

Parks v. LaFace Records[21] also tests the limits of the right of publicity and addresses balancing that right against the First Amendment. The case set forth a variety of tests for addressing the First Amendment considerations—the likelihood of confusion standard used in traditional trademark cases, the alternative avenues test, and the *Rogers v. Grimaldi* test. The court endorsed the last of these, finding that it best accommodates First Amendment concerns. The court invoked this test in evaluating both the false advertising and the right of publicity claims. The court eventually found that fact issues existed as to whether the use of Parks' name had artistic relevance to the song, a key prong in the *Rogers v. Grimaldi* test. This test is clearly more protective of free speech interests than the two alternatives the court considered. For example, the traditional confusion analysis would give no particular emphasis to free speech concerns—instead the standard likelihood of confusion test would simply be applied to the facts of the case. The "alternative avenues" test focuses on whether the speaker has alternative avenues by which to express his or her viewpoint; if there are alternative avenues for expression, then the speaker would have no First Amendment right to invoke the trademark. Nonetheless, some commentators would say that the *Rogers v. Grimaldi* test does not go far enough in protecting speech, while others would argue that it gives too much license to usurp the rights of celebrities.

ETW Corp. v. Jireh Publishing, Inc.,[22] which involved the company that Tiger Woods established to handle his endorsements, also addressed the limits of the right of publicity and the tort's interplay with freedom of expression. The court applied the "transformative elements" test, which is somewhat akin to the fair use analysis used in copyright law (and particularly the Supreme Court's fair use analysis in the 2 Live Crew case, *Campbell v. Acuff–Rose Music, Inc.*[23]). Under this test, the court found that the

---

19. 795 F.Supp. 349 (W.D. Wash. 1992).

20. 875 F.2d 994 (2d Cir. 1989). *But see Presley's Estate v. Russen*, 513 F.Supp. 1339 (D. N.J. 1981) (live stage performance by Elvis Presley impersonator violates right of publicity).

21. 329 F.3d 437 (6th Cir. 2003).

22. 332 F.3d 915 (6th Cir. 2003).

23. 510 U.S. 569 (1994).

use of Tiger Woods' image was sufficiently transformative and therefore did not infringe on his right of publicity. In sum, courts have not definitively determined how to resolve the conflict between the right of publicity and the need for creative expression, and the scope and outer limits of right of publicity claims remain unsettled.

¶ 12.03   Survival of the Right of Publicity

The right of publicity raises a number of other intriguing questions. One of those questions is whether the claim survives the death of the person whose identity was appropriated. As noted above, the right of publicity originated one of the four "privacy" torts identified by Samuel Warren and Louis Brandeis.[24] In light of its origin as a "personal tort," like defamation and other species of invasion of privacy, some courts have held that the claim does not survive death. A number of newer decisions, often interpreting statutes, have held that the right of publicity is primarily a commercial or proprietary interest and therefore the right survives death and is descendable to an individual's estate.

In *State ex rel. Elvis Presley International Memorial Foundation v. Crowell*,[25] the court held that Elvis Presley's right of publicity survives death under Tennessee law. In *McFarland v. Miller*,[26] a suit brought by the estate of George "Spanky" McFarland against a restaurant using his character's name, the court held that the right of publicity claim survives death under New Jersey law. Similarly, in *Martin Luther King, Jr. Center for Social Change, Inc. v. American Heritage Products, Inc.*,[27] the court, applying Georgia law, held that the right of publicity survives death. Perhaps most importantly given the number of celebrities who reside there, California law recognizes the right of publicity after death.[28]

On the other hand, a small number of cases from other states still hold that the right of publicity does not survive death. *Pirone v. MacMillan, Inc.*,[29] a suit involving Babe Ruth photographs, held that the New York statute governing right of publicity was limited to living persons. In *Southeast Bank, N.A. v. Lawrence*,[30] a suit by a representative of the Tennessee Williams estate sought to prevent naming a theater after the deceased playwright, the court held that right of publicity does not survive death under Florida law. Finally,

24. *See* Samuel D. Warren & Louis D. Brandeis, "The Right to Privacy," 4 HARV. L. REV. 193 (1890).

25. 733 S.W.2d 89 (Tenn. Ct. App. 1987).

26. 14 F.3d 912 (3d Cir. 1994).

27. 694 F.2d 674 (11th Cir. 1983).

28. *See Joplin Enterprises v. Allen*, 795 F.Supp. 349 (W.D. Wash. 1992) (publicity rights survive under California law).

29. 894 F.2d 579 (2d Cir. 1990).

30. 66 N.Y.2d 910, 498 N.Y.S.2d 775, 489 N.E.2d 744 (1985).

in *Reeves v. United Artists Corp.*,[31] the court held that Ohio law does not permit right of publicity to survive death in a suit by a deceased boxer's widow.

31.   765 F.2d 79 (6th Cir. 1985).

Chapter 13

PATENTABLE SUBJECT MATTER

Table of Section

PATENT & TRADE SECRET LAW

"I knew that a country without a patent office and good patent laws was just a crab, and couldn't travel any way but sideways or backways. ... The first thing you want in a new country, is a patent office; then work up your school system; and after that, out with your paper."

—Mark Twain, A CONNECTICUT YANKEE IN KING ARTHUR'S COURT, Chapter 9.

¶ 13.01   Overview

Patents offer the strongest possible form of intellectual property protection—an exclusive right to make, use, sell, offer to sell, or import the patented invention anywhere in the United States for the duration of the patent. Foreign patents offer similarly broad protections. Unlike trade secret law, there is no defense of reverse engineering or independent creation. This exclusive right is sometimes called a "legal monopoly"—which does not necessarily mean that a patent holder possesses real economic power, though such power may exist if a patent covers a unique and highly desirable new product. Historically, United States patent law owes much to English law. In the 1500s, the British Crown issued "letters pat-

278

ent," which gave individuals economic monopolies over production or sale of goods within the kingdom. These Crown monopolies were typically granted without regard to whether the goods were novel or previously available. The ensuing price increases and shortages eventually led Parliament to enact the Statute of Monopolies,[1] which deemed that "all grants of monopolies ... are contrary to your majesty's laws" and "are altogether contrary to the laws of this realm, and so are and shall be utterly void and of none effect, and in no wise to be put in use or execution."[2] The Statute created an exception for "letters patents and grants of privilege for the term of fourteen years or under, hereafter to be made, of the sole working or making of any manner of new manufactures within this realm to the true and first inventor and inventors of such manufactures." Thus, these early patents were granted for new inventions for terms of fourteen years.

Like the Statute of Monopolies, the United States Constitution recognizes the value of limited patent terms for inventors. The Patent & Copyright Clause, Article I, Section 8, Clause 8 of the United States Constitution, grants Congress the power "To promote the Progress of Science and useful Arts, by securing for limited Times to Authors and Inventors the exclusive Right to their respective Writings and Discoveries." As stated in *Kewanee Oil Co. v. Bicron Corp.*,[3] this congressional power is exercised in the hope that "[the] productive effort thereby fostered will have a positive effect on society through the introduction of new products and processes of manufacture into the economy, and the emanations by way of increased employment and better lives for our citizens."

The first patent statute was the Patent Act of 1790.[4] In 1793, Congress broadened the patent laws, and in 1836 it created the Patent Office, which was given the responsibility of examining patent applications. Ornamental designs were given patent protection in 1842, and plant patents were authorized in 1930 and 1954. Congress significantly revised the patent laws in the most recent comprehensive re-enactment—the Patent Act of 1952.[5] Since that time, amendments to the patent laws have focused on lengthening the duration of patents and harmonizing patent law in light of international treaties. Most recently, Congress enacted the 2011 Leahy–Smith America Invents Act ("AIA"), which changes the governing rules for the novelty (or newness) of patentable inventions and for the importance of prompt filing of applications, as well

---

1. 21 Jac. I, c. 3 (1623).

2. This translation from the early English is found at: http://ipmall.info/hosted_resources/lipa/patents/English_Statute1623.pdf (last visited June 10, 2012).

3. 416 U.S. 470, 480 (1974).

4. Act of April 10, 1790, ch.7, 1 Stat. 109.

5. Act of July 19, 1952, ch. 950, 66 Stat. 797.

as making a number of other substantive and procedural changes in the law governing patents and in the process for obtaining patent protection. These important new changes are discussed in relevant parts of the text of this section of the book.

In return for being given a statutory right to exclude others from the claimed invention, patent law requires disclosure of the invention to the public as part of the patent application and approval process. One can peruse the specific details of every issued patent on the Patent & Trademark Office (PTO or "Patent Office") website, www.uspto.gov. The Patent Office disclosure includes detailed descriptions of each patent, along with accompanying drawings and specifications. Moreover, although patent protection is broader in scope than other forms of Intellectual Property protection, it is much shorter in duration and more difficult to obtain than trademark or copyright protection.

To be patentable, an invention must meet stringent statutory standards. Two crucial requisites are the novelty and non-obviousness requirements. To meet the novelty standard, an invention must not be found in the prior art—the base of existing public knowledge. In contrast, copyright law merely requires originality, meaning only that the work must not itself have been copied from others. Non-obviousness requires that the invention differ from the prior art in a meaningful way—what is sometimes called an inventive step—a requirement discussed more fully below. Because of the demanding nature of these statutory standards, the process of obtaining patent protection is far more rigorous than the process of obtaining any other form of intellectual property protection. Even after issuance by the Patent Office, a patent is vulnerable to legal challenge in court, and historically approximately half of all litigated patents are ultimately found to be invalid in federal court.[6]

To determine whether the claimed invention is eligible for patent protection, it is important to conduct a patent search in order to determine whether the invention is part of the "prior art," that is, information that is already known or claimed in prior patents. If the invention is in fact novel or new, then the inventor, a patent attorney, or a patent agent can file a patent application with the PTO (at least if all other patentability requirements are

---

6. The percentage has varied considerably over the years. *See* John R. Allison & Mark A. Lemley, Empirical Evidence on the Validity of Litigated Patents, 26 A.I.P.L.A. Q.J. 185, 205–07 (1998) (65 percent of patents held to be invalid in the 1970s, and 46 percent held invalid between 1989 to 1996); Robert P. Merges, Commercial Success and Patent Standards: Economic Perspectives on Innovation, 76 Cal. L. Rev. 805, 821 (1988) (between 1982 and 1985, "the court invalidated only forty-four percent of the patents it adjudicated on appeal from trial courts, a marked contrast to the old invalidation rate of approximately sixty-six percent").

also met). The patent application includes claims, specifications, and drawings.

The heart of a patent application or of an issued patent is the section that addresses the patent claims. These claims attempt to set forth in words the metes and bounds of the invention, in much the same way that a legal description of real estate identifies the boundaries of a piece of land. The PTO responds to the patent application (known as an "office action"), which may narrow or reject patent claims. The patent applicant, in turn, can seek to amend or challenge the PTO's determination, after which the PTO either issues or denies the patent. In 2012, Congress made some modifications to the patent prosecution process in the Leahy–Smith America Invents Act ("AIA"). Specifically, the AIA is intended to make the PTO process more effective by allowing third parties to submit relevant prior art (specifically, patents and printed publications) at any time during the patent application process or as to an issued patent. The AIA also establishes a post-patent grant review process available for nine months after the date of the patent grant (or reissue). The AIA also modifies *inter partes* patent reexamination proceedings (renaming them "inter partes review") for proceedings commenced after September 16, 2012. See AIA § 6(a)–(c) (to be codified at 35 U.S.C. §§ 311–319).

Section 251 of the Patent Act allows patents to be reissued in the event of certain errors or problems in the initial application process:

> Whenever any patent is, through error without any deceptive intention, deemed wholly or partly inoperative or invalid, by reason of a defective specification or drawing, or by reason of the patentee claiming more or less than he had a right to claim in the patent, the Director shall, on the surrender of such patent and the payment of the fee required by law, reissue the patent for the invention disclosed in the original patent, and in accordance with a new and amended application, for the unexpired part of the term of the original patent. No new matter shall be introduced into the application for reissue.

The AIA deleted the limitation that the applicant must have acted "without any deceptive intention" in order to obtain a reissue patent.

The patent application process can involve extended interactions with the PTO, taking two to five years in many instances. In its most recent report, the PTO indicated that the first office action (i.e., the first substantive response to the patent application) took an average of 28 months, and the average time frame from application to issuance (or abandonment) was 34 months.[7] Delays in the Patent Office have serious ramifications for the patent holder, as the term of most patents is twenty years from the *application* date. The one exception is a design patent, which lasts for 14 years from the date of patent *issuance.* Thus, for utility and plant patents, Patent Office delays shorten the duration of the patent holder's exclusive rights, although patent law does provide for some extensions of the patent term.

The number of issued patents has dramatically increased in the last three decades. The PTO issued approximately 66,000 patents in 1980. By the year 2000, more than 175,000 patents were issued.[8] In 2011, the PTO issued over 247,000 patents. The issue of patent reform has been the subject of considerable discussion, as there is an argument for more rigorous review of patent applications.[9] The Leahy–Smith America Invents Act ("AIA") takes some steps toward making the patent application process more rigorous, as discussed above (third party submission of prior art to the PTO) and below in Chapter 13, ¶ 13.02 (post-grant review proceeding for review of the validity of covered business method patents).

Once a patent is issued, its contents become public information. This disclosure serves a fundamental purpose of patent law— allowing widespread dissemination of information regarding new and useful inventions. In order to make its patent claims known to its competitors and others in the marketplace, the applicant can state on its product that it has a "patent pending." Once the patent is granted, patent law's "marking" requirement encourages the patent holder to place a notice of the existence of the patent on the product or face the possibility of being precluded from obtaining a monetary damage recovery for infringement. The marking requirement in section 287(a) states:

> Patentees, and persons making, offering for sale, or selling within the United States any patented article for or under them, or importing any patented article into the United States, may give notice to the public that the same is patented, either by fixing thereon the word "patent" or the abbreviation "pat.", together with the number of the patent, or when, from

---

7. *See* http://www.uspto.gov/about/stratplan/ar/2011/par_01.html (last visited August 13, 2012).

8. *See* David A. Balto, *Intellectual Property and Antitrust: General Principles*, 43 IDEA 395 (2003).

9. There may be some justification for the present patent system. *See* Mark A. Lemley, *Rational Ignorance at the Patent Office*, 95 Nw. U. L. Rev. 1495 (2001). For a contrary argument, see Christopher R. Leslie, *The Anticompetitive Effects of Unenforced Invalid Patents*, 91 Minn. L. Rev. 101 (2006). One commentator suggests that misuse law might remedy the problem of improvidently granted technology patents. *See* Eugene R. Quinn, Jr., *Abusing Intellectual Property Rights in Cyberspace: Patent Misuse Revisited*, 28 Wm. Mitchell L. Rev. 955 (2002).

the character of the article, this cannot be done, by fixing to it, or to the package wherein one or more of them is contained, a label containing a like notice. In the event of failure so to mark, no damages shall be recovered by the patentee in any action for infringement, except on proof that the infringer was notified of the infringement and continued to infringe thereafter, in which event damages may be recovered only for infringement occurring after such notice. Filing of an action for infringement shall constitute such notice.

A spate of litigation has taken place regarding "false marking," an issue that is discussed in Chapter 17, ¶ 17.02.

The question of whether a patent application is made public before it is issued is a complicated one. The following quotation from the PTO website explains the governing rules:

> Publication of patent applications is required by the American Inventors Protection Act of 1999 for most plant and utility patent applications filed on or after November 29, 2000. On filing of a plant or utility application on or after November 29, 2000, an applicant may request that the application not be published, but only if the invention has not been and will not be the subject of an application filed in a foreign country that requires publication 18 months after filing (or earlier claimed priority date) or under the Patent Cooperation Treaty. Publication occurs after the expiration of an 18–month period following the earliest effective filing date or priority date claimed by an application. Following publication, the application for patent is no longer held in confidence by the Office and any member of the public may request access to the entire file history of the application.[10]

Federal courts have exclusive jurisdiction over patent cases: "The district courts shall have original jurisdiction of any civil action arising under any Act of Congress relating to patents, plant variety protection, copyrights and trademarks. Such jurisdiction shall be exclusive of the courts of the states in patent, plant variety protection and copyright cases."[11]

A relatively unusual aspect of patent law jurisdiction is that the U.S. Court of Appeals for the Federal Circuit has exclusive nationwide jurisdiction over all patent appeals, in accordance with 28 U.S.C. § 1295:

> The United States Court of Appeals for the Federal Circuit shall have exclusive jurisdiction—

10. http://www.uspto.gov/patents/resources/general_info_concerning_patents.jsp#heading-13 (last visited June 10, 2012). *See also* AIA § 19 (pre-cluding state court jurisdiction over patent and plant variety protection claims).

11. 28 U.S.C. § 1338.

(1) of an appeal from a final decision of a district court of the United States, the District Court of Guam, the District Court of the Virgin Islands, or the District Court for the Northern Mariana Islands, in any civil action arising under, or in any civil action in which a party has asserted a compulsory counterclaim arising under, any Act of Congress relating to patents or plant variety protections; . . . .

Thus, appeals from Patent Office determinations, as well as appeals from any district court's patent infringement rulings, must be filed in the Federal Circuit, rather than the regional court of appeals in which the parties are located or in which the case was litigated. In effect, decisions of the Federal Circuit on patent law issues are controlling throughout the United States unless they are overruled by the Supreme Court (or by the Federal Circuit itself sitting en banc). Moreover, decisions by the Court of Customs and Patent Appeals (a predecessor of the Federal Circuit) are also considered governing precedent.[12]

In *Kappos v. Hyatt*, 560 U.S. ___, 132 S.Ct. 1690 (2012), the Supreme Court addressed a patent applicant's right to bring a civil action in district court seeking a patent rejected within the PTO's process (as opposed to appealing to the Federal Circuit). The Court held that the patent applicant is entitled to introduce new evidence that was not presented to the PTO, and that the district court should decide any relevant factual questions de novo (i.e., without deference to the PTO's determination).

Terms of Art

Patent law is rife with terms of art—shorthand phrases that relate to central issues in the field. The following is a brief summary of the key terms of art—

prior art—the level of basic and applied knowledge in a particular field, such as the methods and technologies that are standard and generally known in the biotechnology field; prior art includes all publications, patents, and public uses or sales that exist before the "critical date" (the filing date, under the new AIA rules)

person having ordinary skill in the art (sometimes abbreviated *"phosita"*)—a person possessing the technical knowledge of an ordinary person having skills in the relevant field—for example, an understanding of basic and applied chemistry concepts

reduction to practice—having a working prototype of an invention

---

12. *See South Corp. v. United States*, 690 F.2d 1368, 1370 (Fed. Cir. 1982) (adopting as precedent decisions of the predecessor Court of Customs and Patent Appeals).

constructive reduction to practice (also known as *enablement*)—
a description of an invention that is sufficiently detailed to allow a
person having ordinary skill in the art (phosita) to make the
invention

anticipation (or *anticipating event*)—information that is part of
the base of knowledge, basic or applied, in a particular field,
including through material that comes into public use, printed
publications, patents, or general public knowledge; if the information is anticipating as to all elements of the claimed invention, it
will preclude patentability of the same invention.

¶ 13.02   Patentable Subject Matter

There are three types of patents—utility patents, plant patents,
and design patents. Utility patents include new and useful products, processes, or improvements on an existing product or process.
Specifically, section 101 of the Patent Act states simply: "Whoever
invents or discovers any new and useful process, machine, manufacture, or composition of matter, or any new and useful improvement
thereof, may obtain a patent therefor, subject to the conditions and
requirements of this title." The scope of patentable subject matter
does not include abstract ideas or theories, but only useful applications. In other words, patent law generally protects applied science
and technology, but not pure scientific research or abstract ideas.

Utility patents protect the functional aspects of a product.
Historical examples of utility patents include the Wright Brothers'
airplane, Alexander Graham Bell's telephone, and Thomas Edison's
light bulb. In modern times, patent law protects such inventions as
new pharmaceutical products such as the impotence drug Viagra,
biotechnology (such as genetically modified crops or laboratory
mice), and the Apple iPad tablet or the Amazon Kindle Fire
reader.[13]

Although these sorts of inventions are clearly the types of new
and innovative products that one would expect to receive patent
protection, the scope of patentable subject matter is quite a bit
broader than the proverbial better mousetrap. Section 101 of the
Patent Act states: "Whoever invents or discovers any new and
useful process, machine, manufacture, or composition of matter, or
any new and useful improvement thereof, may obtain a patent
therefor, subject to the conditions and requirements of this title."
Essentially this provision grants utility patent protection to three
types of inventions—(1) products (i.e., a machine, manufacture, or
composition of matter), (2) processes (such as a new chemical

13. *See* U.S. Patent No. 6,469,012
(Viagra); U.S. Patent No. 6,204,436 (ge-
netically modified plants); U.S. Patent
No. 4,736,866 (mice); U.S. Design Patent
No. D637,596 (iPad design).

manufacturing process), and (3) improvements on existing products or processes.

Two leading cases illustrate just how far patent law can reach. The first is the Supreme Court's ruling in *Diamond v. Chakrabarty*,[14] which involved a patent application for a genetically engineered bacterium of the genus Pseudomonas. This bacterium was capable of breaking down crude oil, which was of great value in cleaning oil spills more effectively than was possible with naturally occurring bacteria. The Patent Office rejected the bacterium patent on the grounds that it was not patentable subject matter because it was a living thing and because it was a product of nature. The Supreme Court ultimately held that the bacterium was indeed patentable subject matter under 35 U.S.C. § 101.

Congress contemplated that the patent laws would be given wide scope, and that its coverage can "include anything under the sun that is made by man."[15] The Court's analysis is worth extended quotation:

> It is, of course, correct that Congress, not the courts, must define the limits of patentability; but it is equally true that once Congress has spoken it is "the province and duty of the judicial department to say what the law is." Congress has performed its constitutional role in defining patentable subject matter in § 101; we perform ours in construing the language Congress has employed. In so doing, our obligation is to take statutes as we find them, guided, if ambiguity appears, by the legislative history and statutory purpose. Here, we perceive no ambiguity. The subject-matter provisions of the patent law have been cast in broad terms to fulfill the constitutional and statutory goal of promoting "the Progress of Science and the useful Arts" with all that means for the social and economic benefits envisioned by Jefferson. Broad general language is not necessarily ambiguous when congressional objectives require broad terms.
>
> ... This Court frequently has observed that a statute is not to be confined to the "particular [applications] ... contemplated by the legislators."

This is especially true in the field of patent law. A rule that unanticipated inventions are without protection would conflict with the core concept of the patent law that anticipation undermines patentability. Justice Douglas observed that the inventions most benefiting mankind are those that "push back the frontiers of chemistry, physics, and the like." Congress employed broad general

---

14. 447 U.S. 303 (1980).

15. S. Rep. No. 1979, 82d Cong., 2d Sess., 5 (1952); H. R. Rep. No. 1923, 82d Cong., 2d Sess., 6 (1952).

language in drafting § 101 precisely because such inventions are often unforeseeable.[16]

The Supreme Court's decision in *Diamond v. Chakrabarty*, along with advances in technology, have led to an explosion in the number of biotechnology patents sought and issued in the last twenty-five years. From 1990 through 2004, more than 52,000 biotechnology patents have been issued.[17] Some have contended that *Diamond v. Chakrabarty* goes beyond the congressionally intended scope of patent law and has encouraged the development of an industry whose long-term safety and economic consequences are uncertain. Nonetheless, the plain language of section 101 and the overall structure and purpose of the statutory scheme clearly permit the issuance of biotechnology patents. Moreover, the availability of patent protection seems to have fulfilled the general purpose of patent law by encouraging research and development in this important field.[18] Despite some minor problems involving allergic reactions, most biotechnology products thus far appear to offer significant consumer benefits and have not been shown to endanger public health.

Concerns about biotechnology remain the subject of public debate, however, and there are many serious issues. First, some contend that the entire field should be restrained on moral grounds—that modifying the genetic code found in nature is an inappropriate field of human endeavor. More narrowly, many commentators have concerns about the particular ethical issues raised by the application of biotechnology to human and animal subjects. Congress has enacted legislation banning the use of federal appropriations for patents that are directed to or encompass human organisms. Nonetheless, patents have been issued on cloning methods that arguably encompass human cloning.[19]

A second series of concerns relates to the health and safety effects of biotechnology. No widely accepted scientific evidence exists that genetically modified foods pose dangers to humans. It is difficult, however, to conduct long-term studies of the safety of genetically modified foods because of the lack of labelling of most such products. Although there is a federal scheme for labelling "organic" foods, there is no way for a consumer to determine if ordinary food products contain solely conventional ingredients, or

16. 447 U.S. 303 (1980) (citations omitted).

17. *See* David E. Adelman & Kathryn L. DeAngelis, Patent Metrics: the Mismeasure of Innovation in the Biotech Patent Debate, 85 Tex. L. Rev. 1677, 1681 (2007).

18. *Id.* at 1729–30.

19. *See, e.g.,* Pub. L. No. 109–108, 119 Stat. 2290 (2005). *See* Andrew A. Schwartz, the Patent Office Meets the Poison Pill: Why Legal Methods Cannot Be Patented, 20 Harv. J.L. & Tech. 333, 362 & n.199 (2007) (citing human cloning patents).

whether some genetically modified ingredients are included. These genetically modified foods have become a pervasive part of the United States food supply, with some estimates indicating that more than 70 percent of foods in the typical American supermarket contain at least some of these ingredients.[20] This result is not surprising, given that soybean, corn, and cottonseed oil is found in most processed foods, and most of these products are now produced from crops have one or more biotechnology traits. For example, most corn, cotton, and soybeans grown in the United States contain Monsanto's Round–Up Ready herbicide-resistance trait.

A second important patent decision is *State Street Bank & Trust Co. v. Signature Financial Group, Inc.*[21] Written by legendary Judge Giles Sutherland Rich (for whom a patent law moot court competition is named), the Federal Circuit held that business methods can qualify as patentable subject matter under 35 U.S.C. § 101. At issue was the validity of a patent entitled "Data Processing System for Hub and Spoke Financial Services Configuration." The patent was directed to a data processing system which allowed mutual funds to pool their assets in an investment portfolio organized as a partnership in a manner that allowed tracking the results of each fund. Most significantly, the Federal Circuit laid to rest the "business method" exception to statutory subject matter. "Since its inception, the 'business method' exception has merely represented the application of some general, but no longer applicable legal principle, perhaps arising out of the 'requirement for invention'—which was eliminated by § 103. Since the 1952 Patent Act, business methods have been, and should have been, subject to the same legal requirements for patentability as applied to any other process or method."[22]

In reaching this conclusion, Judge Rich quoted Judge Newman's dissent from *In re Schrader*,[23] which stated that the business method exception is "an unwarranted encumbrance to the definition of statutory subject matter in section 101, that [should] be discarded as error-prone, redundant, and obsolete. It merits retirement from the glossary of section 101.... All of the 'doing business' cases could have been decided using the clearer concepts of

---

20. *See, e.g.*, Debra M. Strauss, Genetically Modified Organisms in Food: a Model of Labeling and Monitoring with Positive Implications for International Trade, 40 Int'l Law. 95, 95 (2006) ("At least 70 percent of food products in United States supermarkets—boxed cereals, other grain products, frozen dinners, cooking oils and more—contain GMOs. The Grocery Manufacturers of America (GMA) estimates that 75 percent of all processed foods in the United States contain a GM ingredient, because nearly every product with a corn or soy ingredient, as well as some containing canola or cottonseed oil, has a GM component.").

21.   149 F.3d 1368 (Fed. Cir. 1998), *cert. denied*, 525 U.S. 1093 (1999).

22.   *Id.*

23.   22 F.3d 290, 298 (Fed. Cir.1994) (Newman, J., dissenting).

Title 35. Patentability does not turn on whether the claimed method does 'business' instead of something else, but on whether the method, viewed as a whole, meets the requirements of patentability as set forth in Sections 102, 103, and 112 of the Patent Act." The court also addressed the scope of the mathematical algorithm exception, discussed below, and found that the patent in question involved an application of the algorithm, and thus was not a mere abstract idea which would not be eligible for patent protection.

Like the impact of the decision in *Diamond v. Chakrabarty* on the biotechnology field, the court's holding in *State Street Bank* has prompted a dramatic increase in the number and scope of patents sought for business methods. The Patent Office was flooded with business method patent applications, and often granted such patents despite their dubious validity. Many business method patents covered material that did not satisfy the novelty and non-obviousness standards required by patent law. Patent examiners, overwhelmed by the flood of applications, often granted these patents and did not have sufficient information at their disposal to identify a basis for rejection.

Among the more famous business method patents litigated are the Amazon "one-click" method for purchasing items from a website and the Priceline "reverse auction" method of buying and selling goods and services via the Internet.[24] Both of these patents share the basic idea of applying a known method of doing business—one-stop shopping and reverse auctions—to the Internet. Whether these insights were sufficiently novel and inventive can certainly the subject of some debate and disagreement.

The scope of the Federal Circuit's holding in *State Street Bank* has been the subject of further litigation. In *AT & T Corp. v. Excel Communications, Inc.*,[25] the court held that not only product patent claims involving machines like the patent in *State Street Bank*, but also *process* claims involving business methods can be patentable subject matter. The *Excel* case involved a billing method which used a mathematical algorithm to calculate values for a database record. The court also found that process claims may be patentable despite the absence of a physical transformation feature.

The Supreme Court finally addressed business method patents in *Bilski v. Kappos,* 561 U.S. ___, 130 S.Ct. 3218 (2010). In that case, the Court reaffirmed that business methods are patentable, but found that the particular "hedging" method that was claimed in the patent at issue was an unpatentable abstract idea. The Court

24. *See Amazon.com, Inc. v. Barnesandnoble.com, Inc.*, 239 F.3d 1343 (Fed. Cir. 2001); U.S. Patent No. 5,794,207 (issued August 11, 1998).

25. 172 F.3d 1352 (Fed. Cir.1999), *cert. denied*, 528 U.S. 946 (1999).

rejected the Federal Circuit's approach, however, which focused exclusively on the machine-or-transformation test:

> It may be that the Court of Appeals thought it needed to make the machine-or-transformation test exclusive precisely because its case law had not adequately identified less extreme means of restricting business method patents, including (but not limited to) application of our opinions in *Benson, Flook,* and *Diehr*. In disapproving an exclusive machine-or-transformation test, we by no means foreclose the Federal Circuit's development of other limiting criteria that further the purposes of the Patent Act and are not inconsistent with its text.

The Court did note that the machine-or-transformation test could continue to be a useful tool in analyzing what constitutes patentable subject matter. The test required that a process claim must be tied to a specific machine or must transform a tangible article in some way.

Under section 18 of the AIA, the PTO must establish a transitional post-grant review proceeding for review of the validity of covered business method patents, to be put into place no later than September 16, 2012. A "covered business method patent" is defined in the AIA as "a patent that claims a method or corresponding apparatus for performing data processing or other operations used in the practice, administration, or management of a financial product or service, except that the term does not include patents for technological inventions." The scope of the definition will undoubtedly be the subject of future litigation.

¶ 13.03 Unpatentable Subject Matter—Laws of Nature, Natural Phenomena, Abstract Ideas, Mathematical Algorithms, Printed Matter

Despite the broad scope for patent law suggested by *Diamond v. Chakrabarty* and *State Street Bank,* there are some matters that are ineligible for patent protection. As the Court noted in *Diamond v. Chakrabarty*: "This is not to suggest that § 101 has no limits or that it embraces every discovery. The laws of nature, physical phenomena, and abstract ideas have been held not patentable. Thus, a new mineral discovered in the earth or a new plant found in the wild is not patentable subject matter. Likewise, Einstein could not patent his celebrated law that $E=mc^2$; nor could Newton have patented the law of gravity."[26]

In *Diamond v. Diehr*,[27] the Supreme Court identified three categories of subject matter that are unpatentable—"laws of na-

---

26. 447 U.S. 303 (1980).   **27.** 450 U.S. 175, 185 (1981).

ture, natural phenomena, and abstract ideas." Justice Rehnquist observed:

> This Court has undoubtedly recognized limits to § 101 and every discovery is not embraced within the statutory terms. Excluded from such patent protection are laws of nature, natural phenomena, and abstract ideas. "An idea of itself is not patentable." "A principle, in the abstract, is a fundamental truth; an original cause; a motive; these cannot be patented, as no one can claim in either of them an exclusive right."

As the Court stated in *Diamond v. Chakrabarty*: "[A] new mineral discovered in the earth or a new plant found in the wild is not patentable subject matter. Likewise, Einstein could not patent his celebrated law that $E=mc^2$; nor could Newton have patented the law of gravity. Such discoveries are 'manifestations of . . . nature, free to all men and reserved exclusively to none.' "[28]

The most recent Supreme Court pronouncement on the rule against patenting laws of nature is the 2012 decision in *Mayo Collaborative Servs. v. Prometheus Labs., Inc.*[29] In that case, the Court unanimously held that Prometheus Laboratories' process patent for correlations between blood test results and patient health is not eligible for patent protection because it incorporates laws of nature. The patent hinged upon the relationship between the concentration of metabolites in the blood and the likelihood that a thiopurine drug dosage will prove ineffective or cause harm, which the Court found was a law of nature not subject to patent protection. Allowing such patents, the Court reasoned, would inhibit future research and development.

As noted in *Diamond v. Diehr*, the Court has also found algorithms to be unpatentable, for example one used to convert binary code decimal numbers to equivalent pure binary numbers. "The sole practical application of the algorithm was in connection with the programming of a general purpose digital computer. We defined 'algorithm' as a 'procedure for solving a given type of mathematical problem,' and we concluded that such an algorithm, or mathematical formula, is like a law of nature, which cannot be the subject of a patent."[30] Mathematical algorithms so defined are thus not patentable subject matter to the extent that they are merely abstract ideas. To be patented, the algorithm must be used for some type of practical application—a useful, concrete and tangible result.

Unpatentable mathematical algorithms are merely abstract ideas constituting disembodied concepts or truths that are not

28.   447 U.S. at 309.

29.   132 S.Ct. 1289 (2012).

30.   447 U.S. at 185–86.

useful in a way cognizable under patent law. For example, in *In re Alappat*,[31] the Federal Circuit addressed a patent involving data that was transformed by a machine through a series of mathematical calculations to produce a smooth waveform display on a monitor. The court held that the invention constituted a practical application of an abstract idea (a mathematical algorithm or formula), because it produced the smooth waveform, which was "a useful, concrete and tangible result." Similarly, in *Arrhythmia Research Technology Inc. v. Corazonix Corp.*,[32] the Federal Circuit held that the transformation of electrocardiograph signals from a patient's heartbeat by a machine through a series of mathematical calculations constituted a practical application of an abstract idea, because it produced a useful, concrete or tangible outcome—an assessment of the condition of a patient's heart.

Despite the rule against patents on abstract ideas, the PTO has issued a mathematical patent covering two prime numbers, consisting of 150 and 320 digits, which provide a useful shortcut for code decryption.[33] Both numbers are apparently so large that they are novel in that they had not previously been used in the field. Assuming it is novel and non-obvious, the more difficult question is whether it is consistent with the Court's prohibition on patenting abstract ideas. Nonetheless, the patent appears to have a very practical application within the decryption field.

Another category of material said to be beyond the subject matter of patent law is "printed matter." The Manual of Patent Examining Procedure states that "a mere arrangement of printed matter, though seemingly a 'manufacture,' is rejected as not being within the statutory classes."[34] The key inquiry, according to the Federal Circuit, "is whether there exists any new and unobvious functional relationship between the printed matter and the substrate."[35] The printed matter doctrine applies to cases involving mere arrangements of printed lines, characters, or other material, and but it does not preclude patents on inventions that have functional applications, that are connected to physical features of a product, or that require a machine to process the information. Thus, as long as the printed material relates to a physical object or function of some sort, however, it can be patented. Cases where printed material with a related physical structure was found to be patentable have involved such things as detachable travel coupons and tear-off menu coupons.[36]

31. 33 F.3d 1526, 1554 (Fed. Cir. 1994) (en banc).

32. 958 F.2d 1053 (Fed. Cir.1992).

33. Partial Modular Reduction Patent, U.S. Patent Number 5,373,560.

34. PTO Manual of Patent Examining Procedure § 706.03(a) (8th ed. Oct. 2005).

35. *In re Lowry*, 32 F.3d 1579, 1582 (Fed. Cir. 1994).

36. *See Cincinnati Traction Co. v. Pope*, 210 Fed. 443 (6th Cir. 1913) (de-

Finally, the AIA addressed the patentability of tax planning strategies:

> For purposes of evaluating an invention under section 102 or 103 of [the Patent Act], any strategy for reducing, avoiding, or deferring tax liability, whether known or unknown at the time of the invention or application for patent, shall be deemed insufficient to differentiate a claimed invention from the prior art.[37]

By referencing sections 102 and 103 (novelty and non-obviousness), the AIA effectively precludes what had been a controversial attempt by some to obtain patent protection on tax planning strategies. This provision applies to any patent application pending on September 16, 2011.

¶ 13.04   Utility Patents

The Utility Requirement

The final requisite for granting a utility patent is usefulness, also known as utility (which thus defines this broad category of patents), in contrast to design and plant patents. In *Brenner v. Manson,* a landmark decision on the usefulness requirement for utility patents, Justice Story stated:

> All that the law requires is, that the invention should not be frivolous or injurious to the well-being, good policy, or sound morals of society. The work "useful," therefore, is incorporated into the act in contradistinction to mischievous or immoral. For instance, a new invention to poison people, or to promote debauchery, or to facilitate private assassination, is not a patentable invention. But if the invention steers wide of these objections, whether it be more or less useful is a circumstance very material to the interests of the patentee, but of no importance to the public. If it be not extensively useful, it will silently sink into contempt and disregard.[38]

Similarly, in *E.I. du Pont de Nemours & Co. v. Berkley & Co.,*[39] the court noted that "the defense of nonutility cannot be sustained without proof of total incapacity."

A recurring issue in patent law is whether the courts and the PTO should take into consideration the ethical value or morality of an invention. The question is whether the utility requirement

---

tachable travel coupon); *Rand, McNally & Co. v. Exchange Scrip–Book Co.*, 187 Fed. 984 (7th Cir. 1911) (travel coupons); *Benjamin Menu Card Co. v. Rand, McNally & Co.*, 210 Fed. 285 (N.D. Ill. 1894) (detachable meal coupons).

37. AIA § 14(a).

38. 383 U.S. 519 (1966).

39. 620 F.2d 1247 (8th Cir. 1980). *See also Standard Oil Co. v. Montedison, S.p.A.*, 664 F.2d 356 (3d Cir. 1981).

mandates that an invention be beneficial to society, and an analysis of whether some purposes might be deemed to be harmful or illegitimate. For instance, *Rickard v. Du Bon*[40] was an early decision involving an invention that could be used to facilitate deception or fraud—its sole purpose was to place flecks on tobacco leaves, which would make the tobacco falsely appear to be higher in quality.

More recent cases, however, have rejected this type of ethical inquiry as part of the analysis of an invention's utility. In *Juicy Whip, Inc. v. Orange Bang, Inc.*,[41] the Federal Circuit addressed the extent to which patent law should concern itself with the legitimacy or societal impact of the patent claim. The case involved a utility patent on a beverage machine, which was designed to make it appear that a beverage was being mixed in a visible dispenser when it was not. The court noted that many products involve simulation, citing examples of imitation gold leaf, cubic zirconium imitation diamonds, and imitation leather. Similarly, patents have issued on inventions that create imitation wood laminated flooring and on a process for placing imitation grill marks on food products. Given the broad scope of the Patent Act's coverage under section 101, the Federal Circuit concluded that the invention was patentable. Congress, the court noted, can always carve out unpatentable subject matter if it so chooses, as in the case of certain nuclear weapon technologies.[42] In light of this ruling, inventions that might be used for deception or fraud, or for purposes such as gambling or violence, can still satisfy the utility requirement, as long as they have some purpose that is lawful. In some ways, the question of what type of utility inquiry should be made (by the PTO and the courts) is analogous to the question of what sorts of works should be eligible for protection under copyright law (including pornography).

Aside from the issue of harmful uses, the utility requirement is not particularly demanding, as it allows impractical or inefficient inventions to receive patent protection. Thus, the invention does not have to be superior to the prior art. For example, in *Custom Accessories, Inc. v. Jeffrey–Allan Industries, Inc.*,[43] the court stated: "Finding that an invention is an improvement is not a prerequisite to patentability. It is possible for an invention to be less effective than existing devices but nevertheless meet the statutory criteria for patentability." Allowing these types of inventions to be patented does serve to encourage disclosure of innovations to the public, which may well increase the overall store of public knowledge or lead to further improvements or innovations.

---

40. 103 Fed. 868 (2d Cir. 1900) (finding tobacco-flecking invention unpatentable for lack of utility since its only purpose was to deceive).

41. 185 F.3d 1364 (Fed. Cir. 1999).

42. *See* 42 U.S.C. § 2181(a).

43. 807 F.2d 955, 960 n.12 (Fed. Cir. 1986).

An important issue in patent law is whether to allow patent protection for research tools or discoveries with no current marketplace applications. In effect, these are tools that can aid in the development of useful final products. It seems that the utility requirement can be met if an invention is useful in some way, for instance, in the treatment of animals, at least if the invention might have veterinary uses and those uses are claimed in the patent. The case of *In re Krimmel*[44] involved a drug that was shown to be useful in treating laboratory rabbits (but had not been proven effective in humans). The court held that the utility requirement was satisfied:

> We wish to point out that this court is aware of the common practice of using "experimental animals" in considerable variety for the evaluation of chemical compounds for possible pharmaceutical applications prior to clinical testing on humans. It is also our understanding that a demonstration that a compound has desirable or beneficial properties in the prevention, alleviation, or cure of some disease or manifestation of a disease in experimental animals does not necessarily mean that the compound will have the same properties when used with humans. With this information in mind, we hold that when an applicant for a patent has alleged in his patent application that a new and unobvious chemical compound exhibits some useful pharmaceutical property and when this property has been established by statistically significant tests with "standard experimental animals," sufficient statutory utility for the compounds has been presented. By "standard experimental animals," we mean whatever animal is usually used by those skilled in the art to establish the particular pharmaceutical application in question. These may be mice in one case, rabbits in another, chickens in another, and monkeys in another.[45]

Inventions that provide entertainment, such as games, are patentable. In *Cusano v. Kotler,*[46] the court stated: "Because of the cultural and prophylactic importance of games in our social structure, and the additional relevant factor of the huge annual expenditure for recreation we can properly conclude that the creation of a new game conforms to the patent requirement of being useful."

Medical Patents

Under United States law, patents can be issued on medical procedures, such as a new method for treating a physical ailment. To prevent physicians from being liable for patent infringement when they carry out treatment, however, section 287(c) of the Patent Act immunizes medical practitioners for liability for the

---

44. 292 F.2d 948 (C.C.P.A. 1961).   **46.** 159 F.2d 159, 162 (3d Cir. 1947).
45. *Id.* at 952.

unauthorized use of medical and surgical procedures: "With respect to a medical practitioner's performance of a medical activity that constitutes an infringement under section 271(a) or (b) of this title, the provisions of sections 281, 283, 284, and 285 of this title shall not apply against the medical practitioner or against a related health care entity with respect to such medical activity."[47] The statute defines medical activity as "the performance of a medical or surgical procedure on a body, but shall not include (i) the use of a patented machine, manufacture, or composition of matter in violation of such patent, (ii) the practice of a patented use of a composition of matter in violation of such patent, or (iii) the practice of a process in violation of a biotechnology patent." The immunity thus applies to medical procedures, but not to the underlying physical products that might be used in the course of medical treatment, such as a medical device or a pharmaceutical product.

A medical practitioner is defined as "any natural person who is licensed by a State to provide the medical activity described in subsection (c)(1) or who is acting under the direction of such person in the performance of the medical activity." A "related health care entity" is "an entity with which a medical practitioner has a professional affiliation under which the medical practitioner performs the medical activity, including but not limited to a nursing home, hospital, university, medical school, health maintenance organization, group medical practice, or a medical clinic." The statute applies to treatment of "a human body, organ or cadaver, or a nonhuman animal used in medical research or instruction directly relating to the treatment of humans." Given this language, the law does not generally exempt veterinarians from liability.

The statute is expressly inapplicable to the following categories of persons or entities:

> to the activities of any person, or employee or agent of such person (regardless of whether such person is a tax exempt organization under section 501(c) of the Internal Revenue Code), who is engaged in the commercial development, manufacture, sale, importation, or distribution of a machine, manufacture, or composition of matter or the provision of pharmacy or clinical laboratory services (other than clinical laboratory services provided in a physician's office), where such activities are:

> (A) directly related to the commercial development, manufacture, sale, importation, or distribution of a machine, manufacture, or composition of matter or the provision of pharmacy or

---

47. This provision was enacted in 1996. *See* Pub. L. No. 104–208, 104th Cong., 2d Sess., § 101(a) (1996).

clinical laboratory services (other than clinical laboratory services provided in a physician's office), and (B) regulated under the Federal Food, Drug, and Cosmetic Act, the Public Health Service Act, or the Clinical Laboratories Improvement Act."

The statute is also inapplicable to patents filed prior to September 30, 1996.

The scope of patent protection for medical procedures and for medical advances generally is one of the more controversial aspects of patent law.[48] The law in many foreign countries preclude patenting of medical procedures categorically. Yet there is a clear conflict between providing incentives for medical research by granting traditional patent protection for medical and drug innovations and making those advances widely available once they have been developed. It is in fact the classic public good problem that patent law is designed to help address, except that many believe revolutionary drugs and other medical products should be made available to poor patients worldwide despite their inability to pay.

¶ 13.05   Plant Patents & the Plant Variety Protection Act of 1970

Plant patents protect distinct plant varieties that are asexually reproduced. These plant varieties receive protection under the Plant Patent Act of 1930 ("PPA"). Sexually reproduced plants, in contrast, are eligible for protection under the Plant Variety Protection Act of 1970 ("PVPA").[49] The distinction between these two forms of protection hinges upon the method by which the new plant variety was developed. Asexual reproduction includes methods such as cutting, budding, and grafting. As the Federal Circuit stated in *Imazio Nursery Inc. v. Dania Greenhouses*,[50] the Plant Patent Act "requires asexual reproduction of the patented plant for there to be infringement. It is necessarily a defense to plant patent infringement that the alleged infringing plant is not an asexual reproduction of the patented plant. Part of this proof could be, thus, that the defendant independently developed the allegedly infringing plant." This independent development defense would not apply in cases involving utility patents.

Sexual reproduction, on the other hand, involves traditional cross-breeding of plant varieties and is covered by the PVPA. The

---

48. Examples of useful articles on the subject include Mary T. Griffin, "AIDS Drugs & the Pharmaceutical Industry: A Need for Reform," 17 Am. J. L. & Med. 363 (1991); William D. Noonan, "Patenting Medical and Surgical Procedures," 77 J. Pat. & Trademark Off. Soc'y 651 (1995); Wendy W. Yang,

"Note: Patent Policy and Medical Procedure Patents: The Case for Statutory Exclusion From Patentability," 1 B.U. J. Sci. & Tech. L. 5 (1995).

49. 7 U.S.C. §§ 2321–2582.

50. 69 F.3d 1560, 1570 (Fed. Cir. 1995).

rights of plant breeders in sexually-reproduced plants are protected with certificates issued under the PVPA. The PVPA is not part of the patent system, but offers patent-like protection. To be eligible, the plant must be new, distinct, uniform, and stable (i.e., it must "breed true").[51] The Plant Patent Act did not cover plant breeding because it was believed that new varieties could not be reproduced true-to-type through seedlings. By 1970, however, true-to-type reproduction was possible and the PVPA was enacted to protect such efforts. The PVPA has two important exceptions—plants may be used by other breeders to perform research, and farmers are permitted to save and replant seeds.[52]

Congress enacted specific protections for plants for two main reasons. First, it was thought at the time that plants, even when artificially bred, were products of nature for purposes of the patent law. Second, plants were thought not amenable to the "written description" requirement of the patent law.[53] In essence, identifying a plant in a patent would not necessarily enable one skilled in the art to replicate it. When it enacted the Plant Patent Act, Congress addressed both of these concerns. First, it stated that efforts of a plant breeder in aid of nature constituted a patentable invention.[54] Second, section 162 provides that the written description requirement was satisfied by a reasonably complete description: "No plant patent shall be declared invalid for noncompliance with section 112 of this title if the description is as complete as is reasonably possible. The claim in the specification shall be in formal terms to the plant shown and described."

Section 161 of the Plant Patent Act does not contain a utility requirement for plant patents. Instead it requires distinctness—that the plant be a distinct new variety: "Whoever invents or discovers and asexually reproduces any distinct and new variety of plant, including cultivated sports, mutants, hybrids, and newly found seedlings, other than a tuber propagated plant or a plant found in an uncultivated state, may obtain a patent therefor, subject to the conditions and requirements of this title."[55]

To somewhat complicate the application of patent law to plants, there is a third way in which some plants can receive

---

51. 7 U.S.C. § 2402(a) ("[T]he variety, when reproduced, will remain unchanged with regard to the essential and distinctive characteristics of the variety with a reasonable degree of reliability commensurate with that of varieties of the same category in which the same breeding method is employed").

52. 7 U.S.C. §§ 2543–44.

53. *See* 35 U.S.C.A. § 112.

54. S. Rep. No. 315, 71st Cong., 2d Sess., 6–8 (1930); H. R. Rep. No. 1129, 71st Cong., 2d Sess., 7–9 (1930).

55. *See Yoder Bros., Inc. v. California–Florida Plant Corp.*, 537 F.2d 1347 (5th Cir. 1976). *See also* S. Rep. No. 315, 71st Cong., 2d Sess. 4 (1930). If the inventor desires to obtain a utility patent on the new plant, however, then the usefulness requirement must be satisfied.

protection—through a traditional *utility* patent. Utility patent protection is only available if the plant (or more specifically the plant characteristic) is the product of human ingenuity. This requires that the plant characteristic result from genetic engineering or other similar methods of plant modification, as opposed to conventional plant breeding techniques. The concept of utility patent protection for genetically modified plants seems to logically follow from the Supreme Court's biotechnology ruling in *Diamond v. Chakrabarty*, as discussed in ¶ 12.02 above. Just as a genetically modified bacterium can receive utility patent protection, so too might a genetically modified strain of corn or soybeans. The Supreme Court expressly resolved this question in *J.E.M. Ag Supply, Inc. v. Pioneer Hi–Bred International, Inc.*,[56] which held that plants can qualify as patentable subject matter under section 101 of the Patent Act, so long as they meet the ordinary utility patent requirements of novelty, non-obviousness, and usefulness. This holding confirmed the PTO's practice of granting utility patents that satisfy the ordinary patent standard. Utility patent protection is valuable as it provides broader protection for plants than either the PPA or the PVPA. For example, there are no independent development defenses as in the Plant Patent Act, or farmer seed-saving exemptions as under the PVPA.

¶ 13.06　Design Patents

Design patents protect the ornamental appearance of a product. By definition, they do not have a utility requirement, given that functional features of a product cannot be the subject of a design patent. Instead, the plain language of the statute dictates that the design must be ornamental in nature. Section 171 of the Patent Act states: "Whoever invents any new, original, and ornamental design for an article of manufacture may obtain a patent therefor, subject to the conditions and requirements of this title." Examples of design patent subject matter include the appearance or ornamental features of athletic shoe uppers, an Apple iPad tablet, or a distinctive beverage container.

The design patent laws were intended to give encouragement to the decorative arts—the focus is on the appearance of a product as opposed to its functional aspects. An early Supreme Court decision, *Gorham Mfg. Company v. White*,[57] explains the types of features that might be covered by a design patent: "It is a new and original design for a manufacture, whether of metal or other material; a new and original design for a bust, statue, bas relief, or composition in alto or basso relievo; a new or original impression or ornament to be placed on any article of manufacture; a new and

56. 534 U.S. 124 (2001).　　　　　　**57.** 81 U.S. (14 Wall.) 511 (1871).

original design for the printing of woollen, silk, cotton, or other fabrics; a new and useful pattern, print, or picture, to be either worked into, or on, any article of manufacture; or a new and original shape or configuration of any article of manufacture." A more current definition can be found in the Patent Office's Manual: "the subject matter of a design patent application may relate to the configuration or shape of an article, to the surface ornamentation applied an the article, or to the combination of configuration and surface ornamentation."[58]

It is important to note that design patents are regularly granted for the appearance or ornamental aspects of functional products, but not on the functional features or aspects of those products (which of course may be protected by utility patents). In *Avia Group International, Inc. v. L.A. Gear California, Inc.*,[59] the Federal Circuit addressed design patents on a running shoe. Various aspects of the appearance of the running shoe were the subject of the design patent, including the overall appearance of the sole and uppers, the location and arrangement of perforations and stitching, the swirl pattern on the shoe, and the black and white colors of the shoe. The court addressed the issue of whether these elements were primarily ornamental (and thus eligible for design patent protection) or primarily functional and thus ineligible for design patent protection. The court noted that the appearance of the shoe was not dictated by functional considerations, and that there were many alternative designs that could be placed on the shoe. Thus, the design patent was found to be valid. In *Pacific Furniture Manufacturing Co. v. Preview Furniture Corp.*,[60] the court upheld design patent claims on the appearance of "upholstered armchairs comprising several essential elements: arms, a back and a seat cushion. The chairs also embody a swivel base platform upon which the chair can pivot and which is invisible to the viewer of the chair, and a box member upon which the seat cushion rests and which conceals the swivel base from view."

On the other hand, if the appearance of the product is dictated by functional considerations, then it cannot be the subject of a design patent. For example, *In re Carletti*[61] involved an application for a design patent on a gasket that was part of a closure assembly for gasoline drums and other similar containers. The court upheld the rejection of the design patent application, finding that its appearance was dictated by functional considerations—the ease and effectiveness of the gasket to seal containers:

---

58. U.S. Patent & Trademark Office, Manual of Patent Examining Procedure § 1502 (2001).

59. 853 F.2d 1557 (Fed. Cir. 1988).

60. 800 F.2d 1111, 1112 (Fed. Cir. 1986).

61. 328 F.2d 1020 (C.C.P.A. 1964).

It is clear that appellants never invented an "ornamental design." The appearance of appellants' gasket seems as much dictated by functional considerations as is the appearance of a piece of rope, which, too, has ribs and grooves nicely arranged. The fact that it is attractive or pleasant to behold is not enough. Many well-constructed articles of manufacture whose configurations are dictated solely by function are pleasing to look upon, for example a hex-nut, a ball bearing, a golf club, or a fishing rod, the pleasure depending largely on one's interests. But it has long been settled that when a configuration is the result of functional considerations only, the resulting design is not patentable as an ornamental design for the simple reason that it is not "ornamental"—was not created for the purpose of ornamenting.[62]

The existence of alternative designs for a product is a critical factor in determining whether a feature is ornamental or functional. The Federal Circuit, in *Berry Sterling Corp. v. Pescor Plastics, Inc.*,[63] held that a number of other factors are also important in assessing whether a design is dictated by functional considerations:

The presence of alternative designs may or may not assist in determining whether the challenged design can overcome a functionality challenge. Consideration of alternative designs, if present, is a useful tool that may allow a court to conclude that a challenged design is not invalid for functionality. As such, alternative designs join the list of other appropriate considerations for assessing whether the patented design as a whole— its overall appearance—was dictated by functional considerations. Other appropriate considerations might include: whether the protected design represents the best design; whether alternative designs would adversely affect the utility of the specified article; whether there are any concomitant utility patents; whether the advertising touts particular features of the design as having specific utility; and whether there are any elements in the design or an overall appearance clearly not dictated by function.

An important issue regarding ornamentality is the extent to which the design must have aesthetic appeal. Courts should be loathe to make that type of subjective judgment. Instead, the better view is that the ornamentation inquiry should be limited to differentiating between non-functional designs eligible for design patent protection and functional features that would be precluded from the ambit of the design patent scheme. Of course, the design patent

62. *Id.* at 1022. 63. 122 F.3d 1452, 1456 (Fed. Cir. 1997).

would also have to satisfy the other requisites for patentability, including novelty and non-obviousness.

Interestingly, although a design must be ornamental to qualify for this type of patent protection, it need not necessarily be visible in its ordinary or final uses, as long as its appearance is a "matter of concern" at some point in its commercial life. *In re Webb*[64] dealt with an ornamental design for a hip prosthesis, which is no longer visible once it is put into place in the body of a patient. The Federal Circuit held that the product's "appearance is observed by potential and actual purchasers, surgeons, nurses, operating room staff, and other hospital personnel." Therefore, it was eligible for design patent protection despite its lack of visibility when in final use. In other words, a feature that is hidden in its final use may still be patentable if its appearance is a "matter of concern" at some point in its commercial life. Similarly, the court in *Larson v. Classic Corp.*,[65] held that the design of a waterbed was protectable because customers took its appearance into account when making their decision to purchase a particular waterbed, even if the design would then be covered in ordinary use. On the other hand, the appearance of a product that is unlikely to be selected based on its appearance would not qualify for design patent protection. For example, *In re Stevens*[66] held that the design of internal vacuum cleaner parts are ineligible for design patent protection.

Providing patent protect for ornamental and non-functional designs presents a distinct possibility of overlapping protection with copyright law. The Supreme Court has recognized the potentially overlapping "statutory subject matter" in the fields of copyrights and design patents. In *Mazer v. Stein*,[67] which concerned copyright protection for statuettes used as lamp bases, the Court stated: "We do hold that the patentability of the statuettes, fitted as lamps or unfitted, does not bar copyright as works of art. Neither the Copyright Statute nor any other says that because a thing is patentable it may not be copyrighted. We should not so hold."

The overlap between copyright and design patent law presents the inevitable question of interest to designers who wish to maximize the Intellectual Property protections for their work—can a designer obtain *both* a design patent and a copyright on design features? Although one might think that intellectual property law might require the designer to elect one or the other form of protection, the courts have not so held. In *Application of Richard*

---

64. 916 F.2d 1553, 1557–58 (Fed. Cir. 1990).

65. 683 F.Supp. 1202 (N.D. Ill. 1988).

66. 173 F.2d 1015, 81 U.S.P.Q. 362 (C.C.P.A. 1949).

67. 347 U.S. 201, 217 (1954).

Q. Yardley,[68] the court stated: "We believe that the 'election of protection' doctrine is in direct conflict with the clear intent of Congress manifested in the two statutory provisions.... The Congress has provided that subject matter of the type involved in this appeal is 'statutory subject matter' under the copyright statute and is 'statutory subject matter' under the design patent statute, but the Congress has not provided that an author-inventor must elect between securing a copyright or securing a design patent. Therefore, we conclude that it would be contrary to the intent of Congress to hold that an author-inventor must elect between the two available modes of securing exclusive rights."

The court in this case went on to address whether dual protection of this type would frustrate or further the policies behind the Intellectual Property Clause: "We agree with the board's view that the framers of the Constitution recognized a distinction between 'authors' and 'inventors' and 'writings' and 'discoveries.' But, we do not think that the constitutional provision requires an election. The Congress, through its legislation under the authority of the Constitution, has interpreted the Constitution as authorizing an area of overlap where a certain type of creation may be the subject matter of a copyright and the subject matter of a design patent. We see nothing in that legislation which is contradictory and repugnant to the intent of the framers of the Constitution. Congress has not required an author-inventor to elect between the two modes which it has provided for securing exclusive rights on the type of subject matter here involved. If anything, the concurrent availability of both modes of securing exclusive rights aids in achieving the stated purpose of the constitutional provision."[69]

Finally, with regard to the treatment of design patents under patent law generally, section 171 of the Patent Act provides that "[t]he provisions of this title relating to patents for inventions shall apply to patents for designs, except as otherwise provided." Thus, the analysis of the requirements for patent protection, infringement, defenses, remedies, and other aspects of design patent law is generally the same as that used in the case of utility patents.

¶ 13.07   Novelty Under Section 102(a)

Patent law provides exclusive rights to inventors of new products, plants, or designs. Once a patent is granted by the U.S. Patent & Trademark Office ("PTO"), it gives the inventor the exclusive right to make, use, sell, offer to sell, or import the patented invention. In order to be entitled to this exclusive right, the patent

---

68. 493 F.2d 1389 (C.C.P.A. 1974).   **69.** *Application of Richard Q. Yardley*, 493 F.2d 1389 (C.C.P.A. 1974).

applicant must first meet the novelty requirement set forth in section 102. The invention must, in plain terms, be something new to the public and the marketplace. *When* the invention must be new and *where* it must be new are issues that will soon change. Section 102(a) of the Patent Act sets forth the novelty requirement applicable to patent applications with an effective filing date *prior to* March 16, 2013: "A person shall be entitled to a patent unless—(a) the invention was known or used by others in this country, or patented or described in a printed publication in this or a foreign country, before the invention thereof by the applicant for patent...."

One major change put into place under the AIA is the change in the geographic definition of what constitutes prior art for purposes of determining novelty. Under prior law, as quoted above, public uses or sales were only bars when they took place within the United States, whereas patented or published material worldwide would be taken into account. Post–AIA, prior art includes worldwide information that "was patented, described in a printed publication, or in public use, on sale, or otherwise available to the public before the effective filing date of the claimed invention." There is an exception for prior-filed patent applications under section 102(a)(2). This change takes effect on March 16, 2013. Thus, as a practical matter, both sets of rules will continue to be relevant, because pre-AIA patents will be in force over the next two decades and will be governed by the preexisting novelty rules.

In light of the AIA's amendments to section 102, third-party public uses serve as an immediate bar to patenting, unless the inventor publicly disclosed the invention before the third-party use took place. See 35 U.S.C. § 102(a) & (b)(1)(B) (as amended by the AIA). If the inventor engages in the public use, there continues to be a one-year grace period for filing the application. See 35 U.S.C. § 102(b)(1)(A) (as amended by the AIA).

Section 102, as amended by the AIA, contains two grace periods. First, the inventor's own disclosures will not bar a patent for one year under § 102(b)(1)(A), although third party disclosures are anticipating. Second, if the inventor makes a public disclosure of the invention, he or she gains priority and has one year in which to file the application. During this one-year post-public disclosure grace period, the actions of third parties (whether in using disclosing, or filing application for the invention) do not cause any loss of rights by the inventor.

Public Knowledge or Prior Use

If information is already publicly known in the United States, whether to the general public or to those skilled in the relevant art (i.e., those possessing the general knowledge in the relevant field of endeavor), then it cannot be patented. Specifically, pre-AIA section 102 bars patenting if the invention was "known or used by others" before the date of invention by the applicant. The information must be accessible to the public in some way for it to be anticipating (i.e., in order for it to preclude patenting on grounds of lack of novelty). Thus, for example, a manuscript sitting in a publisher's office, to which the public would have no access, does not constitute public knowledge (and is not yet in the form of a printed publication). Similarly, a memorandum or formula held in secrecy in a corporate office would not constitute public knowledge.

Connecticut Valley Enterprises, Inc. v. United States[70] addresses prior use—in other words when someone other than the patent applicant was making use of the invention before the patent applicant conceived of the invention. The court noted that the prior knowledge or use "must be of a complete and operative device. The prior knowledge or use in order to negative novelty must also be accessible to the public." Many technologies, particularly in fields related to defense or aerospace industries, are contained only in classified or secret documents, materials, or processes. With one exception below, information of this sort is generally not deemed to be prior knowledge for purposes of section 102(a), because it is not *publicly* known or used. This proposition makes sense because this information is not publicly accessible and therefore is not part of the existing store of public knowledge that does not warrant patent protection for lack of novelty. Section 155 of the Atomic Energy Act of 1954[71] establishes an exception to the general rule that limits the scope of anticipating prior knowledge to information that is publicly available. Section 155 provides: "In connection with applications for patents covered by this subchapter, the fact that the invention or discovery was known or used before shall be a bar to the patenting of such invention or discovery even though such prior knowledge or use was under secrecy within the atomic energy program of the United States."

Logically, in order for an invention to have been truly in use, it follows that it must have been in actual operation. In other words, to use the patent law term of art, it must be "reduced to practice." In contrast, courts have not required a reduction to practice in cases involving an invention prior to its conception by the patent applicant (*see* pre-AIA section 102(a)), because in these instances it is not necessary for a working prototype to exist. Instead, a constructive reduction to practice suffices in showing prior knowledge—there must be a complete description of the invention that is sufficiently detailed to permit a person reasonably skilled in the art

70. 348 F.2d 949 (Ct.Cl.1965).   **71.** 42 U.S.C. § 2185.

to make the invention. This point was recognized in the case of *In re Borst*.[72]

Patented or Described in a Printed Publication

As previously noted, prior to the effective date of the AIA, section 102(a) provides: "A person shall be entitled to a patent unless—(a) the invention was known or used by others in this country, or patented or described in a printed publication in this or a foreign country, before the invention thereof by the applicant for patent. . . ." It is critical to notice that prior knowledge or use bars patentability pre-AIA, only if the knowledge or use takes place in the United States. With regard to material that is patented or printed, in contrast, United States patent law takes into account information available anywhere in the world.

This distinction reflects a deliberate congressional choice, under pre-AIA law, as expressed in the plain meaning of the statute. It provides that if an invention is known or used abroad prior to it being conceived of by the United States patent applicant, *it is still novel and eligible for patent protection (i.e., it is not anticipated).* In contrast, the invention is not novel (i.e., is deemed to be anticipated) if it is already patented or printed anywhere in the world prior to the patent applicant's conception date. This latter rule is in place *both* before and after enactment of the AIA.

As noted above, post-AIA, prior art includes worldwide information that "was patented, described in a printed publication, or in public use, on sale, or otherwise available to the public before the effective filing date of the claimed invention." There is an exception for prior-filed patent applications under section 102(a)(2). This change takes effect on March 16, 2013.

So in practice this statutory distinction means that someone can patent information that is known or used abroad (as long as it is not known or used in the United States). Several criticisms are frequently made about this outcome. First, some contend that this permits United States patent law to cover traditional knowledge found in Third World or other foreign cultures. Second, it gives United States patent holders the ability to patent material that may not be patentable elsewhere in the world.

These criticisms, though valid factually, seem to ignore the clear congressional purpose—rewarding patent applicants who bring to the United States information that is not known or used in the United States. This contribution is valuable, as it increases the public store of knowledge in this country. Thus, even if something is not totally novel anywhere in the world, it might be novel from the standpoint of the American marketplace. In contrast, once an

---

72. 345 F.2d 851 (C.C.P.A. 1965).

innovation is patented or available in printed publications, then it is readily accessible in the United States, and thus no one can still claim that it is novel from the perspective of the American market. Moreover, it might be difficult to determine and prove what is known or used worldwide, even with advances in communications and technology. Finally, to the extent that information abroad is now more readily accessible because of the Internet and other improvements in communication, it is much more likely that the information will either already be known or used in the United States or will be deemed an anticipating "printed publication" from abroad.

Determining what constitutes a printed publication is much more difficult than it might seem, particularly given technological changes in the last two decades. A good starting point is the case of *In re Wyer*.[73] At issue in that case was whether information (no patent had been issued) filed in the Australian Patent Office could be deemed a printed publication.

> It has been stated by this and other courts that to constitute a "printed publication," as that term is used in § 102, a reference must be both "printed" and "published." With regard to the "printing" requirement, it has been stated that the "only realistic distinction that we can see as between 'handwritten' and 'printed' publications relates to the method of producing them." In other words, the requirement of printing increases the probability that a reference will be available to the public, for "Congress no doubt reasoned that one would not go to the trouble of printing a given description of a thing unless it was desired to print a number of copies of it."

> The "publication requirement," said to be "so connected with (the 'printing' requirement) that treatment of the one cannot be satisfactorily done without overstepping into the bounds of the other," has been equated with public accessibility to the "printed document." On the other hand, there are a number of cases which eschew this two-tiered approach and view the unitary concept of "printed publication" in the context of dissemination or accessibility alone.[74]

The court concluded that the focus of the analysis "should be [on the] public dissemination of the document, and its availability and accessibility to persons skilled in the subject matter or art."[75] A printed publication need not be a published document having widespread distribution. Indeed, a single copy of a printed docu-

73. 655 F.2d 221 (C.C.P.A. 1981).   **75.** *Id.*
74. *Id.* at 225.

ment found in a library or archive may be deemed a "publication" for purposes of section 102(a), as long as the material is available to researchers exercising reasonable diligence and is properly indexed in the library or archive.[76]

The Internet poses a significant challenge in determining what constitutes a printed publication. Logic would suggest that anything that is available and retrievable by persons in the United States on the Internet should constitute information barring patent protection under United States law. Thus, for example, if one can sit at a computer in the United States and conduct a search on Google that successfully retrieves a particular piece of information posted on a website in Ghana, should it not be deemed to be a printed publication?[77] To the extent the law reaches this conclusion, however, then the distinction between assessing knowledge in the United States and printed publications anywhere in the world ceases to be very meaningful.

In other words, given that most information in existence anywhere in the world is or soon will be available on the Internet, then it will bar patent protection as a printed publication. It does seem that we have reached this point as of 2012, as nearly all information worldwide is now accessible on the Internet. This reality may have prompted Congress to include in the AIA a bar to patenting inventions "otherwise available to the public."

With regard to whether a work is patented anywhere in the world, information that comes within the scope of what is patented anywhere in the world is rather straightforward. The patented information must be available to the general public in some way and must be enabling.[78]

Design patents and plant patents have the same novelty requirements as in the case of utility patents. Plant patent cases present some challenges because the description of a plant may not necessarily permit a person having ordinary skill in the art (phosita) to replicate the plant.[79] Despite this fact, if the plant is previously patented, it cannot be patented again. Similarly, if the description is specific enough to enable it to be reproduced, it would appear to mean the plant is publicly known and thus is anticipated.

---

76. *See, e.g., In re Cronyn*, 890 F.2d 1158, 1160–61 (Fed. Cir. 1989); *In re Hall*, 781 F.2d 897 (Fed. Cir. 1986).

77. *See generally Symantec Corp. v. Computer Associates Intern., Inc.*, 2006 WL 3950278 (E.D.Mich. 2006) (upholding admissibility of material posted on the Internet as prior art).

78. *See United States v. Adams*, 383 U.S. 39 (1966).

79. *See generally In re LeGrice*, 301 F.2d 929 (C.C.P.A. 1962) (noting that photographs and descriptions of a plant do not enable replication of it under section 102(b)).

¶ 13.08 Statutory Bars

Public Use Bar Under Section 102(b)

Section 102(b) sets forth statutory bars under federal patent law: "A person shall be entitled to a patent unless—. . . (b) the invention was patented or described in a printed publication in this or a foreign country or in public use or on sale in this country, more than one year prior to the date of the application for patent in the United States. . . ." These rules essentially require the inventor to proceed diligently in filing its patent application after initiating any of the enumerated activities. *Baxter International, Inc. v. COBE Laboratories, Inc.*[80] suggests four policies underlying the rule: "(1) discouraging the removal, from the public domain, of inventions that the public reasonably has come to believe are freely available; (2) favoring the prompt and widespread disclosure of inventions; (3) allowing the inventor a reasonable amount of time following sales activity to determine the potential economic value of a patent; and (4) prohibiting the inventor from commercially exploiting the invention for a period greater than the statutorily prescribed time." Awareness of these rules is important not only for patent law practitioners, but also for any business advisor as these rules can trap unwary inventors into forfeiting their patent rights.

For example, a public use by the inventor or third parties more than a year before the application date results in forfeiture of an otherwise valid United States patent. This rule, though seemingly harsh, mandates that the patent applicant quickly and expeditiously file an application, and thus is similar in purpose to a statute of limitations. Moreover, although the one-year window might seem brief, it is in fact generous compared to many foreign patent systems, which do not contain any such grace period. Judge Hand's decision in *Metallizing Engineering Co. v. Kenyon Bearing & Auto Parts Co.*[81] addressed the issue of public use, noting that "it is a condition upon an inventor's right to a patent that he shall not exploit his discovery competitively after it is ready for patenting; he must content himself with either secrecy, or legal monopoly. It is true that for the limited period of two years he was allowed to do so, possibly in order to give him time to prepare an application; and even that has been recently cut down by half. But if he goes beyond that period of probation, he forfeits his right regardless of how little the public may have learned about the invention; just as he can forfeit it by too long concealment, even without exploiting the invention at all." Judge Hand notes that this rule reflects congres-

---

80. 88 F.3d 1054, 1058 (Fed. Cir. 1996).

81. 153 F.2d 516, 520 (2d Cir.), *cert. denied,* 328 U.S. 840 (1946).

sional policy "that it is part of the consideration for a patent that the public shall as soon as possible begin to enjoy the disclosure."[82]

The public use, as mentioned above, can be conducted either by the inventor or by a third party. By its terms, the use must be public, an issue which has generated some litigation. For instance, in a divided opinion, the court in *Baxter International, Inc. v. COBE Laboratories, Inc.*[83] held that a public use took place when a third party made use of a centrifuge in a research laboratory. The court found no evidence that observers were bound by confidentiality obligations, and thus the use was deemed public in nature. On the other hand, if the use was actually conducted under conditions of secrecy, then the one-year bar is not triggered.[84] Note that a "public use" only becomes a pre-AIA statutory bar if it occurs in this county, as discussed above.

Experimental Uses

Experimental uses do not fall within the category of invalidating public uses under pre-AIA section 102(b) (and possibly post-AIA as well), but the scope of the experimental use exception requires a careful analysis. The experimental use exception recognizes the common sense idea that an inventor often seeks to test the invention to assure that it works properly. This type of experimentation is entirely proper and should not trigger a one-year bar that might lead to forfeiture of rights to the invention. In *Baxter International*, the court found that the use in question was not experimental. The invention was a blood-processing centrifuge. Tests were conducted by a third party to determine if the centrifuge would have additional uses, and the court concluded that these tests would not fall within the experimental use exception. The court focused on the fact that the additional applications for the centrifuge were not recited in the patent application and that the inventor did not have any direction or control over the third-party testing: "The experimental use doctrine operates in the inventor's favor to allow *the inventor* to refine his invention or to assess its value relative to the time and expense of prosecuting a patent application. If it is not the inventor or someone under his control or 'surveillance' who does these things, there appears to us no reason why he should be entitled to rely upon them to avoid the statute." The court therefore held that the "public testing before the critical date by a third party for his own unique purposes of an invention previously reduced to practice and obtained from someone other than the patentee, when such testing is independent of and not controlled by the patentee, is an invalidating public use, not an experimental

82. *Id.*

83. 88 F.3d 1054 (Fed. Cir. 1996).

84. *See W.L. Gore & Assoc., Inc. v. Garlock Inc.*, 721 F.2d 1540, 1550 (Fed.

Cir. 1983), *cert. denied*, 469 U.S. 851 (1984).

use."[85] The court also identified a series of factors for assessing whether a use is experimental:

> An analysis of experimental use, which is also a question of law, requires consideration of the totality of the circumstances and the policies underlying the public use bar. Evidentiary factors in determining if a use is experimental include the length of the test period, whether the inventor received payment for the testing, any agreement by the user to maintain the use confidential, any records of testing, whether persons other than the inventor performed the testing, the number of tests, and the length of the test period in relation to tests of similar devices.[86]

In *Madey v. Duke University*,[87] the Federal Circuit addressed the issue in the context of a private research university. The court determined that, regardless of whether a university engages in research for commercial gain, its research furthers the university's "legitimate business objectives," which include educating students and obtaining research grants. The Federal Circuit therefore held that the experimental use exception does not generally shield universities engaged in research from liability for patent infringement:

> In the present case, the district court attached too great a weight to the non-profit, educational status of Duke, effectively suppressing the fact that Duke's acts appear to be in accordance with any reasonable interpretation of Duke's legitimate business objectives. On remand, the district court will have to significantly narrow and limit its conception of the experimental use defense. The correct focus should not be on the non-profit status of Duke but on the legitimate business Duke is involved in and whether or not the use was solely for amusement, to satisfy idle curiosity, or for strictly philosophical inquiry.[88]

Thus, regardless of whether a particular institution is seeking commercial gain, the court focused the analysis on whether the use was in furtherance of its legitimate business or whether it is solely for amusement, to satisfy idle curiosity, or for strictly philosophical inquiry. The court noted that the non-profit status of the user is not determinative.

It is also important to distinguish between experimental uses and test marketing of a product. Determining whether a product will be profitable or successful in the marketplace or among consumer is not experimental. Thus, test marketing of a product will

85. 88 F.3d at 1060–61.

86. 88 F.3d at 1060.

87. 307 F.3d 1351 (Fed. Cir. 2002).

88. 88 F.3d at 1362–63.

trigger the one-year bar. For example, the Federal Circuit's *In re Smith* decision[89] noted that the experimental use exception "does not include market testing where the inventor is attempting to gauge consumer demand for his claimed invention. The purpose of such activities is commercial exploitation and not experimentation." The court held that the inventor failed to meet its burden of showing that the public use fell within the experimental use exception.

On–Sale Bar Under Section 102(b)

In *Pfaff v. Wells Electronics, Inc.*, 525 U.S. 55 (1998), the Supreme Court held that section 102(b)'s "on sale" bar can be triggered even without a reduction to practice. *Pfaff* addressed the applicability of the on-sale bar in a case where the invention was offered for sale without an accompanying working prototype. The Supreme Court held that the invention did not have to be "reduced to practice" for an offer for sale to take place. Thus, the triggering event can be either an offer to sell a working prototype or an offer accompanied by a sufficient description to allow one skilled in the art to produce the invention. Recall the earlier discussion of the *Borst* decision in ¶ 13.07, which found prior public knowledge does not require an actual reduction to practice under section 102(a). In cases involving prior knowledge, like cases involving the on sale bar, the existence of a working prototype is not critical in determining whether the claimed invention is novel. In contrast, an actual reduction to practice is required in order for a work to be deemed in prior use under section 102. Prior use implies the actual existence of a working prototype of the invention.

Significantly, the on-sale bar is not triggered by an offer to license or assign future patent rights to an invention, as distinguished from an offer to sell the underlying product or process itself.[90] This distinction sensibly differentiates between an attempt to license intellectual property as opposed to an offer to sell the product itself, or products produced from the process. In the latter case, the inventor is placing the fruits of the invention into the market. Once the inventor makes such an offer, the policy behind the on-sale bar is triggered—preventing the extension of the patent monopoly when the inventor has begun to exploit the invention before filing a patent application. Offers to license or assign, on the other hand, do not place the product into the market in a manner that ought to trigger the on-sale bar.

89. 714 F.2d 1127, 1136–37 (Fed. Cir. 1983).

90. *Moleculon Research Corp. v. CBS, Inc.*, 793 F.2d 1261 (Fed. Cir. 1986), *cert. denied*, 479 U.S. 1030 (1987).

¶ 13.09   Other Requirements of Sections 102 & 104

Abandonment Under Section 102(c)

Section 102(c) of the Patent Act states: "A person shall be entitled to a patent unless—... (c) he has abandoned the invention...." *Moore v. United States*[91] summarizes the focus of this inquiry: "Abandonment is an affirmative defense which must be proven by clear and convincing evidence. Abandonment presupposes a deliberate, though not necessarily an express, surrender of any rights to a patent. To abandon the invention, the inventor must intend a dedication to the public. This intent may be express, as by a declaration by the inventor, or implied as by the actions or inactions of the inventor. Delay alone is not a sufficient basis from which to infer the requisite intent."

Foreign Patents Under Section 102(d)

Patent applications governed by the pre-AIA novelty rules will continue to be subject to section 102(d). Section 102(d) addresses foreign patent applications, stating: "A person shall be entitled to a patent unless—... (d) the invention was first patented or caused to be patented, or was the subject of an inventor's certificate, by the applicant or his legal representatives or assigns in a foreign country prior to the date of the application for patent in this country on an application for patent or inventor's certificate filed more than twelve months before the filing of the application in the United States...." Like the on-sale bars for public uses and sales, this provision encourages diligent filing of patents in the United States.

This provision was the subject of the decision in the *In re Kathawala*[92] case. The Federal Circuit held that because Kathawala had filed and obtained Greek and Spanish patent applications on his invention more than one year before he filed his United States patent application, section 102(d) barred his United States patent. The court rejected the inventor's three arguments against this result. First, the court found that it was irrelevant whether the Greek patent was actually invalid under Greek law. The important fact is that the patent application was filed and granted, and the court rejected the idea that the PTO should delve into the actual validity of patents under foreign law. Second, Kathawala contended that the Spanish patent was not publicly available until after he had filed his United States patent application. Once again, the court held that the key question is whether the foreign patent had in fact been granted. Finally, the inventor argued that the Spanish patent did not claim all features sought to be patented in the United States (apparently because some elements were not patenta-

---

91. 1977 WL 22793, 194 U.S.P.Q. 423 (Ct. Cl. 1977).

92. 9 F.3d 942 (Fed. Cir. 1993).

ble under Spanish law). The court held that the section 102(d) bar still applied because these elements were part of the same invention that was disclosed in the Spanish patent application.

Pending Patent Applications Under Section 102(e)

Patent applications governed by the pre-AIA novelty rules will continue to be subject to section 102(e). Section 102(e) of the Patent Act states: "A person shall be entitled to a patent unless— ... (e) the invention was described in—(1) an application for patent, published under section 122(b), by another filed in the United States before the invention by the applicant for patent or (2) a patent granted on an application for patent by another filed in the United States before the invention by the applicant for patent, except that an international application filed under the treaty defined in section 351(a) shall have the effects for the purposes of this subsection of an application filed in the United States only if the international application designated the United States and was published under Article 21(2) of such treaty in the English language...." Note that material in patent applications that are published pursuant to section 122 of the Patent Act are deemed prior art as of the date of application.

This statute codified the rule announced in *Alexander Milburn Co. v. Davis–Bournonville Co.,*[93] which held that a pending patent application containing the anticipating material precludes patentability. A later inventor, the Supreme Court noted, should not benefit from delays in the Patent Office. Material contained in international patent applications sought under the Patent Cooperation Treaty (PCT) are also considered prior art, if they have been filed in English and seek to claim patent protection in the United States.

Post-AIA law retains section 102(e)'s basic idea of patent rights going to the first of two pending applications in section 102(a)(2).

Inventorship (Derivation) Under Section 102(f)

There is no counterpart to section 102(f) in the new section 102, as revised by the AIA. Nonetheless, only the "true inventor" is entitled to a patent. If someone has improperly derived the invention from the true inventor, that individual does not have ownership rights in the patent, even if he or she was the first to file a patent application. If there is a dispute over the identity of the true inventor, AIA § 3(i) (to be codified at 35 U.S.C. § 135) establishes a "derivation proceeding." These proceedings can be brought as to patents filed after March 16, 2013.

With regard to patents filed before the effective date of this part of the AIA, section 102(f) still governs, and it states: "A person

93. 270 U.S. 390 (1926).

shall be entitled to a patent unless— . . . (f) he did not himself invent the subject matter sought to be patented. . . ." The essence of invention under United States law is conception—developing a detailed and specific concept. The conception must involve a sufficiently detailed and practical invention that actually achieves the result in question. Thus, for example, the theoretical idea of instantaneous travel through space depicted in a science fiction work such as Star Trek is not a conception for purposes of patent law, as the concept is not set forth in a manner that actually allows for or enables such travel.

Once the invention is conceived of in the very practical sense required by patent law, the person or persons involved in this creative process are deemed the rightful inventors unless they either fail to exercise reasonable diligence or are found to have abandoned, suppressed, or concealed the invention. In other words, until the recent AIA amendments take effect (as noted above), the first to conceive of an invention *generally* owned all rights to it even if that inventor is not the first to reduce the invention to practice (i.e., make a prototype) or the first to file a patent application. There are two qualifications on this general rule—the first party to conceive of the invention can lose its priority if it fails to exercise reasonable diligence in reducing the invention to practice or if it abandons, suppresses, or conceals the invention. Once again, the AIA changes this rule, as noted above.

Applegate v. Scherer[94] indicates that conception of the complete invention is the *sine qua non* of invention. As the court noted: "Appellants seem to propose that there cannot be a conception of an invention of the type here involved in the absence of knowledge that the invention will work. Such knowledge, necessarily, can rest only on an actual reduction to practice. To adopt this proposition would mean, as a practical matter, that one could never communicate an invention thought up by him to another who is to try it out, for, when the tester succeeds, the one who does no more than exercise ordinary skill would be rewarded and the innovator would not be an idea so clearly defined in the inventor's mind that only ordinary skill would be necessary to reduce the invention to practice." A technician or mechanic who follows an inventor's specific instructions in reducing the invention to practice is thus not a co-inventor under this standard. Inventorship is discussed further as it relates to patent ownership issues in Chapter 13, ¶ 13.01.

Under the post-AIA section 100(f), inventorship continues to be a general requirement: "The term 'inventor' means the individual or, if a joint invention, the individuals collectively who invented or discovered the subject matter of the invention." However, as of

---

94.   332 F.2d 571 (C.C.P.A. 1964).

September 15, 2012, the AIA eliminates a long-standing "deceptive intention" proviso regarding misidentification of inventors. AIA § 20. For infringement actions or other proceedings commenced on or after September 16, 2012, improper identification of inventors will no longer constitute grounds for invalidating a patent.

In *Collective Conception of the Invention: In Vanderbilt University v. ICOS Corp.*, 601 F.3d 1297, 1303 (Fed. Cir. 2010), the Federal Circuit recently discussed the standard for joint inventorship under section 116:

> A primary focus of section 116 has thus always been on collaboration and joint behavior. A person must contribute to the conception of the claimed invention to qualify as a joint inventor. Yet, each contributor need not have their own contemporaneous picture of the final claimed invention in order to qualify as joint inventors. Rather, "the qualitative contribution of each collaborator is the key—each inventor must contribute to the joint arrival at a definite and permanent idea of the invention as it will be used in practice." The interplay between conception and collaboration requires that each co-inventor engage with the other co-inventors to contribute to a joint conception.

Finally, the AIA made an important clarification regarding the ability of assignees to file patent applications. AIA § 4, codified in section 118 of the Patent Act, allows an application to be filed by a "person to whom the inventor has assigned or is under an obligation to assign the invention." Section 115, as revised by the AIA, requires that patent applications name all inventors and provide a declaration of inventorship from each inventor, but if an inventor who is obligated to assign the invention refuses to provide the required declaration, the patent applicant may submit a substitute statement on behalf of that inventor.

Priority Under Section 102(g)

Section 102(g), which will no longer be relevant once the AIA takes full effect, will still continue to apply to patent claims filed before March 16, 2013. Once the AIA takes effect, of course, priority will be based solely on the "first to file or publicly disclose" rule.

Thus, for purposes of patents filed before the effective date of this portion of the AIA, section 102(g) still provides the governing law. It states: "A person shall be entitled to a patent unless—. . . (g)(1)during the course of an interference conducted under section 135 or section 291, another inventor involved therein establishes, to the extent permitted in section 104, that before such person's invention thereof the invention was made by such other inventor and not abandoned, suppressed, or concealed, or (2) before such person's invention thereof, the invention was made in this country by another inventor who had not abandoned, suppressed, or concealed it. In determining priority of invention under this subsection, there shall be considered not only the respective dates of conception and reduction to practice of the invention, but also the reasonable diligence of one who was first to conceive and last to reduce to practice, from a time prior to conception by the other."

A leading case under section 102(g) is *Paulik v. Rizkalla.*[95] Paulik reduced the invention to practice in 1970, but work on the patent application did not begin until January or February 1975. Rizkalla filed his patent application in March 1975, and sought priority based on that date. Paulik's patent application was filed in June 1975. The court ultimately held that the first inventor, Paulik, had not abandoned, suppressed, or concealed the invention, and thus was entitled to priority (i.e., received all rights to the invention). The court noted that "[t]here is no impediment in the law to holding that a long period of inactivity need not be a fatal forfeiture, if the first inventor resumes work on the invention before the second inventor enters the field. We deem this result to be a fairer implementation of national patent policy, while in full accord with the letter and spirit of section 102(g)."[96] The court also noted that forfeitures under this provision typically occur only when the first inventor was spurred to action by the second inventor:

> The decisions applying section 102(g) balanced the law and policy favoring the first person to make an invention, against equitable considerations when more than one person had made the same invention: in each case where the court deprived the de facto first inventor of the right to the patent, the second inventor had entered the field during a period of either inactivity or deliberate concealment by the first inventor. Often the first inventor had been spurred to file a patent application by news of the second inventor's activities. Although "spurring" is not necessary to a finding of suppression or concealment, the courts' frequent references to spurring indicate their concern with this equitable factor.[97]

The issue of what constitutes sufficient evidence that a first inventor has abandoned, suppressed, or concealed the invention is highly fact specific. Consider the case of two inventors, Perkins and Kwon. Both independently conceive of and develop an invention involving a golf swing sensor. Perkins is the first to conceive of the invention, but Kwon files the first patent application during a period of time in which Perkins is diligently working to reduce the

---

95. 760 F.2d 1270 (Fed. Cir. 1985).   **97.** *Id.* at 1275.
96. *Id.* at 1271.

invention to practice. Until to this point, it would be clear that Perkins still has the rights to the patent. But if Kwon begins marketing the product and it takes Perkins more than a year to file the patent application after Kwon's marketing activities began, then Perkins is no longer entitled to the patent, as a result of the section 102(b) on-sale statutory bar. Kwon, of course, was not the first to conceive of the invention, and assuming Perkins' reasonable diligence, section 102(g) provides that Kwon cannot obtain the patent either.[98] On the other hand, because of the way the operative language of the statutes address foreign activities, the outcome would be different if the inventors' activities took place abroad. If Kwon's sales efforts had taken place abroad, the on-sale bar would not apply, and Perkins' patent would be valid. Alternatively, if Perkins' inventive activity had taken place abroad, then section 102(g) would not preclude Kwon from obtaining United States patent rights.

Inventions Made Abroad Under Section 104

Section 104(a) states:

(1) PROCEEDINGS.—In proceedings in the Patent and Trademark Office, in the courts, and before any other competent authority, an applicant for a patent, or a patentee, may not establish a date of invention by reference to knowledge or use thereof, or other activity with respect thereto, in a foreign country other than a NAFTA country or a WTO member country, except as provided in sections 119 and 365 of this title.

(2) RIGHTS.—If an invention was made by a person, civil or military—

  (A) while domiciled in the United States, and serving in any other country in connection with operations by or on behalf of the United States,

  (B) while domiciled in a NAFTA country and serving in another country in connection with operations by or on behalf of that NAFTA country, or

  (C) while domiciled in a WTO member country and serving in another country in connection with operations by or on behalf of that WTO member country, that person shall be entitled to the same rights of priority in the United States with respect to such invention as if such invention had been made in the United States, that NAFTA country, or that WTO member country, as the case may be.

(3) USE OF INFORMATION.—To the extent that any information in a NAFTA country or a WTO member country

98. *See Perkins v. Kwon,* 886 F.2d
325 (Fed. Cir. 1989).

concerning knowledge, use, or other activity relevant to proving or disproving a date of invention has not been made
available for use in a proceeding in the Patent and Trademark
Office, a court, or any other competent authority to the same
extent as such information could be made available in the
United States, the Director, court, or such other authority shall
draw appropriate inferences, or take other action permitted by
statute, rule, or regulation, in favor of the party that requested
the information in the proceeding.

This provision, which applies to both foreign and domestic inventors, is designed to avoid problems of proof or fraud regarding
inventive activity abroad. It also encourages prompt filing of United
States patents or of foreign patent applications under section 119.
The term "NAFTA country," as used in the statute, has the
meaning given that term in section 2(4) of the North American
Free Trade Agreement Implementation Act. The term "WTO member country" has the meaning given that term in section 2(10) of
the Uruguay Round Agreements Act. After the 2013 effective date
of the AIA, this provision will be relevant only to patent applications filed prior to the AIA's effective date.

¶ 13.10 Nonobviousness Under Section 103

The novelty inquiry looks to similarities between the invention
and prior art, whereas nonobviousness assesses differences between
the prior art and the claimed invention. In other words, in order to
be novel an invention must not be anticipated—it must not already
by part of the public store of knowledge found in patents or printed
publications worldwide, or in public use or known within the
United States. Specifically, a claimed invention is novel if no single
piece of prior art contains each and every element of the claim. The
nonobviousness requirement, in contrast, presupposes that no one
piece of prior art contains all the elements of a claim. Nonobviousness involves a qualitative judgment regarding the differences between all of the prior art and the claimed invention—and those
differences must be sufficiently inventive or substantial. The claim
must involve a significant creative or inventive step beyond what
was already known.

With regard to patents filed before March 16, 2013, section
103(a) sets forth the general nonobviousness requirement: "A patent may not be obtained though the invention is not identically
disclosed or described as set forth in section 102 of this title, if the
differences between the subject matter sought to be patented and
the prior art are such that the subject matter as a whole would
have been obvious at the time the invention was made to a person
having ordinary skill in the art to which said subject matter

pertains. Patentability shall not be negatived by the manner in which the invention was made."

For effective patent filing dates on or after March 16, 2013, the AIA modifies section 103 slightly as follows: "A patent for a claimed invention may not be obtained, notwithstanding that the claimed invention is not identically disclosed as set forth in section 102, if the differences between the claimed invention and the prior art are such that the claimed invention as a whole would have been obvious *before the effective filing date of the claimed invention* to a person having ordinary skill in the art to which the claimed invention pertains. Patentability shall not be negated by the manner in which the invention was made." The key change, highlighted in the quote, is that nonobviousness will be measured as of the date of filing of a patent claim, rather than as of the invention date.

Graham v. John Deere Co.[99] is the paradigm case addressing nonobviousness. The Court set forth the following framework for assessing whether section 103 is satisfied: "Under § 103, the scope and content of the prior art are to be determined; differences between the prior art and the claims at issue are to be ascertained; and the level of ordinary skill in the pertinent art resolved. Against this background the obviousness or nonobviousness of the subject matter is determined. Such secondary considerations as commercial success, long felt but unsolved needs, failure of others, etc., might be utilized to give light to the circumstances surrounding the origin of the subject matter sought to be patented."[100]

In many countries, the nonobviousness requirement is known as the requirement of inventiveness or an inventive step. The essence of the requirement is the concept that a patent applicant is entitled to the benefits of a patent only if the claimed invention is a significant improvement over preexisting technology. The first stage in making this assessment is to determine the what constitutes prior art. This inquiry is similar to the assessment of prior art for purposes of the novelty requirement. If a court, or patent examiner, conducts this analysis and concludes the claimed subject matter was obvious, the claim is invalid under § 103.

More recently, the Supreme Court has returned to the subject of nonobviousness in the 2007 case of *KSR International Co. v. Teleflex Inc.*[101] The Court addressed a patent on an adjustable automobile pedal mechanism with an electronic throttle control which can alter the speed of the engine. The Court took the case to assess whether the Federal Circuit's gloss on the nonobviousness inquiry properly interpreted section 103:

99. 383 U.S. 1 (1966).
100. *Id.* at 17–18.

101. 550 U.S. 398, 127 S.Ct. 1727 (2007).

Seeking to resolve the question of obviousness with more uniformity and consistency, the Court of Appeals for the Federal Circuit has employed an approach referred to by the parties as the "teaching, suggestion, or motivation" test (TSM test), under which a patent claim is only proved obvious if "some motivation or suggestion to combine the prior art teachings" can be found in the prior art, the nature of the problem, or the knowledge of a person having ordinary skill in the art.[102]

The Court rejected the Federal Circuit's TSM test:

Throughout this Court's engagement with the question of obviousness, our cases have set forth an expansive and flexible approach inconsistent with the way the Court of Appeals applied its TSM test here. To be sure, *Graham* recognized the need for "uniformity and definiteness." Yet the principles laid down in *Graham* reaffirmed the "functional approach" of *Hotchkiss*. To this end, *Graham* set forth a broad inquiry and invited courts, where appropriate, to look at any secondary considerations that would prove instructive.[103]

The Court acknowledged that the TSM test was a helpful insight that had analytical value, but should not be determinative: "a patent composed of several elements is not proved obvious merely by demonstrating that each of its elements was, independently, known in the prior art. Although common sense directs one to look with care at a patent application that claims as innovation the combination of two known devices according to their established functions, it can be important to identify a reason that would have prompted a person of ordinary skill in the relevant field to combine the elements in the way the claimed new invention does. This is so because inventions in most, if not all, instances rely upon building blocks long since uncovered, and claimed discoveries almost of necessity will be combinations of what, in some sense, is already known."[104] Thus, the Court reaffirmed that the *Graham* analytical framework, as set forth above, should be used to analyze nonobviousness questions. If the claimed invention is merely an aggregation or a combination of elements or features that were individually known to persons skilled in the art, *KSR* seems to make it more difficult to show that the invention was nonobvious than under the Federal Circuit's TSM test.

McGinley v. Franklin Sports, Inc. is a useful illustration of the nonobviousness inquiry in the context of a patent on a baseball designed for training purposes and containing color-coded markings to assist in placement of fingers to deliver various pitches. In a

---

102. *Id.*, 127 S.Ct. at 1734 (citing *Al–Site Corp. v. VSI Int'l, Inc.*, 174 F.3d 1308, 1323–1324 (Fed. Cir. 1999)).

103. *Id.* at 1739.

104. *Id.* at 1741.

divided opinion, the court upheld a finding that the invention met the nonobviousness requirement.

The nonobviousness requirement under the Plant Patent Act is somewhat vague. Section 161 of the Act states: "Whoever invents or discovers and asexually reproduces any distinct and new variety of plant, including cultivated sports, mutants, hybrids, and newly found seedlings, other than a tuber propagated plant or a plant found in an uncultivated state, may obtain a patent therefor, subject to the conditions and requirements of this title. The provisions of this title relating to patents for inventions shall apply to patents for plants, except as otherwise provided." By its terms, the statute seems to incorporate a non-obviousness requirement, although it is difficult to assess whether this inquiry involves anything more than a showing of distinctness. A PVPA certificate does not require a showing of nonobviousness.

Pre-AIA section 103(b) addresses biotechnological process patents, and states:

(1) Notwithstanding subsection (a), and upon timely election by the applicant for patent to proceed under this subsection, a biotechnological process using or resulting in a composition of matter that is novel under section 102 and nonobvious under subsection (a) of this section shall be considered nonobvious if—(A) claims to the process and the composition of matter are contained in either the same application for patent or in separate applications having the same effective filing date; and (B) the composition of matter, and the process at the time it was invented, were owned by the same person or subject to an obligation of assignment to the same person. (2) A patent issued on a process under paragraph (1)—(A) shall also contain the claims to the composition of matter used in or made by that process, or (B) shall, if such composition of matter is claimed in another patent, be set to expire on the same date as such other patent, notwithstanding section 154. The term "biotechnological process" as used in this provision means any of the following three types of subject matter: "(A) a process of genetically altering or otherwise inducing a single- or multi-celled organism to—(i) express an exogenous nucleotide sequence, (ii) inhibit, eliminate, augment, or alter expression of an endogenous nucleotide sequence, or (iii) express a specific physiological characteristic not naturally associated with said organism; (B) cell fusion procedures yielding a cell line that expresses a specific protein, such as a monoclonal antibody; and (C) a method of using a product produced by a process defined by subparagraph (A) or (B), or a combination of subparagraphs (A) and (B).[105]

105. 35 U.S.C. § 103(b).

Pre-AIA section 103(c) addresses nonobviousness involving related inventors. It states:

Subject matter developed by another person, which qualifies as prior art only under one or more of subsections (e), (f), and (g) of section 102 of this title, shall not preclude patentability under this section where the subject matter and the claimed invention were, at the time the claimed invention was made, owned by the same person or subject to an obligation of assignment to the same person.

(2) For purposes of this subsection, subject matter developed by another person and a claimed invention shall be deemed to have been owned by the same person or subject to an obligation of assignment to the same person if—

(A) the claimed invention was made by or on behalf of parties to a joint research agreement that was in effect on or before the date the claimed invention was made;

(B) the claimed invention was made as a result of activities undertaken within the scope of the joint research agreement; and

(C) the application for patent for the claimed invention discloses or is amended to disclose the names of the parties to the joint research agreement.

(3) For purposes of paragraph (2), the term "joint research agreement" means a written contract, grant, or cooperative agreement entered into by two or more persons or entities for the performance of experimental, developmental, or research work in the field of the claimed invention.

The *In re Foster*[106] decision held that the section 102(b) statutory bar applies when the information that has fallen into public use or on sale renders the claimed invention obvious more than one year prior to the inventor's application date. The Federal Circuit reaffirmed this principle in a case involving vertically perforated business forms, which the court deemed obvious given the product placed on sale more than one year prior to the application date. The court held that the patent was therefore barred under section 102(b).

Post-AIA section 102 contains language that excludes certain commonly controlled prior art activities from being a bar to an invention's novelty. Thus, post-AIA section 103 eliminates the two

---

106.   343 F.2d 980 (C.C.P.A. 1965).

pre-AIA provisions (sections 103(b)–(c)) that were designed to avoid an obviousness bar for some commonly controlled inventions.

Finally, to reiterate, for applications containing a claim whose effective filing date is on or after March 16, 2013, a claimed invention within that application will be unpatentable if the invention as a whole would have been obvious before the effective filing date of the claimed invention. The post-AIA change moves the date on which obviousness will be judged, but it does not change the basic nature of the obviousness inquiry.

¶ 13.11 Written Description Under Section 112

Section 112 of the Patent Act states: "The specification shall contain a written description of the invention, and of the manner and process of making and using it, in such full, clear, concise, and exact terms as to enable any person skilled in the art to which it pertains, or with which it is most nearly connected, to make and use the same, and shall set forth the best mode contemplated by the inventor of carrying out his invention." This provision contains two separate and distinct requirements related to the disclosures in a patent application—(1) an enabling written description of the invention (enablement) and (2) disclosure of the best mode for practicing the claimed invention. Both requirements promote the informational goals of patent law, as they require sufficient disclosure of the claimed invention to allow others to study the invention during the patent term and to imitate it after the patent has expired it. Thus, section 112 is solidly anchored in the Intellectual Property Clause's purpose of promoting the progress of the useful arts.

The AIA includes another major change regarding the relevance of the best mode requirement. For litigation commenced on or after September 16, 2011, the "failure to disclose the best mode shall not be a basis on which any claim of a patent may be canceled or held invalid or otherwise unenforceable." See AIA § 15 (amending 35 U.S.C. § 282, which included best mode defense). Inventors continue to be required to disclose the best mode in the patent prosecution process, but the best mode requirement will no longer serve as a defense in future patent litigation. Because patent cases filed before the effective date of this change will continue to be litigated for some time, this book will continue to discuss the best mode requirement, which will still be relevant as a potential defense in those cases.

The court in *Christianson v. Colt Industries Operating Corp.*[107] addressed the requirements of section 112 in the context of a dispute regarding patented components of the M–16 military rifle.

---

107. 870 F.2d 1292 (7th Cir. 1989), *cert. denied*, 493 U.S. 822 (1989).

The essence of the dispute concerned whether the patent holder failed to satisfy section 112 because it had not disclosed specifications and tolerances that would be permit the components to be interchangeable with all other M–16 rifles, which would be important in marketing the components as replacement parts. The court summarized the enablement requirement of section 112 as follows:

> A patent is enabling when the disclosures made in the patent application are sufficient to allow a person skilled in the art to make and use the claimed invention. The requirement is designed to ensure that the subject matter of the claimed invention is generally in the possession of the public and ready to be reproduced following the expiration of the patent period. To determine whether the disclosure is enabling, a two-part analysis is employed. First, we must delimit the scope of the claimed invention. Second, we must look to the disclosures made in the patent to ascertain whether, given that level of disclosure, a person skilled in the art could successfully reproduce the claimed invention in its entire scope. Because only the claimed invention receives patent law protection, the disclosures need generally be no greater than the claim. If the invention can be reproduced in its entire scope, then the patent specifications are enabling.[108]

The court held that the specifications and tolerances that were not disclosed were not integral parts of the invention. The claimed invention consisted of rifle parts, and did not mention interchangeability with M–16 rifles. Of course, as a practical matter, the challenge for anyone seeking to replicate the invention and market it for the replacement part market involves a massive reverse engineering task. But this result is typical for many inventions— the patent holder will claim and disclose the final product but will not disclose the manufacturing techniques used to achieve the final result. These techniques, which might include specifications or tolerances in the case of parts, can be maintained as trade secrets.

More recently, in *Ariad Pharmaceuticals, Inc. v. Eli Lilly & Co.*, 598 F.3d 1336, 1352 (Fed. Cir. 2010), the Federal Circuit discussed the distinction between the written description requirement and the enablement requirement: "although written description and enablement often rise and fall together, requiring a written description of the invention plays a vital role in curtailing claims that do not require undue experimentation to make and use, and thus satisfy enablement, but that have not been invented, and thus cannot be described." *See also Boston Scientific Corp. v.*

---

108.   *Id.* at 1299. *See Spectra–Physics, Inc. v. Coherent, Inc.*, 827 F.2d 1524, 1532 (Fed. Cir.), *cert. denied*, 484 U.S. 954 (1987); *DeGeorge v. Bernier*, 768 F.2d 1318, 1323–24 (Fed. Cir. 1985).

Johnson & Johnson, 647 F.3d 1353 (Fed. Cir. 2011) (invalidating claims for lack of written description); *Centocor Ortho Biotech, Inc. v. Abbott Labs.*, 636 F.3d 1341, 1348 (Fed.Cir. 2011) ("A mere wish or plan for obtaining the claimed invention is not adequate written description.").

A relatively recent enablement case is *Sitrick v. Dreamworks,* 516 F.3d 993 (Fed. Cir. 2008), which involved an entertainment system that could integrate user-provided images and audio into existing audiovisual works. The patent holder sought to argue that its claims encompassed not just video games, but also motion pictures. The Federal Circuit affirmed the lower court's determination that the specifications were enabling only for video games, thus limited the scope of the patent and precluding its coverage in the case of movies.

The best mode requirement, which continues to have relevance as a defense in cases filed before the effective date of the AIA (as mentioned above), is an entirely subjective inquiry into the actual knowledge of the inventor at the time the patent application is filed. As the *Christianson* court stated:

> Section 112 requires that "the specification ... set forth the best mode contemplated by the inventor of carrying out the invention." Thus, if the applicant develops specific instrumentalities or techniques which are recognized as the best way to carry out the invention, then the best mode requirement obliges the applicant to disclose that information. The requirement contains a subjective standard; we will find non-compliance only if the patentee has concealed, whether knowingly or unwittingly, his or her preferred embodiment of the claimed invention. Again, the focus of the best mode requirement, as it was with the enablement requirement, is on the claimed invention.[109]

Thus, if the inventor knows of another manner of setting forth the invention but genuinely does not believe that it is superior, the best mode requirement has been satisfied. Information acquired by the inventor after the filing of the patent application also need not be disclosed. Similarly, knowledge possessed by an assignee of the patent but unknown to the inventor at the time of filing is not required to be disclosed to satisfy the best mode requirement.[110]

The written description requirement can be difficult to satisfy in some areas of inventive activity. For example, consider the

---

109. *Id.* at 1301 (citing *Spectra–Physics, Inc.*, 827 F.2d at 1537; *DeGeorge*, 768 F.2d at 1324).

110. *See Texas Instruments, Inc. v. ITC*, 871 F.2d 1054, 1060 (Fed. Cir.

1989); *Glaxo Inc. v. Novopharm, Ltd.*, 52 F.3d 1043 (Fed. Cir. 1995), *cert. denied*, 516 U.S. 988 (1995).

challenge of how to provide an enabling disclosure of a biotechnology invention. Two methods of disclosing the invention have been recognized by the Federal Circuit. The patent applicant can either provide a detailed description of the structure and characteristics of the invention, or it can reference a deposit of the biological materials located in a depository that is accessible to the public. The court in *Enzo Biochem, Inc. v. Gen–Probe, Inc.*[111] noted:

> The practice of depositing biological material arose primarily to satisfy the enablement requirement of § 112, ¶ 1. For example, in *In re Argoudelis*, the patent application claimed antibiotic compounds that were produced by a microorganism. The applicants deposited the microorganism because they could not "sufficiently disclose by written word how to obtain the microorganism starting material from nature." By making the biological material accessible to the public, they enabled the public to make and use the claimed antibiotics. In *Amgen*, we noted the relevance of deposit practice to satisfaction of the enablement requirement but rejected the defendants' argument that a deposit was necessary in that case to satisfy the best mode requirement of § 112.[112]

The court held that reference in a patent specification to a deposit of genetic material may suffice to describe that material and concluded that the district court erred in finding the patent invalid as a matter of law for failure to meet the written description requirement of section 112. More recently, in *Falko–Gunter Falkner v. Inglis*,[113] the court further elaborated on the written description requirement in the biotechnology context.

In *Racing Strollers, Inc. v. TRI Industries, Inc.*,[114] the Federal Circuit held that the best mode requirement is inapplicable to an application for a design patent, because a design has only one mode and is described only by illustrations of its appearance. To satisfy section 112 in the context of an ornamental design, the patent should contains illustrations, in any form, that depict the ornamental design being claimed. Section 162 addresses the issue with regard to plant patents: "No plant patent shall be declared invalid for noncompliance with section 112 of this title if the description is as complete as is reasonably possible."[115]

¶ 13.12   Double Patenting & Terminal Disclaimers

The doctrine of double patenting reflects the common sense idea that an inventor is precluded from patenting the same inven-

111. 323 F.3d 956, 965 (Fed. Cir. 2002).

112. *Id.* at 965.

113. 448 F.3d 1357, 1366–68 (Fed. Cir. 2006).

114. 878 F.2d 1418, 1420 (Fed. Cir. 1989).

115. 35 U.S.C. § 162.

tion more than once, or for that matter an obvious modification of the original invention. The doctrine prevents the patent holder from extending the patent term by filing more than one patent on the same essential invention. The case of *In re Longi*[116] illustrates the point. In that case, the Federal Circuit discussed the rule in detail:

> A double patenting rejection precludes one person from obtaining more than one valid patent for either (a) the "same invention," or (b) an "obvious" modification of the same invention. A rejection based on double patenting of the "same invention" type finds its support in the language of 35 U.S.C. § 101 ... Thus, the term "same invention," in this context means an invention drawn to identical subject matter. On the other hand, a rejection based upon double patenting of the obviousness type ((b), *supra*) is a judicially created doctrine grounded in public policy (a policy reflected in the patent statute) rather than based purely on the precise terms of the statute. The purpose of this rejection is to prevent the extension of the term of a patent, even where an express statutory basis for the rejection is missing, by prohibiting the issuance of the claims in a second patent not patentably distinct from the claims of the first patent.[117]

If the material is disclosed, but not claimed, in a prior patent, no double patenting has taken place, because the particular invention has been the subject of only one patent claim. In order to avoid invalidation of a patent on grounds of double patenting, the inventor can make use of terminal disclaimers. Terminal disclaimers are filed in accordance with PTO Rule 321, which states:

> (a) A patentee owning the whole or any sectional interest in a patent may disclaim any complete claim or claims in a patent. In like manner any patentee may disclaim or dedicate to the public the entire term, or any terminal part of the term, of the patent granted. Such disclaimer is binding upon the grantee and its successors or assigns. A notice of the disclaimer is published in the Official Gazette and attached to the printed copies of the specification....

> (b) An applicant or assignee may disclaim or dedicate to the public the entire term, or any terminal part of the term, of a patent to be granted. Such terminal disclaimer is binding upon the grantee and its successors or assigns....

> (c) A terminal disclaimer, when filed to obviate judicially created double patenting in a patent application or in a reexamina-

116. 759 F.2d 887 (Fed. Cir. 1985). **117.** *Id.* at 892.

tion proceeding except as provided for in paragraph (d) of this section, must:

(1) Comply with the provisions of paragraphs (b)(2) through (b)(4) of this section;

(2) Be signed in accordance with paragraph (b)(1) of this section if filed in a patent application or in accordance with paragraph (a)(1) of this section if filed in a reexamination proceeding; and

(3) Include a provision that any patent granted on that application or any patent subject to the reexamination proceeding shall be enforceable only for and during such period that said patent is commonly owned with the application or patent which formed the basis for the judicially created double patenting.

(d) A terminal disclaimer, when filed in a patent application or in a reexamination proceeding to obviate double patenting based upon a patent or application that is not commonly owned but was disqualified under 35 U.S.C. 103(c) as resulting from activities undertaken within the scope of a joint research agreement, must:

(1) Comply with the provisions of paragraphs (b)(2) through (b)(4) of this section;

(2) Be signed in accordance with paragraph (b)(1) of this section if filed in a patent application or be signed in accordance with paragraph (a)(1) of this section if filed in a reexamination proceeding; and

(3) Include a provision waiving the right to separately enforce any patent granted on that application or any patent subject to the reexamination proceeding and the patent or any patent granted on the application which formed the basis for the double patenting, and that any patent granted on that application or any patent subject to the reexamination proceeding shall be enforceable only for and during such period that said patent and the patent, or any patent granted on the application, which formed the basis for the double patenting are not separately enforced.[118]

There is no specific time limit for filing of terminal disclaimers, but courts have refused to take them into consideration when filed after the Board has upheld the patent examiner's rejection of a claim.[119]

---

118. 37 C.F.R. § 1.321.

119. *See, e.g., In re Heyl*, 379 F.2d 1018, 1020 (C.C.P.A. 1967).

Not only might a claim of double patenting arise when the same invention is claimed in two or more utility patents, but the issue can also arise when similar features are claimed in both a design patent and a utility patent. In *Carman Industries, Inc. v. Wahl*,[120] the court addressed design and utility patents both directed to bin flow promoters. The design patent claimed the visible external surface configuration of the bin flow promoter, while the utility patent claimed the internal construction of the flow promoter. The court found that these two patents covered entirely different features of the same product, and that is was possible to practice each invention without using the other. The court then addressed the somewhat more subtle issue of whether the interior construction of the device would have been obvious to one skilled in the art when viewing the exterior appearance of it, as claimed in the design patent. The court held that even if the internal configuration would indeed be obvious, it still did not give rise to a case of double patenting, given that the two patents claimed different features of the product. This conclusion is sensible, given that a patent holder is not improperly double dipping merely because it seeks a design patent on ornamental features and a utility patent on functional features of the same integrated product.

Finally, if an inventor seeks to patent the very same plant as both a utility patent and a plant patent, this action would seem to constitute double patenting. Whether the same is true of material patented and claimed in a PVPA certificate is somewhat less clear, however, as PVPA protection is not considered the equivalent of patent protection.

120.   724 F.2d 932 (Fed. Cir. 1983).

Chapter 14

PATENT OWNERSHIP

Table of Sections

¶ 14.01   Inventorship

The touchstone of inventorship is conception—thus an inventor is a person who conceives of a definite, concrete, practical solution to a problem, even if the inventor has not yet reduced this solution to practice (i.e., built a prototype). United States patent law traditionally required the inventor(s) to be named in the patent application. This did not mean, however, that rights to the invention could not then be transferred to others.

Traditionally United States patent law has given the first inventor the exclusive rights to the invention. In contrast, many foreign countries grant patent rights to the first to file a patent application in the relevant patent office. In 2011, however, Congress passed the Leahy–Smith America Invents Act ("AIA").[1] The AIA changes the governing rule for patent priority, taking effect in March 2013. After that date, the United States will shift from a "first to invent" rule to a "first inventor to file or to publicly disclose" rule.

The new version of section 102 of the Patent Act, when fully in effect, will state:

(a) NOVELTY; PRIOR ART.—A person shall be entitled to a patent unless—

(1) the claimed invention was patented, described in a printed publication, or in public use, on sale, or otherwise available to the public before the effective filing date of the claimed invention; or

---

1. Pub. L. No. 112–29, 125 Stat. 284 (2011).

(2) the claimed invention was described in a patent issued under section 151, or in an application for patent published or deemed published under section 122(b), in which the patent or application, as the case may be, names another inventor and was effectively filed before the effective filing date of the claimed invention.

(b) EXCEPTIONS.—

(1) DISCLOSURES MADE 1 YEAR OR LESS BEFORE THE EFFECTIVE FILING DATE OF THE CLAIMED INVENTION.—A disclosure made 1 year or less before the effective filing date of a claimed invention shall not be prior art to the claimed invention under subsection (a)(1) if—

(A) the disclosure was made by the inventor or joint inventor or by another who obtained the subject matter disclosed directly or indirectly from the inventor or a joint inventor; or

(B) the subject matter disclosed had, before such disclosure, been publicly disclosed by the inventor or a joint inventor or another who obtained the subject matter disclosed directly or indirectly from the inventor or a joint inventor.

(2) DISCLOSURES APPEARING IN APPLICATIONS AND PATENTS.—A disclosure shall not be prior art to a claimed invention under subsection (a)(2) if—

(A) the subject matter disclosed was obtained directly or indirectly from the inventor or a joint inventor;

(B) the subject matter disclosed had, before such subject matter was effectively filed under subsection (a)(2), been publicly disclosed by the inventor or a joint inventor or another who obtained the subject matter disclosed directly or indirectly from the inventor or a joint inventor; or

(C) the subject matter disclosed and the claimed invention, not later than the effective filing date of the claimed invention, were owned by the same person or subject to an obligation of assignment to the same person.

(c) COMMON OWNERSHIP UNDER JOINT RESEARCH AGREEMENTS.—Subject matter disclosed and a claimed invention shall be deemed to have been owned by the same person or subject to an obligation of assignment to the same person in applying the provisions of subsection (b)(2)(C) if—

(1) the subject matter disclosed was developed and the claimed invention was made by, or on behalf of, 1 or more parties to a joint research agreement that was in effect on or before the effective filing date of the claimed invention;

(2) the claimed invention was made as a result of activities undertaken within the scope of the joint research agreement; and

(3) the application for patent for the claimed invention discloses or is amended to disclose the names of the parties to the joint research agreement.

(d) PATENTS AND PUBLISHED APPLICATIONS EFFECTIVE AS PRIOR ART.—For purposes of determining whether a patent or application for patent is prior art to a claimed invention under subsection (a)(2), such patent or application shall be considered to have been effectively filed, with respect to any subject matter described in the patent or application—

(1) if paragraph (2) does not apply, as of the actual filing date of the patent or the application for patent; or

(2) if the patent or application for patent is entitled to claim a right of priority under section 119, 365(a), or 365(b), or to claim the benefit of an earlier filing date under section 120, 121, or 365(c), based upon 1 or more prior filed applications for patent, as of the filing date of the earliest such application that describes the subject matter.

The "the effective filing date" for a claimed invention is defined in section 100, as amended by the AIA, as follows:

(A) if subparagraph (B) does not apply, the actual filing date of the patent or the application for the patent containing a claim to the invention; or

(B) the filing date of the earliest application for which the patent or application is entitled, as to such invention, to a right of priority under section 119, 365(a), or 365(b) or to the benefit of an earlier filing date under section 120, 121, or 365(c).

In other words, the "effective filing date" is either the actual filing date or the date when an earlier application of one of the following types was filed:

— foreign applications under § 119,

— Patent Cooperation Treaty ("PCT") applications under § 365,

— domestic provisional applications under § 119(e), or

— an earlier domestic application that has been continued under § 120 or divided under § 121.

Frequently, an assignment is an express or implied aspect of the contractual relationship between the inventor and the inventor's employer. Thus, the patent will be applied for in the name of the research & development employee who invented it, but then will be assigned to the company that employed that research scientist. Pre-AIA sections 115 and 118 permit parties to whom a patent has been assigned to file a patent application on the inventor's behalf if the inventor is unable or unwilling to do so, and section 116 permits one or more joint inventors to file an application on behalf of all joint inventors. Section 116 states in relevant part:

> If a joint inventor refuses to join in an application for patent or cannot be found or reached after diligent effort, the application may be made by the other inventor on behalf of himself and the omitted inventor. The Director, on proof of the pertinent facts and after such notice to the omitted inventor as he prescribes, may grant a patent to the inventor making the application, subject to the same rights which the omitted inventor would have had if he had been joined. The omitted inventor may subsequently join in the application.

Patent reform efforts have also focused on the ability of an assignee of an invention to file the patent application directly, thereby simplifying the process and recognizing the underlying reality of many research laboratory contexts. AIA § 4, codified in section 118 of the Patent Act, allows a patent application to be filed by a "person to whom the inventor has assigned or is under an obligation to assign the invention." Section 115, as revised by the AIA, requires that patent applications name all inventors and provide a declaration of inventorship from each inventor, but if an inventor who is obligated to assign the invention refuses to provide the required declaration, the patent applicant may submit a substitute statement on behalf of that inventor.

¶ 14.02   Joint Inventors

The development of a particular invention is often a collaborative process involving two or more people. Section 116 of the Patent Act states in relevant part:

> When an invention is made by two or more persons jointly, they shall apply for patent jointly and each make the required oath, except as otherwise provided in this title. Inventors may apply for a patent jointly even though (1) they did not physically work together or at the same time, (2) each did not make the same type or amount of contribution, or (3) each did not make a contribution to the subject matter of every claim of the patent.

A frequently litigated issue is the extent to which a person must participate in the inventive process to warrant the status of an inventor. In *Burroughs Wellcome Co. v. Barr Laboratories, Inc.*,[2] the Federal Circuit addressed this issue in the context of patents on AZT drugs used to treat HIV. As section 116 indicates, inventors need not work together in the same place or at the same time in order to achieve the status of joint inventors. Nor need they make the same type or amount of contribution to the inventive process. On the other hand, individuals who act as mere helpers or as a "pair of hands"—persons carrying out ministerial tasks—are not joint inventors.

As discussed above, the touchstone of invention is conception—developing an idea that is definite and permanent enough to enable a person having ordinary skill in the art (phosita) to carry out the invention. The inventors are those who have developed a specific, concrete, and practical solution to a problem, not merely a general concept or goal. They must be able to describe the invention with sufficient particularity to permit it to be carried out (i.e., reduced to practice). Thus, an invention is not complete if there is uncertainty that renders the concept indefinite or speculative. In *Burroughs Wellcome*, the central issue was whether National Institutes of Health (NIH) scientists played a role in developing the invention or whether their contributions (in the form of NIH test results) came after-the-fact—after the Burroughs–Wellcome scientists had developed a specific, concrete invention. With regard to the drug patents at issue in the case, the court found that the Burroughs–Wellcome inventors had fully conceptualized the invention and in fact had prepared a draft patent application, and thus that the NIH scientists who conducted testing (results of which were not presented until after conception of the invention) were not joint inventors. With regard to the process patents at issue in the case, on the other hand, the court remanded because the specific conception of the process might not have been fully finalized until after the NIH test results were completed.[3]

In determining if joint inventors are involved, courts seek objective corroboration of the inventor's contribution. This can take a variety of forms—a reduction to practice or prototype might be prepared, or the corroboration may involve analysis of laboratory notebooks or notes, audio or video recordings, or third-party eyewitness testimony. In this manner, the court can verify the steps taken in conceiving a definite and permanent invention.

Joint inventorship requires at least some degree of collaboration or connection between the inventors. For example, in *Kimberly–Clark Corp. v. Procter & Gamble Distributing Co.*,[4] the parties were engaged in a dispute over priority of invention involving leak-

---

2. 40 F.3d 1223 (Fed. Cir. 1994).   **4.** 973 F.2d 911 (Fed. Cir. 1992).

3. *Id.* at 1227–32.

proof diapers. P & G sought to establish that the inventor of its patent, Lawson, was a joint inventor with other individuals at P & G, including one Buell. The purpose of making this assertion was that it would give the P & G patent priority over the conflicting Kimberly–Clark patent. Unfortunately for P & G, however, its inventor Lawson was completely unaware of the earlier activities of Buell and other P & G inventors. In light of the lack of any collaboration with the other P & G inventors, the court held that Lawson was therefore the sole inventor of the P & G patent. The practical effect of this decision was that P & G was precluded from amending its patent under section 256 to add Buell as a joint inventor. Being unable to do so meant that the Lawson patent was invalid, because the Kimberly–Clark patent predated Lawson's inventive activity.

If two or more inventors are found to be joint inventors, they have equal and undivided interests in the patent. There is no allocation of patent rights based on the relative type or quantity of contributions made by each joint inventor. This can lead to seemingly anomalous outcomes, as illustrated by *Ethicon, Inc. v. United States Surgical Corp.,*[5] where an inventor who contributed to two out of 55 patent claims was nonetheless deemed a joint inventor for all purposes, with an equal and undivided interest in the patent. Yet this outcome reflects the sensible policy that it would be cumbersome and inefficient to try to determine the relative ownership shares of joint inventors.

Plant patent protection involves somewhat different inventive process. The development of a patentable plant variety involves a three-step process. First, it is necessary to either cultivate or discover the new variety; then characteristics that make the variety new and distinct must be recognized; and finally there must be asexual reproduction of the variety to preserve the unique traits. It is not sufficient to simply discover or learn of the existence of a plant variety. Instead, the key is to identify the plant's distinct characteristics and to replicate them by asexual reproduction.[6]

¶ 14.03 Shop Rights

There are three types of employment relationships that have implications for ownership of an invention. A research and development employee is hired specifically to perform research functions within the scope of his or her duties, and it is well understood that the fruits of these inventive labors should inure to the benefit of the employer. Thus, the inventions developed by research and development employees within the scope of their duties are general-

5. 135 F.3d 1456 (Fed. Cir. 1998), cert. denied, 525 U.S. 923 (1998).

6. *See Ex parte Moore*, 115 U.S.P.Q. 145 (PTO Bd. App. 1957).

ly assigned to their employers and are then wholly owned by the employer. At the other end of the spectrum, an employee whose duties do not involve research and development and who develops an invention on the employee's own time and using the employee's own materials is entitled to full ownership of any resulting inventions. The third situation—known as shop rights—involves an employee whose duties do not involve research and development, but who develops an invention on company time, using the employer's materials, or both.

The Supreme Court defined the employer's "shop rights" with regard to ideas and inventions of employees who are not specifically hired to perform research and development, in *United States v. Dubilier Condenser Corp.,*[7] stating as follows:

> Recognition of the nature of the act of invention also defines the limits of the so-called shop right, which, shortly stated, is that, where a servant, during his hours of employment, working with his master's materials and appliances, conceives and perfects an invention for which he obtains a patent, he must accord his master a nonexclusive right to practice the invention. This is an application of equitable principles. Since the servant uses his master's time, facilities, and materials to attain a concrete result, the latter is in equity entitled to use that which embodies his own property and to duplicate it as often as he may find occasion to employ similar appliances in his business. But the employer in such a case has no equity to demand a conveyance of the invention, which is the original conception of the employee alone, in which the employer had no part. This remains the property of him who conceived it, together with the right conferred by the patent, to exclude all others than the employer from the accruing benefits.

In effect, this doctrine confers upon employers a free and nonexclusive license to use the employee's innovation. As Judge Wisdom put it in *Hobbs v. United States,*[8] "[t]he classic shop rights doctrine ordains that when an employee makes and reduces to practice an invention on his employer's time, using his employer's tools and the services of other employees, the employer is the recipient of an implied, nonexclusive, royalty-free license."

The shop rights doctrine is based upon several policies—"First, it seems only fair that when an employee has used his employer's time and equipment to make an invention, the employer should be able to use the device without paying a royalty. Second, under the doctrine of estoppel if an employee encourages his employer to use an invention, and then stands by and allows him to construct and

---

7.　289 U.S. 178, 188–89 (1933) (citations omitted).

8.　376 F.2d 488, 495 (5th Cir. 1967) (Wisdom, J.).

operate the new device without making any claim for compensation or royalties, it would not be equitable to allow the employee later to assert a claim for royalties or other compensation."[9] A third policy rationale for the shop rights doctrine is the concept of implied consent. In effect, the employee has implicitly consented to allow the employer limited use of the invention based on the employee's acceptance of assistance or resources from the employer while developing the invention.[10]

A helpful formulation of the shop right doctrine can be found in *E.J. McKernan Co. v. Gregory*: "The history of litigation involving employer-employee rights in inventions indicates that, absent a specific agreement, an employer's rights arise from the inventor's employment status. Those inventions made by an employee 'employed to invent' are typically the property of the employer, while those made by other employees in 'general employment' of a noninventive nature, using the employer's property, are typically property of the employee but subject to a nontransferable shop right in favor of the employer."[11]

As the court noted in *Grip Nut Co. v. Sharp*,[12] "the shop right is automatically and equitably the result of using plaintiff's time, labor and materials in developing the inventions." In *Brown v. L.V. Marks & Sons Co.*,[13] the court stated that "estoppel is no longer an essential element in establishing shop rights. Frequently it is present and must strengthen the case but there may be shop rights to a discovery in industry without past development. There is a vested property right which equity fixes in the invention at its inception. Where the employee makes his discovery while working with the employer's tools, machinery and materials and on the employer's time the interest or shop right in favor of the employer attaches immediately."

Some states have enacted statutes specifically addressing the relative rights of employers and employees. An Illinois law, for example, states as follows:

> (1) A provision in an employment agreement which provides that an employee shall assign or offer to assign any of the employee's rights in an invention to the employer does not apply to an invention for which no equipment, supplies, facilities, or trade secret information of the employer was used and which was developed entirely on the employee's own time, unless (a) the invention relates (i) to the business of the

---

9. *Id.* at 495.

10. *See Solomons v. United States*, 137 U.S. 342 (1890).

11. 252 Ill.App.3d 514, 191 Ill.Dec. 391, 623 N.E.2d 981, 1003–04 (1993).

12. 150 F.2d 192, 196–97 (7th Cir. 1945).

13. 64 F.Supp. 352 (E.D. Ky. 1946).

employer, or (ii) to the employer's actual or demonstrably anticipated research or development, or (b) the invention results from any work performed by the employee for the employer. Any provision which purports to apply to such an invention is to that extent against the public policy of this State and is to that extent void and unenforceable. The employee shall bear the burden of proof in establishing that his invention qualifies under this subsection.

(2) An employer shall not require a provision made void and unenforceable by subsection (1) of this Section as a condition of employment or continuing employment. This Act shall not preempt existing common law applicable to any shop rights of employers with respect to employees who have not signed an employment agreement.

(3) If an employment agreement entered into after January 1, 1984, contains a provision requiring the employee to assign any of the employee's rights in any invention to the employer, the employer must also, at the time the agreement is made, provide a written notification to the employee that the agreement does not apply to an invention for which no equipment, supplies, facility, or trade secret information of the employer was used and which was developed entirely on the employee's own time, unless (a) the invention relates (i) to the business of the employer, or (ii) to the employer's actual or demonstrably anticipated research or development, or (b) the invention results from any work performed by the employee for the employer.[14]

The federal government asserts broader rights in the inventions of its employees by virtue of an Executive Order. In effect, this Executive Order places ownership of all employee inventions in the hands of the federal government if the employee is hired for research & development, or uses employer time or resources to develop the invention.[15]

There are also specific federal provisions governing the allocation of rights for patents developed in the course of federally funded research. The law, known as the Bayh–Dole University & Small Business Patent Procedure Act of 1980,[16] gives the federal government a non-exclusive license to use the invention, largely akin to a shop right. It also allows the institution receiving federal funds to retain ownership of the patents, as long as they share revenue with inventors and use their proceeds for further research. The Supreme Court recently addressed patent ownership in *Board of Trustees of*

---

14. Ill. Comp. Stat. Ann. Chapter 765, Section 1060/2 (formerly cited as IL ST CH 140 ¶ 302).

15. *See* 37 C.F.R.§ 501.6 (codifying Executive Order 10096).

16. 35 U.S.C. §§ 200 *et seq.*

the Leland Stanford Junior Univ. v. Roche Molecular Sys., Inc., 131 S.Ct. 2188 (2011). The Court rejected a university's argument that the Bayh–Dole Act gave it ownership of federally funded inventions. The Court affirmed the traditional rule that initial ownership of an invention lies with the inventors.

The broad scope of the shop rights doctrine was highlighted in *Grip Nut Co. v. Sharp:*

> We are fortified in this belief since the principle has been established that if an employee in the course of his employment makes an invention using his employer's time and materials, the employer has a free indefeasible license and shop right under the invention and any patent covering the invention, which shop right is co-extensive with the business requirements of the employer; that is to say, because the servant uses his master's time, facilities and materials to attain a concrete result, the employer is entitled to use that which embodies his own property and to duplicate it as often as he may find occasion to employ similar appliances in his business.[17]

With regard to transfers of an employer's shop rights, however, most cases indicate that shop rights may not be transferred or assigned. In *Dowse v. Federal Rubber Co.,*[18] the court noted, in the context of a case in which a company had received an assignment of all shop rights held by the assignor corporation, that the shop right "was only personal to it, incapable of being assigned." More recently, the court in *Kennedy v. Wright,*[19] reiterated the rule that "where the employee utilizes company time and facilities in perfecting the patent, the employer has at most a shop right—a royalty-free, non-exclusive and *non-assignable* license to use the invention."

Aside from the implied or default allocation of rights under the shop right doctrine, cases generally recognize that the contract between the parties governs the ownership and scope of rights to innovations: "The respective rights and obligations of employer and employee touching an invention conceived by an employee arising out of his employment spring from the contract of employment."[20] This subject is more fully discussed below.

¶ 14.04 Assignment

Patents can be assigned, conveyed by operation of law (for example, in bankruptcy), or passed on by will or the laws of intestate succession. Frequently, individual inventors assign their

17. 150 F.2d 192, 196–97 (7th Cir. 1945) (citations omitted).

18. 254 Fed. 308, 309 (N.D. Ill.1918).

19. 676 F.Supp. 888 (C.D. Ill. 1988) (emphasis added).

20. *Landrum v. J. F. Pritchard & Co.*, 139 Ga.App. 393, 228 S.E.2d 290, 394 (1976).

inventions to their employers or to others who can more efficiently manufacture and market the product. Section 261 states:

> Subject to the provisions of this title, patents shall have the attributes of personal property. Applications for patent, patents, or any interest therein, shall be assignable in law by an instrument in writing. The applicant, patentee, or his assigns or legal representatives may in like manner grant and convey an exclusive right under his application for patent, or patents, to the whole or any specified part of the United States.

> A certificate of acknowledgment under the hand and official seal of a person authorized to administer oaths within the United States, or, in a foreign country, of a diplomatic or consular officer of the United States or an officer authorized to administer oaths whose authority is proved by a certificate of a diplomatic or consular officer of the United States, or apostille of an official designated by a foreign country which, by treaty or convention, accords like effect to apostilles of designated officials in the United States, shall be prima facie evidence of the execution of an assignment, grant, or conveyance of a patent or application for patent.

> An assignment, grant, or conveyance shall be void as against any subsequent purchaser or mortgagee for a valuable consideration, without notice, unless it is recorded in the Patent and Trademark Office within three months from its date or prior to the date of such subsequent purchase or mortgage.

¶ 14.05　Duration

The current term for utility and plant patents is twenty years from the patent application date. Section 154(a)(2) of the Patent Act states: "Subject to the payment of fees under this title, such grant shall be for a term beginning on the date on which the patent issues and ending 20 years from the date on which the application for the patent was filed in the United States or, if the application contains a specific reference to an earlier filed application or applications under section 120, 121, or 365(c) of this title, from the date on which the earliest such application was filed." This term is the result of the Uruguay Round Agreements Act of 1994 ("URAA"), which established the present term for patents sought after June 8, 1995. Prior to the URAA, the standard patent term was seventeen years from the date of patent *issuance*. A patent cannot be enforced, however, until it has been issued by the PTO. Thus, the delay that occurs while a patent application is being examined reduces the actual term of the patent, often by a period of several years. Moreover, the patent holder is not entitled to bring suit until the patent is issued, and then only for infringing activity taking place during the patent term. As a result, the actual patent term may or may not be longer than under prior law, depending on the extent of the delay in gaining patent issuance.

Unlike utility and plant patents, design patents were not extended under the URAA, and are thus still governed by the prior law regarding the patent term. The utility patent term is therefore keyed to the issuance date of the patent, rather than to the application date. Moreover, the term for design patents is only fourteen years. Section 173 of the Patent Act states: "Patents for designs shall be granted for the term of fourteen years from the date of grant."

Section 154(b) does allow for term adjustments and extensions in specified cases involving Patent Office delays:

(b) ADJUSTMENT OF PATENT TERM.—

(1) PATENT TERM GUARANTEES.—

(A) GUARANTEE OF PROMPT PATENT AND TRADEMARK OFFICE RESPONSES.—Subject to the limitations under paragraph (2), if the issue of an original patent is delayed due to the failure of the Patent and Trademark Office to—

(i) provide at least one of the notifications under section 132 of this title or a notice of allowance under section 151 of this title not later than 14 months after—(I) the date on which an application was filed under section 111(a) of this title; or (II) the date on which an international application fulfilled the requirements of section 371of this title; (ii) respond to a reply under section 132, or to an appeal taken under section 134, within 4 months after the date on which the reply was filed or the appeal was taken; (iii) act on an application within 4 months after the date of a decision by the Board of Patent Appeals and Interferences under section 134 or 135 or a decision by a Federal court under section 141, 145, or 146 in a case in which allowable claims remain in the application; or (iv) issue a patent within 4 months after the date on which the issue fee was paid under section 151 and all outstanding requirements were satisfied, the term of the patent shall be extended 1 day for each day after the end of the period specified in clause (i), (ii), (iii), or (iv), as the case may be, until the action described in such clause is taken.

(B) GUARANTEE OF NO MORE THAN 3–YEAR AP-PLICATION PENDENCY.—Subject to the limitations under paragraph (2), if the issue of an original patent is delayed due to the failure of the United States Patent and Trademark Office to issue a patent within 3 years after the actual filing date of the application in the United States, not including—

(i) any time consumed by continued examination of the application requested by the applicant under section 132(b); (ii) any time consumed by a proceeding under section 135(a), any time consumed by the imposition of an order under section 181, or any time consumed by appellate review by the Board of Patent Appeals and Interferences or by a Federal court; or (iii) any delay in the processing of the application by the United States Patent and Trademark Office requested by the applicant except as permitted by paragraph (3)(C), the term of the patent shall be extended 1 day for each day after the end of that 3–year period until the patent is issued.

(C) GUARANTEE OR ADJUSTMENTS FOR DE-LAYS DUE TO INTERFERENCES, SECRECY OR-DERS, AND APPEALS.—Subject to the limitations under paragraph (2), if the issue of an original patent is delayed due to—

(i) a proceeding under section 135(a); (ii) the imposition of an order under section 181; or (iii) appellate review by the Board of Patent Appeals and Interferences or by a Federal court in a case in which the patent was issued under a decision in the review reversing an adverse determination of patentability, the term of the patent shall be extended 1 day for each day of the pendency of the proceeding, order, or review, as the case may be.

The extensions under section 154(b) are limited in cases where the patent applicant has not exercised reasonable diligence in the patent application process.

Moreover, the Drug Price Competition & Patent Term Restoration Act of 1984,[21] also known as the Hatch–Waxman Act, allows the patent term for drugs, medical devices, foods, or additives to be extended if the product's entry into the market was delayed by regulatory review under applicable food and drug laws.

---

21. 35 U.S.C. § 156.

Aside from the specific term extensions described above, patents cannot be extended or renewed. Once the patent expires, the innovation is in the public domain, where it can be freely used by others without payment or permission. Many patent holders seek to have some continuing patent protection by patenting improvements on their existing products, but the basic underlying invention would still be in the public domain. This result is consistent with the operative language and fundamental purpose of the Intellectual Property Clause, which permits patent protection for "limited Times."

Chapter 15

PATENT INFRINGEMENT

Table of Sections

"To coin a phrase, the name of the game is the claim."

—Judge Giles S. Rich, Extent of Protection and Interpretation of Claims—American Perspectives, 21 INT'L REV. INDUS. PROP. & COPYRIGHT L. 497, 499 (1990).

¶ 15.01   Literal Infringement & the Doctrine of Equivalents

Patent infringement occurs when a party makes, uses, sells, offers to sell, or imports the product into the United States. Section 271(a) of the Patent Act states: "Except as otherwise provided in this title, whoever without authority makes, uses, offers to sell, or sells any patented invention, within the United States, or imports into the United States any patented invention during the term of the patent therefor, infringes the patent." This provision governs utility and design patents. Plant patents, in contrast, are infringed when the plant is asexually reproduced, or if the resulting plant is used, sold, offered to be sold, or imported. Section 163 states: "In the case of a plant patent, the grant shall include the right to exclude others from asexually reproducing the plant, and from using, offering for sale, or selling the plant so reproduced, or any of its parts, throughout the United States, or from importing the plant so reproduced, or any parts thereof, into the United States."

The PTO does not enforce patents. Instead, the patent holder must enforce the patent through litigation in federal court, which has exclusive jurisdiction over patent suits. The patent holder may also seek relief from the International Trade Commission, which can preclude the importation of infringing goods.[1] Appeals from patent cases are heard solely by the U.S. Court of Appeals for the Federal Circuit, with final review potentially available in the Supreme Court.

---

1. 19 U.S.C. § 1337.

The patent holder must show that the defendant's product (known as the accused device) is identical to the claimed invention, or substantially equivalent to the claimed invention. Judge Giles S. Rich's observation is apt: "To coin a phrase, the name of the game is the claim."[2] Judge Robert Mayer put is this way: "Anyone who wants to know what a patent protects must first read its claims, for they are the measure of its scope."[3] If the accused device is identical, the defendant has committed literal infringement. If it is substantially similar, it may infringe under the doctrine of equivalents.

The Supreme Court has recognized the importance of claim construction in the development of a uniform national patent system. In *Markman v. Westview Instruments, Inc.*,[4] Justice Souter noted: "The two elements of a simple patent case, construing the patent and determining whether infringement occurred, were characterized by the former patent practitioner, Justice Curtis. 'The first is a question of law, to be determined by the court, construing the letters-patent, and the description of the invention and specification of claim annexed to them. The second is a question of fact, to be submitted to a jury.' "144[5] The Court had taken certiorari to determine "whether the interpretation of a so-called patent claim, the portion of the patent document that defines the scope of the patentee's rights, is a matter of law reserved entirely for the court, or subject to a Seventh Amendment guarantee that a jury will determine the meaning of any disputed term of art about which expert testimony is offered. We hold that the construction of a patent, including terms of art within its claim, is exclusively within the province of the court."[6] Since the Court's ruling in this case, hearings before district judges at which matters of claim construction are resolved are known as *Markman* hearings.

Once the claim construction has been carried out, the issue becomes whether the accused device "reads on" or is literally identical to the one or more of the patent claims. Because of the concern that an alleged infringer might avoid liability by making insignificant changes to its product, the doctrine of equivalents is designed to address this situation. The Supreme Court delineated the doctrine of equivalents in *Graver Tank & Mfg. Co. v. Linde Air*

---

2. Judge Giles S. Rich, Extent of Protection and Interpretation of Claims—American Perspectives, 21 INT'L REV. INDUS. PROP. & COPYRIGHT L. 497, 499 (1990).

3. *Markman v. Westview Instruments, Inc.* (*Markman II*), 52 F.3d 967, 990 (Fed. Cir. 1995) (Mayer, J., concurring) (citing *Aro Mfg. Co. v. Convertible*

Top Replacement Co., 365 U.S. 336, 339).

4. 517 U.S. 370 (1996).

5. *Id.* at 384 (quoting *Winans v. Denmead*, 56 U.S. 330, 15 How. 330, 338, 14 L.Ed. 717 (1854)).

6. *Id.* at 372.

Products Co.,[7] holding that a product or process that does not literally infringe upon a patent claim can nonetheless be found to infringe if there is equivalence between the accused product or process and the patent claims. *Graver Tank* involved the application of the doctrine of equivalents to an accused chemical composition used in welding. The accused product differed from the patented welding material because of the substitution of one chemical element. Thus, there was no literal infringement, but the Court focused on "whether the substitution ... is a change of such substance as to make the doctrine of equivalents inapplicable; or conversely, whether under the circumstances the change was so insubstantial that the trial court's invocation of the doctrine of equivalents was justified."[8]

A number of considerations are taken into account by the doctrine of equivalents:

What constitutes equivalency must be determined against the context of the patent, the prior art, and the particular circumstances of the case. Equivalence, in the patent law, is not the prisoner of a formula and is not an absolute to be considered in a vacuum. It does not require complete identity for every purpose and in every respect. In determining equivalents, things equal to the same thing may not be equal to each other and, by the same token, things for most purposes different may sometimes be equivalents. Consideration must be given to the purpose for which an ingredient is used in a patent, the qualities it has when combined with the other ingredients, and the function which it is intended to perform. An important factor is whether persons reasonably skilled in the art would have known of the interchangeability of an ingredient not contained in the patent with one that was.[9]

The Supreme Court reaffirmed the vitality of the doctrine of equivalents in *Warner–Jenkinson Co., Inc. v. Hilton Davis Chemical Co.*[10] The Court in that case declined to determine the precise definition of the doctrine—one formulation focused on whether the accused device performs substantially the same function in substantially the same way to achieve substantially the same result, while another test focused on whether there were insubstantial differences between the accused device and the claimed invention. Justice Thomas' opinion declined to resolve the issue:

Both the parties and the Federal Circuit spend considerable time arguing whether the so-called "triple identity" test-focusing on the function served by a particular claim element, the

7.   339 U.S. 605, 609 (1950).   9.   *Id.* at 609.

8.   *Id.* at 610.   10.   520 U.S. 17, 39–40 (1997).

way that element serves that function, and the result thus obtained by that element-is a suitable method for determining equivalence, or whether an "insubstantial differences" approach is better. There seems to be substantial agreement that, while the triple identity test may be suitable for analyzing mechanical devices, it often provides a poor framework for analyzing other products or processes. On the other hand, the insubstantial differences test offers little additional guidance as to what might render any given difference "insubstantial."

In our view, the particular linguistic framework used is less important than whether the test is probative of the essential inquiry: Does the accused product or process contain elements identical or equivalent to each claimed element of the patented invention? Different linguistic frameworks may be more suitable to different cases, depending on their particular facts. A focus on individual elements and a special vigilance against allowing the concept of equivalence to eliminate completely any such elements should reduce considerably the imprecision of whatever language is used. An analysis of the role played by each element in the context of the specific patent claim will thus inform the inquiry as to whether a substitute element matches the function, way, and result of the claimed element, or whether the substitute element plays a role substantially different from the claimed element.[11]

Justice Thomas concluded that the doctrine "should be applied as an objective inquiry on an element-by-element basis."[12]

The doctrine of equivalents is cabined by the principle of prosecution history estoppel (sometimes known as file wrapper estoppel). The court in *Autogiro Co. of America v. United States* addressed the role of the prosecution history or file wrapper:

The file wrapper contains the entire record of the proceedings in the Patent Office from the first application papers to the issued patent. Since all express representations of the patent applicant made to induce a patent grant are in the file wrapper, this material provides an accurate charting of the patent's preissuance history. One use of the file wrapper is file wrapper estoppel, which is the application of familiar estoppel principles to Patent Office prosecution and patent infringement litigation.[13]

Prosecution history estoppel comes into play when the patent applicant has made amendments to its application to avoid prior art or to address other objections (such as obviousness) that might

11. *Id.*
12. *Id.*

13. 384 F.2d 391, 398–99 (Ct. Cl. 1967).

render the claimed subject matter unpatentable. In this situation, the patent holder cannot then use the doctrine of equivalents to reassert claims given up in the patent application process.[14] For example, in *Keystone Driller Co. v. Northwest Engineering Corp.*,[15] the allegedly infringing equivalent element was part of the prior art that formed the basis for the rejection of some patent claims. The revised claims did not include the element, and the Court applied the prosecution history estoppel doctrine to prevent use of the doctrine of equivalents to encompass the element. More recently, in *Warner–Jenkinson,* the Court stated: "Prosecution history estoppel continues to be available as a defense to infringement, but if the patent holder demonstrates that an amendment required during prosecution had a purpose unrelated to patentability, a court must consider that purpose in order to decide whether an estoppel is precluded. Where the patent holder is unable to establish such a purpose, a court should presume that the purpose behind the required amendment is such that prosecution history estoppel would apply."[16]

The Supreme Court revisited these questions in the 2002 case of *Festo Corp. v. Shoketsu Kinzoku Kogyo Kabushiki Co., Ltd.*[17] Justice Kennedy's opinion for the Court held that prosecution history estoppel applies to any amendment made to satisfy the requirements of patent law, but that the amendment is not an absolute bar to a claim of infringement under the doctrine of equivalents. Instead, the patent holder has the burden of proving that the particular amendment did not surrender the equivalent material at issue.

The reverse doctrine of equivalents, in contrast, can be applied when the accused device falls within the literal terms of the patent claims, but in fact accomplishes the desired result in a substantially different way. In this situation, as noted in *Graver Tank & Mfg. Co. v. Linde Air Products Co.*,[18] the accused device does not infringe the patent. Thus, the doctrine can both broaden and narrow the scope of material covered by a particular patent.

¶ 15.02   Direct Infringers & Secondary Liability

Direct infringement involves a direct violation of one of the patent holder's enumerated exclusive rights. In other words, the defendant is liable if it has made, used, sold, offered to sell, or imported the claimed invention within the United States. Third parties can also be liable if they actively induce patent infringement or if they are contributory infringers. Section 271(b) states: "Who-

---

14. *Exhibit Supply Co. v. Ace Patents Corp.*, 315 U.S. 126, 136 (1942).

15.   294 U.S. 42, 48 (1935).

16.   520 U.S. at 40–41.

17.   535 U.S. 722 (2002).

18.   339 U.S. 605, 608–09 (1950).

ever actively induces infringement of a patent shall be liable as an infringer." Active inducement involves any action that knowingly causes, urges, encourages, or aids in the patent infringement. A recent Supreme Court ruling clarifies the standard for inducement liability. In *Global–Tech Appliances, Inc. v. SEB S.A.*, 131 S.Ct. 2060 (2011), the Court held that willful blindness as to the infringing nature of the acts being induced satisfies the requirement of knowledge, but that mere deliberate indifference to a known risk was insufficient to establish liability for inducement.

Contributory infringement is actionable under section 271(c): "Whoever offers to sell or sells within the United States or imports into the United States a component of a patented machine, manufacture, combination, or composition, or a material or apparatus for use in practicing a patented process, constituting a material part of the invention, knowing the same to be especially made or especially adapted for use in an infringement of such patent, and not a staple article or commodity of commerce suitable for substantial noninfringing use, shall be liable as a contributory infringer." Thus, contributory infringement liability involves knowingly providing components that are specially made to facilitate infringement, and is actionable upon a showing that the component had no substantial non-infringing use.

Chapter 16

PATENT DEFENSES

Table of Sections

¶ 16.01   Invalidity & Non–Infringement

A patent is presumed to be valid under 35 U.S.C. § 282, which states:

> A patent shall be presumed valid. Each claim of a patent (whether in independent, dependent, or multiple dependent form) shall be presumed valid independently of the validity of other claims; dependent or multiple dependent claims shall be presumed valid even though dependent upon an invalid claim. Notwithstanding the preceding sentence, if a claim to a composition of matter is held invalid and that claim was the basis of a determination of nonobviousness under section 103(b)(1), the process shall no longer be considered nonobvious solely on the basis of section 103(b)(1). The burden of establishing invalidity of a patent or any claim thereof shall rest on the party asserting such invalidity.

As the Federal Circuit stated in *WMS Gaming, Inc. v. International Game Technology,*[1] this presumption can be overcome only by facts supported by clear and convincing evidence to the contrary.

Among the grounds on which the patent might be deemed invalid or not infringed are:

(1) the invention was known or used by others in this country, or patented or described in a printed publication in this or a foreign country, before the invention date under section 102;

---

1.   184 F.3d 1339, 1355 (Fed. Cir. 1999).

(2) the invention was patented or described in a printed publication in this or a foreign country or in public use or on sale in this country, more than one year prior to the date of the application for patent in the United States under section 102;

(3) the patent holder is not the true inventor, or other inventorship issues;

(4) the invention fails the non-obviousness requirement of section 103; and

(5) the patent does not satisfy the written description requirement, is indefinite, or does not set forth the best mode contemplated by the inventor for carrying out the invention under section 112.

Each of these defenses goes to negating one of the requisites for patent protection discussed in Chapter 12. Similarly, the defendant can show that the accused device does not come within the patent claims either literally or under the doctrine of equivalents. These issues are addressed in Chapter 15, ¶ 15.01.

¶ 16.02   Fraud & Inequitable Conduct

The Federal Circuit, in *Nobelpharma AB v. Implant Innovations, Inc.*,[2] explained the difference between inequitable conduct in the PTO and fraud: "Inequitable conduct is thus an equitable defense in a patent infringement action and serves as a shield, while a more serious finding of fraud potentially exposes a patentee to antitrust liability and thus serves as a sword."

The court noted that remedies for inequitable conduct can include unenforceability of the affected patent and possible attorney fees.[3] If the patent is fraudulently obtained, it can not only be invalidated but also can lead to liability under federal antitrust law, as the Supreme Court recognized in *Walker Process Equipment, Inc. v. Food Machinery & Chemical Corp.*[4] This type of claim is generally known as a *Walker Process* claim. As the Federal Circuit has noted, "[s]imply put, *Walker Process* fraud is a more serious offense than inequitable conduct."[5]

A finding of fraud can be premised on a knowing, willful and intentional act, misrepresentation, or omission before the PTO. As the *Nobelpharma* court noted, "if the evidence shows that the asserted patent was acquired by means of either a fraudulent misrepresentation or a fraudulent omission and that the party asserting the patent was aware of the fraud when bringing suit, such conduct can expose a patentee to liability under the antitrust

---

2.   141 F.3d 1059 (Fed. Cir. 1998).

3.   *Id.* at 1069 (citing 35 U.S.C. §§ 282, 285).

4.   382 U.S. 172 (1965).

5.   *Nobelpharma*, 141 F.3d at 1069.

laws."[6] To satisfy *Walker Process*, "the misrepresentation or omission must evidence a clear intent to deceive the examiner and thereby cause the PTO to grant an invalid patent. In contrast, a conclusion of inequitable conduct may be based on evidence of a lesser misrepresentation or an omission, such as omission of a reference that would merely have been considered important to the patentability of a claim by a reasonable examiner. A finding of *Walker Process* fraud requires higher threshold showings of both intent and materiality than does a finding of inequitable conduct."[7]

¶ 16.03   Exhaustion/First Sale Doctrine

The unconditional sale of a patented article exhausts the patent holder's rights to that particular product, just as in the case of the first sale doctrine in copyright law. The owner of that particular product is thus free to make use of or dispose of the product in whatever way it chooses without violating the inventor's otherwise exclusive right to make, use, sell, offer to sell, or import the product. This defense is known as exhaustion of rights or first sale. The Supreme Court considered the scope of the exhaustion defense in *Quanta Computer, Inc. v. LG Electronics, Inc.*[8] The question at issue was: "Whether patent rights are exhausted by a licensee's authorized sale of a patented product to an authorized purchaser, where that product has no reasonable use other than in practicing the patented invention."

The Court reaffirmed the vitality of the first sale doctrine, holding that the first sale of products produced by a patented process under a license exhausted the plaintiff's patent rights, including both product and process claims. Significantly, the Court held that there was an authorized sale even though the license agreement was limited in scope (specifically, it did not permit Intel to sell its products for use in combination with non-Intel products). The Court concluded as follows:

> The authorized sale of an article that substantially embodies a patent exhausts the patent holder's rights and prevents the patent holder from invoking patent law to control postsale use of the article. Here, LGE licensed Intel to practice any of its patents and to sell products practicing those patents. Intel's microprocessors and chipsets substantially embodied the LGE Patents because they had no reasonable noninfringing use and included all the inventive aspects of the patented methods. Nothing in the License Agreement limited Intel's ability to sell its products practicing the LGE Patents. Intel's authorized sale to Quanta thus took its products outside the scope of the

---

6. *Id.* at 1070.

7. *Id.*

8. 553 U.S. 617, 128 S.Ct. 2109 (2008).

patent monopoly, and as a result, LGE can no longer assert its patent rights against Quanta.

In *Static Control Components, Inc. v. Lexmark Int'l, Inc.*, 615 F. Supp. 2d 575 (E.D. Ky. 2009), a district court held that *Quanta* implicitly overrules prior Federal Circuit precedent, which stood for the proposition that a patent owner can restrict the application of the first sale doctrine by contractual provisions authorizing only a conditional. The Court did not expressly do so, as it avoided treating the Intel license as a conditional license. As a result, the issue remains open to debate.

¶ 16.04   Express or Implied License

An express license granted by the patent holder is of course a defense to a claim of patent infringement. Federal Circuit precedent indicates that implied licenses require a two-part showing: "This court [has] set out two requirements for the grant of an implied license by virtue of a sale of nonpatented equipment used to practice a patented invention. First, the equipment involved must have no noninfringing uses. . . . Second, the circumstances of the sale must 'plainly indicate that the grant of a license should be inferred.' "[9]

¶ 16.05   Patent Misuse

The misuse doctrine in patent law plays a fundamental role in delineating the boundaries of Intellectual Property rights. Often Intellectual Property owners seek to obtain rights or otherwise seek benefits that are not within the scope of the rights granted to them by Congress. The misuse doctrine covers behavior in which a patent owner attempts to extend its power beyond the boundaries of the lawful rights under the patent.[10] The unlawful monopoly extension could include extension to other products or extension in the physical or temporal scope of the patent, or the imposition of anticompetitive terms in contracts or licenses. A key point is that a misuse claim does not require the same scrupulous showings of standing, antitrust injury, and possibly even anticompetitive effect as would be required in a garden variety antitrust case. One of the central questions still left unclear in the case law is whether misuse rules extend to substantive conduct that is not condemned under antitrust principles, and if so, how to give definition to the misuse doctrine.

9. *Met–Coil Systems Corp. v. Korners Unlimited, Inc.*, 803 F.2d 684, 686 (Fed. Cir. 1986) (quoting *Bandag, Inc. v. Al Bolser's Tire Stores, Inc.*, 750 F.2d 903 (Fed. Cir. 1984)).

10. *Zenith Radio Corp. v. Hazeltine Research, Inc.*, 395 U.S. 100, 140 (1969).

One point that appears to be settled is the proposition that patent owners are not categorically exempt from standard antitrust analysis. As the Federal Circuit succinctly stated: "Intellectual property rights do not confer a privilege to violate the antitrust laws."[11] Moreover, there is substantial overlap between the doctrine of patent misuse and the antitrust laws. The two areas of law are not, however, coextensive. If a patent holder commits an antitrust violation in the exercise of its patent monopoly, it almost by definition also commits patent misuse (as long as there is a nexus to the patent). Nonetheless, conduct that falls short of an actual violation of the antitrust laws might still constitute patent misuse, although this outcome is controversial.

Moreover, patent misuse is an equitable doctrine—akin to the doctrine of unclean hands or in pari delicto—and thus the affirmative defense of patent misuse can be asserted by parties who do not satisfy the requirements of antitrust standing or antitrust injury under the Sherman and Clayton Acts. Further, a party accused of patent infringement is legally entitled to assert the patent misuse defense even that party was not the subject of the conduct alleged to be misuse.

Thus, for example, defendants in patent cases can raise the misuse defense even though they were not bound by the contractual provisions found to constitute patent misuse. The rationale is that the courts should not enforce patent rights which are being exercised in violation of public policy.[12] Thus, the misuse doctrine can be invoked defensively by an alleged infringer even if that infringer does not have formal antitrust standing—it may not have been the direct target of the conduct claimed to be misuse.

Congress has narrowed the scope of the patent misuse defense, which is restricted in some instances by 35 U.S.C. § 271(d), which states:

> No patent owner otherwise entitled to relief for infringement or contributory infringement of a patent shall be denied relief or deemed guilty of misuse or illegal extension of the patent right by reason of his having done one or more of the following: (1) derived revenue from acts which if performed by another without his consent would constitute contributory infringement of the patent; (2) licensed or authorized another to perform acts which if performed without his consent would constitute contributory infringement of the patent; (3) sought to enforce his patent rights against infringement or contributo-

11. *In re Indep. Serv. Orgs. Antitrust Litig.*, 203 F.3d 1322, 1325 (Fed. Cir. 2000).

12. *See Morton Salt Co. v. G.S. Suppiger*, 314 U.S. 488 (1942); *Compton v.*

Metal Products, Inc., 453 F.2d 38 (4th Cir. 1971), *cert. denied*, 406 U.S. 968 (1972).

ry infringement; (4) refused to license or use any rights to the patent; or (5) conditioned the license of any rights to the patent or the sale of the patented product on the acquisition of a license to rights in another patent or purchase of a separate product, unless, in view of the circumstances, the patent owner has market power in the relevant market for the patent or patented product on which the license or sale is conditioned.[13]

Thus, Congress has statutorily modified the misuse doctrine, so that in a tying case it is necessary to show market power in order to show misuse. Market power is typically proven by showing that the defendant possesses substantial market share in an economically relevant product (or service) and geographic market with entry barriers, or through direct evidence of the power to control prices in the relevant market. This modification of the misuse doctrine is consistent with the development of antitrust tying law under the Sherman and Clayton Acts. Similarly, this provision immunizes a patent owner from a finding of misuse based solely on its refusal to license its patent to a particular party. The amendment has a narrow and particular effect—a patent owner does not commit misuse if it refuses to license its technology to a particular party. Thus, for example, the defendant cannot assert a misuse claim on the mere ground that the patent owner refuses to license its technology to the defendant.

¶ 16.06 Other Defenses

Other defenses available in patent cases include:

— laches and estoppel, which are equitable doctrines regarding undue delay upon which the defendant detrimentally relied, or actions by the patent owner that reasonably preclude enforcement of the patent;

— inequitable conduct before the Patent & Trademark Office (PTO), which is discussed below;

— shop rights, which are addressed in Chapter 13, ¶ 13.02;

— immunity for medical practitioners, which is addressed in Chapter 12, ¶ 12.04;

---

13. For commentary on the contributory infringement/misuse issue, see Samuel Oddi, Contributory Infringement/Patent Misuse: Metaphysics and Metamorphosis, 44 U. PITT. L. REV. 73 (1982); Cathlyn Joan Steiner, Patents—Contributory Infringement and Patent Misuse under 35 U.S.C. § 271 (1980), 56 WASH. L. REV. 523 (1981); Note, Contributory Infringement and Misuse—The Effect of Section 271 of the Patent Act of 1952, 66 HARV. L. REV. 909 (1953); Tom Arnold & Louis Riley, Contributory Infringement and Patent Misuse: The Enactment of § 271 and its Subsequent Amendments, 76 J. PAT. & TRADEMARK OFF. SOC'Y 357 (1994). Finally, a comprehensive treatment can be found in 1 HERBERT HOVENKAMP, MARK D. JANIS & MARK A. LEMLEY, INTELLECTUAL PROPERTY & ANTITRUST: AN ANALYSIS OF ANTITRUST PRINCIPLES APPLIED TO INTELLECTUAL PROPERTY LAW, Chapter 21 (2002 & 2005 Supp.).

— good faith prior users of business methods, discussed below;[14]

— federal government and government contractor limitations on liability;[15] and

— state governmental immunity under the Eleventh Amendment.

The Federal Circuit narrowed the defense of inequitable conduct in *Therasense, Inc. v. Becton, Dickinson & Co.*, 649 F.3d 1276, 1290 (Fed. Cir. 2011) (en banc). The court held that inequitable conduct only takes place when the patent owner omits or misrepresents material information during the patent prosecution and the conduct my be deliberate, with specific intent to deceive the PTO. The defendant must prove inequitable conduct by clear and convincing evidence.

Recent amendments have expanded the good faith prior user defense, taking effect for patents issued on or after September 16, 2011. The defense applies if three condition are met: (1) it must involve "subject matter consisting of a process, or consisting of a machine, manufacture, or composition of matter used in a manufacturing or other commercial process, that would otherwise infringe a claimed invention being asserted," (2) the subject matter must have been "commercially used" by a person "acting in good faith" in connection with "an internal commercial use or an actual arm's length sale or other arm's length commercial transfer of a useful end result of such commercial use," and (3) the commercial use occurred at least one year before the effective filing date of the claimed invention or the date of public disclosure of the claimed invention under an exception in section 102(b) (as amended by the AIA), whichever date is earlier. See AIA § 5(a) (to be codified at 35 U.S.C. § 273(a)). The defense is limited to the prior commercial user itself and is non-transferable, other than by assignment of an on-going business in its entirety.

The ability to recover damages in patent cases is limited to a period of six years prior to filing of the action for infringement.[16]

14. 35 U.S.C. § 273.   **16.** 35 U.S.C.A. § 286.

15. 28 U.S.C. § 1498.

Chapter 17

PATENT REMEDIES

Table of Sections

¶ 17.01 Injunctions

Injunctive relief is ordinarily the most important patent remedy because it permits the patent holder to maintain its exclusivity in the marketplace, which is the essence of the patent reward. Section 283 states: "The several courts having jurisdiction of cases under this title may grant injunctions in accordance with the principles of equity to prevent the violation of any right secured by patent, on such terms as the court deems reasonable."

In *eBay, Inc. v. Merc Exchange, LLC.*,[1] the Supreme Court held that a patent holder must make the traditional showing in order to receive equitable relief: "(1) that it has suffered an irreparable injury; (2) that remedies available at law, such as monetary damages, are inadequate to compensate for that injury; (3) that, considering the balance of hardships between the plaintiff and defendant, a remedy in equity is warranted; and (4) that the public interest would not be disserved by a permanent injunction." The Court rejected the Federal Circuit's presumption that injunctions should be granted except in unusual cases.

The Court's decision in *eBay* makes it clear that injunctions are only granted when the four-part showing is made. In practical effect, the patent owner is likely to be able to make this showing in most, though not all, cases. The Federal Circuit made this point in its post-*eBay* decision in *Robert Bosch LLC v. Pylon Mfg. Corp.*,[2] where the court stated: "Although the Supreme Court disapproved of this court's absolute reliance on the patentee's right to exclude as a basis for our prior rule favoring injunctions, that does not mean that the nature of patent rights has no place in the appropri-

---

1. 547 U.S. 388, 393–94 (2006).

2. 659 F.3d 1142, 1149 (Fed. Cir. 2011).

ate equitable analysis." In other words, because patent rights generally involve a right to exclude others from making, using, selling, offering to sell, or importing the patented invention, the patent owner will be able to make the four-part showing required by *eBay* in most cases.

¶ 17.02 Damages

Section 284 sets forth the damages recovery available to patent holders: "Upon finding for the claimant the court shall award the claimant damages adequate to compensate for the infringement but in no event less than a reasonable royalty for the use made of the invention by the infringer, together with interest and costs as fixed by the court." The Federal Circuit discussed this provision in *Rite–Hite Corp. v. Kelley Co., Inc.*,[3] stating:

> The statute thus mandates that a claimant receive damages "adequate" to compensate for infringement. Section 284 further instructs that a damage award shall be "in no event less than a reasonable royalty"; the purpose of this alternative is not to direct the form of compensation, but to set a floor below which damage awards may not fall. Thus, the language of the statute is expansive rather than limiting. It affirmatively states that damages must be adequate, while providing only a lower limit and no other limitation.

> The Supreme Court spoke to the question of patent damages in *General Motors*, stating that, in enacting § 284, Congress sought to "ensure that the patent owner would in fact receive full compensation for 'any damages' [the patentee] suffered as a result of the infringement." Thus, while the statutory text states tersely that the patentee receive "adequate" damages, the Supreme Court has interpreted this to mean that "adequate" damages should approximate those damages that will *fully compensate* the patentee for infringement.[4]

The court in *Panduit Corp. v. Stahlin Brothers Fibre Works, Inc.*[5] articulated a frequently used four-factor for establishing damages based on lost profits damages: (1) demand for the patented product; (2) absence of acceptable non-infringing substitutes; (3) manufacturing and marketing capability to exploit the demand; and (4) the amount of the profit it would have made. This showing establishes that the patent holder would have earned the lost profits "but for" the defendant's infringing acts.[6]

3. 56 F.3d 1538 (Fed. Cir.), cert. denied, 516 U.S. 867 (1995).

4. *Id.* at 1544–45 (quoting *General Motors Corp. v. Devex Corp.*, 461 U.S. 648 (1983)).

5. 575 F.2d 1152, 1156 (6th Cir. 1978).

6. *See Kaufman Co. v. Lantech, Inc.*, 926 F.2d 1136, 1141 (Fed. Cir.1991).

Section 284 expressly contemplates the use of expert testimony to determine a reasonable royalty, the minimum recovery to which patent holders are entitled: "The court may receive expert testimony as an aid to the determination of damages or of what royalty would be reasonable under the circumstances."

In cases involving willful infringement, treble damages can be recovered. Section 284 states in relevant part: "When the damages are not found by a jury, the court shall assess them. In either event the court may increase the damages up to three times the amount found or assessed. Increased damages under this paragraph shall not apply to provisional rights under section 154(d) of this title." The Federal Circuit discussed the willfulness issue in *Knorr–Bremse Systeme Fuer Nutzfahrzeuge GmbH v. Dana Corp.*[7] Another AIA change in patent law is new section 298 of the Patent Act (AIA § 17(a)), effective for patents issued on or after September 16, 2012:

> The failure of an infringer to obtain the advice of counsel with respect to any allegedly infringed patent, or the failure of the infringer to present such advice to the court or jury, may not be used to prove that the accused infringer willfully infringed the patent or that the infringer intended to induce infringement of the patent.

The ability to recover damages in patent cases is limited to a period of six years prior to filing of the action for infringement.[8] Finally, damages can be limited if the patent holder fails to satisfy the marking requirement of section 287(a). The marking requirement is addressed in Chapter 13, ¶ 13.01. The AIA quelled litigation under section 292 of the Patent Act, which had allowed any person to sue for a fine of up to $500 for every false marking offense, with the recovery split between the plaintiff and the government. The AIA allows recovery only for compensatory damages by "a person who has suffered a competitive injury" as a result of false marking. AIA § 16(b). The government retains the ability to sue for the $500 penalty for each false marking offense. The amendment applies to both pending and future cases.

¶ 17.03   Costs and Attorneys Fees

Section 285 allows for the recovery of reasonable attorneys fees in exceptional cases: "The court in exceptional cases may award reasonable attorney fees to the prevailing party." This provision can be invoked in cases of willful infringement or in other situations involving litigation conduct that might warrant a fee award.

---

7.   383 F.3d 1337 (Fed. Cir. 2004).   **8.**   35 U.S.C.A. § 286.

Chapter 18

TRADE SECRET LAW

Table of Sections

¶ 18.01   Trade Secret Subject Matter

A trade secret can involve almost any kind of proprietary information that has value to a firm, that is maintained making use of reasonable secrecy measures, and that is not common knowledge. In other words, the subject matter of trade secrets is extremely broad. Thus, a trade secret can involve any type of information, such as technical or non-technical data, a formula, a pattern, a compilation (a collection of data or information), a computer program, a device or product, a method or technique, a drawing, a process (such as a manufacturing or fabrication process), financial data, or a list of actual or potential customers, prospects, or suppliers.

Given the wide variety of information that may be protected under its auspices, trade secret law can encompass material that might be within the scope of patent or copyright law. For example, a secret formula that enables a manufacturer to produce a chemical or a prescription drug is a trade secret—the particular steps involved in manufacturing the chemical or the drug, the raw materials or ingredients involved, and the techniques used to mix or prepare the chemical or the drug can all potentially be considered to be trade secrets. To the extent that the manufacturer takes steps to protect this information, it may have a legal claim if anyone unlawfully attempts to obtain or use the process. Similarly, a new product may be a trade secret, at least until the product is placed on the market (at which time the manufacturer may have obtained patent protection for the product). Even data concerning a product—such as the results of tests used to determine a device's efficacy, safety, and marketability—may constitute a trade secret (again, until and unless the information is publicly disclosed).

Thus, a company might make use of trade secret law during preliminary stages of product development, while eventually seeking patent protection for some or all aspects of its proprietary information. Subject to the requirements of patent law (for example, requiring patent applications to be filed within one year of public use or of placing a product on sale), both fields of Intellectual Property law can be invoked when appropriate. Of course, to the extent material is disclosed or claimed in a patent, it ceases to be eligible for trade secret protection. Nonetheless, a company might seek to claim patent protection for aspects of its product that will be apparent or easily reverse engineered upon marketing and sale of the product, while retaining trade secret protection on aspects of the manufacturing process that are not readily reverse engineered. Unlike patent law, which provides exclusive rights against any party that makes, uses, sells, offers to sell, or imports the invention, trade secret law does not prevent competition from those who independently develop or reverse engineer the invention.

Trade secret law originated at least as early as Roman times, when the law provided a remedy against persons who induced an employee to divulge confidential information belonging to an employer. With the advent of the Industrial Revolution in the 1800s, the basic outlines of modern trade secret law began to emerge, largely in response to the growing importance of industrial technology. Although the protectability of trade secrets is governed by state law, there are federal criminal law provisions governing economic espionage and intentional theft of trade secrets. The federal provisions include very substantial fines (up to $5,000,000 to $10,000,000 under two provisions), extensive prison terms (up to 10 years and 15 years under two provisions), and criminal forfeiture.[1]

Two requisites must be proven in order to establish the existence of a protected trade secret. First, the information must be sufficiently secret that the firm derives some economic value or advantage, either actual or potential, from the information. In other words, the information must not be generally known to other persons who can obtain economic value from its disclosure or use. This requirement focuses on *the kind of information* that is claimed to be a trade secret—if it gives the firm an advantage or "edge" over competitors who do not possess the information, then it very likely will qualify as a trade secret. The second requirement for trade secret protection is that the firm possessing the trade secret must make efforts that are reasonable under the circumstances to maintain its secrecy or confidentiality. This requirement focuses on *affirmative steps taken by a company to protect its trade secrets.*

---

1. 18 U.S.C. §§ 1831–39.

Assuming that the information sought to be protected is sufficiently secret to provide its owner with a business advantage over
competitors that do not have the information and assuming that
sufficient secrecy measures have been taken, almost any kind of
information can qualify as a trade secret. A trade secret can relate
to technical matters such as the composition or design of a product,
a method of manufacture, or the know-how necessary to perform a
particular operation or service. For example, a new product or
product development information can be protectable as a trade
secret. If the particular product and product development information in question fulfills the requirements of the trade secret law, it
would qualify for protection as long as it is maintained in secrecy.
Suppose a manufacturer of medical devices develops a new artificial
heart valve. The valve differs from and is in some ways superior to
those produced by other firms. The valve takes several years to
develop and during this time it is maintained in secrecy and is not
placed on the market. The heart valve is a trade secret. While the
heart valve is still in the development stage, the manufacturer
conducts confidential research into the valve's safety and efficacy.
The research data and findings are maintained in secrecy and are
not published. The product data and findings can qualify as trade
secrets. Similarly, a pharmaceutical products manufacturer might
conduct studies to determine the effectiveness of various substances
in treating cancer. In addition to finding valuable products, the
company will identify many "dead ends," or substances that are
ineffective. The company might maintain a confidential database of
this information solely for use by its researchers, so as to prevent
duplication of effort. This information could also be considered a
trade secret. Reasonable secrecy measures are discussed below in
¶ 18.02.

In contrast to the patent law requirement of novelty, trade
secret law generally requires only relative secrecy. If several competitors lawfully possess a trade secret, while several others do not,
the information can still qualify as a trade secret. The secrecy
requirement is satisfied if it would be difficult or costly for others
who could exploit the information to obtain it. Put another way,
novelty is not required—the information need not be completely
novel or new. As the Restatement (Third) of Unfair Competition
explains: "The rule stated in this Section requires only secrecy
sufficient to confer an actual or potential economic advantage on
one who possesses the information. Thus, the requirement of
secrecy is satisfied if it would be difficult or costly for others who
could exploit the information to acquire it without resort to the
wrongful conduct proscribed under § 40. Novelty in the patent law
sense is not required."[2]

2. THE RESTATEMENT (THIRD) OF UNFAIR
COMPETITION § 39, comment f. *See gener-* *ally Kewanee Oil Co. v. Bicron Corp.,*
416 U.S. 470 (1974).

The secrecy question depends heavily on the state of the art in the field and the degree to which the information is unique or at least difficult to replicate. For example, suppose a company designs and sells computer systems to banks and other financial institutions. In the course of its business, the company creates computer programs, service manuals, and technical bulletins, which compile technical information and procedures. This information, if maintained in secrecy, would qualify as a trade secret. Even if portions of the information compiled by the company are generally known, the company's efforts in gathering and compiling that information into a useful form may be sufficient to establish a protectable trade secret. The focus is on the degree of secrecy of the information sought to be protected.

The key to determining whether the information qualifies as a trade secret is the ease with which the information can be duplicated without involving considerable time, effort, or expense. The trade secret must be sufficiently secret that its owner derives some economic value or advantage, actual or potential, from the fact that the information is not generally known to competitors or others who might use it. Thus, whether a particular piece of information qualifies as trade secret depends fundamentally on secrecy of the information in its particular industry context. The requirement is somewhat flexible. Thus, a trade secret can exist in a combination of characteristics and components, as long as that combination provides a competitive advantage.

On the other hand, as the Court noted in *Kewanee Oil Co. v. Bicron Corp.*,[3] if the information can readily be duplicated by anyone with general skills and knowledge in the field, it is not a protectable trade secret. For instance, as illustrated by *George S. May International Co. v. International Profit Associates*,[4] if the information contained in the manuals of a consulting firm is of a very general nature, which anyone with accounting, finance, or sales knowledge could easily duplicate, it would not qualify as a trade secret.

Similarly, if information is easily discerned, widely known, or obvious, it cannot qualify as a trade secret. Information that is well-known and generally used in an industry is not protectable because it would accord a firm possessing that information with no particular advantage over others. For example, a company's customer tracking methods, such as use of follow-up letters and deletion of customer names after second failure to respond, were found not to

---

3. 416 U.S. 470 (1974).

4. 256 Ill.App.3d 779, 256 Ill.App.3d 779, 195 Ill.Dec. 183, 628 N.E.2d 647 (1993).

be protected in *Computer Care v. Service Systems Enterprises, Inc.*[5] The court concluded that these business methods were not sufficiently secret to be protected; there was no evidence that they were not generally available in the industry, and no evidence that these business methods would not be obvious to someone entering business.

In *Noah v. Enesco Corp.*,[6] an artist developed a concept for a line of "Noah's Ark" figurines. The idea was not new and was generally known to those in the industry. The court held that the artist's idea did not a qualify as a trade secret. Similarly, in *Composite Marine Propellers, Inc. v. Van Der Woude*,[7] the Seventh Circuit held that a manufacturer of marine propellers did not establish that its competitors had misappropriated a trade secret consisting of a "gas counter backpressure" molding technique. The court found that the technology was commonly known and had actually been shown to the plaintiff by another firm.

On the other hand, if the information is secret and sufficient secrecy measures have been taken, trade secret protection can encompass almost any kind of information. The law in most states does not require that information be continuously used in a business (i.e., of long-term value) to be protectable as a trade secret, although a few states still follow the prior rule (which only protected information that is regularly used in a business). Thus, under the majority rule, even if certain information is only used on a one-time or short-term basis, it will still qualify for trade secret protection, as long as the requisites of trade secret law are met. For instance, suppose a construction company is about to enter a secret bid in order to obtain a lucrative government contract. An employee from that company breaks into a safe and obtains the bid information, which he sells to a competing bidder. The competing bidder undercuts the company's bid by a hundred dollars and obtains the contract. A trade secret violation has arguably occurred under the trade secret laws of most states. For example, in *Inflight Newspapers, Inc. v. Magazines In–Flight, LLC*,[8] held that an airline magazine distributor's secret bids were protectable trade secrets because information would permit underbidding. In *Martin Marietta Corp. v. Dalton*,[9] a government contractor's Navy bid was a trade secret because it contained confidential cost, pricing, and strategy infor-

---

5. 982 F.2d 1063, 1071–74 (7th Cir. 1992).

6. 911 F.Supp. 299 (N.D. Ill. 1995).

7. 962 F.2d 1263, 1267 (7th Cir. 1992). *See also Web Communications Group, Inc. v. Gateway 2000, Inc.*, 889 F.Supp. 316 (N.D. Ill. 1995) (information that is well-known and generally used in the industry is not protectable).

8. 990 F.Supp. 119 (E.D.N.Y. 1997).

9. 974 F.Supp. 37 (D.D.C. 1997). *See also Economy Roofing & Insulating Co. v. Zumaris*, 538 N.W.2d 641 (Iowa 1995) (customer correspondence, bids and estimates, customer and pricing lists, and cost and profit information are protectable trade secrets).

mation, and thus bids could not be revealed under the trade secret exemption to the Freedom of Information Act (FOIA).

This broader conception of trade secret law is reflected in the Uniform Trade Secrets Act (UTSA), which as been adopted by 46 states and the District of Columbia as of March 14, 2012.[10] The UTSA expanded the scope of trade secret protection, particularly as to one-time information and other information that is not continuously used in a business. Traditionally, this type of information was not protectable as a trade secret, but the UTSA extends protection as long as the other requirements of trade secret law are met. Typically, this information is only used once, yet competitors would obtain a substantial business advantage if they knew the amount of other bid, enabling them to undercut the bid if they wish to do so. Examples of cases applying the contrary rule include *State ex rel. The Plain Dealer v. Ohio Department of Insurance*,[11] which held that draft contracts, bids, and letters of negotiation are not trade secrets under Ohio law.

Customer lists present close questions of protectability under the UTSA, particularly as to whether the information is not generally known or readily ascertainable. The central question is whether the content of the customer list could be ascertained or easily obtained from public sources, such as phone directories or trade publications. When the information is difficult to obtain, trade secret protection has generally been available, assuming the other requisites are met. For example, in *Stampede Tool Warehouse, Inc. v. May*,[12] the court held that a list of automotive "jobbers" was a trade secret given the time, effort, and expense required to compile list. The information was not readily duplicated from any one source, and the employer took secrecy measures to guard the information. In *Elmer Miller, Inc. v. Landis*,[13] the court held that a tailoring shop's competitors could not duplicate customer list without significant expenditure of time, effort, and expense. The list

---

10. http://www.nccusl.org/Acts.aspx (last visited March 14, 2012). Governor Chris Christie of New Jersey signed his state's version of the UTSA into law in early 2012. A UTSA bill has been introduced in Massachusetts, but has not been enacted as this book goes to press. New York, North Carolina, and Texas have not adopted the UTSA.

11. 80 Ohio St.3d 513, 687 N.E.2d 661 (1997) (citing *Wisconsin Electric Power Co. v. Public Service Commission of Wisconsin*, 110 Wis.2d 530, 329 N.W.2d 178 (1983)). *See also MQS Inspection, Inc. v. Bielecki*, 963 F.Supp. 771 (E.D. Wis. 1995) (customer lists,

bids, pricing formulas, and marketing information not protectable trade secrets under Wisconsin law).

12. 272 Ill.App.3d 580, 209 Ill.Dec. 281, 651 N.E.2d 209 (1995), *appeal denied*, 163 Ill.2d 589, 212 Ill.Dec. 438, 657 N.E.2d 639 (1995). *See also Morlife, Inc. v. Perry*, 56 Cal.App.4th 1514, 66 Cal. Rptr.2d 731 (Ct. App. 1997) (customer list protected as trade secret).

13. 253 Ill.App.3d 129, 192 Ill.Dec. 378, 625 N.E.2d 338 (1993), *appeal denied*, 154 Ill.2d 559, 197 Ill.Dec. 485, 631 N.E.2d 707 (1994).

was secret enough for owner to derive value from it, and owner had made reasonable efforts to maintain secrecy of information.

On the other hand, if the customer list is easily duplicated, it will not qualify as a trade secret. In *Curtis 1000, Inc. v. Suess*,[14] a customer list was deemed unprotectable as a trade secret when the information contained in it was readily obtainable from the telephone book, mailing lists, trade publications, and association directories, or could be obtained by simply driving down streets. Similarly, in *Hamer Holding Group, Inc. v. Elmore*,[15] the could that a customer list that was derived from a Secretary of State's list was not trade secret, because anyone with access to Secretary's list or phone directory could have easily duplicated it.

¶ 18.02   Reasonable Secrecy Measures

The Requirement of Reasonable Secrecy Measures

Whether particular actions taken to protect a trade secret are sufficient to satisfy this standard is ordinarily a jury question. A firm seeking to protect its trade secrets should consider a variety of secrecy measures. Any secrecy measure will involve some cost or inconvenience, and thus a balancing of the benefits of a particular measure against its cost is necessary. The UTSA requires only reasonable secrecy measures. A firm might consider adoption of some or all of the following measures: (1) external physical security measures to protect the plant from incursion; (2) internal physical security measures to prevent employees and visitors from gaining access to areas in which proprietary information is kept; (3) confidentiality agreements or clauses for all employees, customers, suppliers, and other third parties who have access to any trade secret information; (4) prohibiting persons who are not bound by these agreement from gaining access to trade secret information; (5) requiring employees with access to proprietary information to sign reasonable covenants not to compete; (6) keeping trade secret information "under lock and key," including securing all documents and insuring that computers have password protection; (7) identifying and labeling all confidential information; and (8) maintaining a policy of informing all incoming and departing employees of the firm's trade secret policies and of the particular types of

14.   843 F.Supp. 441 (C.D. Ill. 1994), *aff'd*, 24 F.3d 941 (7th Cir. 1994).

15.   202 Ill.App.3d 994, 148 Ill.Dec. 310, 560 N.E.2d 907 (1990), *appeal denied*, 136 Ill.2d 544, 153 Ill.Dec. 373, 567 N.E.2d 331 (1991). *See also Inflight Newspapers, Inc. v. Magazines In-Flight, LLC*, 990 F.Supp. 119 (E.D.N.Y. 1997) (airline magazine distributor's customers lists were not protectable trade secrets); *AmeriGas Propane, L.P. v. T–Bo Propane, Inc.*, 972 F.Supp. 685 (S.D. Ga. 1997) (propane dealer's customer list was not protectable trade secret under Georgia law).

information considered to be trade secrets (and to which the employee has had or will have access).

As the RESTATEMENT (THIRD) OF UNFAIR COMPETITION § 39, comment g, states: "Precautions taken to maintain the secrecy of information are relevant in determining whether the information qualifies for protection as a trade secret. Precautions to maintain secrecy may take many forms, including physical security designed to prevent unauthorized access, procedures intended to limit disclosure based upon the 'need to know,' and measures that emphasize to recipients the confidential nature of the information such as nondisclosure agreements, signs, and restrictive legends."[16]

The failure to take reasonable secrecy measures has serious ramifications. For instance, in *Electro–Craft Corp. v. Controlled Motion, Inc.*,[17] an employee departed to form his own firm in competition with his former employer, taking proprietary information with him. The court held that the employer did have the type of information normally protected under the law of trade secrets, but that it failed to take adequate measures to protect those secrets. The case illustrates how a careless firm can forfeit its proprietary rights, even in a situation in which the former employee rapidly replicates the trade secret information (clearly borrowing from the former employer). The case discussion includes a number of proposed secrecy measures that the court viewed as reasonable in the circumstances. In *Web Communications Group, Inc. v. Gateway 2000, Inc.*,[18] the court held that a marketing firm took insufficient steps to protect the confidentiality of its ideas for an advertising insert to be used in a magazine. The court noted that documents related to the insert bore no confidentiality stamp or designation, although the company's practice was to stamp as "confidential" all protected materials. Further, the company did not have non-disclosure or confidentiality agreements with its customers regarding the project, and disclosed the idea to suppliers and printers, including one of the company's own competitors. This absence of secrecy measures was fatal to the company's trade secret claim. In *George*

---

16. *See generally Colson Co. v. Wittel*, 210 Ill.App.3d 1030, 155 Ill.Dec. 471, 569 N.E.2d 1082 (1991) (noting that employer took steps to keep customer information from becoming generally known to others within the company except on "need-to-know" basis, although ultimately denying trade secret claim on other grounds), *appeal denied*, 141 Ill.2d 537, 162 Ill.Dec. 484, 580 N.E.2d 110 (1991); *Curtis 1000, Inc. v. Suess*, 843 F.Supp. 441 (C.D. Ill. 1994) (noting that a customer list can qualify as a trade secret if it is sufficiently secret that its owner derives economic value from it

and it is known only to salesman who filled orders and not available to other employees, the general public, or competitors), *aff'd*, 24 F.3d 941 (7th Cir. 1994); *Elmer Miller, Inc. v. Landis*, 253 Ill.App.3d 129, 192 Ill.Dec. 378, 625 N.E.2d 338 (1993) (holding that tailoring shop made reasonable efforts to maintain secrecy of information), *appeal denied*, 154 Ill.2d 559, 197 Ill.Dec. 485, 631 N.E.2d 707 (1994).

17. 332 N.W.2d 890 (Minn. 1983).

18. 889 F.Supp. 316 (N.D. Ill. 1995).

S. May International Co. v. International Profit Associates,[19] the court found a failure to take necessary secrecy measures, given that the firm gave out information to thousands of trainees before any confidentiality agreements were executed, sign-out policies for manuals were not shown to have been enforced, and the firm failed to identify confidential portions of manuals, which contained much commonly known material.

A variety of secrecy measures may be necessary, depending on the circumstances. In *Mangren Research & Development Corp. v. National Chemical Co.*,[20] which involved a secret formula, the employer required each employee to sign a confidentiality agreement. It also informed each employee of the trade secret status of the formula. Moreover, only employees were permitted in the laboratory, and the firm regularly replaced identifying ingredient labels with coded labels when the ingredients were delivered to the premises. The court held that these secrecy measures were sufficient to support a jury's finding that the plaintiff had taken reasonable secrecy measures, despite the defendant's assertion to the contrary. The defendant had argued that the company's trade secret measures were insufficient because all six of the company's employees knew the trade secret and a keen observer might have been able to identify the formula's ingredients before the coded labels were applied.

A wide range of protective measures can be taken to protect proprietary information. If patent protection is available, it is certainly a powerful form of protection, albeit one of limited duration. Confidentiality agreements and non-competition agreements enable a firm to protect its trade secrets by contracting with those with whom it deals. General secrecy measures enable the firm to prevent disclosure of information to parties not bound by express or implied confidentiality duties. By adopting a full panoply of protections, suited to the individual circumstances of a business, a firm can maximize the practical and legal protection of its proprietary information. The discussion below highlights several particular secrecy measures that a firm might consider: confidentiality agreements, limits on access to trade secrets, labeling of confidential information, and non-competition agreements.

Confidentiality Agreements.

Case law clearly supports the use of confidentiality agreements to bind recipients of a company's trade secret information.[21] Confi-

19. 256 Ill.App.3d 779, 195 Ill.Dec. 183, 628 N.E.2d 647 (1993), *appeal denied,* 156 Ill.2d 557, 202 Ill.Dec. 921, 638 N.E.2d 1115 (1994).

20. 87 F.3d 937 (7th Cir. 1996).

21. *See* RESTATEMENT (THIRD) OF UNFAIR COMPETITION § 39, comment g ("Precautions to maintain secrecy ... includ[e] ... measures that emphasize to recipients the confidential nature of the

dentiality agreements are also sometimes known as non-disclosure agreements (or NDAs). A confidentially agreement or NDA is an agreement in which a party (such as an employee, supplier, or customer) agrees that he or she will not disclose any secret or confidential information, knowledge, or data belonging to the company. The agreement generally requires that the party agree not to disclose the information either directly or indirectly, unless the party has the express, written permission of the company allowing him or her to do so. Generally, these agreements also require that the party turn over all confidential information received from the firm when and if the employment relationship (or other business relationship, such as customer-supplier) terminates. Thus, the party generally agrees to turn over notes, memoranda, notebooks, drawings, computer files and other data, and the like.

These confidentiality agreements are significant because they permit the company to divulge its trade secrets to those who need to know the information in order to assist the company in achieving its objectives. For example, the company's research and development employees may need access to research data in order to do their work, or an engineering firm may need to know some details of a trade secret manufacturing process in order to build a plant to proper specifications. In these circumstances, the company can obtain a confidentiality agreement as part of the employment or other business transaction, and then it can divulge the trade secret with some degree of assurance that it will have a legal remedy in the event that the employee or other party divulges the information to others without permission.

The partial disclosure of trade secrets to third parties who are under obligations of confidentiality does not destroy the trade secret status of the computer programs, compilations, and technical information. For example, suppose a computer software development firm has a valuable trade secret, and requires every party with access to the trade secret to sign confidentiality agreements obligating the third parties to take reasonable secrecy measures and not to divulge or use the information in any impermissible way. In this instance, the company has successfully taken sufficient measures to protect its trade secrets.[22] On the other hand, if the company reveals confidential information to suppliers, customers, and others without signed confidentiality agreements, the recipients have no reason to know that the information was a trade secret. In this situation, the company clearly has not taken sufficient secrecy measures.

---

information such as nondisclosure agreements, signs, and restrictive legends.").

22. See *ISC–Bunker Ramo Corp. v. Altech, Inc.*, 765 F.Supp. 1310 (N.D. Ill. 1990).

Limiting Access to Trade Secrets.

Controlling access to trade secrets has both practical and legal benefits. On a practical level, the fewer people who know about a particular item of information, the lower the chance that someone will divulge it. As a matter of trade secret law, limiting access on a need-to-know basis is imperative. Thus, employees should only have access to trade secret information that is relevant to their own job responsibilities. Similarly, third parties should only have access to trade secret information when it is necessary. All parties—both employees and third parties—given access to the information should be required to sign confidentiality agreements or clauses. Parties who have not signed such an agreement should not be given access to trade secrets. Further, a company seeking to maximize its trade secrets protection should consider the additional step of requiring that those who are given access to trade secrets must sign reasonable non-competition agreements.

Specific measures to insure that only persons with a need to know have access to trade secrets will depend on the nature and circumstances of a particular business operation. As to external security, it certainly is important for a firm to insure that sufficient steps are taken to prevent incursion into areas in which trade secrets are kept. Some of these physical security measures are likely to have already been taken for other reasons, such as for employee and visitor safety. Thus, most plants and research facilities will have physical barriers preventing unauthorized access, such as fences, gates, guard houses, and emergency exits that are locked to the outside (and which set off an alarm when opened from the inside). Visitors should not be permitted to wander the hallways. Depending on the size of the operation, badges or entry cards may be used to restrict access. A particularly significant danger is the "plant tour." Whether formal and organized or informal and spontaneous, it is important to consider the ramifications of allowing visitors to enter areas of a facility in which trade secrets are kept. The best approach is to limit such tours, if permitted at all, to areas in which no trade secret information is kept or is accessible.

In addition to access measures involving outsiders, a company should insure that only persons with a "need to know" be given access to trade secret information within the company. In a small operation with very few people, it may be necessary for all persons to have access to trade secrets, or it may be impossible to prevent them from gaining access in some manner. In a larger operation, such as one organized into departments, it is certainly necessary to prevent people from unrelated departments from gaining access to trade secrets that they do not need to know. Even persons from the same department may not need access to all trade secrets in that area or department.

Labeling Confidential Information.

Trade secret law clearly indicates that the owner of a trade secret should specifically identify material that it claims is protected.[23] Some trade secret information might obviously be considered a secret, while in other cases it will not be intuitively obvious that the company considers a particular item of information to be a trade secret. The best course of action is therefore to conduct an audit or review of all potential proprietary information and then to identify the information as such, label it in some appropriate manner, and inform those with access to the information of its protected status. Some practical steps may include placing signs in restricted areas, adding restrictive legends to important information, stamping documents as "confidential," password protection, and encryption. Where feasible, the company may consider encoding information to prevent unwarranted disclosure. Steps should be taken to protect computer data, such as password protection and encryption.

A consistent policy of identifying, labeling, and securing trade secret material can enhance a firm's practical and legal ability to protect its trade secrets. Once that policy is adopted, it is then imperative that all documents and files pertaining to the trade secrets be so marked. The failure to follow a policy of regularly and consistently marking proprietary information could lead to the inference that undesignated materials are not considered trade secrets.

Non–Competition Agreements.

Another important method of protecting trade secret information, as well as simply preventing current employees from becoming future competitors (or from joining an existing competitor), is to require that employees who have access to proprietary information sign a non-competition agreement. These agreements, also known as covenants not to compete, can serve to protect the owner of trade secret information. A non-competition agreement is an agreement in which an employee (or other party) agrees that he or she will not compete with the company for a certain period of time after the employee's departure from the company. These agreements, which are frequently part of an overall employment agreement, preclude the employee from leaving the firm and immediately

---

23. *See* Restatement (Third) of Unfair Competition § 39, comment d ("An agreement between the parties that characterizes specific information as a 'trade secret' can be an important although not necessarily conclusive factor in determining whether the information qualifies for protection as a trade secret under this Section."); Restatement (Third) of Unfair Competition § 39, comment g ("Precautions to maintain secrecy ... includ[e] ... measures that emphasize to recipients the confidential nature of the information such as nondisclosure agreements, signs, and restrictive legends.").

becoming a competitor (or joining an existing competitor) of his or her former employer. The agreements generally prevent the former employee from becoming associated with a competitor in any capacity, such as employee, investor, lender, director, officer, partner, independent contractor, consultant, or owner (basically in any capacity calling for the party to provide personal services or to become involved in ownership, management, or control of a competing business). These agreements are typically for a specific period of time, such as six months, one year, or three years, after which the former employee is free to engage in a competing business in any capacity. There is also commonly a geographic limitation on the scope of the non-competition agreement. In other words, the party agreeing to be bound is prohibited from competing with the company in a specifically identified geographic area, which is frequently the area in which the company does business. Depending on the type of business involved, a company may seek to bar competition within a specific geographic radius (such as twenty-five miles), within a metropolitan area, within a state, within a region, or even in the entire United States or worldwide. If the former employee relocates outside the geographic area identified in the agreement, then he or she is free to begin competing with the former employer immediately. Finally, non-competition agreements generally have a limitation regarding the types of businesses that are considered to be in competition with the employer/company.

Non-competition agreements are an effective way to prevent an employee (or other party) from obtaining a trade secret from a company and then making use of that information in direct competition with the firm. In some instances, it may be the only effective way to protect proprietary information. For example, in one case, the court noted that the only way in which an employer can prevent its former employee, a salesman, from soliciting the employer's customers is to obtain an agreement restricting the salesman from competing for customers upon termination of his employment.[24] Sales leads are typically freely given to sales employees and in some cases may be developed by the employee himself or herself, and thus trade secret law would not provide any protection to the employer.

Not only might a covenant not to compete be effective against former employees, it can also provide protection when trade secret information is divulged to suppliers, customers, or others who might need access to that information. Again, the covenant will help assure that the recipient of the trade secret information

---

24. *Colson Co. v. Wittel*, 210 Ill. App.3d 1030, 155 Ill.Dec. 471, 569 N.E.2d 1082 (1991), *appeal denied,* 141 Ill.2d 537, 162 Ill.Dec. 484, 580 N.E.2d 110 (1991).

cannot immediately make use of it in competition with the owner of the trade secret.

It should be noted that courts are often critical of non-competition agreements, construing them strictly and refusing to enforce agreements that are overly broad or that are overreaching in scope or length. The covenant must further a legitimate interest of the employer, must be reasonable in scope and duration, must not unduly burden the employee, and must not be contrary to public policy (which can include considerations of whether the covenant creates a monopoly or interferes with other public policies, such as the attorney-client or physician-patient relationship). Some courts will not "blue pencil" or modify a covenant not to compete that is found to be unreasonable; instead, the agreement will be found to be invalid. Other courts, however, do apply the blue-pencil rule and will modify terms that are found to be unduly burdensome or unreasonable, thus leaving the overall agreement intact and allowing enforcement as modified.

¶ 18.03   Trade Secret Infringement

Trade secret law does not automatically allow recovery against parties who are making use of information claimed to be a trade secret. To prove a violation of the trade secret law, the plaintiff must show several facts. First, it must be established that the information qualified as a secret, as discussed in ¶ 18.01 above. Second, the company must show that the trade secret was misappropriated or taken by some unlawful means, rather than independently developed or lawfully obtained from third source. Third, the company must show that the trade secret was used in the appropriator's business, or at least obtained or disclosed in an unlawful manner.[25]

There are several ways in which a company can show the second element noted above (that the information was taken unlawfully). THE RESTATEMENT (THIRD) OF UNFAIR COMPETITION, section 38, sets forth a helpful statement of the elements necessary to prove infringement of a trade secret:

One is subject to liability for the appropriation of another's trade secret if:

(a) the actor acquires by means that are improper under the rule stated in § 43 information that the actor knows or has reason to know is the other's trade secret; or

---

25. *See Composite Marine Propellers, Inc. v. Van Der Woude*, 962 F.2d 1263 (7th Cir. 1992); *Flavorchem Corp. v.* *Mission Flavors and Fragrances, Inc.*, 939 F.Supp. 593 (N.D. Ill. 1996).

(b) the actor uses or discloses the other's trade secret without the other's consent and, at the time of the use or disclosure,

(1) the actor knows or has reason to know that the information is a trade secret that the actor acquired under circumstances creating a duty of confidence owed by the actor to the other under the rule stated in § 41; or

(2) the actor knows or has reason to know that the information is a trade secret that the actor acquired by means that are improper under the rule stated in § 43; or

(3) the actor knows or has reason to know that the information is a trade secret that the actor acquired from or through a person who acquired it by means that are improper under the rule stated in § 43 or whose disclosure of the trade secret constituted a breach of a duty of confidence owed to the other under the rule stated in § 41; or

(4) the actor knows or has reason to know that the information is a trade secret that the actor acquired through an accident or mistake, unless the acquisition was the result of the other's failure to take reasonable precautions to maintain the secrecy of the information.

Thus, a trade secret plaintiff might show that information was taken as a result of the breach or inducement of a breach of a confidential relationship or other duty to maintain secrecy or limit use. If a confidentiality agreement was breached (or a third party encouraged the breach of such an agreement), the company has made the required showing. For example, suppose a manufacturer of MRI machines develops a more efficient process for producing these machines. It discloses this information to a production manager employed by the company, who is bound by a confidentiality agreement. It also discloses the information in confidence to an engineering firm hired to design and build a plant where the machine will be produced. The employee forms a competing business and the engineering firm divulges the trade secret information to another competitor, and both competitors then make use of the trade secret. The employee and the engineering firm have breached a confidential relationship and committed a trade secret violation.

A trade secret violation can also be shown if someone receives trade secret information knowing (or having reason to know based on the circumstances) that it is an unlawfully or sometimes even an accidentally revealed trade secret. This form of liability for receiving trade secret information strengthens the protection that trade secret law provides. It is worth considering, however, the extent to which liability for mistakenly revealed trade secrets should be tempered by the principle that owners of trade secrets have an obligation to take reasonable secrecy measures.

Section 41 of the RESTATEMENT (THIRD) OF UNFAIR COMPETITION describes situations in which a duty of confidence can be found:

A person to whom a trade secret has been disclosed owes a duty of confidence to the owner of the trade secret for purposes of the rule stated in § 40 if:

(a) the person made an express promise of confidentiality prior to the disclosure of the trade secret; or

(b) the trade secret was disclosed to the person under circumstances in which the relationship between the parties to the disclosure or the other facts surrounding the disclosure justify the conclusions that, at the time of the disclosure,

(1) the person knew or had reason to know that the disclosure was intended to be in confidence, and

(2) the other party to the disclosure was reasonable in inferring that the person consented to an obligation of confidentiality.

A trade secret violation occurs if a party obtains a trade secret by breach of confidence or by using other improper means or methods, such as theft, bribery, misrepresentation, or espionage using electronic or other means. The classic case analyzing the alleged usurpation of trade secrets by "improper means" is *E.I. duPont deNemours & Co. v. Christopher.*[26] The central question raised by the case is what means of discovery are proper and what methods are impermissible for purposes of trade secret law. A competitor of duPont, the chemical manufacturer, hired the Christophers to fly a plane over a duPont plant while it was under construction. On the plane was a highly sophisticated telephoto camera that took pictures of the plant design, revealing the trade secret to the competitor. The court held that despite the lack of violation of any generally applicable laws (such as trespass or aviation law), the fly-over constituted an improper means of obtaining the trade secrets.

The "improper means" standard addresses situations in which there is no binding duty of confidentiality between the parties, but the defendant's action is alleged to be improper in some manner. It is difficult to provide a workable standard for defining improper means, because there is no way to anticipate the methods a competitor might use to uncover a trade secret. Some methods are clearly improper because they violate existing laws, such as discovery of information through fraud, trespass, eavesdropping, or wiretapping.

26.   431 F.2d 1012 (5th Cir. 1970).

When a competitor uses methods having ambiguous legitimacy, as in *duPont,* the court adopted the Restatement standard, which focuses on whether the means used "fall below the generally accepted standards of commercial morality and reasonable conduct."[27] More generally, the court focused its standard on the extent of reasonable secrecy measures that a firm can be expected to take. If the defendant engages in a method of discovery that would breach the wall of reasonable secrecy measures, it is more likely that the means used will be deemed improper.

Under section 43 of the RESTATEMENT (THIRD) OF UNFAIR COMPETITION, " '[i]mproper' means of acquiring another's trade secret . . . include theft, fraud, unauthorized interception of communications, inducement of or knowing participation in a breach of confidence, and other means either wrongful in themselves or wrongful under the circumstances of the case. Independent discovery and analysis of publicly available products or information are not improper means of acquisition."

On the other hand, there are some ways in which a competitor or other third party can lawfully duplicate a company's trade secrets. Reverse engineering and independent development are the two most common lawful means. Reverse engineering occurs when someone starts with a known product and works backward in order to understand how the product works or how it was made. For example, a competitor can lawfully engage in chemical analysis of a chemical compound produced by another firm in an effort to duplicate that compound. Assuming that the company does not possess a patent monopoly (a federally granted exclusive right to the invention), the competitor is free to engage in reverse engineering and then to produce the same product using the same process. Similarly, if a competitor independently discovers a trade secret simply as a result of its own efforts, it is free to use that process (again, assuming no patent is involved).[28] In these situations involving reverse engineering or independent development, it may well be that *both* the original owner of the trade secret and the competitor who developed the information later possess the same legally protectable trade secret, which they can then enforce against any other party that might unlawfully seek to obtain it.

Despite its emphasis on secrecy, trade secret law has been found to not be preempted by federal patent law. *Kewanee Oil Co. v. Bicron Corp.*[29] is a landmark Supreme Court decision that held that federal patent law does not preempt state trade secret protec-

27. RESTATEMENT OF TORTS § 757, comment f.

28. *See Kewanee Oil Co. v. Bicron Corp.*, 416 U.S. 470 (1974).

29. 416 U.S. 470 (1974).

tion. The case discussed the principles and policies underlying these two important areas of law, eventually concluding that trade secret law does not unduly impinge upon patent law's policies favoring public disclosure of innovations. The policies underlying trade secret law include creating incentives for the development of useful innovations, maintaining standards for commercial behavior, and insuring the efficient distribution of proprietary information. Patent law similarly seeks to encourage innovation, but it also requires disclosure of new inventions to the public upon issuance of a patent, so that others may be spurred to innovate further and so that the patented information will ultimately enter the public domain.

Thus, there is a certain degree of conflict between the patent law policy of requiring disclosure and the trade secret policy favoring confidentiality measures. There are some instances in which a firm might opt to utilize trade secret protection in the hope that its proprietary information might be protected in perpetuity, or at least for much longer than the patent term. This may be particularly feasible in the case of a secret process that can be hidden from competitors and that is not readily susceptible to reverse engineering. For example, in *Lamb–Weston, Inc. v. McCain Foods, Ltd.*[30] the plaintiff obtained patent protection for aspects of its curly-fry making machine which could readily be subject to reverse engineering (such as the shape and overall external appearance of the blade in this case), while retaining trade secret protection for the process by which the blade is made (the specifications, materials, and the steps in the actual manufacturing process). The manufacturing process is not readily subject to reverse engineering, and thus may allow for protection as a trade secret for a potentially longer duration than the limited patent term. A firm that takes the trade secret route is at risk, however, of losing any exclusive rights under patent law (consider, for example, the Patent Act's statutory bars under section 102). Moreover, at any time, a competitor might independently develop or reverse engineer the process, or a scientist or other expert might publish an article describing the process for all to read and implement.

¶ 18.04   Defenses & Remedies

Trade secret cases can be defended by showing that the plaintiff failed to establish one of the elements of its case in chief—the existence of a trade secret, maintenance of it through reasonable secrecy measures, and infringement by breach of confidence or improper means (or other actionable conduct). Trade secret rights can be lost, abandoned, or waived in a number of ways. Trade

30.   941 F.2d 970 (9th Cir. 1991).

secrets can be lawfully discovered by reverse engineering or independent discovery. Thus, defenses based on reverse engineering or independent development can be asserted, as the scope of rights under trade secret law is limited to cases in which the information is somehow improperly obtained, unlike patent law—which provides "rights against the world." In addition, if the information becomes sufficiently well known that it ceases to provide a competitive advantage, it may cease to be a protectable trade secret. Further, if the information is revealed in a patent, it ceases to be a trade secret (although it could then be protected under federal patent law).

A firm's failure to take reasonable secrecy measures or a voluntary, non-confidential disclosure may result in abandonment or waiver of the trade secret. Thus, one way in which trade secret protection can be inadvertently waived or lost is through a voluntary disclosure to a third party. Any disclosures that are made should always be in the context of an express, written confidential relationship. Thus, for instance, a corporation's partial disclosure of computer trade secrets to third parties who were under obligations of confidentiality does not waive the trade secret status of computer programs, compilations, and technical information. On the other hand, providing third parties with trade secret information *not in confidence* will result in a waiver or loss of trade secret rights. A waiver of trade secret rights can also occur if the owner of the trade secret permits another to use the trade secret by agreement (again, without an assurance of confidentiality).

One court has noted that the owner of a trade secret commercial oven did not abandon the secret by selling hundreds of ovens to parties who were not subject to confidentiality agreements, because on those facts the secret interrelationship of the oven's component parts could not be reverse engineered in a reasonable period of time.[31] The key in that case was that the sale of the ovens did not disclose the secret technology, even if others attempted to discover it by reverse engineering. The court did note that if a trade secret owner failed to take reasonable precautions to prevent a trade secret from falling into the hands of competitors, the trade secret would be deemed to have been abandoned. Thus, in *Thermal Zone Products Corp. v. Echo Engineering, Ltd.*,[32] another case also involving the sale of ovens without a confidentiality agreement, the court decided that this action resulted in an abandonment of the trade secret in the oven. In that case, the court concluded that the oven

---

31. *See Thermodyne Food Service Products, Inc. v. McDonald's Corp.*, 940 F.Supp. 1300 (N.D. Ill. 1996).

32. 1993 WL 358148 (N.D. Ill. 1993) (sale of ovens without confidentiality agreement results in abandonment of trade secret in oven).

could easily be reverse engineered, and thus the company had "let the cat out of the bag."

Thus, placing a product on the market can ordinarily lead to a waiver or loss of trade secret rights, particularly as to the nature, design, and function of the product itself. There may still be some trade secret aspects related to the manufacturing process necessary to develop the product, but the product itself can be freely imitated. Of course, if a trade secret owner has successfully obtained patent protection for a particular innovation, it can proceed to market that product under the protection of the patent. At that point, trade secret protection will cease and the manufacturer's remedy is under patent law (as to the subject matter of the patent). In some circumstances, the manufacturer might retain trade secret protection for a secret manufacturing process while having concurrent patent protection for the final product.

Finally, a variety of standard defenses can be asserted. For example, if a firm becomes aware of a trade secret violation and fails to pursue the trade secret claim within the applicable statute of limitations (a time limit imposed by state law), it will be barred from relief. Laches and other equitable defenses may also be asserted.

With regard to remedies, successful trade secret plaintiffs can recover compensatory damages as well as injunctive relief. The duration of injunctive relief is frequently litigated. As the court noted in *Lamb–Weston, Inc. v. McCain Foods, Ltd.*,[33] the plaintiff is only entitled to an injunction lasting as long as the "head start" that the defendant received. In other words, the injunction should reflect the time period that would have been needed to reverse engineer the product without the benefit of the trade secret that was obtained.

33. 941 F.2d 970 (9th Cir. 1991).

Chapter 19

IDEA PROTECTION & MISAPPROPRIATION

Table of Sections

"If you ever have the good fortune to create a great advertising campaign, you will soon see another agency steal it. This is irritating, but don't let it worry you; nobody has ever built a brand by imitating somebody else's advertising."

— David Oglivy. ENTREPRENEUR, April 2012, at 14.

"He who receives an idea from me, receives instruction himself without lessening mine; as he who lights his taper at mine receives light without darkening me."

— Thomas Jefferson, Letter from Thomas Jefferson to Isaac McPherson (Aug. 13, 1813).

¶ 19.01 Express Contract

Ideas might be called the "poor stepchild" of Intellectual Property law. Copyright law specifically disavows any protection for ideas in the express language of section 102 of the Copyright Act. Clear patent law precedent also establishes that an abstract idea or concept is not eligible for patent protection. Trademark law protects branding ideas but only if they have been used in commerce or for a limited time in an intent-to-use trademark application; once again, abstract marketing or branding ideas do not receive trademark protection. Trade secret law might protect an idea, but only if it provides a business advantage over competitors, it is the subject of reasonable secrecy measures, and it is not generally known or used in the industry. So the question becomes how does a party protect an idea and how can that idea be conveyed or transferred to the party who has the greatest willingness to pay for it. Contract law provides the principal avenue for protection of ideas.

Standard contract law principles and theories can be brought to bear in cases involving the dissemination of ideas between parties in commercial transactions. If there is a binding contract between the parties, courts generally honor the terms of the parties' agreement. Ideas can simply be conveyed by contract to those who wish to use them. So long as there is bargained for consideration and mutual assent, this type of transaction is routine. Most courts will not inquire into the adequacy of the consideration—i.e., the extent to which the idea conveyed is sufficiently novel, unique, and concrete. In some states, however, a contract in which one party agrees to compensate the other for providing an idea must involve an idea that is novel in order to be enforceable.[1]

Often the terms of the parties' agreement will not be entirely clear. The case of *Sellers v. American Broadcasting Co.*[2] illustrates the typical outcome of a case involving the issue of "idea protection"—whether can someone protect their right to an idea for which they claim authorship or ownership. As the case law demonstrates, the answer to this question is—not very often. Most plaintiffs' claims for protection of an idea are unsuccessful, regardless of the theory or theories they assert. *Sellers* illustrates the common scenario—an unsophisticated individual contacts a major broadcasting company offering an idea in return for compensation. ABC and Geraldo Rivera actually signed an agreement and appear to have seriously entertained the plaintiff's story that Elvis Presley died of a cortisone overdose and was perhaps the victim of a conspiracy by his doctor. In the end, however, the defendants did not use the story, though they did a report on Elvis that was sufficiently close that it impelled the plaintiff to conclude that ABC must have relied on his story. The case presents a good discussion of one of the better theories of recovery for idea protection, the express contract claim. Unfortunately for the plaintiff in this case, because ABC did not actually use the precise story that he set forth, his contract claim had no chance to succeed. It is clear that Sellers would have had a much stronger case if Rivera and ABC had used his "cortisone" story and had not lived up to the terms of their contract. Sellers would have had potential claims of breach of contract and misappropriation. Although novelty would certainly be an issue, particularly as to the misappropriation theory, Sellers would very likely have gotten to a jury.

The most famous dispute over idea protection is undoubtedly the litigation between the Winklevoss brothers and Mark Zuckerberg, based on the assertion that Mr. Zuckerberg misappropriated the idea for Facebook from them. This dispute was a topic in the movie, "The Social Network," as well as a series of lawsuits that

1. For a thorough analysis of these issues, see Larissa Katz, A Powers-based Approach to the Protection of Ideas, 23 CARDOZO ARTS & ENT. L.J. 687 (2006).

2. 668 F.2d 1207 (11th Cir. 1982).

ultimately resulting in a settlement and payment to the Winklevoss plaintiffs.[3]

¶ 19.02   Misappropriation

The Supreme Court recognized the misappropriation theory in the landmark case of *International News Service v. Associated Press*.[4] INS copied material in AP news reports published in the eastern United States and distributed news stories to western states based on the information they copied. The Court recognized a claim for unfair competition when a competitor appropriates news for use in direction competition:

> In doing this defendant, by its very act, admits that it is taking material that has been acquired by complainant as the result of organization and the expenditure of labor, skill, and money, and which is salable by complainant for money, and that defendant in appropriating it and selling it as its own is endeavoring to reap where it has not sown, and by disposing of it to newspapers that are competitors of complainant's members is appropriating to itself the harvest of those who have sown. Stripped of all disguises, the process amounts to an unauthorized interference with the normal operation of complainant's legitimate business precisely at the point where the profit is to be reaped, in order to divert a material portion of the profit from those who have earned it to those who have not; with special advantage to defendant in the competition because of the fact that it is not burdened with any part of the expense of gathering the news. The transaction speaks for itself, and a court of equity ought not to hesitate long in characterizing it as unfair competition in business.[5]

The *INS v. AP* theory, which is sometimes known as a claim for misappropriation of a competitor's intangible trade values, has rarely been invoked with success in later decisions. Indeed, the RESTATEMENT (THIRD) OF UNFAIR COMPETITION endorses the view that this legal theory should be abolished:

> Although the decision has been frequently cited, it has been sparingly applied. Notwithstanding its longevity, the decision has had little enduring effect. In many cases it has been invoked when narrower rules of unfair competition would have achieved the same result. In most of the areas in which it has been expansively applied, its application has now been supplanted by legislation.

3. *See ConnectU v. Zuckerberg*, 522 F.3d 82, 86 (1st Cir. 2008).

4. 248 U.S. 215 (1918).

5. *Id.* at 239–40.

The rule stated in this Section limits common law tort liability for appropriations of intangible trade values to cases involving an appropriation of trade secrets, an appropriation of the commercial value of another's identity, or an appropriation of a work of authorship that is not fixed in a tangible medium of expression and thus protectable under common law copyright. Although courts have occasionally invoked the *INS* decision on an ad hoc basis to grant relief against other commercial appropriations, they have not articulated coherent principles for its application. It is clear that no general rule of law prohibits the appropriation of a competitor's ideas, innovations, or other intangible assets once they become publicly known. In addition, the federal patent and copyright statutes now preempt a considerable portion of the domain in which the common law tort might otherwise apply. The better approach, and the one most likely to achieve an appropriate balance between the competing interests, does not recognize a residual common law tort of misappropriation.[6]

Judge Richard Posner has written on the subject of misappropriation, suggesting that the concept as a free-standing cause of action should be discarded.[7] The author of this book has also written on this topic, and endorses the same view.[8] The theory may be viewed as questionable given its "uncertain doctrinal underpinnings and concomitant susceptibility to metastasis, as well as its pre-*Erie* origins, and its potential for conflict with the Intellectual Property Clause or federal doctrinal law. Yet the case is far from dead."[9]

Another recent case analyzing the misappropriation theory is *Barclays Capital Inc. v. THEFLYONTHEWALL.COM, Inc.*, 650 F.3d 876 (2d Cir. 2011). The defendant copied and disseminated on the Internet investment research gathered at considerable expense by the plaintiff banks. The court held that the misappropriation claim was preempted by section 301 of the Copyright Act.

Prior to the *Barclays* case, the court in *National Basketball Association v. Motorola, Inc.*[10] The National Basketball Association (NBA) sought an injunction preventing the manufacturer of a hand-held pager from transmitting NBA basketball scores or other data about games in progress via the pagers, absent authorization

---

6. RESTATEMENT (THIRD) OF UNFAIR COMPETITION, § 38, comment b.

7. *See* Richard A. Posner, Misappropriation: A Dirge, 40 HOUS. L. REV. 621 (2003).

8. *See* Gary Myers, "The Restatement's Rejection of the Misappropriation Tort: A Victory for the Public Domain," 47 S.C. L. REV. 673 (1996).

9. LANGE, LAFRANCE, MYERS, & LOCKRIDGE, INTELLECTUAL PROPERTY: CASES & MATERIALS, at 26. For further discussion of this subject, see DAVID LANGE & H. JEFFERSON POWELL, NO LAW: INTELLECTUAL PROPERTY IN THE IMAGE OF AN ABSOLUTE FIRST AMENDMENT, at 8–24, 149–67 (Stanford University Press 2009).

10. 105 F.3d 841 (2d Cir. 1997).

from the NBA. The district court issued a permanent injunction in the NBA's favor. The Second Circuit reversed and dismissed the NBA's claim for misappropriation, holding that only a narrow "hot news" misappropriation claim survived preemption for actions concerning material within the realm of copyright. The court found the additional elements that allowed a "hot news" claim to survive preemption were: (1) the plaintiff generates or gathers information at some cost; (2) the information is time sensitive; (3) the defendant's use of the information constitutes free riding upon the plaintiff's investment; (4) the defendant is in direct competition with the plaintiff; and (5) the free rider problem will so reduce incentives to produce the information that its existence or quality of the information would be substantially threatened. These factors were not found to be present in the case of the NBA, because the pagers did not in any meaningful way threaten the NBA's ability to continue to provide its primary products (professional basketball games and related products) and the defendant was not free riding on the NBA's proposed pager system.

¶ 19.03   Unjust Enrichment or Quasi–Contract

Courts have sometimes applied a theory of unjust enrichment or quasi-contract to provide compensation for the submission of a valuable idea. The rationales for this theory of recovery are the existence of an implied contract between the parties to compensate the developer of the idea and the prevention of unjust enrichment of the recipient of the idea. For example, in *Monumental Properties of Georgia, Inc. v. Frontier Disposal, Inc.,*[11] a Georgia court recognized a claim for relief for the misappropriation or conversion of an unpatented or unpatentable product or idea. The invention in *Monumental Properties* was a unique design for a garbage disposal system. The plaintiff's right of recovery was based upon the property right to one's mental labors. In order to recover, the plaintiff must show that the design or idea was exclusive (i.e., not available in the market place), and that the duty to provide compensation for the design or idea arose out of a contract, course of dealing, or confidential relationship existing between the parties.

The court applied and clarified the claim in a case involving an employee who asserted an unjust enrichment theory in *Wilson v. Barton & Ludwig, Inc.*[12] In that case, an employee brought suit against a former employer, claiming the wrongful appropriation of an idea or plan for leasing and managing residential rental property. The court held that the plan was not novel, which was an essential element of the claim. The plan did not create anything new to the real estate industry, but was merely a somewhat better

---

11. 159 Ga.App. 35, 37, 282 S.E.2d 660 (1981).

12. 163 Ga.App. 721, 296 S.E.2d 74, 220 U.S.P.Q. 375 (1982).

than existing business methods. The court set forth the following elements and analysis in reaching this conclusion:

> In contrast with *Monumental Properties* where the misappropriated idea was a product design, the instant case involves an idea that is more abstract—a business management concept. While we have found no Georgia case addressing the exact fact situation before us now, we adopt the clear and concise expression of the elements essential to a recovery for the wrongful appropriation of an abstract idea as set forth in *Official Airlines Schedule Information Service, Inc. (OASIS) v. Eastern Air Lines, Inc.*, 333 F.2d 672 (5th Cir. 1964): "[T]he idea must be novel; (2) the disclosure of the idea must be made in confidence, and (3) the idea must be adopted and made use of by the defendant." A fourth essential element which we also adopt is that the idea be sufficiently concrete in its development to be usable.[13]

Matarese v. Moore–McCormack Lines, Inc. illustrates a rare success story for a plaintiff in idea protection cases, as the plaintiff ultimately prevailed on a quasi-contract or unjust enrichment claim. The plaintiff was a stevedore who was encouraged by his supervisor to develop a highly valuable invention used in handling cargo. Instead of being compensated as promised, he was later fired. The plaintiff was unable to recover on a more conventional express or implied contract theory because the supervisor with whom he worked lacked the authority to bind the company under New York law at the time.

Given that a conventional contract theory was unavailable, the court awarded relief on the equitable principle of unjust enrichment or quasi-contract. The court established strict requirements for application of the concept. In particular, the innovations in question in *Matarese* here were highly concrete, original to the plaintiff, and very valuable. The defendant voluntarily invited the plaintiff to present his ideas, obtaining his daily assistance in placing them into service, promised compensation, and then refused to pay and instead fired him. Thus, there was a course of dealing between the parties, the defendant sought disclosure of the information, the defendant's employee made a promise of compensation (albeit perhaps without authority to do so), the plaintiff's invention was novel, concrete, and in fact patentable, the defendant made extensive use of it, and the defendant failed to compensate the plaintiff for the use. It is rare to find this combination of facts.

---

13. *Id.*, 296 S.E.2d at 76 (citing *Hamilton National Bank v. Belt*, 210 F.2d 706, 708 (D.C. Cir.1953)).

The law of "shop right," discussed in the patent law discussion in Chapter 14, ¶ 14.02, has some relevance to an understanding of the *Matarese* decision. The plaintiff in that case had obtained patents on his invention, but those patent rights could not be invoked against his former employer in light of the shot right doctrine, because he had developed the inventions on company time and made use of employer-provided materials in developing it. Thus, the plaintiff had no other recourse other than the state law theory he pursued in this case.

Frequently, those who submit ideas fail to take steps necessary to protect their interests in compensation by gratuitously disclosing the concept. Plaintiffs often assert a variety of legal theories—express contract, implied contract, copyright, quasi-contract, and fraud. Although there are circumstances in which each of these theories of recovery can provide relief, the elements of each claim must be proven. Often, unsophisticated parties do not receive compensation and cannot prevail under any applicable legal theory. *Downey v. General Foods Corp.*[14] illustrates an instance in which a claim is asserted based on the submission of an idea of making use of the term "wiggle" in connection with Jello. The case addresses two lines of defense: a lack of novelty in the plaintiff's idea and the independent creation defense. *Downey* held that a claim cannot be asserted unless the idea is novel and original, which was not the case here given prior references to "wiggling" Jello products. Further, the defendant had a strong case based on evidence that its advertising agency had independently developed the same idea and that the ad agency had no access to the plaintiff's idea. The case also illustrates one way in which a company might protect itself from idea submission claims through the use of an idea submission form. Some companies simply refuse to accept or consider unsolicited ideas.

Persons who possess ideas will find it difficult to market them for licensing or use. On the one hand, no company will promise compensation without having first evaluated an idea. On the other hand, the party submitting an idea will fear that it will be used by the recipient without compensation, and thus will be reluctant to disclose the idea without a binding contract. This catch–22 situation presents a difficult challenge for an attorney representing either party.

Companies that wish to avoid most litigation over idea submissions can simply refuse to accept or consider unsolicited ideas. An individual within the firm can be designated to handle these refusals; that individual should not have any substantive contact with people within the company who are responsible for developing

14. 31 N.Y.2d 56, 334 N.Y.S.2d 874, 286 N.E.2d 257 (1972).

ideas. The drawback to this approach is that the company is closed to new ideas. An alternative approach is to require anyone submitting an idea for consideration by the company to sign contracts specifying the terms under which the company will deal. Finally, some companies provide specified rewards or cash bonuses to employees (and sometimes others) who provide the company with useful ideas that are utilized.

Chapter 20

SUI GENERIS INTELLECTUAL PROPERTY RIGHTS

Table of Sections

SUI GENERIS RIGHTS

¶ 20.01 Laws Currently in Effect

A number of *sui generis* statutory Intellectual Property rights have been enacted under federal law. A *sui generis* form of protection is essentially a free-standing or unique form of Intellectual Property. Two examples of *sui generis* laws are the Semiconductor Chip Protection Act of 1984 and The Vessel Hull Design Protection Act of 1998. The Anticybersquatting Consumer Protection Act is another statutory scheme that warrants discussion, as it plays an important role in protecting trademark rights in the context of domain names.

Semiconductor Chip Protection Act

The Semi–Conductor Chip Protection Act of 1984 protects original mask works and related semiconductor products upon proper registration with the Copyright Office. A mask work is a two or three-dimensional layout or topography of an integrated circuit, i.e. the arrangement on a chip of various semiconductor devices (e.g., transistors and resistors).

Vessel Hull Design Protection Act

The Vessel Hull Design Protection Act was enacted in the aftermath of the Supreme Court's decision in *Bonito Boats v. Thunder Craft Boats.*[1] In that 1989 case, the Court applied Intellectual Property preemption principles and held that state misappropriation-based unfair competition laws are preempted when they purport to forbid copying or misappropriation of patentable subject matter. At issue was a Florida law that provided patent-like protec-

---

1. 489 U.S. 141 (1989).

389

tion for boat hull designs. Congress then enacted specific legislation to protect boat hull designs under federal law. The Vessel Hull Design Protection Act, Title 17, Chapter 13 of the United States Code, was enacted on October 28, 1998 and provides protection for original designs of vessel hulls. The law grants an owner of an original vessel hull design exclusive rights provided that application for registration of the design with the Copyright Office is made within two years of the design being made public. The law protects vessel hull designs embodied in actual vessel hulls that are publicly exhibited, publicly distributed, or offered for sale or sold to the public on or after October 28, 1998.

The Anticybersquatting Consumer Protection Act

The tremendous growth of Internet usage and its advent as a medium for substantial commercial and recreational activity has led businesses to establish websites making use of their trademarks as domain names. This practice, of course, serves as a valuable marketing tool, allowing consumers to identify quickly a company's website by entering the familiar trademark (rather than having to locate the website indirectly through a search engine such as Google). To protect their marks, firms have asserted trademark rights when others have made use of the mark as a domain name.[2] In *Brookfield Communications, Inc. v. West Coast Entertainment Corp.*,[3] the court held that the mere registration of a domain name is insufficient to establish rights in the term as a mark, requiring instead a traditional "first to use" analysis (in the absence of an intent to use application, discussed in Chapter 8, ¶ 8.02).

The potential use of a trademarked name as a domain name quickly led to the practice of "cybersquatting," in which a third party registers a domain name using an individual or company name and thus prevents the use of that domain name in the eventual hope of turning a profit, usually by selling the right to the domain name to the trademark owner. Courts have used traditional trademark law and dilution analysis to prevent this practice, as illustrated by the leading early case of *Panavision International, L.P. v. Toeppen*,[4] in which the court found that Toeppen's registration of "panavision.com" diluted Panavision's trademark.

Late in 1999, Congress enacted the Anticybersquatting Consumer Protection Act[5] to provide more effective remedies in this

2. *See, e.g., Cardservice International, Inc. v. McGee*, 950 F.Supp. 737 (E.D. Va. 1997) (finding infringement of registered "Card Service" mark by the defendant's use of "cardservice.com"); *Washington Speaker's Bureau v. Leading Authorities, Inc.*, 33 F. Supp. 2d 488 (E.D. Va. 1999) (finding that defendant's domain name infringed plaintiff's unregistered trademark).

3. 174 F.3d 1036 (9th Cir. 1999).

4. 141 F.3d 1316 (9th Cir. 1998).

5. Pub. L. No. 106–113 (1999) (codified at 15 U.S.C. § 1125(d)(1)(A)).

situation.[6] The legislation adds a new section 43(d) to the Lanham Act, with remedies for cybersquatting. It makes actionable the registration, trafficking, or use of a domain name when the domain name dilutes a famous mark, or is confusingly similar to the mark of another. The Act requires a showing of a bad faith intent to profit and delineates nine factors for determination of that intent.

Courts have also addressed the use of trademarks as metatags, i.e., lines of code buried in the HTML code used in websites. Metatags are not visible to the consumer or viewer (unless the viewer specially seeks to view the HTML code), but they do serve as "key words" for purposes of search engines. The use of a trademark as a metatag without the trademark owner's consent may also infringe on a trademark, unless it is done in a manner constituting fair use.[7]

The statute is quoted in full below:

. . .

(d) Cyberpiracy prevention

(1)(A) A person shall be liable in a civil action by the owner of a mark, including a personal name which is protected as a mark under this section, if, without regard to the goods or services of the parties, that person

(i) has a bad faith intent to profit from that mark, including a personal name which is protected as a mark under this section; and

(ii) registers, traffics in, or uses a domain name that—

(I) in the case of a mark that is distinctive at the time of registration of the domain name, is identical or confusingly similar to that mark;

(II) in the case of a famous mark that is famous at the time of registration of the domain name, is identical or confusingly similar to or dilutive of that mark; or

(III) is a trademark, word, or name protected by reason of section 706 of Title 18 or section 220506 of Title 36.

---

6. *See Sporty's Farm, L.L.C. v. Sportsman's Market, Inc.*, 202 F.3d 489 (2d Cir. 2000). QUOTE

7. *See, e.g., Brookfield Communications, Inc. v. West Coast Entertainment Corp.*, 174 F.3d 1036 (9th Cir. 1999) (use of "moviebuff" as metatag infringes registered trademark by diverting consumers to defendant's website; term was not used in a fair use or descriptive manner).

(B)(i) In determining whether a person has a bad faith intent described under subparagraph (a), a court may consider factors such as, but not limited to

(I) the trademark or other intellectual property rights of the person, if any, in the domain name;

(II) the extent to which the domain name consists of the legal name of the person or a name that is otherwise commonly used to identify that person;

(III) the person's prior use, if any, of the domain name in connection with the bona fide offering of any goods or services;

(IV) the person's bona fide noncommercial or fair use of the mark in a site accessible under the domain name;

(V) the person's intent to divert consumers from the mark owner's online location to a site accessible under the domain name that could harm the goodwill represented by the mark, either for commercial gain or with the intent to tarnish or disparage the mark, by creating a likelihood of confusion as to the source, sponsorship, affiliation, or endorsement of the site;

(VI) the person's offer to transfer, sell, or otherwise assign the domain name to the mark owner or any third party for financial gain without having used, or having an intent to use, the domain name in the bona fide offering of any goods or services, or the person's prior conduct indicating a pattern of such conduct;

(VII) the person's provision of material and misleading false contact information when applying for the registration of the domain name, the person's intentional failure to maintain accurate contact information, or the person's prior conduct indicating a pattern of such conduct;

(VIII) the person's registration or acquisition of multiple domain names which the person knows are identical or confusingly similar to marks of others that are distinctive at the time of registration of such domain names, or dilutive of famous marks of others that are famous at the time of registration of such domain names, without regard to the goods or services of the parties; and

(IX) the extent to which the mark incorporated in the person's domain name registration is or is not distinctive and famous within the meaning of subsection (c)(1) of this section.

(ii) Bad faith intent described under subparagraph (A) shall not be found in any case in which the court determines that the person believed and had reasonable grounds to believe that the use of the domain name was a fair use or otherwise lawful.

(C) In any civil action involving the registration, trafficking, or use of a domain name under this paragraph, a court may order the forfeiture or cancellation of the domain name or the transfer of the domain name to the owner of the mark.

(D) A person shall be liable for using a domain name under subparagraph (A) only if that person is the domain name registrant or that registrant's authorized licensee.

(E) As used in this paragraph, the term "traffics in" refers to transactions that include, but are not limited to, sales, purchases, loans, pledges, licenses, exchanges of currency, and any other transfer for consideration or receipt in exchange for consideration.

(2)(A) The owner of a mark may file an in rem civil action against a domain name in the judicial district in which the domain name registrar, domain name registry, or other domain name authority that registered or assigned the domain name is located if

(i) the domain name violates any right of the owner of a mark registered in the Patent and Trademark Office, or protected under subsection (a) or (c); and

(ii) the court finds that the owner—

(I) is not able to obtain in personam jurisdiction over a person who would have been a defendant in a civil action under paragraph (1); or

(II) through due diligence was not able to find a person who would have been a defendant in a civil action under paragraph (1) by—

(aa) sending a notice of the alleged violation and intent to proceed under this paragraph to the registrant of the domain name at the postal and e-mail address provided by the registrant to the registrar; and

(bb) publishing notice of the action as the court may direct promptly after filing the action.

(B) The actions under subparagraph (A)(ii) shall constitute service of process.

(C) In an in rem action under this paragraph, a domain name shall be deemed to have its situs in the judicial district in which

(i) the domain name registrar, registry, or other domain name authority that registered or assigned the domain name is located; or

(ii) documents sufficient to establish control and authority regarding the disposition of the registration and use of the domain name are deposited with the court.

(D)(i) The remedies in an in rem action under this paragraph shall be limited to a court order for the forfeiture or cancellation of the domain name or the transfer of the domain name to the owner of the mark. upon receipt of written notification of a filed, stamped copy of a complaint filed by the owner of a mark in a United States district court under this paragraph, the domain name registrar, domain name registry, or other domain name authority shall

(I) expeditiously deposit with the court documents sufficient to establish the court's control and authority regarding the disposition of the registration and use of the domain name to the court; and

(II) not transfer, suspend, or otherwise modify the domain name during the pendency of the action, except upon order of the court.

(ii) The domain name registrar or registry or other domain name authority shall not be liable for injunctive or monetary relief under this paragraph except in the case of bad faith or reckless disregard, which includes a willful failure to comply with any such court order.

(3) The civil action established under paragraph (1) and the in rem action established under paragraph (2), and any remedy available under either such action, shall be in addition to any other civil action or remedy otherwise applicable.

(4) The in rem jurisdiction established under paragraph (2) shall be in addition to any other jurisdiction that otherwise exists, whether in rem or in personam.

¶ 20.02   Proposed Laws

Database Protection

In its 1991 decision in *Feist Publications, Inc. v. Rural Telephone Service Co.*,[8] the Supreme Court held that copyright law does not protect laboriously gathered and maintained factual compilations if they do not possess a minimum level of creativity in their selection or arrangement. *Feist* thus prevents many factual databases from receiving copyright protection, and has led to proposals for *sui generis* protection for databases. Bills that have been regularly proposed in Congress to provide specialized legal protection to the creators of databases, as the European Union has already done.[9] Factual databases are eligible for protection under the EU Database Directive. To date, Congress has not enacted similar protection under United States law.

Were Congress to enact a database law, a preliminary question involves the source of its authority to do so. The Court in *Feist* clearly established that the Intellectual Property Clause does not authorize copyright protection for works that do not satisfy a minimum standard of creativity, as well as that the Copyright Act does not cover such works. In that sense, the ruling in *Feist* has a constitutional, as well as statutory, dimension. The Intellectual Property Clause states: "to Promote the Progress of Science and useful Arts, by securing for limited Times to Authors and Inventors the exclusive Right to their respective Writings and Discoveries."[10]

---

8. 499 U.S. 340 (1991).

9. *See* Jonathan Band & Makoto Kono, "The Database Protection Debate in the 106th Congress," 62 Ohio St. L.J. 869 (2001); Jane C. Ginsburg, "Copyright, Common Law, and Sui Generis Protection of Databases in the United States and Abroad," 66 U. Cinc. L. Rev. 151 (1997); J.H. Reichman & Pamela Samuelson, "Intellectual Property Rights in Data?" 50 Vand. L.Rev. 51 (1997).

10. U.S. Const., Art. I, § 8, cl. 8.

By its terms, copyrights can only be granted to those who qualify as authors of a writing.

The constitutional holding of *Feist* would imply that the Intellectual Property Clause would not provide Article I authority to Congress for a database protection law. The alternative, of course, is for Congress to anchor the protection database law in its Commerce Power. The development, marketing, and sale of databases would be activity in interstate and foreign commerce, and thus is arguably within Congress' power to regulate. It would appear the High Court would uphold such a law as long as it was not deemed to be an attempt to take an end-run around the limitations on congressional power in the Intellectual Property Clause.

Fashion Design Protection

Traditionally, fashion designs have been viewed as mere crafts or useful objects that do not warrant copyright protection. The fashion industry has generally flourished in spite of this general lack of copyright protection, but with increasing levels of style piracy, there have been calls from some in the industry for stronger Intellectual Property protection.[11] One proposal would provide copyright-like protection for original clothing designs—the Design Piracy Prohibition Act.[12] To date, no fashion bill has been enacted. In the past, the fashion industry has attempted to self-police imitators through boycotts of retailers who sold pirated designs, but this led to a well-known antitrust case, *Fashion Originators' Guild of America, Inc. v. FTC*,[13] which held that the group boycott violated section 1 of the Sherman Act.

SOPA & PIPA

It seems appropriate to conclude this book with a brief discussion of two proposed bills that generated a widely publicized controversy in 2012. The Stop On–Line Piracy Act (SOPA) and the Protect Intellectual Property Act (PIPA) were proposed bills designed to improve enforcement of IP rights, particularly focusing on the infringing activities of entities operating abroad. Advocated primarily by Hollywood corporations, it included provisions dealing with payment processing, as well as obligations for website operators and search engines. After a massive response from Silicon Valley companies and Internet users, who argued that these bills would stifle commerce and discourse on the Internet, much of the congressional support for SOPA and PIPA dissolved. Opponents of

---

11. *See* Kal Raustiala & Christopher Sprigman, The Piracy Paradox: Innovation and Intellectual Property in Fashion Design, 92 VA. L. REV. 1687 (2006) (questioning the need for copyright protection in fashion design). *See also* Julie P. Tsai, Fashioning Protection: A Note on the Protection of Fashion Designs in the United States, 9 LEWIS & CLARK L. REV. 447, 447 (2005).

12. H.R. 5055, 109th Cong. (2006).

13. 312 U.S. 457 (1941).

SOPA and PIPA have proposed an alternative to address some of the concerns of copyright owners, the Online Protection and Enforcement of Digital Trade Act (OPEN Act). As of this writing, no legislation has been enacted to address these issues.

The controversy surrounding SOPA and PIPA highlights the central challenge of Intellectual Property law—how to protect the legitimate interests of creators and of society by rewarding innovation and creativity, while at the same time allowing for the development of a robust competitive economy and a free and open society, particularly on the Internet. Technology has posed a challenge to Intellectual Property law since the days of the first printing presses. Today, those challenges are even more pressing and potentially devastating, as demonstrated by the severe contraction of the music industry. Yet, these changes can provide opportunities for new forms of creativity and of commerce. As IP law develops, it is important to maintain an awareness of the balance, avoiding both extreme overprotection of rights-holders and blatant free riding on the creative efforts of others.

Table of Cases

H

Haas Outdoors, Inc. v. Oak Country Camo., Inc., 957 F.Supp. 835 (N.D.Miss.1997)—¶ **9.03, n. 40.**

Halicki v. United Artists Communications, Inc., 812 F.2d 1213 (9th Cir. 1987)—¶ **4.03, n. 49.**

Hall, In re, 781 F.2d 897 (Fed.Cir. 1986)—¶ **13.07, n. 76.**

Hamer Holding Group, Inc. v. Elmore, 202 Ill.App.3d 994, 148 Ill.Dec. 310, 560 N.E.2d 907 (Ill.App. 1 Dist. 1990)—¶ **18.01, n. 15.**

Hamilton Nat. Bank v. Belt, 210 F.2d 706, 93 U.S.App.D.C. 168 (D.C.Cir. 1953)—¶ **19.03, n. 13.**

Hard Rock Cafe Licensing Corp. v. Concession Services, Inc., 955 F.2d 1143 (7th Cir.1992)—¶ **11.01, n. 3.**

Harjo v. Pro Football Inc., 1994 WL 262249 (Trademark Tr. & App. Bd.1994)—§ **7.10, n. 84.**

Harper & Row Publishers, Inc. v. Nation Enterprises, 471 U.S. 539, 105 S.Ct. 2218, 85 L.Ed.2d 588 (1985)—¶ **2.03, n. 10; ¶ 5.02, n. 7.**

Hasbro Bradley, Inc. v. Sparkle Toys, Inc., 780 F.2d 189 (2nd Cir.1985)—§ **3.03, n. 16.**

Hearst Corp., In re, 982 F.2d 493 (Fed. Cir.1992)—¶ **9.01, n. 5.**

Heartsprings, Inc. v. Heartspring, Inc., 143 F.3d 550 (10th Cir.1998)—§ **9.01, n. 18.**

Heaton Distributing Co. v. Union Tank Car Co., 387 F.2d 477 (8th Cir. 1967)—§ **11.03, n. 19.**

Hemingway's Estate v. Random House, Inc., 23 N.Y.2d 341, 296 N.Y.S.2d 771, 244 N.E.2d 250 (N.Y.1968)—¶ **2.07, n. 75.**

Henri's Food Products Co., Inc. v. Kraft, Inc., 717 F.2d 352 (7th Cir.1983)—¶ **9.01, n. 13.**

Herbert Rosenthal Jewelry Corp. v. Kalpakian, 446 F.2d 738 (9th Cir. 1971)—§ **2.05, n. 66.**

Heyl, Application of, 54 C.C.P.A. 1608, 379 F.2d 1018 (Cust. & Pat.App. 1967)—¶ **13.12, n. 119.**

Hines, In re, 1994 WL 587037 (Trademark Tr. & App. Bd.1994)—¶ **7.10, n. 82.**

Hi–Tech Video Productions, Inc. v. Capital Cities/ABC, Inc., 58 F.3d 1093 (6th Cir.1995)—¶ **3.02, n. 10.**

Hobbs v. United States, 376 F.2d 488 (5th Cir.1967)—¶ **14.03, n. 8.**

Hoehling v. Universal City Studios, Inc., 618 F.2d 972 (2nd Cir.1980)—§ **2.04, n. 56.**

Holiday Inns, Inc. v. Alberding, 683 F.2d 931 (5th Cir.1982)—¶ **11.03, n. 6.**

Holiday Inns, Inc. v. Holiday Out In America, 481 F.2d 445 (5th Cir. 1973)—§ **9.01, n. 7.**

Holiday Inns, Inc. v. Trump, 617 F.Supp. 1443 (D.N.J.1985)—¶ **7.05, n. 42.**

Horgan v. Macmillan, Inc., 789 F.2d 157 (2nd Cir.1986)—¶ **4.02, n. 2.**

House of Windsor, Incorporated, In re, 1983 WL 51833 (Trademark Tr. & App. Bd.1983)—¶ **7.10, n. 86.**

Houts v. Universal City Studios, Inc., 603 F.Supp. 26 (C.D.Cal.1984)—¶ **2.04, n. 57.**

Humble Oil & Refining Co. v. American Oil Co., 405 F.2d 803 (8th Cir. 1969)—§ **9.01, n. 12.**

I

Imazio Nursery, Inc. v. Dania Greenhouses, 69 F.3d 1560 (Fed.Cir. 1995)—§ **13.05, n. 50.**

Imperial Residential Design, Inc. v. Palms Development Group, Inc., 70 F.3d 96 (11th Cir.1995)—¶ **3.05, n. 23, 25.**

Independent Service Organizations Antitrust Litigation, In re, 203 F.3d 1322 (Fed.Cir.2000)—¶ **5.07, n. 39; ¶ 16.05, n. 11.**

Indianapolis Colts, Inc. v. Metropolitan Baltimore Football Club Ltd. Partnership., 34 F.3d 410 (7th Cir. 1994)—¶ **10.01.**

Indonesian Imports, Inc. v. Old Navy, Inc., 1999 WL 179680 (N.D.Cal. 1999)—§ **10.02, n. 13.**

Inflight Newspapers, Inc. v. Magazines In–Flight, LLC, 990 F.Supp. 119 (E.D.N.Y.1997)—¶ **18.01, n. 8, 15.**

In re (see name of party)

Intel Corp. v. Terabyte Intern., Inc., 6 F.3d 614 (9th Cir.1993)—¶ **10.05, n. 26.**

International Jensen, Inc. v. Metrosound U.S.A., Inc., 4 F.3d 819 (9th Cir. 1993)—¶ **7.09, n. 79.**

International Kennel Club of Chicago, Inc. v. Mighty Star, Inc., 846 F.2d 1079 (7th Cir.1988)—¶ **7.04, n. 26; ¶ 9.01, n. 11.**

International News Service v. Associated Press, 248 U.S. 215, 39 S.Ct. 68, 63 L.Ed. 211 (1918)—¶ **19.02, n. 4.**

Inwood Laboratories, Inc. v. Ives Laboratories, Inc., 456 U.S. 844, 102 S.Ct. 2182, 72 L.Ed.2d 606 (1982)—¶ **7.04, n. 25; ¶ 11.01, n. 2.**

Q

R

S

Index

References are to Pages

415

†